DIMITRI D. LAZO

NEWTON D. BAKER
America at War

IN TWO VOLUMES
VOLUME II

BAKER AND PERSHING IN FRANCE

NEWTON D. BAKER

America at War

BASED ON THE PERSONAL PAPERS OF THE SECRETARY
OF WAR IN THE WORLD WAR; HIS CORRESPONDENCE
WITH THE PRESIDENT AND IMPORTANT LEADERS
AT HOME AND ABROAD; THE CONFIDENTIAL
CABLEGRAMS BETWEEN THE WAR DE-
PARTMENT AND HEADQUARTERS IN
FRANCE; THE MINUTES OF THE
WAR INDUSTRIES BOARD, AND
OTHER FIRST-HAND MATERIAL

by

FREDERICK PALMER

VOLUME II

With Illustrations

DODD, MEAD & COMPANY

New York   *1931*

PRINTED IN THE UNITED STATES OF AMERICA
BY THE VAIL-BALLOU PRESS, INC., BINGHAMTON, N. Y.

CONTENTS

CONTENTS

CONTENTS

ILLUSTRATIONS

NEWTON D. BAKER
America at War

"I am not so concerned as I should be, I fear, about the verdict of history. For the same reason it seems to me unworthy to worry about myself, when so many thousands participated in the World War unselfishly and heroically who will find no place at all in the records which we make up and call history."
        NEWTON D. BAKER IN A LETTER TO F. H. GOFF.

XIX

WE MAKE A KING IN FRANCE

"Now that I am going for good," Bliss said upon his departure, "you will want to make the acting Chief of Staff the permanent Chief of Staff."

"I'll not make a permanent Chief of Staff until I know my man," Baker replied.[1]

As I have already mentioned, Baker had desired that Pershing should choose as a successor to Bliss a younger man who had had experience in France.[2] Pershing had chosen Major General John Biddle, a distinguished and personable officer of engineers, embodying fine professional traditions, who had been chief of the War College and commandant at West Point.[3] Biddle was fresh from France, fresh from consultations with Pershing, and should know Pershing's mind. Pershing retained Major General Peyton C. March, whom Baker had favored as Chief of Staff, as Chief of Artillery in the A. E. F. Upon the shoulders of the gracious Biddle as acting Chief of Staff had descended a herculean task. If there were two supermen in the American Army, one ought to be in command in France and the other to be Chief of Staff in Washington. If there were only one, then the need for him was perhaps greater for the next six months in Washington than in France. He must be the Army expert of experts, the superior of the bureaus, the supreme technical coordinator under the General Staff system. A gentlemanly and kindly policy of *laisser faire* would not do; nor would a shorter working day than sixteen hours. He must harden his heart to excuses and spare no one's feelings; he must be a sharp blade that would cut away dead-wood ruthlessly in a period when the parts of the plan were in an uneven state of progress.

Biddle labored under heavy handicaps. The number of staff officers to assist him had been further reduced. Some of those

1

who remained in the War Department were suffering from desk weariness, but they forced their pace as they saw their colleagues departing for France or joining divisions in the cantonments which would one day be on their way "over there."

But being able and willing to work sixteen hours a day did not of itself insure efficiency. At two o'clock in the morning, on his way home, Baker entered a bureau chief's office to find him with a pile of charts on his desk and working out computations on a pad. The habits of peace were still strong upon him. He could not bring himself to delegate details for which he himself was responsible.

"You ought not to be doing that," said Baker. "Your part is to do the thinking."

The time had now come to replace some of the elder bureau chiefs with younger men. Crozier, Chief of Ordnance, and Quartermaster General Sharpe had labored for nine months without a holiday. They were now reckoning that uncertain harvest of filled orders at a time when requirements were leaping beyond the power of production. Survey, production, priority! When production did not keep up with survey, priority knew not on what to reckon. And the period of the survey was practically over. The plan approached its final test. The next stage of execution required fresh energy.

Agitation for more concentrated authority and for more vigorous executives supported Baker in the creation of the War Council, composed of the veteran chiefs of bureaus who were to have time for thinking and for conferences with major heads in all activities. If some of them had been too long in the treadmill to learn to think in the large, the War Council would serve another purpose without raising a row or breaking hearts. We had no baronetcies and peerages with which to reward the veteran chiefs for their great services in the formative period.

When voices were raised under the dome of the Capitol demanding by what authority Baker had created the Council, he said that he might order any officer to any service he pleased. The members of the Council were the Secretary of War and the Assistant Secretary of War; the Chief of Staff; Major General

Henry G. Sharpe, Quartermaster General; Major General
Erasmus M. Weaver, Chief of Coast Artillery; Major General
William Crozier, Chief of Ordnance; and Major General Enoch
H. Crowder, Provost Marshal General.

There was no thought of replacing Crowder. He had become
the indispensable administrator of the draft. Brigadier General
John D. Barrette succeeded Weaver. The two bureaus which had
known the largest expansion and upon which the most depended
were ordnance and supplies. Brigadier General Charles Wheeler
succeeded Crozier as Acting Chief of Ordnance. He planned
reorganization. Would his new plan succeed in hastening production? For experience had proved that reorganization did not
always come up to the promises of the reorganizer.

Major General George W. Goethals was made Quartermaster
General. In spite of his prestige as builder of the Panama Canal,
any suggestion earlier in the War that Goethals, an engineer
officer, should be made Quartermaster General would have
started a chorus of rows sounding down through the Army and
back and forth between the War Department and the Congress.
Now his appointment was acclaimed. Edward R. Stettinius became Surveyor General of Supplies. Goethals, with characteristic directness, immediately declared that either Stettinius must
yield in a conflict of authority, or he himself would retire. Stettinius gracefully yielded. He was soon to become Second Assistant Secretary of War; but, as a member of the firm of J. Pierpont
Morgan & Company, which stood for Wall Street, his appointment earlier would have drawn all the fire away from the other
dollar-a-year men.

In the American Expeditionary Force, the coming of highly
centralized authority, which though dangerous in peace may
be essential in war, did not have to wait until the opinion of a
democracy had become convinced of its necessity. A dictatorship had been created for Pershing the day that he sailed. In our
world in France his nod was law. No American in all history had
ever been delegated so much power. His character, his personal
method, his strength and limitations, his outlook on life made
the mould in which his army was formed. As winter closed in,

the divisions drilling in the Lorraine sector were finding "sunny" France the falsest bit of all war propaganda. There was no heat in their billets in French houses near the manure pile; no way of drying our soldiers' clothes, saturated with the cold mist even when it was not raining. They drilled to numb exhaustion in the mud to become automatic machines of flesh and blood in mechanical warfare. Word might come that none other than Pershing himself was to inspect a regiment; and they stood in the mud for hours after the time set for his arrival, waiting for the ever-busy Commander-in-Chief to appear.

Letters from home were weeks late and received out of the order in which they were sent, for nearly all the mail ships had become cargo ships and distribution was slow. The few Y. M. C. A. canteens that had been set up expected payment for cigarettes and chocolates from soldiers who had no change. When Edward C. Carter, head of the Y. M. C. A., protested to Pershing against the "Y" becoming a sales organization, Pershing's sharp question was, "Are you here to serve or not?" Carter answered that he was there to serve. Pershing said his soldiers should not be objects of charity. They were not to be pauperized. He had set himself a stern model for making the first professional army in our history.

WEST POINT DISCIPLINE IN THE A. E. F.

To the sons of a non-military nation who were sent to learn war under him, Pershing said:

"The standards for the American Army will be those of West Point. The rigid attention, the upright bearing, attention to detail, uncomplaining obedience to instruction required of the cadet will be required of every officer and soldier of our armies in France." [4]

The Commander-in-Chief blocked this out on his own pad in his square letters. He was not, as Washington, Grant, and Lee had been, under the handicap of having to deal with volunteer armies which must be recruited by volunteering. Officer or soldier, the man who arrived in France must know that he was now

a "pleb" beginning the fundamentals no less than if he had
been under the shadow of the gray walls on the Hudson. Many
Regular officers thought that as it took four years at West Point
to make an officer, it should take at least three to make a trained
soldier. West Point, in its proud professional cult, had kept the
watchfires of discipline burning in the democracy; and now they
were to light the drill-ground of the masses of our manhood. It
was not enough in the A. E. F. that you should salute your superior when you met him if he were going in the opposite direction; you must also salute him if you passed him when he
was going in the same direction. The French and the British,
who had expected in us the free-and-easy manner of democratic
soldiers, were as astonished by the meticulous detail of our discipline as by the number of our typewriters, and would not have
been surprised if we had adopted the Prussian goosestep in a
march-past before the Commander-in-Chief. French veterans
might slouch along, careless about salutes, in the streets; but
French ways were French ways. Pershing saw the West Point
fundamentals as right for raw American recruits in peace or
war.

Under the censorship there could be no reports to the press
of complaints from the men about the exacting discipline or
about any of their miseries. The intelligence section had its eye
on whimperers. No soldier might write home in critical mood
to his mother or to his Member of Congress. Pershing need receive from home no officer he did not want; he might send back
any officer he pleased.

In spite of the centralization of authority in France under so
able a man, the A. E. F. also suffered from many boards and
many committees. Officers who were used to prolonged dis-
cussions in the conscientious performance of their duties in peace
did not easily drop their habits in war-time. Boards were called
to consider every subject—from whether we should change our
uniform to whether our officers should carry canes in the trenches.
A board decided to stick to the old uniform with the high collar;
even if it lacked pocket-room, it looked more soldierly. Another board compromised on allowing the officers to carry

canes in the trenches, but not out of them. A military police-
man who caught an officer carrying a cane when his unit was
in billets haled him under arrest to local headquarters.

In professional exaltation and the intoxication of tireless industry, under strange auspices and in strange surroundings, the
founding fathers of the A. E. F. formed policies. It was their
day. They were in the presence of a vast conscript army of veteran
experience with the fresh traditions of the Marne and Verdun
against the background of those of the campaigns of Condé,
Turenne, and Napoleon. They, who had maneuvered armies on
paper and in their dreams, would have a vast army of real soldiers to direct in action if the War did not end too soon. America
now, as well as France and Germany, had conscription to supply
them with man-power for their expert fashioning. They sat in
the seats of the mighty over the fresh and coming host while
their veteran Allied colleagues were in command of waning
and scarred hosts. This power had come to them suddenly. A
few months ago they had been the patient servants of democracy
as colonels, majors, and captains in posts or on staff duty in
Washington or in a departmental headquarters. Then the democracy declared war. Only those who had been graduated from
the Staff School were equipped in theory for the organization of
warfare on a large scale. Not all the chiefs of sections in the
A. E. F. had been to Leavenworth. Whether living the life of
Army posts or cloistered in study rooms, they had not had the
opportunity for general culture which Marshal Foch, after all
his experience, bade young officers of the future to avail themselves of in order to be prepared for modern warfare, which
embraced all the industrial and professional activities of the
nation.[5]

"In what especially concerns the army officer, the future
probably will merely accentuate this need of general culture
combined with professional knowledge. As the sphere of war
expands, so should the minds of those waging it broaden. . . .
How, then, can an officer who is not in constant touch with the
spirit of his people hope to turn such resources to good account?
How can he comprehend and direct the social phenomena

which characterize great national wars unless he has some acquaintance with moral and political sciences and possesses that knowledge of history which alone can explain to him the life of nations in the past and in the present? Here again technical acquirements are no longer sufficient; he must complete them with a large addition furnished by other faculties.

"Moreover, as any officer can readily perceive, his mind and character will be far better prepared for a coming war, and his career will be advanced even in time of peace, if he keeps himself—always with a loyal sense of discipline—constantly abreast of the events and problems of his time, instead of confining his interest solely to garrison life, obsessed by thoughts of promotion and careless of developing his higher capacities.

"Without this conception, the regular officer, when war arrives, runs the risk of seeing himself outdistanced by the reserve officer, who can bring to his work—in addition to an indispensable military equipment—faculties and knowledge which a wider life has maintained in fruitful activity."

The world of the officers of our High Command in France was populated entirely by the increasing Army. In that Army were the energy and intelligence of America, represented not only by fresh graduates of our colleges and technical schools, but also by graduates who had had a few years in the world where they had won their laurels in the professions and industry. These were older than the pleb who goes to West Point at sixteen, seventeen, or eighteen; their minds better trained than the minds of the plebs.

The tireless officers of the A. E. F. were out of touch with the moods of their own country and removed from its effort, while the French officer was in his home setting, and the British received his morning paper across the Channel the day it was published. But our Staff leaders would have been dull clay, they would have lacked professional ambition as the hounds of war who must keep lean and keen as statesmanship held them in leash, if they had not thought of themselves as very much a chosen band who were laying the foundations for a great military future for America when she should have a standing army worthy of her importance as a nation. Conscription for this war was to be only the forerunner of conscription in peace, when they should have real flesh-and-blood armies to maneuver in peace so that they might be ready for maneuver in war.

In their own financial incorruptibility and soldierly honor they did not count money costs or industrial delays in a war emergency. America was rich, the richest of nations. All her industrial resources, as well as her man-power, every hammer blow, every turn of a lathe or a car wheel or a ship propeller, every furrow cut by every plough, were at their command. They drew the drafts which Washington cashed. They would have no repetition of the errors of military organization north and south in the Civil War, as they combined the best features of the French and British staff systems, ever keeping in mind the Prussian system which they professionally most admired, in forming an Americanized whole.

Their academic training was bound to express itself in perfectionist terms. It would have been un-American for them not to strive for the best. Such of the able Army minds as had the luck to be in France also now had the opportunity of insisting upon full recognition of their own branches of the service. Infantry, cavalry, artillery, tank, aviation, and machine-gun enthusiasts had differences which delayed recommendations, and changed them after they were made.

Soon there were casualties among the chosen few who were striving with prodigious industry to apply their theories in practice. Some did not develop up to their peace reputations. All had a final refuge for passing bucks—Washington. Our people were not really in the War. Our army authorities at home were evidently lax in their discipline over soldiers and the public. Why were officers at home so stupid? Why was Washington retaining able officers who should be in France? Why were not more troops arriving? Why wasn't shipping up to the requirements of the force we already had in France? Every officer who tried to communicate over the telephone in France wondered when America would send poles and wires and string the wires and set up a *real* telephone system.

The traditional feeling of the Army posts toward the War

Department became a part of *esprit de corps* now no less than in frontier days. Asking for more than you expect to get, in order to get something, was no less in order as a part of the system of administration.

THE REGULARS RULE INDUSTRY

Geographical necessity had compelled Pershing to place his headquarters at Chaumont, a small town with as villainous a winter climate as ever tried the nerves of overworked men. Chaumont, more than a hundred miles back from the trenches, was five hundred miles from our ports in France. The man who a few months previously had been in command of ten thousand men at Colonia Dublon in Mexico not only had to form an army of one million or two million men overseas, but in building his line of communications he was the head of an industrial enterprise which was without precedent in its complexity and size for the distance from its home base. This enterprise, too, must be militarized. Engineers, foremen, railroad managers, train dispatchers, and all other technical experts and commanders, all who served the Army in France must be in uniform, under military discipline.

"Through channels" meant that a Regular chief alone reported direct to the Commander-in-Chief for any department. The chief baker of the A. E. F. was a Regular. At first soldiers were the telephone operators. But this branch of civil training again brought women to the front. Women telephone operators as well as nurses could step into service without previous military training.

Ever calling for more specialists from civil life, Pershing held to his policy that the chief of every branch must be a Regular, on the ground that the Regular alone knew how to co-operate with other branches in co-ordinating all in military power at the front. No important proposal by any reserve officer, although he might be master of a most technical calling in which no Regular officer had been trained, could become effective without the approval of a Regular superior. And among Pershing's able staff chiefs was no man who had ever had the opportunity of acquiring anything like the experience of many civilians in large enterprises in construction, in handling of vast quantities of freight by railroad or ship, in the organization and direction of labor in small or large groups. The documented revelation of the difficulties of making war three thousand miles from home is in the cablegrams of requisitions from the A. E. F. with their minute specifications. Aside from armament and routine quartermasters' supplies, they included all the material for building a city and everything to equip it for its daily life.

In the very early period Pershing himself would go personally over these cablegrams to avoid duplications and to subject all of them to the general plan he carried in his mind; but even his industry was not equal, in addition to all his other labors, to their increasing volume. Inevitably the most minute measurements and technical terms were often garbled. After a long cablegram, covering many subjects, had been cut in strips in Washington, and each strip sent to the branch which it concerned, it might bring more than one "rush" telegram from a plant or factory asking just what the strip meant. Did the measurement, for example, mean one-eighth of an inch, or eight inches? This involved further delay in the supply of some article which was essential to the construction plan of some impatient chief in France.

That chief would be especially indignant if he were quite unfamiliar with industrial production, whose processes in a great plant he might disrupt by writing a single line on a pad on his desk. Naturally, in his preoccupation with his task, he might regard the docks of our Atlantic coast ports as a combined department store and warehouse. To his thinking, all that a clerk had to do when a requisition from France came in was to pull down from a shelf, or remove from a bin, a thousand motor trucks, four miles of pipe, two thousand mules, sixteen laundry machines, fourteen bakeries, ten cement-mixers, or a thousand miles of telephone wire. If last week's order of 10,000 eight-inch bolts was changed to 12,000 six-inch bolts, then the clerk had only to take 12,000 bolts out of the six-inch bin instead of 10,000 out of the eight-inch bin. Meanwhile, it might happen that there was a shortage of both kinds of bolts at home, and local construction projects were calling for more no less lustily than the A. E. F. In that case, the priority for the A. E. F. demand over the domestic might delay the construction of some article which was more essential for immediate delivery in France than the 12,000 six-inch bolts which, to the chief who had ordered them, were vital to winning the War. On the other hand, if the 10,000 eight-inch bolts had already been shipped before the change of specifications came, this might lead to blasphemous utterances in France to the effect that the folks in the War Department could not read plain English.

With the submarine zone between the two, there was a bottleneck in French ports as well as in American. Troop ships had taken as long as five weeks for a turn-around, and cargo ships as long as nine weeks. Unloading in France was exasperatingly slow. France had no labor to spare for stevedoring. The French army and French private interests were bound to press for priority over the needs of an army which was not yet in action. The French port, municipal, and prefectural authorities had been under the strain of three years of war. Our State Department sent long communications to the War Department as to the system by which we should pay port dues for our transports and cargo ships. Local authorities even thought that regimental trains in passing through their villages and towns should pay *octroi* duties.

There were many things to be settled before the relations of the American Army in France could be established on a regular working basis—even if the disaster of Caporetto had not complicated the situation. The French had not only to supply reinforcements to the Italian army through the winter of 1917–18, but must hold in readiness a large reserve of rolling stock for concentrations against the German offensives. Men who were sweating blood to complete their parts in the vast Service of Supply enterprise in France had their raw nerves lacerated by the difficulties of dealing with foreign officials through interpreters. They must have permission from local authorities for the use of land or a building. The mayor might refer the matter to the prefect, who in turn might refer it to Paris, with permission eventually secured only through intervention by our Headquarters at Chaumont.

If we were to unload ships rapidly on the other side we must have labor and build docks. Why didn't Washington send the labor, and the material for the docks? Labor also required transport, and it had to be fed—sometimes housed—after it arrived; and the material had to be provided, shipped by rail to an American port, and then wait for a ship. Naturally, the staff in France, which saw itself as the first scientific staff that the nation had ever had, was bound to view that antiquated staff system in Washington as failing in its part; while the staff in Washington faced a problem that had no precedent in the British, French, German, Italian, or Russian staff systems. It had to adapt itself to local conditions no less than other staffs. When at General Headquarters in France, I shared its irritations; I had its viewpoint. Then, when I was with the troops and heard what Line officers said about the G. H. Q. staff, I shared their irritation and got their viewpoint. Finally, during a month in the United States, December–January, 1917–1918, I learned what the viewpoint was at home.

CONGESTION AT THE PORTS

In French seaports I was reminded of the critical period in the Panama Canal project and the confusion at the port of Colon. The chaos along our lines of communication in France was like the chaos of the unfinished works across the twenty-mile strip of the Isthmus. The situation in Hoboken, though less chaotic, recalled that at Tampa in 1898 during the Spanish War. American energy was crowding men and supplies through the bottleneck on this side, and the same brand of energy in the A. E. F. was trying to pull it through the bottleneck on the other side and then push it into the interior of France with utterly inadequate transport. Pershing informed Washington in a cable that it might be better to stop sending timber for docks and send railroad cars instead.[6] Meanwhile he was hastening the repair of French cars. He would communicate definitely when he had

THE $3,000,000,000 PUNCH

SWEETHEARTS and WIVES
WILL SEE HOW CITIZENS
OF NEW YORK HAVE BEEN
MADE INTO SOLDIERS
AT CAMP UPTON.

HIPPODROME
SUNDAY DEC. 9
AFTERNOON and EVENING
305TH INFANTRY, NATIONAL ARMY
WILL PRESENT
"A DAY at CAMP UPTON"
POPULAR PRICES
AND THE BEST CAUSE IN THE WORLD

ALL MINNESOTA

Must back up
the boys who
are "Somewhere
in France"

BUY
LIBERTY BONDS

Get Behind the Man
Behind the Gun

Save a loaf
a week
help win
the war

U.S. FOOD ADMINISTRATION

WAR POSTERS

more information. And Washington kept on getting out the timber while it considered how the railroads could spare rolling stock.

The fluctuations of the A. E. F. demands were related to those of the Allies and dictated all deliveries in place of the orderly routine of peace in private business. For "over there" was the command that speeded up production in any plant and speeded factories and the railroads in transportation of the A. E. F. requisitions. Once a consignment had reached the port, the railroad's and producer's parts were finished. So supplies piled up at the ports for want of shipping. Articles for which the latest cablegram from France demanded urgent priority were behind stacks of material much nearer the ship's side. Officers who had charge of loading the ships, under stinging reminders of the slow turn-around, madly hastened loading in order to clear a ship for sea. And big troubles found their way up to the Secretary of War. He might have enjoyed inspections of pleasant situations; but the only time he could spare away from Washington must be used to remedy unpleasant ones.

So he answered an alarm sounded from the Hoboken wharves. Major General Francis E. Kernan had worked out our original transportation program, but not in contemplation of so large demands from the A. E. F., and least of all of the Caporetto disaster. The really big mistake of the Secretary of War, the Congress, the War Industries Board, Pershing, and the people of the United States, not to mention all the Allied commanders, was not to have foreseen Caporetto. Such foresight should be included in future preparedness, thus removing from war the element of surprise and chance. And perhaps such an achievement would automatically abolish the Stock Exchange, for then all prices could be charted for a year to come!

Baker saw the Hoboken piers, where production was banked up for the want of ships, as another example of the need of concentrated authority in war-time. In place of French prefectures and English counties we had States, which were far more independent integers in our national whole. New York harbor is bounded by two States. Each wanted to help win the War, no doubt, but State authority had clashed with State authority and with national authority. There were volunteer citizens' organizations, labor, shipping, and railroad organizations, and municipal authorities to be considered. Land and sea were related through the Army and the Navy. The Treasury Department had a hand. There were bitter complaints against incompetent superiors to be analyzed. Strong personal jealousies must be soothed. The demand was for one man, who finally appeared in Brigadier General Frank T. Hines, another Regular of the type who would compose civilian and military differences under Army authority. But for the moment the best that could be done was that one board should take the place of several. Baker did not pass the buck to Hurley of the Shipping Board, who was driving the shipbuilders, or to the Navy for not repairing the boilers of the big German liners and reconditioning them as transports overnight. No administrative genius, but ships only, could really solve the problem.

Some onlookers had confirmation of their view that a Secretary of War should be a "hard-boiled he-man" instead of a sentimental pacifist, when Baker paused on the wharves to watch the soldiers going over the Christmas presents from relatives to men in France. Combustibles and perishables must be removed and the packages securely wrapped up again. Baker appreciated all it meant to have a package some mother had sent from Arizona, from Maine, from a city flat, reach her boy in a French billet. As one of the party with him remarked: "If he gets any relaxation out of that, let him have it. Life is not one grand holiday for him, and his troubles are only beginning." But Christmas presents when the A. E. F. was crying for essentials! That killjoy "priority" would hardly permit the presents to cross France to the billets in time.

Baker even wrote a note to the President about it, saying:

"Many things were in evidence, kid gloves and finery being common among the presents. One box contained dressed birds; many of them contained fruit, bananas, peaches, and pears; and veritable stacks of matches, not deemed safe for transportation, were being taken out. Many packages were in frail boxes, and for these new and stronger boxes were being made."

It was never revealed, so far as I know, who was responsible for shipping the bathtubs, chairs, office desks, cuspidors, filing cabinets, floor wax, and sofas, which Pershing mentions with soldierly indignation.[7] Later, the extensive administrative establishment of the A. E. F. was calling for more desks of the American pattern. Our officers did not find a superfluity of bathtubs in France. Perhaps the bathtubs were unnecessary if we had the cuspidors. Unless my memory fails me, there were cuspidors in the Commander-in-Chief's office and in the offices of others of the High Command. Provided the ejections were accurate, the cuspidors protected the waxed floors of the old French army barracks which had been fitted up as a headquarters at Chaumont. Colonel Benjamin Alvord, the pioneer Adjutant General of the A. E. F., watched over two filing cabinets, from Washington to New York, then across the Atlantic on the *Baltic* to Paris, where, to his chagrin, they were purloined, leaving him to makeshifts until another set should arrive in France. Many filing cabinets were required for the personnel records of the A. E. F., which now occupy so much space in Washington. Iron safes seemed to be serving a very practical purpose in protecting valuable documents from fire.

FILING CABINETS, CUSPIDORS, AND BATHTUBS

Force of habit sometimes led old quartermasters to think in terms of outfitting an Army post, which included living quarters for the officers' families. Pershing might not know of the articles asked for by one subordinate until another subordinate indignantly reported their arrival at a port instead of articles for which he was impatiently waiting. But consignments of bathtubs, filing cabinets, and cuspidors—although they were not more impracticable than the Arctic clothes and equipment for Alaskan service which I saw arrive in Manila in 1900—may have been sent to the docks by mistake. Perhaps they were the nearest cargo at hand to complete a loading under the raucous (not to say blasphemous) urging of the stevedores to get a ship away from a berth so that a waiting one might take its place. Perhaps they were mistaken for Red Cross or Y. M. C. A. or hospital allotments, when it seemed there was nothing on earth which the A. E. F. did not want. Perhaps the officer who put them on board was only just another of the tired men, who are more numerous in war than in peace, with a correspondingly larger range for errors.

There was another case, one of a conspicuous pair of which we heard so often at G. H. Q. that they may be cited as exceptions to the rule, when millions of tons of cargo were being hurried to France in an industrial undertaking unfamiliar to us. Enormous long piles had been ordered for the new docks we were building at Bassens. In order to get them on board in America some transport officer who knew nothing about building docks had them cut in two. He may even have vented his sarcasm on the ignoramus who thought that piles of that length could be shipped on the vessel which must carry them if they were to have priority! Of course cutting them in two made them useless for the purpose for which they had been ordered.

But it is not within human power to explain all the mistakes that we made in the War. Mistakes were a part of our education when everybody was learning in a new school of experience. Only by making mistakes did we get ahead. We were at war, and war is made at the front. Headquarters in France was responsible for the lives of our men, and for victory which should end all the expense and strain.

Yet even the new scientific staff system of Headquarters in France might make mistakes. Even it might be subject to human frailties, to exhausted men and shattered nerves. Indeed, as one who was at G. H. Q. a great deal, while I rarely met staff officers who admitted their own mistakes, I often heard them descanting on the mistakes of their colleagues, which was not surprising in the course of a rapid expansion of inexperienced personnel and the frequent shifting of superiors in all branches. The inevitable delays in stating requirements and changes of mind "over there" were sometimes puzzling to Washington.

I may mention the gantry cranes. These enormous structures

were not to be turned out so speedily as screws and bolts. On July 14, 1917, a cablegram was received ordering "sixty 5-ton, 44-feet-span cranes . . . quickest possible delivery." [8] The manufacturers set to work. After the order had been placed, one board in France decided against the gantries. Another confirmed the original order. But in the middle of April, 1918, a cable was sent to "suspend further shipments of gantry cranes." Eight were on their way to France. The other fifty-two were left on the docks or at the plants. Reconsideration of the availability of the eight began again in May. After hesitation they were installed at Bassens, and finally, on August 16, 1918, came the cable: "Actual experience with gantries has demonstrated efficiency and we will require all of the 52 cranes remaining to be shipped as well as additional cranes (16) for which order will be cabled soon." [9]

THE A. E. F.'S CHANGES OF MIND

Headquarters in France decided that half-ton motor trucks were too small; so all shipments of that type should be immediately stopped. There were one hundred and seventy-eight on the docks or on their way to the ports. At the worst, they were a form of transportation, and the A. E. F. was short of transport. The obliging Biddle, Chief of Staff in Washington, said he would send them on "if they would be of some service." [10] After that, of course, G. H. Q. would have the kind of trucks it wanted. A requisition from the A. E. F. might have to be filled two thousand miles from an Atlantic port. It might necessitate the setting up of new machinery, or require raw material of which there was a desperate shortage. A cancellation might unload trains on their way to ports, and even unload ships. The many changes of mind about aviation will have a place in another chapter.

An animal required more ship space than a man. The request of G. H. Q. that officers' private mounts should be sent to them was the subject of several cablegrams. These horses had to be forwarded to our ports, and then put in stalls to be sent to France; then forwarded from French ports to the of-

ficers wherever the officers happened to be at the time. An
officer might be in some place where he could neither stable
nor use his horse; but someone highly placed in France decided that other things were more pressing—especially after
Caporetto.

The French had suggested that they could supply horses
for some of our divisions, and mules were supposed to be forthcoming from Spain in return for shipments of sulphate of am-
monia, which must have immediate priority. The French and
the Spanish seemed about to make good on their promises;
then they were not; and then they were. French conditions
were subject to all manner of influences, and Spanish conditions to bargaining with a neutral instead of an ally.

Horse stalls were put in cargo ships, taken down, and then
put in again, thus wasting time and tonnage. There were protests from G. H. Q. that horses were sent over without having
had their manes roached, and that the stalls were not built to
prevent the horses from biting one another. Then G. H. Q.
found that a heavier type of horse was required than had been
anticipated, thus preventing light draft horses in the corrals at
the ports from seeing France. The pro-and-con discussion about
the extent of motorization of transport subjected animal
requisitions to several changes. At first sight of one cablegram,
Washington wondered why the A. E. F. should order seven
hundred thousand horse blankets, which implied a wardrobe
of several for every animal we then had in France. But evidently a cipher had been added in transmission by the cable
operator, who was inadvertently doing his part to keep the
horses warm.

Two weeks after Caporetto, when the Allies realized that
they must face a German offensive in the spring on the Western
front, the cavalry advocates had their innings at G. H. Q. in
France. They maintained that aviation and trench warfare
had not eliminated cavalry as a useful branch of the service.
A large cavalry force in France had not previously been in our
plan. We were now asked to organize "one cavalry division

for service in France to arrive when we had five army corps in France." [11] "Such a division would constitute a strategic reserve in case of a combined Allied offensive," when at the time the problem was how to resist the coming enemy offensive. For three years, in hope of such an opportunity for their use in a "break through," the British were stated to have maintained forty thousand and the French thirty thousand cavalry.

Our regular cavalry was largely on the Mexican border, which was still sending in such frequent alarms of threatened raids that the War Department must keep a watchful eye on the Mexican situation. Our regular cavalry officers had been scattered through the Army organization; many of our regular cavalry horses had been assigned to the artillery. Cavalry takes long to train. When the artillery in our cantonments was complaining of lack of enough horses, the cavalry became a competitor in the market. Cavalry officers must be detached from their work against the protests of commanders who thought they had not a fair share of Regular personnel for the training of infantry divisions. In addition to the barracks for cavalrymen and plants for feeding them, we must build new stables for their mounts, which took labor away from the shipbuilding and other plants under construction. The cavalry must be equipped with saddles when there was a shortage of leather and leather-workers, and when the infantry had not yet a sufficient supply of shoes, not to mention that all the officers in France must now be supplied with Sam Browne belts. This is not to imply that the A. E. F. perhaps did not need a cavalry division, but only suggests that the preparation and dispatch of one to France was far from being so simple an additional item to home labor as might be easily imagined at G. H. Q. in France.

It was all in the course of the expansion of the A. E. F. as shaped by broadening experience. By the middle of December when Pershing had become very strongly convinced that "a crisis was coming in the spring," he said that during the coming year our troops

"will be required for defensive and possibly offensive work.
. . . Both French and British are going to lean very hard on
us, and public opinion in both countries will clamor loudly
for American assistance. . . . Consider it of the utmost importance that our best troops be sent over. The National Guard
divisions now here contain a large percentage of raw material
both in officers and men. It will take very hard and persistent
work to get them in shape." [He emphasized the] "importance
of sending regular divsions here for our first-line combat divisions in order to get more time for training our National
Guard and National Army divisions." [12]

The Regular divisions, it should be said, were also largely
composed of recruits; but the idea was that they were Regular
in name and discipline, and were formed in the Regular spirit
and tradition and officered by chosen Regulars. Pershing suggested relieving the Regular regiments in Hawaii and Panama,
which were already much reduced, with National Guard divisions. The answer was that the War Department had "begun
organization of regular regiments into brigades and divisions
about three weeks ago. The third Regular division will sail
about January 1st, and will be followed by other divisions. In
case of any delay in Regular divisions the best of other divisions will be sent to avoid loss of time. The matter of relieving the Regular infantry regiments at Panama and Hawaii
now under consideration." This transfer would take more
shipping and was a further tax on railroads already unequal
to the traffic.

Unforeseen additional demands of the A. E. F., for which
only the War was to blame, interfered with keeping up the
schedule of regular troop movements. In early December Pershing asked for four thousand aviation mechanics to be rushed
to England; five thousand in January; six thousand in February; and thereafter fifteen thousand to be maintained permanently in England, where we should have to house and feed
them.[13] This, of itself, was a force as large as we had had at
Santiago in 1898.

Moreover, he wanted immediately twelve hundred bricklayers, one hundred carpenters, and four hundred laborers to construct aviation quarters in England. But this time the cable operator had slipped off a cipher instead of adding one as he had done in the case of the horse blankets: the number of carpenters was really one thousand, and of laborers four thousand. A fortnight elapsed before the mistake, for which neither G. H. Q. nor Washington was responsible, became known in Washington.

The total of these special units to be in England in December would have filled to capacity any two troop transports we had at the time. They would have packed the *Leviathan,* which was ready for her first trip. The aviation mechanics must be summoned and transported from the flying fields, though we were short of railroad cars. The value of the Draft's classification of man-power was exemplified in the preparedness of the boards to respond to such emergencies; but selection from the lists took time, and every bricklayer or carpenter sent must be taken from unfinished war construction at home, whose chiefs would have resented the loss for any reason except "over there." All the mechanics, after being mobilized, must be organized into construction units under officers, and given places on ships which might instead have been transporting infantry. When there were disasters at sea the A. E. F. had to wait until the articles lost were replaced and shipped again. The more ships we sent, the longer it took to unload them in French ports.

XX

A STERN WINTER OF WAR

THERE might be an autocracy in France, but on this side of the Atlantic we were still a democracy. The Regular officer who served at home received his morning paper and was continuously in touch with the public mood. Inside of a few weeks he might learn more about his own people than he had during all the years since West Point had received him as a plastic youth to be formed in the classic military mould; and if he failed to respond to what he was learning, then co-operation between the civil and the military worlds would suffer.

If it chanced that his part was the humdrum, though highly essential, business of dealing with the recruit munition plants, he heard the roar of industry's wheels rather than the tramp of marching men. The leaders of industry with whom he came in contact were not always reserve officers, awkwardly saluting him as their military superior; and foremen and machine-hands were not khaki-clad sergeants, corporals, or privates.

Or he might be at a cantonment. Here he conducted the primary school of instruction for the draftees, which passed them on to the graduate school in France. The mothers and fathers of the men in his cantonment were more than names on cards to him. They and their friends, their clergymen and Congressmen, visited the camp. Sometimes he had to explain to them why it was that the boys who lived within commuting distance might not sleep at home. And he was training a different type of rookie from the Regular rookie of peace-time, who was used to drilling not more than two or three hours a day. All the classes of men in the new Army came at war's call from civil occupations where they had been used to eight or ten hours of labor a day. They unquestioningly accepted this same number of hours of training as the soldier's routine job; and

22

no Regular officer would slacken their industry by telling them that this was not the usual thing for soldiers.

If the primary lessons in America failed, then there would be failure in France; and the primary lessons would fail if the spirit to endure the drill was not in the new soldiers who reflected, in turn, the spirit of the people. The civilian Secretary of War had reason to understand the difference between leading and driving in a democracy. In the course of a note to Spring-Rice, the British Ambassador, which Baker wrote on October 16, 1917, he remarked:

"The most tyrannical governments rest in a certain sense on popular approval, or at least popular acquiescence; and when that is withdrawn, the government is but a poor feeble thing which must run to any cover it can find."

But democracy had a long, hard road of achievement to travel before the Kaiser was to "run to cover" in Holland in early November, 1918. I quote again from Baker: [1]

"If I had some subtle and instantaneous way of using efficiently all of the good will to help that there is in America, the world could not stand against her for five minutes. Facing the fact that it takes some time to order the process by which so much willingness and good will can be used—that is the difficult part of this situation; and yet it is one of the prices that we pay for democracy.

"It would be perfectly possible to have an ordered and regimented society in which each person would have in his pocket a card, and upon that card directions as to how he is to act under all sorts and conditions of circumstances; and when a national emergency arose, to have the public authority telegraph abroad: Everybody act according to Rule 13. It would be possible to fix by congressional enactment a particular breakfast hour for the human race and prescribe their conduct for every five minutes of the rest of the day; and in certain forms of government this is a more or less popular amusement.

"But one of the characteristics of democracy is that it does not proceed that way. It scatters its people; it allows them to go about here and there, seeking by individual inspiration and

unguided effort to find the avenue of their own highest opportunity and enjoyment. All are busy about their own concerns.
And then, when the national emergency comes, there is no
Rule 13. Everybody has to ask somebody else, 'Well, what are
you going to do? What do you think I can do?'"

Eight months after our entry into the War we were beginning
to understand that the time for "Rule 13" had come; that
everyone must do what his card said he should do; and finally,
that for some of us, "the largest usefulness may come from doing the same thing—just continuing to do it."

The people at home had not read the dispatches of alarm
from Pershing and Bliss, or Bliss's memorandum to Baker.
They knew nothing of the details about that twenty-four division program. But there had been borne in on them during
the winter of 1917–18 that just "showing the flag" in France
and putting through two Liberty Loans might not be enough.
Baker had said before Caporetto, "Some people say they do not
know how long the War will last. I do. It will last until we
win it." [2] Now the nation realized that victory might require
all America's strength as well as Britain's and France's.

It required more imagination for G. H. Q. in France to picture the situation at home than for the people at home to
picture the situation abroad. For the eyes of the people at home
were set on the European front—the news in the communiqués
was beginning to affect our daily lives. Europe, which had been
so remote, had come integrally close to us. Our fortunes, our
comforts, our national future were at stake on battlefields three
thousand miles away.

England, we knew, was grim in winter fog. Her people were
on a strict food ration under police surveillance to save tonnage for war supplies. Her statesmen were reassuring the public
with reports of larger grain reserves than a year ago as a result
of increased acreage in the homeland which had been brought
under cultivation the previous summer. We saw France bent
under her three years' burden, and hungry. In peace-time,
France grew a large portion of her foodstuffs. Now, during war,
while the men were at the front, grandfather and grandmother,

WILLIAM G. McADOO
Director-General of Railroads

EDWARD N. HURLEY
of the Shipping Board

HERBERT HOOVER
Food Administrator

DR. H. A. GARFIELD
Fuel Administrator

mother and children, had allowed none of the fields to go un-
tilled. But a French gastronomic prejudice refused our offer
of cornmeal: it was food for animals.

Before Caporetto the suggestion had been made that we
suspend troop movements in order to release more tonnage to
feed Europe. Assistant Secretary of War William M. Ingraham
had even given the suggestion authority in a way that was
taken by a newspaper man to indicate that we were going to
send no more troops to France. The Committee on Public Information, on being informed that such a statement was about
to be put on the wire, blocked its widespread dissemination by
expeditious action. No news could have been so distressing to
the French soldiers, who had ample rations, and none so heartening to the enemy.

FOOD WOULD NOT WIN THE WAR

Our apprehension about hunger, which Belgian relief work
and the "Food Will Win the War" slogan had gone so far to
establish in our minds, was eased on assurance from Pershing
that his men were well-fed. France was rationed much less than
Great Britain, and Great Britain less than Germany, which
Allied reports pictured as at the point of starvation. Our voluntary rationing, which was quite sufficient, saved our Food Administration from the unpopular business of police regulations
and bread-lines. The thought that we were limiting our pleasure rides in our cars to save gasoline strengthened the fellowship of sacrifice in all things for the common cause. Food was
our easiest problem.

The Congress voted for prohibition. We refused alcoholic
drinks to our soldiers, though wine was a regular part of the
French soldier's rations and rum of the British soldier's. We
would close our saloons though French cafés and British "pubs"
were open. One of the strong arguments for prohibition was
that it would turn energy and material for the production of
liquors and beer into the production of food and munitions.

Meanwhile the War Department continued to accelerate the
movement of draft men to the cantonments, which were not

quite ready to receive such large numbers. Industrial preparation had not been able to keep up with the movement. The
canvass of the Munitions Board in April, 1917, which had
shown that we could not fully supply 1,000,000 men by January 1, had been proven correct. In spite of the pressure on
manufacturers to utilize every available loom and all materials,
we were short 1,000,000 cotton underdrawers, 75,000 hats,
800,000 wool undershirts, 400,000 wool overcoats, as the troops
faced winter in the cantonments.

"This War is being fought in every factory, every workshop,
every home in the country," Baker said, "by those marvelously
subtle processes of modern scientific achievement by which
we are all co-ordinated."

And he said on October 17, before Caporetto: [3]

"I do not love war; yet there are some things dearer than
life. Would we call back the Continental Army? Would we
send Lafayette back to France? Would we take the sword of
Washington out of his hands and break it over our knee? . . .

"Oh, my fellow citizens, suppose a soldier came in here and
said to you: 'Good people, I have been selected to go off and
hazard my life for you. I would like to have a coat, and shoes,
and a hat, and a gun; I would like to have a gas mask; I would
like to have equipment to make my task as safe as possible.'
Everyone in this audience would empty his pockets and pour
out all that he had in order that the soldier might have everything that he needed for his comfort and safety. . . .

"Just for a moment I represent him as an advocate to you.
I am coming to ask you to clothe him and feed him, to pay his
railroad fare, to carry him across the ocean, and to put a gun in
his hand.

"We must realize that we are at war; we must realize that
the very character of our adversary and the aggression which
brought on our own participation mark it as a supreme struggle. Let no man imagine for a moment that a feeble effort will
suffice. If we are in truth to rescue civilization out of this con-
flagration, then every nerve and every muscle, every thought,
every affection, every impulse, every capacity both in us as individuals and collectively in us as a nation, must be devoted

to this undertaking, not only that we may win, but that we may win quickly. For every day that this War continues decreases the wealth of the world by at least $100,000,000 and many thousand lives. So far these have been not your lives, nor mine, nor those of our sons and brothers, but the lives of fellow human beings, much like us, who are entitled to peace and liberty and opportunity in the world, and whose welfare is an essential ingredient, in any wide and popular view, of our own welfare. So, if America can shorten this War by a single day, it is worth the effort that it costs."

And about democracy, which was fighting the War in the name of democracy, he said: [4]

"For we must never forget, when we speak of democracy, that it is not an accomplishment, it is not a thing that has been done. Rather it is a progress, it is a system of growth; and though today we might achieve what our limited vision proclaims to us as the democratic ideal, its quality is such that when we stand on what now seems to us the highest peak in the range, there will ever be greater heights ahead to tempt and inspire us. . . ."

On January 2, 1918, he said in Washington:

"The Army is merely the point of the sword; the handle, and the hand that wields the handle, and the body that controls that hand, and the subsistence of that body, are all just as vitally indispensable to the effective use of that weapon as the point itself. . . . This isn't one man's war, or several men's war, or an army's war. It is a war of *all* the people of the United States. . . . If the German Emperor has any sort of notion that racial differences exist among us, or that religious differences may annoy us, or that sectional or partisan considerations may divide us, let us send him a message that that is not so." [5]

We were entering that stern period which Baker had prophesied to the college presidents in Washington on May 5, 1917, when he said that "our feelings are going to be torn and our nerves made raw." And we were learning, as he had said on July 4, 1917, that "the progress of the art of war is not from year to year but from day to day"—as witness both the effect of Caporetto and the changing requisitions of the A. E. F. for material.

If there should be some fresh demand, such as that for gas masks after the first German attack at Ypres, we had not England's advantage of propinquity. England, as she concentrated on making gas masks, could have them at the front the day after they were finished. We might perhaps not have them there for weeks. The question of how we could best bring all our resources to bear on the enemy was becoming more acute every day, as our spirit became more united and better educated in military realities. Sea spaces were not our only limiting distances. Britain's advantage in bringing her force to bear lay not alone in the narrow stretch of the Channel. Her forty million people lived on a little island. Our one hundred and ten millions were spread from coast to coast between the Canadian and the Mexican borders. Her coal mines, her steel plants, all her munition works, her camps, were much nearer the seacoast than ours, nearer the mouth of the shorter funnel which fed the rapacious hopper of war. Steel billets had to be transported farther to the American maker of rifles and guns than did a new rifle from a British factory to the front. Our grain had to go a thousand or two thousand miles to a port for transport to Europe. Britain's labor was in a congested area, quickly moved from one munition works to another.

"MILITARY NECESSITY" AND A COAL FAMINE

The British railroad system radiated toward the many ports of a seabound country dependent upon oversea trade. Our railroads were already stretched to capacity before we were in the War. Many of our railroad equipment plants had been transformed into munition plants. Railroad labor that was usually occupied in maintenance was building spur tracks, being alienated by the draft and by munition work at high wages, or sent to France to serve the railroad system of the A. E. F. We had insufficient freight cars to keep up with the transport of war material to the factories and the coast. Troops must not only be moved from home to camps and then from camps to the coast, but also back and forth between camps. That new master, "military necessity," had become a nation's train-dispatcher. Army orders called for many unexpected routings of what would have been called "excursions" in peace. Special units that had been mobilized in one camp were dispatched to other camps for further training, as new aviation fields and training centers were established. Large numbers of men were sent from the wintry North to camps vacated in the warmer South by departing divisions. And the divisions from the South waited, as pawns of "military necessity," in chilly northern camps for troop ships delayed by storms or slow disembarkation "over there."

The location of all manner of new enterprises, as well as camps, meant of itself much switching and disorganization of the peace-time transport system both by rail and by water. In nine months the enormous and disconcerting demands had gravely depreciated rolling stock, which since the World War began had not been kept up by peace-time renewals and repairs. Poor maintenance and undermanning were the rule; any railroad that was not in rundown condition had lost caste. Railroad men were proud of what they had accomplished with engines and cars that ought long ago to have gone to the repair shops or been dumped on the scrap-heap. All this meant inefficiency.

In face of the winter crisis and the call for the twenty-four division plan, the War Department program had been disrupted by the insufficiency of home carriers, even though the use of inland waterways had been increased. Munition plants were late in filling orders because raw material did not arrive in time, and the General Staff accordingly was late in meeting the A. E. F. requisitions.

It had been proposed at the outset of the War that the government should take over the railroads, but the railroads had by voluntary action achieved remarkable co-operation which railroad experts thought was sound for the first stage, though they now understood that we had reached another stage. At first

Washington tested public opinion by suggesting a limited control. The response was in tune with the temper of the hour: the people acquiesced in the war-time measure which was to pool all the railroads and run them as though they were a single system. No dissent arose from stockholders and managers of railroads which had to share valuable terminals with competitors having none or inferior ones in the great cities. Evolution had brought us one more dictatorship. Secretary of the Treasury McAdoo, of the many jobs, now took on still another. He became the dictator of all the railroads of America, with Samuel M. Felton, a veteran railroad president, retaining his part as the expert second-in-command.

The nation, which heretofore had worried only about the prices it had to pay for fuel, now worried about getting enough at any price. In spite of all our stores of coal under the earth we had a coal famine. Such is human nature that the war dictator who enforces a schedule of rationing inevitably becomes the target of public criticism; and Fuel Administrator Garfield had a "No" task which should have made him sympathize with the Secretary of War. In the rich United States housewives were standing in line to get rations of coal just as they were in England and Germany for both food and coal; standing in line in order that the A. E. F. and France and Italy might have coal. In Europe the price of coal had risen to sixty, seventy, and eighty dollars a ton. Washington was worried lest Italy might yet drop out of the War for want of coal. Lord Robert Cecil, the British Minister of Blockade, thought that the shortage of coal had been one of the factors in bringing on the Caporetto disaster.

I was colder in a New York City hotel in early January, 1918, than I had been in France. Proclamations by Dr. Garfield were receiving as much headline space as Hoover's or McAdoo's, as he asked for "complete patriotic co-operation" in his system of rationing. In the one of January 18, 1918, he said:

"The main and urgent thing to do is to send to the American forces abroad and to the Allies the food and war supplies which they vitally need. War munitions, food, manufactured articles of every description, lie at our Atlantic ports in tens of thousands of tons, while literally hundreds of ships, waiting loaded with war goods for our men and the Allies, cannot take the seas because their bunkers are empty of coal. The coal to send them on their way is waiting behind the congested freight that has jammed all terminals."

The railroads must first have coal to carry material to the munition plants, and the munition plants must have coal to go on manufacturing. Our soldiers must have it in their cantonments or freeze. The wheels of industry, except those propelled by oil or water power, must have coal. In the public mind coal now outranked food as the means of winning the War.

RAILROADS SNOWBOUND—SHIPS STALLED IN HARBORS

Providence did not favor us with an open winter. The weather continued in a war mood. In regions where normally the thermometer rarely touched zero, this winter it frequently registered many degrees below. Shoveling snow was in order for the soldiers at the cantonments, where drifts covered the drill-grounds. While ships were unable to clear for France, the railroads of the eastern United States, fighting snow and ice, were almost paralyzed by the latter part of January. Passenger trains between New York and Chicago and solid trains of supplies for the Allies were canceled. Flood conditions were a menace, and stopped production in several mines. After ships' bunkers were filled, the ships were often held in port by terrific storms at sea.

We were having workless as well as heatless and meatless days. There had been many kinds of holidays, but none so strange as when Dr. Garfield suspended the operations of some industries in order that the railroads might catch up with the transport of coal and supplies.

When it read the daily papers the public had reason for optimism one day and for pessimism the next. The Italians were reported to have gained ground in an attack, and to have lost another nine thousand prisoners. Winston Churchill declared the situation of the Allies to be perilous. Lloyd George, who knew that it was, had lost none of his facility for cheerful public statement.

One morning we were aghast at a horror that had an aspect more terrible than battle losses. The high explosive, TNT, had become the very symbol of concentrated material power in the depth charges against submarines, in aerial bombs, in the shells that shattered trenches and laid villages in ruins. A cargo of it in a French munition ship in Halifax, that busy war harbor, exploded as one vast charge, wrecking ships and making a shambles of the débris of buildings on shore; and our Red Cross faced here a problem in relief nearer home than stricken Italy. And then out of the East came news that recalled the Crusades. This time the Richard Cœur de Lion was General Allenby, released from the attrition of the Western front for a cavalryman's paradise, as he led his British soldiers into Jerusalem.

But Sir Douglas Haig, Commander-in-Chief of the British army in France, in his report of summer operations, sent out an encouraging word. He said that "the additional strength which the enemy can obtain from the events in Russia and Italy has already been discounted and the ultimate destruction of the enemy field forces brought perceptibly nearer"—while in apprehension over the coming German offensive his confidential dispatches to the War Office pled for more man-power.

To mention other items in a review of the headlines: Trotzky issued a message to the world asking the Allies to make peace, and later resumed peace negotiations with the Germans at Brest-Litovsk; the crisis of the War would come in the next six months; Christmas spirit rose high in the United States in spite of the War; the Germans were reported to be forcing Belgian women to dig German trenches; Socialism was reported to be spreading in Austria; one million more Class A men were now available through the draft; the Senate was criticizing Government railroad control; Lloyd George declared that Britain would fight to the death to recover Alsace-Lorraine for France; German U-boats torpedoed a British hospital ship without warning; German ammunition plants were reported closed for lack of coal; Federal marshals and police were on the lookout for violators of fuel edicts; the Stock Exchange was closed; Pershing reported five men wounded in action; the sale of Thrift Stamps had reached $3,418,376 in New York, and the New York committee expected to have $100,000,000 within a year; and with the Second Liberty Loan drive behind us we were preparing for a drive for funds for the welfare organizations.

Winter was always the period for peace talk in Berlin. Lord Lansdowne, of the British House of Lords, had given it a lead this winter in his letter in late November suggesting a peace of compromise. The Germans chose the Christmas period as favoring propaganda for softening the enemy for Ludendorff's coming blow on the Western front. The Berlin press openly admitted the need of peace; again the Kaiser sent out feelers for a conference—when the Italians were sore beset and America was on the brink of shedding the blood of her youth. Baker said in his weekly review of the military situation:

"Germany's newest peace propaganda, viewed as a forerunner to an offensive in the West, unless a German-made peace is accepted by the Allies and the United States, should not for a moment induce us to slacken our preparations for war. The Germans realize that within a short time our armies will form the principal body of fresh strategic reserves remaining available on the battlefields of Europe. Our armies constitute the reserves of victory."

Yet the peace talk persisted. President Wilson met it with his Fourteen Points, which became the charter of Allied aims to the end of the War. They linked our fortunes and suspense still closer with the Allies' destiny.

WOMEN DOING MEN'S WORK

The women who stood in line for their rations of coal were not wanting for other occupations. In Washington the veteran Anna Howard Shaw and her vigorous young assistant, Hannah Jane Patterson, of the Woman's Division of the Council of

National Defense, were hearing no remarks these days that war was singularly a man's business. Women need no longer complain that sons and brothers were being told what to do while mothers, wives, and sisters were not. British women had passed through the same cycle when the British New Army was forming and when that "brute," Lord Kitchener, could find no more room for women ambulance-drivers or welfare workers at the front when he was rushing the oldest reservists into the trenches in Flanders in the winter of 1914–15 to hold the Germans back from the sea. America had come to the point, which Britain had long since reached, when we could use all our woman-power as well as our man-power.

If the importance of temperance for the soldiers had been a factor in the Congress's passing the Prohibition Act, so women's part in the War had won the final battle for woman suffrage. All the women's committees which had seemed to overlap each other were now finding work to do. As Baker said: [6]

"People are wont to say in America that whenever a grievance arises it is discussed, an organization is formed, its officers get together and appoint a committee, and then it is all over. In a sense that is so. We do multiply committees. We get up societies and associations and leagues until we are sometimes weighted down with the multifariousness of our diverse occupations and interests, and are disposed to question whether many of them may not be futile. Yet I make bold to say that if we were to withdraw from the effective government of the United States the voluntary effort which is represented by such associations, our government would scarcely exist at all."

And to women he said: [7]

"It won't do for us to embrace the hollow figure in which democracy was once a tenant and say, 'This is Democracy.' We must have an image to represent it which is suited to the environment in which the figure is to play a part. . . . In 1789 it might well have been possible to define as a democracy a society in which the family was represented by a single representative—a man; but in 1917, society cannot speak of itself as a democracy unless it forgets its old environment, unless it re-

WOMAN'S COMMITTEE, COUNCIL OF NATIONAL DEFENSE

Left to right: Miss Maude Wetmore, Mrs. J. E. Cowles, Miss Ida M. Tarbell, Mrs. Stanley McCormick, Dr. Anna Howard Shaw, Mrs. Newton D. Baker, Mrs. Carrie Chapman Catt, Mrs. J. R. Lamar, Mrs. Philip N. Moore.

members the change that has taken place. It cannot speak of itself as a democracy unless all the men and women who live under the administration of that government and those institutions are recognized and represented in the Government. . . .

"I have made no careful search of my own mind on the subject, but I think I am prepared to say that, if all the women in America were to stop tonight doing the things that they are doing, and making the sacrifices and contributions they are making toward the conduct of this war, we should have to withdraw from the War. We should at least have to withdraw until we could bring about the entire reorganization of our social and industrial structure. . . ."

To speak of woman's work in the War is to speak of her as doing men's work of all kinds except in combat. Welfare work was her shining rôle. If it took her to France, then she became heroic, and envied by her sisters. But if she was working instead at a canteen at home, she was performing the same service, and often more arduous service than if she had been "over there." The charming young Red Cross woman whom I heard say in France under the Harbord régime in the S. O. S., "I really haven't a thing to do. The officers are so busy that they have not time to dance!" was a favorite of fortune not at all typical of Red Cross women as a whole.

The women who drove cars at home in war work forever removed the suspicion on the part of the superior male in the early days of automobiling that a woman could not be a capable driver. Women who could hardly claim the title of welfare workers were going down the alleys in mining villages to carry their cheer and aid. Under Miss Mary Van Kleeck the women in the Industrial Section of the Ordnance Department were arranging conditions for the employment of women in munition plants. Under Mrs. McAdoo more than a million volunteer women workers assisted in the Liberty Loan drives. Dr. Rosalie S. Norton and a committee of women physicians organized medical service for the women in industry. Under Clara Sears Taylor the Woman's War Work Division of the Committee on Public Information encouraged war activities among women. The woman at the lathe, the woman making shells or gas masks, or in any one of a hundred unaccustomed occupations, just the woman of toil—she was the dough-girl of our part in the War.

And the women were perhaps more sensitive to fluctuations of war emotions than the men, when their men were in the cantonments and the question of whether the divisions which had been forming would ever reach France had been succeeded by the question of when they would go. The truth as to how slowly we were sending troops to France would have been cheering to Hindenburg and Ludendorff as they mobilized their divisions in France. The extra shipping for the twenty-four division program had not been forthcoming. Britain insisted that even if she had it to spare she would not spare it until some definite understanding as to how our man-power was to be used came out of the negotiations between Pershing and the Allied commanders. In December 786,000 deadweight tons of troop and cargo ships were in the service of the A. E. F., and we transported 9,000 men; in January, 863,000 tons and we transported 3,000 fewer men. At this rate we should not have half a million by the end of May.

The nation was gradually settling down to recognize that the two great essentials were man-power and shipping, as they had been from the first. Not coal, not food, not loans, but a "Bridge to France" had now become the slogan for a new national drive. The hand behind the rivet, joining the ship's plates, became the heroic hand of industry. Hog Island was now far from a mad conception of wild extravagance. Why had we been so long in starting it? Why had it been so slow in building? As significant in its place and time as the draft registration day and the landing of our first contingent in France was the day when the first keel was laid at Hog Island. Speed the building of ships; speed the troops and supplies "over there"! And in that stern winter, which had brought us close to the realities of war's strain on our energy and resources, a crisis had arrived in the fortunes of the War Department.

XXI

THE SCAPEGOAT OF IMPATIENCE

REPUBLICANS would not have been human if they had altogether forgotten that a Democratic administration was in office and might gain political profit from national victory; and the Democrats would not have been human if they had readily yielded the power which had been conferred upon them in the previous national election. Soon after our entry into the War, Senator John W. Weeks, Republican, of Massachusetts, and Representative Martin B. Madden, Republican, of Illinois, were talking of a bi-partisan committee on the conduct of the War. Arguments were heard in favor of our starting right and profiting by England's delay in accepting the inevitable—a coalition cabinet formed of leaders from both parties. However, there had been no coalition cabinet in our war of 1812–14, in which we had blundered so badly, or in 1846–48 or 1861–65, or in the Spanish War.

No eminent public man could find in his own experience more decisive reasons for understanding the clumsiness of coalitions or bi-partisan committees in conducting war under our form of government than Elihu Root, former Secretary of War. He said on April 17, 1917: [1]

"We need no coalition government to make us loyal. We will make a coalition, ourselves, with every Democrat in the country. . . . We must have no criticism now. . . . There will be criticism, fault-finding and discontent, but these have been incidental to all wars. It is incidental to our free-and-easy democracy."

William H. Taft, former president and Root's associate in the Roosevelt Cabinet, no less sturdily held the same view. Their old chief spoke no word in favor of bi-partisan responsibility.

When a new national administration comes in on March 4

the attitude of the opposition is to join the nation in good wishes and bide its time until the new administration shall disclose its weaknesses. In time of war this policy becomes a matter of patriotic duty. All men must give their loyal support to the administration policy until such time as its errors shall call for correction or its leaders be proven inefficient.

The President of the United States ever serves two masters. He is chief of a political party as well as the Chief Executive of the nation. Upon our entry into the War, Wilson had become the people's leader in a new and commanding sense. When he went over the party affiliations of the members of the Advisory Commission, he remarked that he might be charged with forming a partisan body.[2] All except two were classified as Republicans or independents, although primarily Chairman Daniel Willard was a railroad man, Julius Rosenwald a merchant, Howard E. Coffin an automobile engineer, Dr. Franklin Martin a leader in medicine, and Walter S. Gifford, the director, an industrial expert and organizer. As for Samuel Gompers, his politics, religion, vocation, and recreation had ever been the cause of labor. Of the group only Bernard Baruch could qualify as a sturdy Democrat, and he, primarily, was a financier and an expert in raw materials. Not one had been active in politics or sought office.

Frank A. Scott, whom Baker had chosen as head of the Munitions Board and later of the War Industries Board, and Stanley King, who made a place for himself on Baker's right hand, were both Republicans. So were Benedict Crowell, who became first Assistant Secretary of War, succeeding William M. Ingraham, and Edward R. Stettinius, John D. Ryan, and Frederick P. Keppel, who became assistant secretaries. That is, they had the reputation of voting the Republican ticket. For the most part they had been as aloof from politics as Daniel Willard or Dr. Martin.

Republicans were saying that, after all, the War Department, when it wanted ability, could find it only in the Republican party; and the Democrats were asking if Baker thought there were no Democrats capable of filling the high official positions to which he assigned Republicans. In accepting his war mandate as so non-partisan that he inquired about a man's fitness for his task without regard to his politics he ran the administrative risk, to use a Presidential phrase, of "having a political enemy in camp" who might develop political ambitions in the Washington atmosphere and use his position to undermine the administration's power. Even Colonel George B. M. Harvey, the most virulent critic of Baker, admitted Baker was non-partisan in his war administration.

It is clear enough, in reading the letters between Baker and Wilson, that the former president of Princeton could not shed his partisanship in war-time quite so readily as could the former Mayor of Cleveland. Indeed, the President once told Baker that Baker would find with time and experience that he was becoming increasingly partisan.

The protests which the President received from party leaders and passed on to Baker included one to the effect that Charles B. Warren—a bitter critic of the President and one of the inner circle of the Republican National Committee—"in view of his indiscreet talk should not be placed in so important and confidential a position." Warren was serving as a major in the Judge Advocate's office in Washington. On May 19, 1917, Baker wrote to the President that "the position of major of the Officers' Reserve Corps in the Judge Advocate General's Corps is not a place of great distinction, nor can the work which Mr. Warren is now doing affect anybody without being first brought to my personal attention, as my legal training makes me rather inquisitive about the legal end of the work done in the department." If, the day after the passage of the Draft Act, Warren had been removed because he was a Republican, it would have aroused criticism to the effect that the draft administration reflected political partisan influences.

Edward N. Hurley, whom the President had appointed to succeed Denman as Chairman of the Shipping Board, was a Democrat who had warmly supported President Wilson as a candidate before the Baltimore Convention in 1912. Hoover, the Food Administrator, had been classified as a Democrat from administration affiliations. As an absentee from his country, with few home connections which were not sentimental or social, Hoover's business and financial associations had been abroad. The Republicanism of Garfield, a college president, who had the most difficult task of all the dollar-a-year administrators except Frank A. Scott, Willard, Hurley, and Baruch later on, must necessarily be somewhat academic. Granted that Hoover had not yet decided as to the political camp in which he should cast his fortunes, Garfield was the only Republican among the dictators.

Vance McCormick, Chairman of the Democratic National Committee, was appointed Chairman of the War Trade Board by the President, and A. Mitchell Palmer, a forthright Democrat, Alien Property Custodian. Both might be subject to the charge that they would be partial to party interest, just as it might have been intimated that the captains of industry could not be quite oblivious of their own business interests. As one dollar-a-year man remarked, "A servant of the government, to start right in time of war, should never have voted, and should never have had any business or executive experience, or any friends!" [3]

The War Department's watchfulness lest any official background should be supplied for partisan opinions extended to the cantonments, which could be such excellent sounding-boards for oratory. There were two distinguished American leaders whose widely different natures had an emotional quality which would make restraint difficult in addressing an audience of citizen soldiers. To refuse to either leader the privilege of the rostrum would offend an immense personal following, who would cry out against partisan discrimination in a land of free speech. Reminders to either of the need of discretion required a good deal of temerity on the part of division commanders. One had resigned as Secretary of State in protest against the President's *Lusitania* note, which the other, as champion of the big stick, had found timorous and shilly-shallying. One was a Fundamentalist and an ardent advocate of national prohibition; the other a modernist who did not mind a little wine for his stomach's sake.

William Jennings Bryan was the cause of a number of letters of complaint in the War Department files after his address to the men at Camp Sherman, when he included in his program for human betterment some items that seemed highly debatable to many of his soldier hearers. The commandant of Camp Sherman had to explain to the War Department that he had had no idea that Bryan would depart from the usual discretion of speakers under the auspices of the Committee on Training Camp Activities. But Bryan, after all, was only delivering one of his regular Chautauqua lectures, quite unconscious that he had overstepped the bounds. The men liked to hear him, just as they liked to hear former President Roosevelt, "Teddy" of the Rough Riders, who had a pulpit singularly to his taste and an audience that stirred him to embattled mood.

"Colonel Roosevelt shot facts and figures, as they had been given to him uncensored, at 18,000 National Army men today. He dealt with the present military conditions of the United States and in repeated sentences hammered reproach at the governmental policy that he held had produced the situation." [4]

He kept saying, "If I am wrong, correct me" to Major General Thomas H. Barry, commanding at Camp Grant, who was in the rather embarrassing position of being challenged to contradict his old Commander-in-Chief, who had given him his star. America's effort had discommoded no Germans yet, said the former President, who as early as September, 1917, had become the leading critic of the War Department.

CHIEF OF THE WHISPERING GALLERY

When the Congress adjourned in mid-October, conscious of duty performed by its long summer vigil and its colossal appropriations, the news from Europe was still favorable. Before the members were back in Washington, in early December, for the opening of the new session, Caporetto had written its warning on the map.

Meanwhile members had been in touch with their constituents, for whom they were the depositories of all sorts of complaints and revelations. They had been moving about and seeing things for themselves in munition plants and cantonments, riding on under-heated trains, and eating meager fare in the dining cars. A few who had been in France added their quota in the exchange of information in the lobbies as the local Washington whispering gallery poured its accumulated views and gossip into legislative ears.

Colonel George B. M. Harvey had become chief of the whispering gallery, not as the result of any concerted movement of the members, and certainly not as a dollar-a-year man actively engaged on an industrial committee, but rather because he had proved his peculiar fitness for the position above all competitors. His own executive experience had been as president of Harper & Brothers' publishing house. Instead of retrieving its fortunes he had left it still deeper in debt and had ended the career of the once-powerful *Harper's Weekly,* which he had made a personal organ for his brilliant paragraphs. Later, Thomas B. Wells, a practical and highly cultivated editor, together with his younger colleagues, so managed the affairs of that old house that its debts were paid off and it was restored to prosperity and its former position in the publishing world. But there was no more scintillant and caustic dinner companion than Colonel Harvey, who delighted to be "in the know." He had received his military title for serving on the Governor's Staff of the State of New Jersey.

The day before I left Washington to go abroad with the pioneer staff of the A. E. F. I met him at the Shoreham Hotel in Washington when we were lunching at adjoining tables. Suddenly I heard him say, in a voice that could be heard across the room:

"I know when Pershing's going and on what ship. It's the *Baltic.*"

Now every one of the *Baltic* party had been enjoined to the

strictest secrecy as to the ship and its time of sailing. All manner of important people lunched every day at the Shoreham,
at tables placed very close together. The enemy's intelligence
service would hardly be unrepresented at this public listening-
post. It would have been somewhat discomfiting if our first
report of Pershing's landing on the other side of the Atlantic
had come to us from the German port of Kiel, accompanied by
the explanation that while there had been room for him, his
Chief of Staff, and his aides on the submarine that had sunk
the *Baltic,* the rest of the Commander-in-Chief's Staff had been
left, under urgent military necessity, in open boats on the
Atlantic. It was conceivably just such an indiscretion as this
that may have informed the Germans that Lord Kitchener was
going to Russia on the cruiser that was sunk in the North Sea,
tragically ending his career. In a lobby of a London restaurant
in 1916 I saw a red-headed, freckled Scotch officer knock down
a man who had been voicing his knowledge of the plans of the
British army in France. But we were not so deep in the War as
the British had been at that time of heavy British casualties.
The whispering gallery had the compensating tidbit that some
stupid quartermaster's clerk or officer's "striker" of that stupid
War Department had "given the show away, anyhow," by label-
ing some baggage for "General Pershing.—S.S. *Baltic.*" But to
no intelligence section of any army would this have justified
so highly sagacious a leader of opinion as Harvey in openly
violating the injunction to secrecy.

At the turn of the year Harvey, who was editor of *The North
American Review,* established as its adjunct a war weekly which
became widely known as *Harvey's Weekly.* This voice of the
whispering gallery and organ of urgent criticism gained a wide
circulation. The "nobby little Secretary of War" and "chattering ex-Pacifist" became Harvey's particular target. "Of all Cabinet members Mr. Baker will prove the least effective during
the progress of actual warfare. We assume, therefore, that he
will be sent as our representative on the Supreme War Council." And again: "It goes without saying that all the multifari-
ous documents that issue from the War Department cannot be

passed upon, much less edited, by a man of sense." Again: "As long as Newton Baker remains Secretary of War we cannot hope to reach a state of efficiency that will give us strength to beat the Hun." At first, Harvey approved of the War Council, but later he referred to it as a "group of superannuated generals whom he [Baker] has been forced to decapitate as bureau chiefs." Baker glanced through the pages of one copy of *Harvey's Weekly* which was shown to him, without feeling any of the anger it had aroused among his friends.

"I hope that I have more first-hand information about the War Department than Colonel Harvey has," he remarked.[5]

Harvey furnished scandal as well as comment at Baker's expense. His weekly intimated that the War Department had become a nest of nepotism and the Secretary of War a war-profiteer. Harvey had discovered that Baker's brother, H. D. Baker, was interested in the Engel Aircraft Company, which had a contract with the government. Harvey continued for weeks to exploit his triumph in having forced the end of this sordid business by his exposure. But it happened that his brother's connection with the company had been discovered by Baker before Harvey learned of it. There had reached Baker a copy of a letter from a man who had been asked to buy stock in the company, in which the brother's interest was mentioned. Baker acted instantly by sending through Major General George O. Squier, Chief of the Signal Corps, the following telegram to the company:

"By direction of the Secretary of War your contract for aircraft is hereby canceled."

The company promptly protested that it had gone ahead with its contract in good faith at a time when every possible source of production of aircraft should be doing its utmost. Then Baker sent Eugene Meyer, Jr., to Cleveland to make further investigation as to the company's financing and methods, and gave him a letter to F. H. Goff, President of the Cleveland Trust Company, in which he said:

"I am asking Mr. Meyer to take the situation up with you in the hope that you will find it possible to ask two or three men of the highest character and responsibility in Cleveland to act with you in bringing about the immediate, complete, and final separation of my brother from all interest in this company and its affairs, such separation to be without profit of any kind to him. I have not discussed the matter with my brother, but Mr. Meyer tells me that he has expressed a desire to do anything necessary to remove the embarrassment and all grounds of doubt on the subject. I will be deeply grateful for your interest and help in this matter."

Meyer found that the way in which the broker who was selling the stock had used the brother's name had been unauthorized by either the brother or the company; that the company was composed of reliable business men; that "the Department of Equipment of the Signal Corps reports that the Engel Aircraft Company should start delivery on its contracts about the first week in February, and that the company is doing its work with efficiency and promises to become one of the most valuable concerns in the production of spare parts, with the possibility of being used to advantage in the assembly of complete planes."

The reports about the company's methods of business and financing and the nature of the work it was doing make a section of the Baker files nearly an inch thick. After the brother had withdrawn from the company, receiving nothing except the money he had put in and his salary, the company was reinstated in its contracts on the advice of Meyer and Goff and the equipment officers of the Signal Corps. In this case Baker regarded himself as very much his brother's keeper.

"IF BAKER DOESN'T BREAK, WE'LL BREAK HIM"

By midwinter the members of the whispering gallery confidently passed the word, "If Baker doesn't break, we'll break him." Some of the callers who brought to the gallery first-hand observations reported him to be looking tired and careworn. Their impression was warranted if they saw him as he rose from his desk after midnight; but his gift of falling asleep the moment he was in a horizontal position still brought him fresh to his office in the morning. His hour at home for luncheon and dinner in the quiet of Georgetown gave him a new draft of strength for the next session of the long day's routine. At eleven at night he might telephone to Mrs. Baker that he would not be home until three, as this apparently was to be one of his busy days.

All the suggestions for "speeding up the War" and plans for reorganization were deluging his office. "What can I do? What can I do now?" had been succeeded in some cases by "If you had accepted my plan, we should not now be having chaos." True, the War Industries Board was in its new office building, which had risen in three weeks, and other temporary office buildings were soon to be completed. But that did not stop the cries from all directions, "Why don't we get what we want?" and "Why can't this be straightened out?" in the midst of the winter's blizzards. The questions became stentorian when they reached Baker's desk. Important men who were charged with not doing their parts, or even with selfish motives or profiteering, demanded in their hurt pride and hot indignation a hearing before the Secretary. The draft boards were passing up problems to him.

Every plan of reorganization seemed to require legislation by the Congress; and a bill must be drawn for its consideration, and in such a way and accompanied by such argument and address, as to hasten its passage. A way must be found to condemn property for artillery proving grounds, powder plants, and for many other purposes when the owners refused to agree to rent or sell. A telegram asking for no further action about barges on the Mississippi until the sender could be heard might lie beside a telegram protesting that delay was fatal to the local situation. There were telegrams about ocean shipping troubles, and others expressing suspicion of men of German blood, the latter requiring conferences with Colonel Ralph H. Van Deman of the intelligence service, who had in hand the trying and complicated business of espionage and counter-espionage.

RECREATION ROOM IN A CANTONMENT

The Allied ambassadors and chiefs of staff of Allied missions had burning appeals which they did not wish to commit to paper, and preferred to make in person. Distinguished officers of the Allies and representatives of Allied war industries had suggestions which might be valuable if the proponents could agree as to the changes which were needed to speed up our war work. And often the conclusion was that what might do in England or France would not do in America, for reasons of national psychology, just as what would do in England might not do in France. Sometimes a question arose as to how far the Allied personage represented his government and how far himself.

Communications for the Secretary of War's information from the State Department were more frequent as the Allied crisis became more acute. Wouldn't Baker remind Pershing that Belgian feelings had been hurt because he had sent no liaison officer to the Belgian army? Wouldn't Baker soften Pershing's stubborn attitude toward the amalgamation of our troops with the British and French armies?

From a question of rank and procedure, he turned to one of the allocation of authority between two chiefs; then to transport; then to artillery; then to hospitalization; then to a member of Congress or a delegation. In each case his concentration was such as to make one who had to go often to him say, "My part in the War was to him the whole War for the moment."

Less than ever might decisions be delayed in the quest of perfectionism as a nation rampant sought direction for its energy in that time of national apprehension. A Secretary of War could not stand for hours at the fork of the roads, hearing arguments whether to take the road to the right or the left, when both led to the same goal on a life-and-death hurry call. If he took the road to the right and there was delay, the champions of the road to the left might pause long enough, as they helped to pull the car out of a slough, to let it be known to the whispering gallery that their forebodings had been fully justified. There must be the courage to make mistakes, but it must be a reasoned and not a blind and impulsive courage. His critics were saying that he delegated too much authority; that he was trying to do too much himself. They described his rapidity of decision as mere facility in snap judgments without any real understanding of his problems. No man's enemies could have wished on him a worse "damned if you do and damned if you don't" job than the one the Secretary of War had during the winter of 1917–18.

He was between the extremists who wanted conscientious objectors excused, and the extremists who wanted them shot; between the press calling for more publicity and the Army calling for absolute secrecy; between the industrialists demanding more skilled labor to fill building and munition contracts, and the Staff who did not want to part with men half-trained as soldiers; between the staff and the bureaus; the military hierarchy and the War Industries Board; the public's and the soldiers' conception of the way the War should be fought; between winter storms delaying traffic and the coal famine.

He had confidential moments of philosophizing when he dwelt on the part to which destiny had assigned him. Why should there be this incredible orgy enveloping the world in death, misery, and waste, prostituting the reason and the better instincts of mankind? Why should he be in command of the processes of organizing death and destruction instead of solving problems of civic betterment back in Cleveland? Those who believed that a Secretary of War should glory in war, be a partisan of war as war, look fierce and murderous, could they have heard him in these moments, would have had their conviction confirmed that here was softness when the emergency demanded strength. Yet these sentiments were the same that we, who knew the front, were familiar with in the minds of the men who were doing the fighting from the Piave to the English Channel; and just as they took their places to go over the top to carry on the orgy, Baker applied the merciless logic of piling up man-power and weapons as the only means to victory.

I think that men who have seen much of war generally agree that the bloodthirstiest warriors are those who have no arms except emotion.

The members of the whispering gallery did not see much of Baker, personally. Many of them really wanted to do more than whisper to help win the War; but neither a bureau chief nor the War Industries Board had been able to find a place in the organization for their volunteer efforts. Others who casually saw Baker, looking even slighter than he was, sunk in his chair as he listened to callers, thought the little fellow appeared to be cowed by his enormous task; but, predisposed as they were against him, they might be set to wondering when he called Jimmy Durbin and dictated a sharply defined decision without changing his pose. There could be no misinterpretation of any of his orders. Pershing said that out of all the letters and cables he received from Baker he had never been in doubt of the meaning of a single sentence.[6]

SERENE UNDER FIRE

I have found that those working with Baker invariably had a deep personal devotion to him, and all spoke of his unflinching loyalty to his subordinates, and said that his only weakness was kindness. Strangely enough, I have never met anyone who ever saw him break into a passion—though his "No!" could be so short. All were familiar with his remark, "A's burdens are heavy—make allowances for him," or "B's tired! See that he gets a day off!" When a subordinate had done well, all honor to him. Let the world know it.

When a subordinate failed, Baker seemed to take it for granted that the blame rested upon himself. "What was a Secretary of War for?" War meant concentration of authority. He never complained that the hard winter was against him; but the whispering gallery seemed inclined, in moments when it was short of a better complaint, to think that he was even responsible for the weather. That stupid War Department! The water pipes had been laid on top of the ground in a Southern camp, and had burst in a cold snap—in a region where the thermometer had not registered below freezing for many years.

In the face of the coming storm, as the clouds thickened and the forks of lightning were shooting at Baker's head, he kept on the treadmill, smoking his pipe, having his whimsical moments when it did not seem to very solemn people that he was taking his task seriously enough, never pompous, never indefinite in his language, never mumbling, never grumbling, bearing his burdens as they came with a certain jauntiness. He was something of an enigma even to those who knew him best and who were gripped to him by an extraordinary affection, but not an enigma to the clerks and attendants who circulated a paper of good wishes on his birthday. They had learned to like him for his own sake as a kind, fair, considerate chief, who had no "side" when all "Who's Who" still seemed to be racing in the War Department corridors to the tune of the jingle of the new generals' spurs.

"In face of all this maddening business," Edward R. Stettinius exclaimed one day as he paced the Chief of Staff's room, "how can the Secretary keep so serene?" [7]

But the members of the whispering gallery who were close to Harvey were saying, as I remember, that Baker's serenity was merely mental coma under the weight of a responsibility whose true nature he was incapable of grasping.

No subject caused more speculation in the whispering gallery than the actual number of men we had in France. Pessimistic estimates placed it as low as fifty thousand in early December. With the public eager to know the truth, and the press eager to report it, Baker turned public curiosity to skepticism in some quarters when he said in his annual report, "It would, of course, be unwise to attempt any enumeration of the forces overseas."

Then, on December 15, the newspaper headlines had the assurance on the authority of the Secretary of War that we had a quarter of a million men in France. Of course this was flashed as news to London. Pershing sent a cablegram on December 16 saying that our General Bartlett had stopped publication of the report in England, and that "there are 137,000 officers and men here." [8] Optimistic broadsides of the American press about America's part in France had been embarrassing to Pershing, who did not wish his strength to be overestimated. The Allied missions in Washington and the Allied statesmen were equally concerned that it should be emphasized for the sake of morale. No one of our Allies had ever stated the number of their troops on the line or under arms.

Baker had actually said that there were more than 100,000 men overseas. Many members of the whispering gallery thought that we had fewer than a hundred thousand. On the basis of the report of a quarter of a million they had Baker convicted of falsehood. He was charged with using the excuse of military secrecy as a smokescreen to hide the War Department's failure. Did anyone think that the Germans did not know, through their wonderful spy system, how many troops we had in France? That they did not know just what we were doing in every detail? It was only Americans who were being kept in the dark.

COMPLAINTS AGAINST MILITARY SECRECY

But the records were to show that the Germans did not know. They were much confused. The Allied commands and Pershing's staff in France were more insistent upon secrecy than our staff at home. The value of such secrecy had been sensationally demonstrated through Ludendorff's concealment of his plan and his mobilization for the Caporetto attack, and was being expressed at the moment in Allied mystification as to the number of divisions the Germans were massing on the Western front and where their blow would come. It was being laboriously proven every day in the intelligence section of every army as experts painstakingly sifted, tested, and checked off bits of information from every source. Often some seemingly unimportant item became the missing part that completed the picture puzzle.

Censorship is one of the penalties of war, a part of its armor, just as propaganda is one of its weapons and one of its most loathsome features. What an outcry there would have been against the "ex-Pacifist" if he had regarded nothing as confidential! He would have been accused of betraying our Allies to the enemy, of informing the enemy of our plans, the number and location of our own and the Allied troops, so that the enemy would know where to hit us by surprise. One of the ironies of the War was the criticism by the militarists of the "ex-Pacifist" for his militaristic methods.

But the members of the Congress, so warrantably accustomed to having their questions answered by all government offices, were wroth to find that the Capitol was shut out from the truth by the fog of war. Those soldier men, busily stamping documents "Secret and Confidential," would not, even in the strictest confidence, answer a vital question by an eminent senator. As if a senator could not keep a secret! Of course, he understood it could not be spread among the large membership of the Lower House. If it had been, its possession would have lost exclusiveness. Yet senators knew how often everything of importance in an executive session appeared in the press the next morning; and even Presidents have been surprised to find how much of what passes at meetings of the small circle of the Cabinet becomes public property.

The "I told you so" prophets now found confirmation of their cynical prescience that upon our entry into the War, once the shouting was over, we should face the reckoning in misspent funds, in bad food and clothes for the soldiers, and in a repetition of all the scandals of the Spanish War, as revealed in the inevitable Congressional investigation.

By midwinter of 1917–18 the time for the reckoning appeared to have come. The Congress could not stand by and see the War lost, and lost it would be if half the reports were true. Our law-making branch would not continue to bow to this extra-legal monarch of "legal necessity," enthroned in its star chamber of "military secrecy."

Members had a duty to the sons whose parents were sending letters of specific criticism; to constitutents whose plants were not getting raw material; to able men in their constituencies who were not being used when lesser men were in the parade of milling reserve officers in Washington; to communities which were not receiving their share of coal or railroad service; a duty, too, to get at the truth about the bureau chiefs, the General Staff, the War Industries Board, and the Shipping Board. The big task of investigation fell to the Senate Committee on Military Affairs. It began with the bureau chiefs; all of these had to prepare elaborate detailed statements, with Crozier of the Ordnance receiving the most attention. He wrote:

"Two officers of the Ordnance Department who had most to do with the procurement of machine-guns were obliged to shut themselves up and deny interviews to designers and manufacturers, as well as to their own subordinates, for five days, in order that they might gather from the records the data for refuting the misinformation which had found lodgment in certain minds; and my own testimony before the investigating committee occupied over two hundred printed pages." [9]

MANY SENATORS AND MANY QUESTIONS

After the Committee had finished with the subordinates, Baker's turn came on January tenth. He might expect no partisan support from Senator George E. Chamberlain, Democrat, Chairman of the Committee, whose feud with Representative Hay had put him out of the running as Garrison's possible successor in the Secretaryship. Chamberlain had been an implacable critic of Baker's administration from the outset. In the present crisis he occupied the position of a leader who had broken party bonds for patriotism's sake. The whispering gallery was saying that Chamberlain was to have his day. This prophet should receive his due; this inquisitor would develop the evidence which would strip "the nobby little Secretary of War" to the nakedness of his incapacity for his task.

Among the other senators on the Committee were the veteran Francis E. Warren, ranking Republican member, father-in-law of Pershing; James W. Wadsworth, Jr., Republican, of New York, who had served as a volunteer in the Spanish War; Morris Sheppard, Democrat, of Texas; Gilbert M. Hitchcock, Democrat, of Nebraska; James A. Reed, Democrat, of Missouri, and John W. Weeks, Republican, of Massachusetts.[10]

Baker's attitude might well have been that of the executive in high indignation over the waste of his and the nation's time when he was trying to get on with the War. He might have

spoken some vigorous phrase which would have rung through
the land, picturing to the public mind the clumsy mass tactics
of his critics against a single antagonist. Before a later committee the "Hell and Maria" of Brigadier General Charles M.
Dawes titillated the nation's fancy at Congressional expense.
But that was after the War, when the subject was war expenditures and not soldiers' lives and stopping the German army;
the public was then in a better mood for a joke than it had been
in January, 1918.

Anyhow, "Hell and Maria" was not the Baker way. His attitude was that of respect for the law-making power, a respect
which had a certain disarming quality. The restraint and seriousness of the occasion favored Congressional dignity at its
best. No senator who had a weakness for speaking to the gallery
need indulge in mere smartness to relieve the tedium or make
a yawning newspaper man attentive to the proceedings, which
were assured of broadside headlines. Senators, while they nursed
their questions, were urbanely considerate as they listened to
the Secretary's opening statement, which might have been prepared by assistants for a busy chief. It dwelt upon the enormous
expansion of War Department operations, which I have already
described.

From April 1 to December 1, 1917, our armed forces had
increased from the total of 202,000 officers and men in the
Regulars and National Guard to 1,600,000 in Regulars, Guard,
and National Army, six times the total we had had at any time
in the Spanish War and one and one-half times the force ever
before mobilized by the nation.

The War Department's appropriations for the then current
fiscal year, $7,500,000,000, were fifty times as great as for the
normal year of 1915, and ten times the normal appropriations
for all purposes, one-third the gross value of the products of
all our industries, and twice the total of the operating income
of all our railroads. The Quartermaster's personnel had jumped
from 347 officers to more than 6,000, and its appropriations to
$3,000,000,000, or four times that of all appropriations in 1915.

Two billions of dollars had already been obligated by contracts or disbursements.

"This business involved accounting, determinations of standards, prices, quantities, the creation of new manufacturing facilities, the substitution of materials for insufficient supplies, diversions of labor, the erection of storage warehouses, and difficult and often embarrassing questions of land and water transportation."

The Quartermaster had made 4,160 contracts for 142 different kinds of articles. Aviation appropriations alone were five times normal War Department appropriations. The appropriation for the Ordnance Department alone had been $3,200,000,-000, three times the total value of our iron and steel industries.

After Baker's statement came the questions. Senators generally agreed that the men in the camps were all getting enough nourishing food, although the pies were not such as Mother used to make. So the army was not "starving." That was something, considering the embalmed-beef scandal of the Spanish War, which so many senators remembered. There had been some pneumonia in the camps. There had been some outbreaks of measles, but otherwise no serious epidemics of communicable diseases which are favored by men living so close together. The death-rate in the home camps had been one-third of that in the home camps in the Spanish War.

No senatorial voice was raised against the moral safeguards of the camps and the recreation and entertainment provided in contrast with the saloons and "cribs" of former days. The efficacy of all such measures had documentary proof in the small number of courtmartial cases as compared with the records of the Spanish War. But not all the senators accepted the health conditions as satisfactory when out of the millions in camps and cantonments a certain number were on the sick list. Senator McKellar asked:

"Do you not think it would be wise on the part of the Department to look into these hospital arrangements where so many of the boys are sick? Do you not think it would be a wise public policy?"

Baker replied:

"So wise that it was done a long time ago, and has been constantly continued. I sent Surgeon General Gorgas in person to inspect every camp in which there was an unusual prevalence of disease, and have instructed him to have his medical representative at each camp make constant reports of each need as it is foreseen or arises, and to have every change made in hospitals that should be."

Baker confessed to some satisfaction in the vast sums he had spent before the Congress had appropriated a single cent for the War Department. With public memory so short in peace-time, it was not unnatural that Congressional memory should be short in war-time. Members had forgotten the spring exhibitions of inherent Congressional jealousy of arbitrary executive action; had forgotten their criticisms of the abolition of the slow process of competitive bidding as giving the dollar-a-year men so much power, thus endangering the rightful authority of the trained servants of the nation in the army bureaus. Senators and representatives were not more readily shaken out of their peace habits than are other average middle-aged human beings.

HE WAS EXPECTED TO KNOW EVERY DETAIL

From four to six hours for three days were given to the hearings, Baker returning from each session to catch up with his routine work for the day. He had to meet questions and cross-questions about all the War Department's activities, and about all the kinds of peace production and the many kinds of new production which the War required. He was expected to know the state of progress in every munition factory, and in spruce production in the forests of the Pacific Northwest, and be familiar with every contract of any kind that had been made. Senators who knew wool, cotton, leather, or any kind of manufacturing from expert study of schedules in forming tariff bills, quizzed him about technical details in the making of blankets, uniforms, underclothing, shoes, and other items. He had to explain how artillery was being trained in France; the mechanism of rifles and machine-guns, and of the complicated recuperator of the French field-gun; the difference between the oil and the spring systems of gun recoil; why cantonments were built in certain localities; the causes for railroad delays; and the duties of the British Minister of Munitions.

The questions by senators did not always harmonize, nor did their views. But this was in order in the course of discussion looking for the truth. When one senator said that he had seen men at the camps without uniforms, another corrected him by saying that the men might just have arrived at the camp and not been outfitted yet. Senator Chamberlain thought that Baker had been too considerate of the National Guard, and Senator Frelinghuysen that he had not been considerate enough. He was told that he had ordered too many things, and that he had not ordered enough. He had consulted men of business experience too seldom, and he had consulted them too often. Senator McKellar still insisted that the War Department should not have given up competitive bidding.

Senator Weeks wanted to know why the camps had not yet received the 240 motor trucks to which each division was entitled. Baker replied that they would not be required until the division moved to France. But did not motor-truck drivers need training? Baker replied that 40,000 were receiving special training at Black Point.

Senator Hitchcock inquired if there had been any consideration given to providing hot food for the men in the trenches. There had been. All the devices proposed had been submitted to General Pershing, who knew best the systems in Europe, and his decision was awaited.

When Baker's concern over good working conditions for women and children in factories was cited as a cause of delay in production, Senator Wadsworth called the attention of the Committee to the fact that in his State (New York) the sweat-shop system was forbidden by law.

Senator Weeks asked why there were no rolling kitchens at the camps nine months after we had entered the War. Baker replied that rolling kitchens were not needed at the camps, but only after the divisions went to France. Weeks said they were needed at Spartanburg, where the men had to go thirty miles to the target range; but he could not tell Baker whether the men had been without food while at the target range. Baker did not mention that we had had no rolling kitchens in Cuba or the Philippines; or that, with all the traffic congestion, to move rolling kitchens to the camps and then to the ports would mean wasting transport; or that priority in the production of rolling kitchens, which would not be required until the divisions started for France, was not so important as equipment for the men while in the camps. Questions came so fast that Baker did not always have time to complete his answers. Why did inventors who had devices of all kinds to aid in winning the War have to go to local officers, and then be passed on up from superior to superior, wasting their time? The only reason was that the applicant did not know there was an equipment board in Washington, whose business it was to consider all new mechanical ideas.

Why were laborers on new plants still without housing? There was Locust Point, for example. The answer was that when it was proposed to build many small houses the workmen had preferred to live in Baltimore with their families and near schools. Then boats must be found to carry them back and forth. If that system proved to be unacceptable, houses would have to be built.

Did the War Department have any system of reports on the progress of all branches in production and transport? Yes. On every one, all tabulated. Was it known what progress could be expected in the future? Yes, subject to delays which could not be foreseen. Baker brought blueprints and charts so that the Committee could see the plan and system for themselves. There were many questions about the new War Council and the new Division of Purchase and Storage.

TESTING CANNED FOODS FOR THE ARMY

AN ARMY ROLLING KITCHEN IN FRANCE

Why were our uniforms made of virgin wool? Because the experts had decided that reworked wool could not be profitably used in 16-ounce melton cloth for uniforms. Why had blankets seventy-five percent wool and twenty-five percent cotton? Because this was the best blanket-weight cloth that could be promptly produced.

When somebody charged the Depot Quartermaster in New York with not being open to suggestions, and not giving time to important callers, Baker replied that if the Quartermaster had a fifty-hour day he would not be able to see everybody who wanted to see him. "He is a very busy man—busier than I am," Baker remarked.

"Busier than you are?" asked Senator Weeks.

"I am sure he is. He deals with a vast mass of detail which I deal with from a supervisory point of view."

When Baker was asked if the different chiefs and commanders were doing the best that possibly could be done, he replied:

"There are too many people in the world. I do not know."

He cast no reflections upon other departments of the government for delays; he defended his subordinates. Not once was his serenity ruffled. No senator lost his temper. But senators varied in their ideas of how to conduct an investigation which would "speed up the War."

After reading the scores of pages recording Baker's three days on the national witness-stand, I cannot refrain from a word about Senator Wadsworth, Republican, of New York, who did not ask questions for questions' sake, or to score a point, but apparently only on subjects that he knew, and with a constructive object. He, too, had declared a closed season for partisan politics and personal political interests in a war that was the whole nation's war. When time showed that some of his criticisms were wrong, he admitted his error. His conduct as a member of the Senate Committee on Military Affairs had a thoroughbred quality from beginning to end, and in any future war might be cited as an example for a member of the party that is "out," whether it is the Republican or the Democratic.

It is worth while to quote Baker's own attitude toward investigation in a letter to Judge Westenhaver:

"I don't think that those who criticize the 'delays' of the War Department have any other than a patriotic purpose. Indeed, I share their feelings of deep anxiety to speed our preparation along and bring the full strength of America to bear to end this conflict successfully; and I share, too, their impatience to get rid of all fretting causes of delay. The only difference between them and me, I think, is that, having been busy at the infinite detail of the undertaking for a long time, I have a better realization of the fact that some delays are inherent in the very size and difficulty of the task; and the only thought I come out with is the prayer that my strength may not prove insufficient and that I may not allow my mind to be closed to any helpful suggestion."

THE NATION BECOMES MORE CRITICAL

Meanwhile, what had been the response of the country to his appearance before the Committee? This had no clear national ring. It was a medley of the voices of war emotion, affected by political partisanship and the personal experiences of individuals in their part in winning the War. Supporting opinion thought Baker's answers had been fully convincing, a revelation of magnificent achievement. Hostile opinion, in its varying expressions, saw him as admitting errors, as bragging, as having been too adroit and clever in covering up errors, as too contented and even "insolent" in his optimism.

And he had been optimistic. If a general, a colonel, a captain, a sergeant may never betray the slightest doubt of the complete success of a coming attack, if a football coach may not send his team on the field in a defeatist mood, certainly a Secretary of War must never show pessimism. Yet to some, Baker's serenity had been prejudicial to him; the absence of any thunder or chain-lightning flashes of indignation comported with the view that he lacked the aggressiveness that was necessary for his post.

"The people are anxious, very anxious. There is a pervading fear that calamities and national humiliation will be the penalties for administrative incapacity." [11]

Perhaps if fair weather had come the controversy would have turned in Baker's favor. This would have been unfortunate, as he might not have appeared before the Committee on January 28 in one of the most dramatic and enlightening occasions in parliamentary history. The winter was at its worst in the third week of January. Blizzards piled more snow on doorsteps; housewives stood in the midst of snowstorms or below-zero weather waiting for their rations of coal; the five workless days were upon us, giving people time for thought.

America had appropriated billions, dug deep in her pockets for Liberty Loans and Community Chests, and sent her sons to the training camps. Was it true that her young soldiers were shivering for the lack of winter clothing, that after nine months of effort they had not enough machine-guns nor even enough rifles with which to drill? The people were used to waiting two or three years for a great bridge to be built, or a year or more for a great office building to rise from its foundations and be made ready for occupancy. But this was in peace: we were at war, now. Our people had been kept in the dark about the greatest national undertaking in our history. They had given of all their strength in faithful obedience to Washington's instructions. What was wrong with our government?

Harvey's Weekly said that "the chattering ex-Pacifist" was seated "on top of a pyramid of confusion which he had jumbled together and called a war machine." The indirect fire from the whispering gallery became direct and public fire. The regular battalions of criticism now saw themselves as crusaders heavily reinforced by volunteers. Senator Chamberlain led the Senate agitation to force a change in personnel in the conduct of the War. He had asked few questions at the Committee hearings; but on January 18 he was the principal speaker at a luncheon of nineteen hundred people under the auspices of the National Security League in New York. He said:

"The military establishment of America has fallen down. There is no use to be optimistic about a thing that does not exist. It has almost stopped functioning. Why? Because of inefficiency in every department of the Government of the United States. We are trying to work it out. I speak not as a Democrat but as an American citizen."

Theodore Roosevelt sprang to his feet, leading the prolonged applause at the close of Chamberlain's speech. The old lion, if he might not go to France, was not precluded from roaring at home, and his roar could penetrate every corner of the land. Since the opening of the War the leader of the Bull Moose movement had been restored to his old prestige with his class and to his former regular party standing, so that he was again its leader and was talked of as its next candidate for the Presidency. When he spoke in answer to the outcry of the New York meeting, he dwelt on his own campaign with his Rough Riders. In considering war on land he always reverted to the regimental formation, to the small fighting unit; it never seemed to me that the movement and control of great bodies of troops interested him. But when he considered the Battle of Lake Erie the ships became individual soldiers to him. He would have been a mighty admiral in the days of Drake, or Paul Jones, or Nelson.

"The Santiago campaign was a welter of confusion. I remember perfectly that we sent the guns down on one ship, and the locks to fire them with and the breech-blocks on another ship, which got mislaid on the way down. That was only one example of it. I stated that we were saved from disaster by the incompetency of our foes, and that to go against a well-led, well-trained, well-handled foe under such conditions would have meant ruin. . . ."

He set his audience to roaring with laughter when he recalled William Jennings Bryan's remark that in the event of war "a million Americans would spring to arms between sunrise and sunset." Then he continued: "They have been 'springing' for twelve months now, and have had to spring hard to reach rifles, and have not got any cannon to spring to as yet." But a fact that the Colonel had overlooked was that a rifle for every soldier we could send to France was assured, and also the artillery for the twenty-four division plan.

Roosevelt had dwelt much on "broomstick preparedness." But Leonard Wood had told Baker that it was well to send the men promptly to the camps where they would learn the habits of discipline. Major Palmer E. Pierce, voicing the concurring opinion of the General Staff, had stated to the Munitions Board in April, 1917, that the men might drill with dummy rifles for three months without affecting their preparation seriously, but after that they would be dissatisfied.[12] Roosevelt had stood for the draft in place of the Garrison plan and other patchwork preparedness plans. We had the draft; and in any one of the sixteen national cantonments which had risen in from sixty to ninety days, he had seen more of our youth in training than the whole force we had sent to Santiago. Now he had become the champion of a permanent universal service law. But Baker said that "civilized men must hope that the future has in store a relief from the burden of armament and the destruction and waste of war"; and he did not favor a huge standing army in time of peace. In an article in *The Kansas City Star* under the title "Brayed in a Mortar," Roosevelt took as his text Proverbs XXVII, 22: "Though thou shouldst bray a fool in a mortar among wheat with a pestle, yet will not his foolishness depart from him." In the course of this article he said:

"President Wilson speaks in military matters through his Secretary of War. The sole importance of the Secretary of War's report comes from its being the official declaration of the President. I discuss it as such. . . . Mr. Wilson's administration officially declares that we shall persist in our folly until we are brayed in the mortar of dreadful calamity."

As for universal conscription, this we had for the war that we were now engaged in, which seemed sufficient trouble for the War Department at the moment. Instead of trusting to the Bryan hope of a million men springing to arms, the War Department was following the scientific system, even to the length of opposing Roosevelt's volunteer division as a privilege which might set a precedent for future exceptions. In view of the "welter of confusion of the volunteer system in the Spanish War," Roosevelt, after he became President, had brought before the Congress no bill for universal service in peace. After the World War, when the men were weary of discipline and service in France and the nation was weary of war effort, neither political party adopted a universal service plank in its platform. No important group of either party proposed such a law. An important motivating influence in the public acceptance of the draft in 1917 had been that it was a means to win "the war to end war."

Always one must remember the great services of Roosevelt, and the individual affection we bore him, and consider how hard it was for the old lion, now so near his end, to have no active part in the War; how hard, once having been the dynamo on the inside at Washington, to be on the outside and taking much of his information from the whispering gallery which he himself, when he was so gallantly bearing the burden of responsibility, had so often derided. So far as he quickened the war spirit and war labor, he was a most helpful pulpiteer.

Yet he might have looked back to the days of his own battle for the Panama Canal. The land resounded with attacks upon him for setting up the Republic of Panama, on the basis of Elihu Root's right of eminent domain, to get a free hand for his mighty enterprise in joining the two oceans. People were saying that the Canal could never built; that if it were built, its enormous cost would be foolish waste. Pessimists prophesied that men would die like flies on the Isthmus, and there would be the same sort of scandalous fiasco as had ended the de Lesseps effort. The Congress having authorized the project, there followed the impatient cry to "make the dirt fly," when the Congress was as hesitant about appropriations as it had been in the first two months after our entry into the War.

"Instead of realizing that millions of dollars' worth of machinery must be bought . . . and a great army of men enlisted, drilled, housed, and fed, the Congress could think of nothing but the danger of another scandal like that of the de

Lesseps Company, and so dole out the money in grudging driblets." [13]

While Roosevelt was voicing his own indignation that we were so slow in sending men to France and in preparing munitions, he might have recalled how he traded patronage to senators in hard bargains to get his Canal legislation; remembered the Congressional and editorial jibes over his procrastination as he pondered contradictory engineering reports, after the work was well under way, before he could decide between a sea-level and a lock plan. He too had faced a dark hour when reports from the Isthmus pictured a chaos of banked-up material, half-finished workmen's camps, insurgent labor, and steam-shovels tossing dirt to no purpose. Members of the Canal personnel were resigning and bringing home stories which were bound to discourage other men from taking their places.

Goethals, in his task, had not to work against a time limit; war's sharp spur was not then roweling the public to impatience. The lives of soldiers were not at stake. He had not to compete for labor and materials under war conditions.

Roosevelt's right-hand man, William H. Taft, then Secretary of War, whom he had sent to the Isthmus, returned to say: "I care not whether you are Republicans or Democrats, you want the work done." Voicing his indignation against "the bitter and obviously malicious criticism," he said, "The Canal will be built. All the windy opposition will not obstruct it."

In a special message to the Congress, Roosevelt said:

"Where the slanderers are of foreign birth, I have no concern with them. Where they are Americans, I feel for them the heartiest contempt and indignation; because in a spirit of wanton dishonesty and malice they are trying to interfere with and to hamper the execution of the greatest work of the kind ever attempted, and are seeking to bring to naught the efforts of their countrymen to put to the credit of America one of the giant feats of the ages."

He lived to see all the criticism and dour prophecies confounded; even, with a later generation, to foresee the possibility that the Canal would actually be unequal to the growing traffic. As a prophet of gloom—a part ill-suited to his nature— Roosevelt was to be confounded no less than the men had been who had prophesied so gloomily about the Panama Canal. Possibly one of Baker's shortcomings for his task was that he did not turn on Roosevelt with the same vigorous indignation that Roosevelt had poured on the Canal critics. This would have given Baker's reply as conspicuous headlines as the attack had won; for the way a thing is said often counts in public display for more than what is said. But it was not in Baker to turn on his opponents as "wanton and dishonest." Perhaps the criticisms of Roosevelt a few years before had served to keep his Canal administration up to the mark; and perhaps criticism of the War Department in 1917–18 served a like purpose. The impetuous Rough Rider, when he became President, had faced as widespread apprehension about his ability as an administrator as had the Mayor of Cleveland when he became Secretary of War. Such are historical facts, which are ever rich in parallel and ever enlightening.

"WE NEED A BUTCHER, NOT A BAKER"

At the beginning of the fourth week in January the headquarters of the crusade moved to Washington, upon which public opinion was turning a still fiercer light of inquiry and suggestion. It looked as if the secret prophecy I had made, when Pershing sailed, was already on the way to fulfilment. In view of America's failure to comprehend the seriousness of the Allied situation or the real task in preparing and transporting an army to France, it seemed to me that both Baker and Pershing, however truly they laid their foundations, would eventually be superseded.

Germany had changed chancellors; and the German army had turned from von Moltke to von Falkenhayn, and then to Hindenburg. In Britain Lloyd George had unhorsed Asquith, and a coalition cabinet had been formed whose personnel had undergone many changes. Earl Kitchener had built a war machine for others to drive, and Sir Douglas Haig had suc-

ceeded Sir John French in field command. In France there had
been a succession of premiers, and Joffre had been replaced at
the head of the army by Nivelle, who in turn was replaced by
Pétain.

Again a coalition cabinet was being bruited in Washington.
This was not so practicable under our Constitution as under
the British or the French constitution. In England the King,
and in France the President, as head of the nation above partisan politics, can summon a leader to form a cabinet as
Premier. At any time the parliament of either country may vote
the Premier out of power. But the Congress cannot remove the
President, who is our Premier as well as head of the nation,
except by impeachment, in default of his resignation. He
chooses the members of his Cabinet. President Wilson was
wholly unresponsive to the idea of a coalition cabinet. Meanwhile non-partisanship in the War Department had kept faith
with the principle of using all men regardless of party.

But shouldn't we follow the example of Britain in a Ministry
of Munitions? Doubts were expressed by those who had been
in Britain as to the success of the Ministry of Munitions; and
this suggestion, too, did not meet with Presidential favor. Anyhow, the impatient ones were again calling for a superman—
a "he-man"—who should have full power to make this a
"he-war." "We need a butcher, not a Baker."

Hoover's friends suggested him, but the President apparently thought him well-placed as Food Administrator. The
other supermen proposed included one who, under the strain
of a subordinate position, had to go to a health resort for two
weeks to escape a nervous breakdown. I do not mention his
name, because he did such invaluable service and because he
never thought of himself as a superman, but concluded, after
working a few weeks with Baker, that we already had a great
executive as Secretary of War.

On January 23 Theodore Roosevelt had come to Washington, where his followers gathered around him at Mrs. Long-
worth's house.[14] Some of them favored leaving the administration to conduct the War in its own way, and allowing the

people to find out the bad management. Roosevelt was not so narrow a partisan as that, and was too great a patriot to profit by such partisan strategy. He was for constructive criticism: for a law providing for universal compulsory training in peace; for a War Cabinet, and a Director of Munitions; for legislation limiting all war measures, such as government control of the railroads, to the duration of the War; and against a coalition cabinet.

Senator Chamberlain's speech at the New York luncheon turned out to be only the first trial shots preliminary to his real bombardment in the Senate, where no limits of a luncheon-time would hamper the fullest exposition of his indictment of the War Department. In a speech of three hours' duration he said: [15]

"I noticed in reading the proceedings of the British Parliament not long ago, a member said, and I think he was right, 'You need not be afraid about giving Germany any information.' Germany knows more about America today than many men connected with the department; and so far as I am concerned, my colleagues, I feel that America would be better off if her representatives would come out in the spotlight and let the plain people of this land know what is being done. Then you could rely upon them to rally to the support of the President for the successful prosecution of this war. There is not any question about that. . . .

"Poor bleeding France, my friends—bled white, not only for her own life and for the liberty of her own citizens but for America as well—is today furnishing to our troops as they arrive in France the necessary heavy ordnance and the machine-guns for aircraft and for ground service.

"Why, there is testimony, if I correctly remember it, before the Military Affairs Committee that along some of these fronts the cannon—and heavy cannon, if you please—are located five yards apart for a distance of six miles; and yet America, this great and magnificent country, is dependent upon poor France to deliver the ordnance! . . .

"You senators know that there are soldiers along the Atlantic seaboard who ought to have gone to France six weeks or two months ago. They do not go. Why is it? At Mineola there were a lot of Oregon and other brave boys who went from a Southern encampment to that bleak and barren place, where some of them were kept for over a month in extremely cold weather, not sufficiently clad, and without the comforts that camp life ought to have furnished them, waiting to get over. There must be something wrong somewhere."

It is needless to mention that it was the winter storms as well as the lack of shipping that had delayed the departure of the Oregon men, who were from Chamberlain's own State. In proof of the bad management in the camps and neglect of the sick, without regard to the statistics that showed the low sick-rate, Chamberlain offered letters which included two, whose author's names were not given, testifying to neglect of the dead. He had the ear of the nation—and every word of his speech seemed to be aimed indirectly if not directly at Baker. Representative Medill McCormick, who had just returned from London, reported that the British leaders were saying, "We wonder if you have all the big men whom you might bring together in your government?" [16] Other senators, who had been silent, were turning critical. Senator William S. Kenyon, Republican, of Iowa, who had been lukewarm about our entry into the War, and about the prosecution of our part, returned from France to spread alarm by saying that Germany's plans for world mastery included an indemnity from the United States.

In a letter to Judge Westenhaver, Baker referred to the ill-will of a certain Senator, "who is quite impossibly small and nurses a grievance at my having refused his improper requests," and continued:

"To the outsider or the inexperienced it seems easy to put out the less efficient and put in the more efficient; but the turmoil which would have followed any civilian who would act rashly with an organization as traditional and specialized as the Army would have been tremendous; and after all, there are really few people in the country who could with any confidence have been expected to have all the qualities needed for success in a task requiring not only industrial experience but a knowledge of the Army and of military matters in addition. So I have gone on supplementing and gradually replacing until a more modern group are now practically in control, and neither the Army nor the country feels, so far as I know, that I have presumed to disregard experienced men. The investigations before the Senate Committee seem to me on the whole beneficial.

"There is the usual amount of ineptitude represented by several of the senators who do not know the long and patient preparation necessary to prepare a plant to turn out new things in quantity, and who accordingly think the whole thing is to be disposed of by a surprised look at such slowness. There is, too, the usual eager rush of disappointed contractors and inventors to testify that their merits were overlooked from either inertia or favoritism. There are diplomatic reasons why much cannot be told. The French and English surpluses of artillery which they want to exchange for steel billets but do not want to have talked about; the difficulties we have had with labor questions which it would be unwise and controversial to mention; the very great embarrassment over price; the questions of priority, as between the Allies' needs and our own—all of these have at times been mountains of difficulty, and perhaps the greatest thing we have done at all is the negative thing of not raising rows. . . . Now is not the time to have a public dispute, so I simply ask the senators, when they talk with me privately, to beat the Germans first and then beat me if I still seem to deserve it."

The "negative thing of not raising rows" was quite important in our relations with the Allies; and also in the War Department's relations with the Congress.

President Wilson had answered Chamberlain in a powerful letter defending the War Department; but that did not stay the agitation against Baker. Many of the President's devoted followers thought that he overestimated Baker's ability. The whispering gallery now had a new epithet for Baker—"Newty Cootie." The gallery was certain that Baker would have to go; that the President could not retain him in face of the tide of opinion that was rising against him. Political wiseacres were saying the time had come for a "scapegoat," and that destiny had cast Baker for the part.

But the son of Jeb Stuart's trooper was not of the mind to continue to receive all this fire sitting quietly at his desk. On the previous occasion he had been summoned as a witness to answer senatorial questions. Now he asked the Senate Committee on Military Affairs to hear him again.

XXII

"WHAT MORE CAN WE DO?"

THE word passed quickly about the lobbies of Congress that
Baker was to appear before the Committee again. So numerous
an audience gathered around him upon his arrival at the Capitol
that the hearing was transferred to a larger room than the one
the Committee regularly occupied. When Chairman Chamberlain asked him whether he planned to supplement or correct
what he had previously said at the three days' hearings, Baker
replied that he proposed covering the whole conduct of the
War.[1]

This time he had no prepared statement. A few minutes before he went to the Capitol he drew a sheet of note-paper from
the rack on his desk. Upon it he wrote the heads of his address;
and its appeal was: "What more can we do?" After his return
from the Capitol he dropped the sheet on his desk, and Ralph
Hayes, his private secretary, saved it from the waste-basket as a
personal memento.

". . . For one reason or another the impression has gone out
into the country, to some extent at least, that the War Department has fallen down in addressing itself to the task of conducting this war. I want to address myself to that question. . . .
The country is entitled to know what this war is, what its
problems are, and what steps have been taken to meet these
problems. . . .

"I have a deep sense of obligation to the officers of the Army
and to the civilians who have from the beginning labored in a
way which, certainly in my experience, has never been equaled;
with devotion, self-sacrifice, zeal, spending sleepless nights and
tireless days in an effort to bring up most rapidly and effectively the organization of this great Army and its use in a military enterprise. . . . It would be a tragic thing if this tre-

mendous effort, this wholly unprecedented sacrifice were, in fact, to turn out to deserve the comment that it had fallen down.

"I have not the least doubt that such currency as that feeling has gotten is due in large part to the tremendous impatience of the American people to do this great thing greatly. Every one of you, and every one of us, wants to demonstrate the thing which we know to be true—that our country is great and strong, and in a cause like this will hit like one man at the adversary which has attacked us. And always there is between the beginning of preparation and the final demonstration of its success a period of questioning when everybody, you and I and everybody else, goes through searching of heart to find out whether all has been done that could or ought to have been done; whether anything remains that can be done. And we look back over the past and realize that there have been delays and shortcomings; that there have been things which might have been done better. In so great an enterprise it is impossible for frankness not to find those things.

"But our effort is to learn from them not to repeat; to strengthen what needs strengthening; to supplement what needs supplementing; and, by bringing two things together, our very best effort and the confidence of the country back of that effort, to make our enemies finally feel the strength that is really American.

"The issue of this is far too large for any prejudice or favoritism to any individual. . . . Nor am I here to deny delays, mistakes, shortcomings, or false starts. I think I can say with confidence that where those things have appeared we have sought the remedy; that in many places we have applied the remedy. And the largest purpose I have in being here is to urge that your committee, that the Members of the Senate and the Members of the House, that every citizen in this country, official and unofficial, from the highest to the lowest, should realize that this is their enterprise, and to ask from you and from them every suggestion, every criticism, every constructive thought that occurs to any of you. I ask you, when shortcomings are pointed out to you, whether they are well founded or not, that you will instantly convey them to me, so that I may search out where blame is to be attached, where remedies are to be applied, and where strengthening and improvement of the organization is possible. . . .

"I have understood that Senator Chamberlain felt that there was not a plan for this war. I do not know how far the members of the Committee feel that way; I do not know how far the country feels that way; but I want to say to you that there is a plan; that it is the only plan under the circumstances."

Now he came to the main body of this statement of January 28, 1918, from which I have already quoted at intervals in order to keep the reader current with facts and factors in the forming and execution of the War Department's plan, about which the public at the time was in the dark.

". . . We were coming into a war which had been going on for two and one-half years, in which the greatest military experts, all the inventive genius, all of the industrial capacity of those greatest countries in the world had been for two and one-half years solving the problem of what kind of war it was to be and where it was to be waged.

"It was not for us to decide where our theater of war should be. That theater was France. It was not for us to decide our line of communications. That line was across three thousand miles of ocean, one end of it infested with submarines. It was not for us to decide whether we should have the maneuvering of large bodies of troops in the open. There lay the antagonists in the trenches on opposite sides of No Man's Land at a death-grapple with one another. Our antagonist was on the other side of that line, and our problem was and is to get over there and get him. . . . They said to us: This is a moving picture; it is something that nobody can paint and give you an idea of. It is not a static thing. . . . France was a white sheet of paper, so far as we were concerned, and on that we had not only to write an army . . . we had to go back to the planting of corn in France in order that we might make a harvest."

Baker now spoke of various things that it had not been possible to mention publicly before this time: the effect on our plans of the failure of the spring offensive of the French in

1. Introduction

2. Chamberlain letters

3. Ordnance dept.

Rifles. Conference Scott Bliss Baker Crozier Pershing

Machine Guns.

Cannon

4 Q.M.G.

Food

Clothing

5 Cantonment sites

Air & gas

Hospitals

Medical advisers

Sickness

6 Plans of War

7.

8 Health care &c.

BAKER'S NOTES FOR HIS TALK BEFORE THE SENATE
COMMITTEE ON MILITARY AFFAIRS, JANUARY 28, 1918

1917; and the effect of the Russian collapse. By this time, too, he could even refer to the Italian defeat, though not as a disaster. No Allied nation ever publicly admitted that it had had a military disaster, not even when privately it was presenting to the other Allies a picture of such utter despair that only generous aid in men and in funds would keep its people in the War.

There had been much talk at the previous hearings about our lack of artillery. Senators had been alarmed at the prospect of our men going into battle unarmed. Now Baker cleared the situation about guns by stating the readiness of the French to supply all the troops we could send abroad with sufficient artillery.

"Why have you not felt it proper," Chamberlain asked, "to let the public into your confidence with reference to these things that you are telling us now?"

"Senator, I confess I have hesitated and I still hesitate. . . . Field Marshal von Hindenburg is quoted as saying in contemptuous fashion of us, that we have advertised our preparations for this war in an unworthy manner."

This, too, was characteristic. One of Baker's weaknesses as Secretary of War was that he was a poor propagandist. The Committee on Public Information found him difficult in this respect.

Chamberlain wanted to know how many men we had in France. Senator Henry L. Meyers, Democrat, of Montana, cut in with a question as to whether British, French, and German armies stated their numbers. Baker said he could not himself ascertain in definite figures the totals of British or French on their fronts; and he would not tell how many men we had in France.

The name of Theodore Roosevelt inevitably came up. The magazine of which he was contributing editor had said in August, 1917, that "we should strain energy to get 50,000 to 100,000 men to France this year, and by next year, 1918, we should have 500,000 men to send over, or any part of 500,000 men we could ship."

Baker made this comment:

"Now, instead of having 50,000 or 100,000 men in France in 1917, we have many more men than that in France, and instead of having a half million men whom we could ship to France if we could find any way to do it in 1918, we shall have more than one-half million men in France early in 1918; and, if the transportation facilities are available, we have one and one-half million who in 1918 can be shipped to France."

READY TO SEND THE MEN FAST

Then he took up the charge that he had raised an army faster than he could supply and care for it. Speaking of his plan formed early in 1917, he said:

"I did not then know, nor can I know now, how rapidly it may be necessary for us to send men to France. . . . I know what our present plan is, but I do not know but that tomorrow it might turn out that it would be wise to double the rate at which we are sending them. There are now in the United States 16 National Guard camps and 16 National Army camps, filled with men who are ready to go if necessary. I have sacrificed something for that. I have not willingly sacrificed the health of anybody, but I have intended, if it was humanly possible, to be ready when the call came. And if I had delayed to call out these troops until the last button was on the last coat, and the call had come in November, or December, or January, 'Send them and send them fast,' and they were still at home waiting for tailors, I would have felt a crushing load of guilt and responsibility."

If he had told of the Allied pressure for our man-power in January, 1918, protests would soon have been coming down the corridors from the State Department, from the Allies, and direct from Pershing, against a statement that would encourage German morale—when any day the German army might begin its offensive on the Western front. Baker was walking on eggs in trying to take the public into his confidence. His revelations of Allied relations must be historical rather than contemporaneous.

"And yet I was not callous about it. I asked those agencies with which we were dealing in this matter how fast we could expect supplies. They gave me the forecast as to the future. They relied upon their estimate of production. I relied upon their estimate of production. Men who were called upon to take contracts for the production of clothing and the making of garments, not unnaturally perhaps, overestimated their capacity for production."

He was bold enough to mention that there had been some labor difficulties and delays in transportation due to "a winter the like of which none of us has seen since we were children"; but without implying that the Caporetto disaster had interfered with altogether adequate supplies for ourselves.

"Suppose I had taken the other counsel. There were two alternatives: either we could go into this War as other nations go into wars, summoning the countryside and assembling them into camps, working out their problems afterwards—which was one suggestion at the time; or we could wait until the last element of preparation had been made before summoning the men. The unwisdom, I think, of either of these courses is obvious. What we tried to do—and the responsibility for it I think I must personally accept, because I was conscious of the grounds on which it lay—what we tried to do was to summon the men out as rapidly as they could be taken care of, with the best knowledge we could get of the capacity of the industry of this country. It is not unknown to any member of this Committee that when the draft army came to be assembled, we delayed calling out its units sometimes a couple of weeks, sometimes more than that, in order that at each camp no man would be received who could not be taken care of; and the last element of the first 600,000 or 700,000 men selected by the draft, the last element of these men intended originally to have come out in November or December, will not, in fact, report to the camp until the 15th of February, in order that production may catch up and be adequate for their entertainment and protection when they come."

As for the two letters from persons whose names Chamberlain might not give, describing neglect of the dead, Baker said that, pending receipt of the names, he would mention the case of an American who was killed on the Toronto flying-field, where we had an aviation group under Canadian instruction. The British and Canadian practice was to remove the clothes of the dead and wrap the body in a winding-sheet. An order had been sent to Toronto to follow the American practice in the case of further deaths.

With reference to Senator Chamberlain's charge of incompetent and even cruel treatment given by doctors to sick soldiers in the camps, which led to fatal results, Baker said:

"There are two cases which in my judgment illustrate the attitude of the department on this subject. The first is that of a lieutenant, charged with neglect of patients at the base hospital at Camp Beauregard, Louisiana. He was court-martialed and sentenced to be dismissed. The other case is that of another lieutenant, charged with neglect of patients, court-martialed, and sentenced to be dismissed. Their cases present substantially the same facts. In one case, an ambulance drove up and a man was brought in claiming to be sick. The doctor made a hasty examination, looked at him, felt his pulse, or something of that kind, and ordered him back, saying that he was not sick. In other words, the doctor did not do the things he ought to have done; he did not examine the patient and diagnose his difficulty in either of these cases, and the result was that in both of them severe illness developed, and death resulted.

"When those cases came to me, I had them reviewed by the Judge Advocate General to see what further could be done. A court-martial organized in accordance with the laws of the Army and of the land had sat upon these cases and apportioned the punishment as dismissal from the Army. But when the Judge Advocate General reviewed it for me he came to the conclusion that that sort of neglect went much deeper, and recommended that both of those cases be sent back to the court-martial which had tried them, and that such imprisonment as could be added under the statutes of this country for that kind of neglect should be added to the penalty of dismissal."

Two cases out of more than a million men in a hastily organized army with its hastily expanded medical corps!

Baker quoted a letter from Mary Roberts Rinehart, who had
seen conditions in European camps and hospitals before our
entry into the War, and for four months had been going from
camp to camp in the United States. The letter carried conviction
through her fame as a writer, her character, training, and experience.

". . . I know something about hospitals. I took a nurse's
training as a girl. I married a member of my hospital staff, and
I have been for many years constantly in touch with hospitals. . . . I want drastic punishment applied to any man, of
no matter what rank, who is found guilty of negligence in the
care, physical or moral, of our boys. And I want immediate
remedy of conditions that require remedy. . . . We will not
rest, we women, until we have all [the inefficients] removed.
But that, I know, will be at once. It must be at once. . . . I
have a son in an army cantonment. He enlisted as a private. He
would receive, if he became ill, the same treatment as any other
man in our new army. And I should have not only no hesitation in placing him in the cantonment hospital, but I should
do it in absolute confidence. As a matter of fact he has already
spent a few days there with an infected knee and received the
best of care. . . . Of cruelty and indifference I have found
none. On the contrary, I have found the medical staffs of the
hospitals both efficient and humane. . . . Nursing is on the
same high plane. Wards are large and airy. Beds are comfortable. I have found exquisite cleanliness everywhere. . . . I
have examined storerooms and kitchens and watched diets being served under the direction of a woman dietician."

There had been a lack of supplies, Mrs. Rinehart said, and
hospitals had not always been quite ready; doctors and nurses
had put up with hardships. But these things were being rem-
edied. She would like to see more trained women nurses in
place of hospital orderlies. But how many more could our
undermanned civil hospitals spare?

Baker concluded his talk:

"And, now, let me be frank with you, and let your judgment be frank with me about this: Has any army in history ever, since the beginning of time, been so raised and cared for as this army has been? Can the picture be duplicated?

"So far as I am personally concerned, I know what is ahead of us. I know what American feeling about this war is. Everybody is impatient to do as much as he can. There will be no division of counsel; there will be all the criticism there ought to be upon shortcomings and failures; there will be, so far as the War Department is concerned, a continuing effort at self-improvement, and a hospitality toward every suggestion for improvement from outside."

Chamberlain said: "I know that you must be tired. The Committee has been very much impressed."

DEMOCRACY JUSTIFIES ITS METHODS

Indeed, all who had listened had been much impressed, and the people were to be, too, when they read the full reports of Baker's talk in the morning papers. There was corresponding relief among members of the Cabinet and in the White House itself. Democrats, who had complained of Baker's non-partisanship, could not deny that it might have been of service to a Democratic administration. The agitation for a coalition cabinet ceased. Baker was not breaking; nor was he to be broken.

It is interesting to note that the proposal of Senator Ollie M. James, Democrat, of Kentucky, to have Baker's statement printed in *The Congressional Record* met the opposition of Senator Jacob H. Gallinger, Republican, of New Hampshire, and Senator Reed Smoot, Republican, of Utah. Gallinger, who was the more persistent of the two in his objection, said the statement as printed in the Committee's hearings could be franked by any Senator in as large numbers as he pleased; whereas few people ever read the *Record*. Anyhow, he thought that the hearings of the first three days should be included with Baker's later statement. To this James agreed. The Democratic Vice President, Thomas R. Marshall, ordered that both should have a place in the *Record;* and accordingly the report of the investigation of the conduct of the nation's greatest war effort was included in the minutes of the national legislature with other speeches and testimony which now seem to be of relatively less historical consequence.

In his second statement Baker had anticipated so many questions that few were asked; and even in a larger degree than in the earlier hearing the whole had been on a high plane. Senators who had reports two weeks before of lack of supplies at the cantonments found that in the meantime supplies had arrived. The weather had turned in Baker's favor. The sun had come out, leaving the snow-shovels idle. People were not suffering from such bitter cold on fuelless days. Traffic congestion had been measurably relieved.

All complaints had now been threshed out according to the best parliamentary precedents of the forum, the hall of nobles, the hall of the commoners, the town meeting, or the house of burgesses, with the modern press as the sounding board for a committee of a Congress which represented more than one hundred million people. Sometimes the system seems to require far too many words. It allows small minds as well as great minds to be heard. But all the suspicions that arrest war energy under an autocracy had been aired. The democracy could now proceed with fresh confidence to its mighty task. The whispering gallery, which has a much busier and more thrilling time under an autocracy, could turn to a new item.

Daniel Willard, veteran of industrial preparedness, had resigned as chairman of the War Industries Board, deeply to the regret of his colleagues and of Baker. The whispering gallery had the list of a dozen supermen fit to succeed him, but could not unite on one. Those who were supermen to their own followings were not so to the followings of other supermen. "No, he will not do." "He is too short-tempered," or "too slow," or "too tactless." "He is not a business man." "He knows only transport." "He is a financier, and doesn't know production." "Too many enemies." "Not an administrator." "The Congress would never have him." "Too young to hold the respect of older captains of industry." "Past his prime." "He knows he is a superman; that kind will never do."

Willard thought he could now do better work by returning to his railroad. As chief of industrial output he had reached a point where his efficiency suffered from want of sufficient authority. His resignation was an act of wisdom and courage which was to be a powerful factor in winning for his successor the free hand which the law had denied to Willard himself.

DRAFTING THE OVERMAN ACT

There had been much comment on the power of the President under the Constitution, and its extension for war purposes by the National Defense Act, which had given a false impression to the public. "Extra-legality" could not cover the present need, which could be met only by an act of the Congress. No one was in a better position than Baker to realize the importance of more concentration; no one had so intimately pressing reasons for being its partisan. On January 24, 1918, three days before he asked for the hearing before the Senate Committee, we find him writing a letter to the President, enclosing the copy of a bill to be presented to the Congress by General Crowder. This was the Overman Act, which was not to be passed until May twentieth. In the files, too, are Baker's interlineations of Crowder's draft of the bill. They include the phrase "more efficient administration" as the appealing and sufficing public reason for the Act, and also the one which authorizes such distribution of executive functions as the President "may deem necessary," which meant that the President would be supremely and personally responsible for all our war effort. Some of Baker's assistants and members of the War Industries Board thought that the Congress would be better occupied in passing such legislation than in investigating Baker.

The investigation, however, had cleared the way for the bill. And the public agitation and discussion had had a part in preparing the Congress for the eventual decision that there was an emergency for granting the President unprecedented power over the civil life of the nation. But this would not be granted by the nation's representatives without some support more solid than a passing wave of public emotion, executive requests, or innuendoes from the whispering gallery.

Meanwhile, Baker must continue to make the most of the authority that existed. On February 1, three days after his address to the Senate Committee, he informed the President of the result of his conference with Bernard Baruch about a reorganization of the War Industries Board. "We recognize that the present question is the appointment of a successor to Mr. Willard, and that the redistribution of power will have to be delayed until the President is empowered by legislation, but the immediate organization could begin and suitable distribution of power could be made later when the legislation is assured."

The new chairman of the War Industries Board must naturally be chosen from among the men who had already been tried out in the co-ordination of business and government under war conditions. In a letter to the President on January 24, Baker had suggested three names.

There was Baruch, with whom he had just been in conference, the pioneer of raw materials on the War Industries Board. The objection to him, from members of the Cabinet among others, was that he was primarily a financier and not a business executive. Clarence M. Wooley, President of the American Radiator Company, who was with the War Trade Board, had risen round by round up the ladder as a business organizer. So had John D. Ryan, President of the Anaconda Copper Company. Ryan's business connections, when the nation was consuming so much copper, might be considered a handicap in certain quarters. Also, some of the copper interests thought that Ryan, when he was working for the nation, might lean over backward so far that he would not give the copper industry a fair deal. Ryan, no less than Baruch, wanted more authority, the authority that Willard lacked, and so hesitated to take the appointment. But Ryan wrote to Baker that he would not be obstinate; he would try to work it out along present lines if he were drafted. Baruch's attitude was the same. The President took his time, more than a month, before he made his choice, which was Baruch.

Another change in chiefs was also in order; a change which some angles of War Department opinion thought had been too long delayed. For a new Chief of Staff Baker turned to the same man whom he had originally had in mind when he was considering a successor to Bliss. The most important of all the many cables across the Atlantic about personnel was sent on January twenty-sixth.[2] It had the usual signature of "McCain" as Adjutant General, but with the name "Baker" added. This meant that it was personally sent by Baker to Pershing.

"Can Major General Peyton C. March be spared to return to this country as Acting Chief of Staff? If he can, direct his immediate return. I feel it urgently necessary to have him. Please reply."

This had an unusually peremptory tone for a message from the Secretary of War to the Commander-in-Chief.

THE NAVY WAS DOING ITS PART

Through the long months of preparation, any word from the Navy Department on the other side of the building, reporting the safe arrival of another transport after passing through the submarine zone, always brought relief to the War Department. There had been no repetition of the jealousies, the differences, and the ructions between the Army and Navy which had been common in the Spanish War. Again the discrimination between the historical precedents to be avoided and those to be followed had served a good purpose. Upon our entry into the War, Baker, Secretary Daniels of the Navy, Major General H. L. Scott, Chief of Staff of the Army, and Admiral W. S. Benson, Chief of Operations of the Navy, had a conference on the subject of Army and Navy relations. Baker said that as the Navy was the first line of defense, it should have priority over the Army for steel for a year; after that, the Army, which should then be in action in force, might ask for priority.

THE *LEVIATHAN* CARRIES ELEVEN THOUSAND MEN

LAST LETTERS HOME BEFORE THE TRANSPORT SAILED

All questions about overlapping authority should be settled between Scott and Benson in a liberal give-and-take manner. If they came to an impasse, the difficulty was to be referred up to Baker and Daniels. Scott and then Bliss, and Bliss's successor, and the sagacious Benson kept the good faith of the sister services so well that they rarely had a problem for their chiefs. Once the soldier was on board ship, it was the business of seamen to take him across the Atlantic, while the soldier took charge of his own transport once he was on land again. There were no land-admirals or sea-generals. If Secretary Daniels were away from his desk, the broad-gauge and engaging Franklin Roosevelt, Assistant Secretary, became Acting Secretary to expedite business.

Yet always there hung over both departments the apprehension that some transport would be sunk; and on February 5 the dreaded news arrived. The British liner *Tuscania,* acting as an American transport, had been torpedoed off the north coast of Ireland on her way to Liverpool. According to the first report it seemed certain that all the soldiers on board had been lost. For the first time his assistants saw the Secretary very much shaken. His imagination painted the picture in all its horror. As yet we had had relatively few casualties at the front, and now two thousand men, after all their training in anticipation of the day when they should face the enemy, had gone down like rats in a trap without even arriving over there! It would be a triumph proclaiming to Ludendorff's army, forming for its great spring drive, the assurance that the American army would be drowned on the way to the front.

Happily, a later cable said that all but a few of the men had been safely brought ashore. The relief over this came at a time when Secretary Daniels had the best news that England had received for a year: the submarine losses for January were down to 318,000 tons, although there was still a margin of tonnage destroyed over the tonnage coming from the world's shipyards.[3] Heavier losses might come with the longer days of spring; but British and American naval co-operation, the adoption of the convoy system, and the depth bombs, were promising to win

the day. In France four of our divisions were now having, or
had had, trench experience: the 1st, 2nd, 26th, and 42nd. We
were looking up at Mont Sec in the miserable sector at Toul.

But Pershing no sooner disposed of one trouble than he was
beset by two or three more. At first the French had said that
we could not use Brest as a port. After Caporetto they had
changed their minds and thought we could get 20,000 men
and 6,000 tons of supplies ashore monthly "if not too much
bunching." [4] The old German *Vaterland,* which we had re-
christened the *Leviathan,* could carry 11,000 men, which certainly would have been regarded as "bunching" by the port
authorities at Brest. But we must supply the lighters and tug-
boats for disembarkation. So we started them across the Atlantic in perilous weather. At one time it was suggested that we
make the *Leviathan* a station ship at Brest. As no coal was
available at Brest, she and other big transports had to go to
England for coal for the return voyage, which meant three
trips through the danger zone. Ships must also have ballast for
the homeward voyage. Brest could not supply enough. But
Pershing hoped less would be required, since the ships would
not roll so much after the winter storms were over and summer weather came. Water ballast might be the only solution
unless the French would supply sand barges. He cabled January 5, "The general situation at our ports is becoming very
serious. We are not able to handle transports quickly enough
to get full service from the limited amount of tonnage that up
to the present seems available for military use." [5] On February
20 he was cabled that our ships must install water-ballast systems before next fall. He was unloading "approximately 8,000
tons at all ports, but owing to shortage of railroad cars evacuating only about 3,000 tons" from the ports to the Army.[6]

Meanwhile, the *Leviathan* and other reconditioned German
passenger ships were on the way. The British were establishing
depots for our men in passing through England. Their busy
cross-Channel fleet was ferrying across all it could to France.
We might augment the fleet by sending ships from home while
France bargained for some with Norway and Sweden. Three of

her great liners would soon be in our ports at our service as troop transports.

"We'll load all you send," said Brigadier General Frank T. Hines, who had just been appointed Chief of the Embarkation Service, and kept his word.[7]

But our men must have food and transport in France, where cargo piled up at the ports. With the Senate investigation over, with General March coming to be Chief of Staff, with the Overman Act on the President's desk and before the Congress, home preparations now permitted Baker's interest to shift overseas. He might gratify Pershing's wish that he come to France and see conditions for himself. But this required permission from his own superior officer. On February 20, 1918, he wrote to the President:

"I have come more and more to realize the need of an actual inspection of ports, transportation and storage facilities, and camps overseas.

"Of course, we are constantly having officers of the several Armies returning from France with information and recommendations; but they frequently serve only to illustrate the impossibility of securing a complete view of the situation by any other course than a personal inspection.

"In addition to this, the relatives and friends of our soldiers are deeply concerned to know the conditions under which these soldiers live and the environment in which they find themselves. It will be of importance if I can give comforting assurances as the result of an actual visit to the camps; and it may be that I can suggest betterments as the result of our experience here where great encampments have been built up, and a most wholesome and helpful environment provided with the co-operation of all the helpful and sympathetic agencies which the people of the country have placed at our disposal."

The President replied two days later that the comprehensive view Baker would bring back would be serviceable to all concerned, and suggested that it would gratify the Italian military and people if he would visit Italy, however briefly.

Further reminders of the enormous contribution of supplies

as well as man-power continued to arrive in cables from Pershing in the week before Baker sailed: "This storage system will require one hundred twenty-five miles of track per month with eight switches and frogs per mile for at least three months." The French had 20,000 useless locomotives and 30,000 useless freight cars that they could not repair. We must hurry over immediately "4,800 car and locomotive repair-shop troops, with necessary tools and equipment . . . and American freight cars at rate of fifteen hundred per month and locomotives at rate of seventy-five per month for the next three months and probably two months thereafter. . . . These shipments of freight cars, locomotives, and track must be given priority over everything except subsistence, clothing and forage." [8] A freight car is a large article to ship, and a locomotive even larger, not to mention that our railroads were short of both and unable to meet home requirements. The French, Pershing said, were in immediate need of 40,000 tons of steel, and short of chrome ore, zinc, tungsten and retort carbon.[9]

A "complete view" of our war situation, which Baker sought in a brief visit, was bound to keep him as busy in France as he had been at home. But the routine of his sixteen-to-eighteen-hour day in the War Department was to be broken for the first time in more than a year. "The Secretary of War leaves Washington today for an indefinite absence." Meanwhile, Benedict Crowell, the Assistant Secretary, would be Acting Secretary of War. The British Secretary of State for War could be at the front from London in four hours, and the French Minister of War had only to motor out to Chantilly to be at French G. H. Q.: but an American Secretary of War must take ten days to reach France, and then more than a day to reach American headquarters. Of course, the whispering gallery could surmise Baker's destination. But the Navy, which was responsible for his safe conduct, would have no definite information given out before his arrival in France.

XXIII

THE SECRETARY SEES THE A. E. F.

THE decks of the cruiser on which Baker crossed the Atlantic were piled high with bags of coal for the return voyage; a reminder of the European fuel shortage. At night he knew the soldier's experience of having the ports closed in order to darken ship through the submarine danger zone.

Not only was he the first American Cabinet officer to visit Europe in the World War, but he was the one who officially represented the final reservoir of man-power for the Allies at a time when the German army was massing for a decisive blow. France would have gladly spread the red carpet of official welcome for him, accompanied by all the ingratiating attentions to distinguished guests in which she is so adept. Baker, however, through the State Department, asked the Allied governments to regard his coming as unofficial.

"It seemed to me of the highest importance that my visit should not be long; that it should be devoted intensively to the study of conditions, and that it should not be interrupted by a round of official courtesies and ceremonial observances. . . . This, of course, also prevented my visit from being a distraction and an embarrassment to the busy civilians and military men of the Allied armies." [1]

At six-thirty on the morning of March 10, Pershing and Bliss awaited him at the railroad station in Paris. He paid a call on the President of France; he met Clemenceau and Joffre and other statesmen and generals, and heard their views and appeals. To all he said that his purpose in France was to learn how he could better support the Commander-in-Chief upon whose judgment he relied. After a single night in Paris, made thrilling for him by a German air-raid, he was forth to see what America had written on the white sheet of paper.

At home, when he went to see a camp or a munition works, he traveled on a regular train; but now he traveled on Pershing's private train with Pershing as his guide, and with a soldier orderly as his personal attendant. It was evident that Baker, though he had been Secretary of War for two years, hardly knew just what to do with a soldier orderly; but no one could gainsay that Patrick Walsh, who had won praise for a pioneer American exploit in trench heroism, was worthy of this honor.

Inspection was to begin where the ships came in, in the base zone of the Services of Supply, which had now set up their own subsidiary kingdom, apart from G. H. Q., under Major General Francis E. Kernan, with his headquarters at Tours, in the center of France. At first, the lines of communication had been called the Service of the Rear. "Those fellows at G. H. Q., thinking they are God Almighty and at the front, although they're a hundred miles from the trenches," had put that further embarrassment upon the toilers who were still farther out of gun range but in no less danger. The chanty which bade mother take down her service flag because her son was in the "S. O. S." would have been even more scornful if he were in the "S. O. R."

Boards and boards had sat at G. H. Q. on the problems of transport and supply, which, at home, also included the problem of production. Mistakes had been corrected, and the correction of the mistakes corrected. Another reorganization had just gone into effect. In making a reorganization Pershing did not have to wait on an act of Congress. He was sure of the support of the press in *The Stars and Stripes,* edited by soldiers of his command.

There was the coast, there was the front, and the distance between the two had to be covered by a system of rail transportation and storage whose size and elaborateness would have been astounding to that great quartermaster, Napoleon, who had built the straight highways of France for the march of his men and the easier roll of the wheels of his artillery and of his commissary wagons. Reorganization could not change the original plan, which showed a breadth of vision corresponding to that of the plan at home. It was grounded in the same capacity for the same expansion as was the draft in increasing our man-power for dispatch to France. Those pioneers, the fathers of the plan, Brigadier General Harry Taylor, of the Regular Engineers, and Colonel William J. Wilgus, formerly chief engineer of the New York Central Railroad, had seen their little band gradually grow into an army through eight long months of labor. Wilgus had preceded Pershing with the pioneer engineering contingent under Colonel William Barclay Parsons, which was our first response to Joffre's call for technical troops. Pershing had asked the War Department to send over a first-class railroad man, and the Department had chosen W. W. Atterbury, Vice President of the Pennsylvania Railroad. But, meanwhile, Pershing had "found a man on the spot" in Wilgus, who worked out the project of a transportation system which would be capable of expansion to care for two million men. It was ready for Atterbury when he arrived, and his appointment made him its chief.

The plan had reached a stage where chaotic piles of material lay alongside projects which were a quarter or half completed, or had sufficient form so that all was not left to the imagination. As at home, a definite outline was developing out of the smudge of the negative. At the time of the Secretary's visit I recalled how six months earlier I had heard some reserve officers, in a tent stacked with blueprints, talk of a vast cold-storage plant on a space where not a handful of earth had been lifted nor a bit of material arrived. Now, the Secretary saw the plant seventy percent complete, set in a spray of spur-tracks.

As he went from place to place one set of the rulers of the local industrial realm succeeded another as his local guides. His derby hat and civilian clothes made a dark outline on the background of the khaki of generals, colonels, and majors surrounding him. They were showing a deference to a civilian which was rare and wonderful in the American world in France. Some may have had the preconception that he was the worst Secretary of War that ever was; and many might have

wanted to violate military etiquette by complaining frankly of
the delay in their projects because their requisitions had not
been promptly filled. But, withal, it was good to have him see
what they were trying to do against odds. In one place the
scene was all American in areas of corrugated iron roofs, except for the tower of an ancient village church in the distance;
and in another our insistent demands for space threatened to
disrupt routine municipal life. The Colossus of America had
one foot set on the home shore while the other strove for a
foothold on the shore of France; one hand stretched its powerful fingers farther and farther into France to deposit there
the material passed across by the other hand.

We were Allies, and yet, in southern and middle France,
where the people were far removed from the front, we appeared as invaders with our motor trucks, our huge machines,
our fractious, persistent energy, which seemed to the French
at times to be wasting itself as prodigally as we wasted our
material. As our project rose and spread to maintain a vast
army in the fall of 1918, the French of that region, in their
tense anticipation of another German blow, wondered if this
colossal industrial demonstration was our idea of how to win
a war. As our soldiers disembarked at Brest and took a more
northerly route to Lorraine, the residents along the lines of
the S. O. S. saw no troop trains coming from the southern
ports.

These Americans were cutting down French forests to make
structures which were of no use to the French, or even to the
Americans themselves if they were not going to remain in
France. Did the French army, in order to fight the Germans,
need ice to store its meat? All these acres of wooden buildings?
A candy factory? Chewing-gum as well as cigarettes? And such
extensive apparatus in order to unload ships? So many new
telephone wires? So many typewriters clicking out such quantities of orders and memoranda?

At the ports Baker saw the ships waiting in dock for labor
to unload them and hasten their return for cargoes on the congested docks at home; he saw piles of material awaiting evacu-

ation to the interior, and he saw new piers already in service, others ready for the cranes that had not yet arrived, and sites that had been chosen for still others in swamps at the water's edge; concrete foundations for new structures set with steel uprights; and lines of fresh earth turned for more spur-tracks.

OUR PIONEERING ENERGY IN AN OLD LAND

Our supply organization had divided the American world in Gaul into three parts or zones. The writing that it was making on the white paper across France followed the line of the railroads toward Lorraine. Theoretically we were always to have a reserve of three months' supplies in France for the A. E. F.: forty-five days at the base ports, thirty days in the intermediate depots, and fifteen days at the advance depots.

In the intermediate zone Baker saw aviation training grounds and other schools; repair shops which had been shipped in parts across the Atlantic, salvage depots, material waiting on the sites of warehouses and empty warehouses waiting for material, warehouses for everything from overseas— caps, uniforms, and shoes, machine-guns, ammunition and medical supplies; shops for the assembling of locomotives, and a ten-thousand-bed hospital under construction.

Then the rapidly conducted traveler went on to the regulating stations of the advance zone which were forming in the midst of more spur-tracks. These drew on the stores of the intermediate zone in their distribution of supplies to the front.

There were places and occasions when it was in order for him to "say something" to assembled groups. Nobody knows how many of these talks he made.

He said to the officers of the S. O. S.:

"You have brought the blueprints of a great conception into being. . . . You come from a pioneering people, and you have brought to France a pioneering energy. You have turned marshes into docks, facing waterways which you will dredge; sent out spurs of railway track; and built warehouses and the necessary supplementary plants for a system which will dispatch along the lines of communication to the front food, clothes, guns, ammunition, and all the enormous amount of complicated material which the resources of our country can supply, to be transported by ships which we are building. We owe it to your devotion and efficiency that the troops in action shall not lack the means of striking blows."

To the officers of the G. H. Q. in the old French barracks at Chaumont, which they had turned into a modern office building, Baker said:

"I have been at one of your artillery schools, where young reserve officers are preparing to support our troops with their gunfire. I have seen your staff school, where another group of reserve officers, including a former Secretary of War, whom I envy, is being trained to assist in your staff work when we shall number our corps in France as we now number our divisions."

This former Secretary of War, laboring diligently and faithfully under officers who had formerly been under his command, was Henry L. Stimson, who became Colonel of the Thirty-first Field Artillery and later Secretary of State in President Hoover's Cabinet.

"I appreciate how you would prefer to leave your desks for the front line, where you could see the direct result of your efforts against the enemy. But you are at least in France, and thereby are the envy of those who are held at their desks in the same kind of work at home. . . . Action has taken the place of study. The problems which you have to solve are no longer those of theory in the movement of imaginary forces, but of fact, in control of the supply and equipment of large bodies of troops in the greatest military undertaking in our history. . . . War is skill against skill, force against force. . . . You are forming an army to fight against a most powerful, skilful foe, who allows nothing to divert him from the main essential. . . . I might say that promotion awaits those who have proven themselves fit to lead in the stern test to come. However, I know that you are not thinking of promotion, but only, in a spirit of soldierly service, how to give the best that is in you to the cause."

He was to see those who were "striking the blows" in the march-past of men who had already been in the trenches on another of the gray winter days of Lorraine. This seems to be the right place to introduce parenthetically the subject of the photograph which was taken of him on a march-past in France. All the generals with him were rigid in the salute of the flag, but Baker's hat was on and one hand was in his pocket. This made a rich morsel for the whispering gallery. *Harvey's Weekly* published it to show that the "ex-Pacifist" was still at heart a pacifist: "Newty-Cooty" would not even show respect to the flag of his country. It was a petty matter, yet the real facts might well be stated here. When the camera's shutter clicked, the color-bearer was not yet abreast of Baker; if it had clicked a second later the photograph would have shown him in a proper civilian attitude of respect. Up to that second, Pershing's big army overcoat beside Baker had hidden the advance of the colors. Even as it was, no one who was present saw anything amiss. And I might add that I have seen other photographs in which Baker's hat was off even before a general had brought his hand to the salute, which is not to imply that an officer of our Army does not respect his flag.

In addressing the men of a division, he said:

"I thought you marched well and drilled well when I last saw you, but what I have seen of you today gives me a new standard of comparison. The mark of the thorough system of our Army in France is upon you. I feel you have all grown to greater manhood, and that the steel of your spirit now has the fighting edge."

TO A COMPANY OF INFANTRY

He had now seen the Army from the recruits arriving at the home cantonments all the way to their billets in France, and the movement of supplies from the American sources to the advance stations. But that was not enough.

Pershing was at first opposed to the Secretary's going into the trenches. A trench might be peaceful for days and then suddenly the enemy artillery might let loose a "hate."

Baker, however, was not of the mind to give up the logical end of his journey, which was an American parapet where he might look out upon No Man's Land. The place chosen for this experience was in the sector occupied by men of his own State of Ohio. It happened that the Commander-in-Chief assigned me to conduct him. I had met the Secretary only in a casual way. When I was sent home on a mission in the winter of 1917–18, I had reported to him. He asked me several questions about conditions in France and then bade me go on with my work. After I had finished this, he gave me travel orders back to G. H. Q. in France.

On the day in which the trenches were to be included as a part of his program, we rose at five. At breakfast we had word that there was a good deal of artillery fire in the Ohio sector. Some of the staff officers present, acting in the spirit of the Commander-in-Chief's instructions, proposed that the visit to the trenches should be given up.

"Gentlemen, I do not want you to risk your lives," said Baker quietly, but in a way that ended further discussion.

After we left the house where we had spent the night, we had gone only a few miles when a company of American infantry took vague form on the road ahead of us out of the mist of dawn. Our car stopped. The captain asked Baker if he would say a few words to the men. Their faces were like moist granite in the mist, and gray like the moist gray road under their feet. The clinging particles of mist gave their khaki and even their steel helmets a gray film. All things seemed to be reduced to a severe outline, all thought to be chilled in the air of a moon-dead world to which spring would never come.

The captain was very proud of his men. They were young and fresh. After all their training they were near the promised land of the trenches where the enemy's welcome of gas, shells, and bullets awaited them. I had seen the young and fresh Frenchmen going to the front in August, 1914, and the young and fresh men of the British New Army, and seen them suddenly grow old in that war which was now so very old. So these young countrymen of mine would in turn grow old in war. I had already become familiar with the sight of them on French roads. They were a part of the routine of feeding flesh into the hopper, a routine which must go until the War was won; a routine in which even the sight of an American Secretary of War alighting from an American Army car on a road in Lorraine to speak to an American company of soldiers had become a part. I had heard scores of speeches to troops by visiting officials and statesmen, and speeches of final instruction and girding by commanding officers to their men before they filed up the communication trenches to take their places for the zero hour in going over the top. The briefest was that of a French colonel on the Marne: "For France! Forward! That is all! Forward!" I had heard a red-faced British colonel say: "You are going into action. You will take your objective. There will be no shell-shock cases in this battalion." An old American Army sergeant had said: "Saying you're hard-boiled won't do. You've got to *be* hard-boiled."

The longest speech had been by a famous orator. This had lasted half an hour, and such was the discipline and fortitude of the soldier listeners that no jaw had dropped in a yawn. Indeed, I had heard so many speeches that I thought I could foretell the nature of Baker's remarks, as a matter of course, just as one could foresee that the dressing stations would soon be busy after an attack began. There were certain things a statesman must say to strengthen the morale of troops in wartime, and many more things he must not say, owing to that instinctive self-censorship which was the potent auxiliary of the formal censorship.

It happened that I had missed Baker's speeches on this trip, some of which I have quoted. I had never heard him speak on an important occasion; and this was not an important occasion to me, this of an impromptu talk to a company of infantry on a road, when companies of infantry had so long been so common on French roads. Certainly, as I knew from his dispatches, the speech would be in excellent English, the phrases would be sutured in a compact whole. If Baker were as sleepy as I was, he would be a marvel if he could utter a dozen coherent sentences.

Then suddenly, I realized that he was not saying what I had expected him to say. The little man, with his hat off, had become a foot taller. I was wide awake now, broken out of the routine, myself young to the War, my imagination soaring high and wide. I had been struck by sentimentality, a lump was tugging in my throat, so much so that my sophistication was conscious of being shamed.

Shafts of all the kinds of sunlight from coast to coast of the homeland had shot across the Atlantic, lightening the mist and glinting on steel. I was seeing the mighty pile of the Alps looking down on all the races in their rivalries, hates, and quarrels, and seeing the Appalachians and the Rockies as very near the Alps in the map of one human scheme. I felt not only the wonder of that company of American soldiers being in France, but I was feeling why they were there and the cause that brought them there and made them so rigid, a cause which was rooted deep in each one and in his part as a citizen of America and the world.

It was very brief, this speech that affected me in such a fashion. I wish that Baker had followed the custom of some eminent men who have stenographers at their elbows lest their remarks should be lost to posterity, or, at least, to the morning paper. Even if I pretended to remember his words I should not try to report sentences which so distinctly had style that they should be given exactly or not at all.

Ralph Hayes, the private secretary of a chief who never wrote out even the most formal of addresses beforehand, could not include this in the collection of Baker's war speeches which he gathered from hearers' memories or the notes of stenographers who happened to be present. It was the effect of the speech that counted—the wells of thought set gushing in my own war-sophisticated mind. Great speeches take distinction from the occasion as well as from their substance. I am sure that Baker's greatest speech was not, as his admirers think, before the Senate Committee, but on a road in Lorraine at seven o'clock in the morning.

After we were back in the car, and the company dissolved in the mist behind us, the usual compliments on such occasions would be in order. "That was fine, Mr. Secretary," or "That did them a lot of good!" I should have been warranted in saying, "I have heard a bit of real eloquence." But I paid him no spoken compliment—and yet, in my silent reflection, the highest.

The master of the day's schedule had arranged that our itinerary on the way to the trenches should not disclose our destination. Our next stop was to witness a practice exhibition of an attack on a strong point by infantry. If Baker made a talk on this occasion, I do not remember it. Then he paid a courtesy call on General de Castelnau, the Commander of the French Army in that region. Castelnau had been the defender of Lorraine, in September, 1914, against the German onslaught whose success would have meant the loss of the Battle of the Marne. He had been Joffre's Chief of Staff in 1916 and his prompt action had been invaluable in the defense of Verdun. Many Frenchmen were aggrieved that he had never received a Marshal's baton.

Simplicity ruled life at Castelnau's headquarters. When he traveled it was always in a compartment of a regular train. That sturdy royalist of the old régime and the former progressive Mayor of Cleveland, who had such widely divergent views about democracy, seemed to come to an easy understanding, possibly because neither had any "side" and Baker knew something about the history of France. The fact that Baker did know history contributed one factor in making him an agreeable companion. Another was that he did not talk all the time nor expect others to do so in a speeding Army automobile. He was, too, quite free from the weakness of some distinguished visitors whom I showed about the front in one period of my service: I would not have minded their taking so little interest in the War if only they had not talked so much about themselves.

After passing through an area of ruined villages and shell-holes, we came to the American division general and other generals, surrounded by staff officers, on a hill whence the start was to have been made for the trenches. An ultimatum accompanied their respectful greeting. The front had suddenly become very active. It was quite out of the question for the Secretary to go farther. They pointed to bursting shells as an insuperable barrier on the road which he was to follow on his way to the trenches. They were responsible for his safe conduct, and they were obviously more concerned about the risk to be taken than the Secretary himself was.

THE SECRETARY SEES THE TRENCHES

Commanding officers had a professional pride in showing a civilian visitor the trenches without his being injured, and were always relieved when they had him safely out of the zone of shellfire. It would not have been pleasant for the staff to have to report that the civil chief of the Army had been killed or wounded in their sector. Having a Secretary of War who was so satisfactory to him, Pershing hardly wanted to take chances with the unknown quantity of a successor. Nor did I want to risk the life of an agreeable traveling companion. However, I knew he wanted to see the trenches, and my directions had been to show him the trenches. I knew the habits of the German artillery from more than three years' experience, which had made me a most expert dodger.

"But that is just a burst of interdictory fire," I remarked. "They put it on that road for only a few minutes at long intervals. The same thing happened yesterday and the day before, didn't it?"

"Yes." Professional candor could not deny that.

"There is no scattering fire in the fields, not in this sector, these days."

"No."

"Well, if there is still fire on that road we can walk around it"—which was about as risky as walking on a solid river bank around a whirlpool.

At this the phalanx of officers turned on me with the stare of superior rank which I might have interpreted as indicating me as an accomplice in the assassination of the Secretary of War, who had been listening to the talk.

"Impossible! There would not be time for him to walk. It is so late already that even if he went along that shelled road by car he would not be back from the trenches in time to keep his other engagements."

Baker might have asserted his right as the official superior of all present by saying, "I am Secretary of War, and I propose to see our soldiers in the trenches." This, if delivered with a proper spirit, would have been good copy for the press.

I was standing to one side of the phalanx of rank. Baker crossed over to me. "I want to go," he said. "Do you think there is any way that we can get by all these solicitous officers?"

It happened that Colonel de Chambrun, the French liaison officer with our G. H. Q., was standing near us; and his recollection that we had an American company in the trenches with the French not far away brought a spontaneous suggestion for the solution of the problem. But still the objectors had a final argument. They were sure there would not be time unless the Secretary missed a part of his schedule.

"We'll make it," said the spirited Chambrun. "I know a short cut."

As the Secretary stepped into Chambrun's French staff car the group we left behind us must have been relieved by the thought that if he were killed or wounded the responsibility would be with a distinguished French officer and an irresponsible American reserve officer. In one respect the French staff certainly led all the Allies—the speed with which they drove their staff cars, a privilege in making war in their own country. We were going fifty miles an hour when we came to a short cut guarded by French sentries. It was a "forbidden" stretch of road over which no traffic was allowed in daylight. The Ger-

man artillery had the range of that gray ribbon across the fields
plotted perfectly by practice shots at passing prey. Without
further explanation than Chambrun's shouted "G. H. Q." in
French, we sped on, now up to seventy miles an hour. Happily, the German gunners were either nodding or not in the
mood to lob a shell at the flying target of our car.

Soon we were in a ruined village which gave into a communication trench. The rest was simple. It was just seeing the
trenches. To those who ever saw them description is superfluous; to those who never saw them description avails little,
as all war-writers knew. The French and Germans had been
dug-in on the same line here for over three years. Nowhere did
the War seem so permanent an institution as in parts of Lorraine where both sides made themselves comfortably at home
in trench life in relief from service in the more active sectors.
The early alarms that the coming German drive might be in
this region had passed, as it was now known that Ludendorff
was making his great concentration to the west.

Baker did the labyrinthine tour. He talked with the men,
asked them questions. His experience was the same as if he had
gone in at the place that was planned for him; only he was
meeting Iowans instead of the Ohioans of his own State. When
he looked out over the parapet of No Man's Land he had
reached the farthest point of his authority as the President's
second-in-command of our armed forces. If he had exposed a
few inches more of his person a German marksman might have
fulfilled Colonel Harvey's wish for a new Secretary of War.
There were four or five shell-bursts, a German mortar threw
in a greeting; but these were two or three hundred yards away.
A French and a German airplane overhead exchanged bursts
of machine-gun fire. Although General Scott thought the Secretary did not know enough to be a second lieutenant, I had the
idea that he was learning a great deal about trench routine.
With no decision about policy and no speeches to make or letters to write, he was having a very good time; a better time, I
concluded, than I was. In fact, peaceful though that trench
was, I was suffering a little from cold feet. I better understood

THE SECRETARY OF WAR SEES THE TRENCHES

the solicitude of the divisional staff. If it should happen that the Germans did throw in a .155 at the right spot, I had an idea that the most rigid of salutes would not quite atone to the Commander-in-Chief for the loss of a Secretary of War whom he had found so satisfactory.

Yet, I should have felt I was doing my part all the better as a conductor if some dust from a shell-burst had been sprinkled on him. However, as we passed back over the forbidden road, the German gunners lobbed over three .105's with excellent aim considering our speed. The closest passed just over the hood of the car and burst about fifteen yards away.

"That was a shell, wasn't it?" Baker asked.

"Yes—about four-inch."

"Then I may say I've been under fire, mayn't I?"

A few minutes later, out of the range of the guns, in a quiet countryside, we stopped at an American cemetery. A burial party was approaching an open grave. The Secretary heard Taps and the volley fired. After that, as he stood in a hospital doorway, he saw an ambulance arriving with wounded.

THE GREAT OFFENSIVE BEGINS

My next distinct memory of my part in his tour was early on March twenty-first. For luncheon that day he was to be at Pétain's headquarters at Chantilly. During the afternoon I was to show Baker over the old battlefield of the Somme. It seemed to me that I knew that ground, Thiépval to Gommecourt and Péronne to Bapaume, as I knew the hills and valleys of the township where I was born. I had seen the British New Army forming in the then quiet sector, its guns going into position, and heard their full-throated rage in the preparatory bombardment before the men went over the top; and then day on day, week on week, I had watched the ordeal of attacks for piecemeal gains, including that day when those strange monsters, the pioneer tanks, first entered the arena.

As our car drew nearer to Chantilly we heard, as the road rose over a hill, a sound that was lost in the valley, a sound louder and louder until it was with us even in the valleys, a sound that even the ears of the novice would have known was no local morning hate of the German guns. As we drew up at Pétain's headquarters the roar had become as distant surf that had no lull between the breakers, a surf of ten thousand breakers on an uneven shore, a roar that was so widespread that it seemed to extend beyond the curve of the earth: the mightiest roar that the engines of man had ever made in all history. There was no need of asking the officers who greeted us about its meaning, no need of their offering a word in explanation. The long-expected German offensive had begun.

The Secretary went to the luncheon, the midday *déjeuner,* with Pétain, Pershing, and others of the mighty; and I to the intelligence mess, with colonels and juniors of my rank, where the talk ran on all manner of subjects, and lightly, discursively, with nothing said in relation to the roar, which one thought, or perhaps imagined, was coming nearer. Only the fact that an orderly spoke to a major, who withdrew, could be taken as indicating any departure from the routine of a quiet day along the whole front.

These officers had learned the value of serenity, not out of staff books, where it is taught so strictly as the first principle of a proper habit of command, but through nearly four years of war, of war that had become the normal day's work. Unless a chief called for him, there was nothing for any officer to do until the reports were in and the orders for the next day's dispositions to be formulated. He would keep fresh for the night's labor to come and not wear himself out in suspense or speculation without information.

With the enemy so rapidly recovering the farther part of the Somme battlefield and his swaths of shellfire reaching deeper and deeper toward Amiens, my part as conductor that day was to be limited to accompanying the Secretary along the rear of the British army in action. At a railroad crossing a St. John's ambulance, driven by a tall, long-shanked Englishwoman, waited alongside our car for the gate to be raised.

"It's come," she said, referring to the roar, "and we know where. That part of the suspense is over."

Baker alighted, examined her ambulance, and asked her many questions about her work.

"Who is he?" she whispered to me as the gates rose.

"The American Secretary of War."

"Your Secretary of War is a delightful and quite inquisitive person. If he doesn't know all about our ambulance service by now, I must have forgotten some detail."

But she was not so much interested in the presence of the Secretary of War on the scene as in that of our Army. Was it coming? And all that day, so critical to Allied fortunes, when the Germans planned to repeat Caporetto on French soil, we did not see one American soldier. Yet if the only military suggestion the Secretary of War ever made to the Commander-in-Chief had been accepted, we should have had four divisions in the battle.

XXIV

THE INTEGRAL ARMY

When the Secretary rode toward Amiens on the afternoon of March 21 I had not read what became to me, thirteen years later, one of the most suggestive of the file of cablegrams between the War Department and G. H. Q. This drops the narrative back, for a fresh start, to the period, four weeks after the Caporetto disaster, when the Allies had become fully aware of the danger which threatened from a great German offensive on the Western front in the spring of 1918. The cable of December 25, 1917, was signed by Baker, which meant that it was not from a subordinate, but from the Secretary of War himself, and would go personally to the Commander-in-Chief. The significant portion begins with the second paragraph, but I quote the whole: [1]

"Both English and French are pressing upon the President their desire to have your forces amalgamated with theirs by regiments and companies, and both express belief in impending heavy drive by Germans somewhere along the line of the Western front. We do not desire loss of identity of our forces but regard that as secondary to the meeting of any critical situation by the most helpful use possible of the troops at your command. The difficulty of course is to determine where the drive or drives of the enemy will take place; and in advance of some knowledge on that question, any redistribution of your forces would be difficult. The President, however, desires you to have full authority to use the forces at your command as you deem wise in consultation with the French and British Commanders-in-Chief.

"It is suggested for your consideration that possibly places might be selected for your forces nearer the junction of the British and French lines which would enable you to throw your strength in whichever direction seemed most necessary.

This suggestion is not, however, pressed beyond whatever merit it has in your judgment, the President's sole purpose being to acquaint you with the representations made here and to authorize you to act with entire freedom in making the best possible disposition and use of your forces for accomplishing the main purposes in view. It is hoped that complete unity and co-ordination of action can be secured in this matter by your conferences with the French and British Commanders. Report result of any conferences you may have with French and British Commanders and line of action that may be agreed upon."

It was an interesting sequel to this cable, written three months previously, that, on the afternoon of March 21, the Secretary passed that "junction of the British and French lines," which had become the object of the main thrust of the attack whose inaugural roar we were hearing.

The United States now had in France four divisions that were fully organized and had trench experience, numerically the equivalent of eight British or French divisions at their present strength. But our four divisions were three hundred miles away at the other end of France in the American sector. This seems the fitting place, therefore, to bring out the salient points of Pershing's long and complicated negotiations for preserving the integrity of his army with reference to home policy and preparations.

On November 13, 1917, four weeks after Caporetto, Pershing wrote that now we could not defer action until 1919, but that we must be prepared for a great effort in 1918.[2] Against 169 divisions for the Allies on the Western front, he anticipated that the Germans could mass 265, including 48 Austrian divisions. (The Austrians, however, were to remain concentrated on the Piave preparing for an offensive against the Italians.)

"As in 1914 and in 1915, we could think of deciding the War by an attack on land," Ludendorff wrote. "Numerically, we had never been so strong in comparison with our enemies. In Germany, the national spirit appeared to be better than with our Allies." [3]

I have already quoted Lloyd George's note of December 2, appealing to Colonel E. M. House to feed our troops into British divisions; "Even half-trained American companies or battalions could fight well if mixed with 2- or 3-year veterans." A memorandum accompanying the note said:

"Obviously Germany has a better chance of winning the War before America can exert her full strength than she will have after. It follows that she may try to win it during the next eight months or so. . . . Would America therefore be ready to help in another way as a temporary measure? . . . She preferred to retain her national identity. No doubt she still desires to do so, but over and above the preparation of her divisions, and without interfering with it, would it be possible for her to provide a company of infantry to replace a British company in such number of British battalions as America could bring over the men?" [4]

REASONS FOR AN ENGLISH-SPEAKING COMBINATION

In his memorandum of December 18, which Bliss brought back to Baker upon his return from his trip with the House Mission, he said:

"We must take note of the deep, growing, and already very strong conviction on the part of Englishmen, both military and civil, that the War must be finally fought out by an Anglo-Saxon combination. If this be true it may become evident by the driving in of a wedge into the French line, which will cause that people to quit—not to make a separate peace, but to be reduced to a state of inaction, leaving the others to fight it out."

Pétain, the French Commander-in-Chief, told him that "the French losses have been approximately 2,600,000 men killed, died of wounds, permanently incapacitated, and prisoners." If we decided to go in with the British, this would enable the weary French to contract and strengthen their line. On this point, however, Bliss, ever the accurate, impartial reporter, wrote that at the War Office in London he was "informed that only with the greatest difficulty could they [the British] prevail

upon the French to let them have additional front." But, on
the contrary, in an interview on the same subject Bliss had
with the French Premier, "M. Clemenceau said (to use his own
words), 'We have a devil of a time getting them [the British] to
take over more front.' "

When Bliss sounded the call for "men, as many as possible
and as soon as possible" and "tonnage necessary to transport
them," he had in mind that the British had the ships and that
transport was a matter between the British and the Americans.
To quote him again:

"If the French could be brought to look upon the Anglo-
Saxon union as having no ulterior object, other than a certain
defeat of the enemy, it would be greatly to be desired. The
situation, as it is, is fraught with possible great danger.

"So earnest are General Robertson [Chief of the British
Imperial Staff] and Sir Douglas Haig [British Commander-in-
Chief] in this matter that, in my interview with them, they have
urged amalgamating bodies of our troops with theirs. Sir Douglas Haig even said that he would give command of these mixed
organizations to American officers and that as rapidly as our
units became sufficient in number to form complete divisions
they would be separated for this purpose."

No commander had better reasons than Haig, out of his experience, for appreciating the mistake of infiltrating troops of
another nation into his army. The British army included the
rivalries of the English, the Scotch, the Welsh and the Irish;
and within these racial groups were the Guard, County, and
Highland and Lowland regiments. From the Dominions came
the high-spirited Canadians, Australians, New Zealanders, and
South Africans, who regarded themselves as belonging to distinctive, self-governing commonwealths, even nations, within
the Empire. The Canadians and Australians had their own
separate corps under their home commanders; and the New
Zealanders their own division. A Canadian or an Australian
did not always see eye to eye with a Cockney in their relations
in action or behind the lines. The rivalry between the Canadians and Australians approached a feud. In addition to these

elements, whose differences of character and outlook Haig had to compose, he had at one time under him native Indian regiments of antipathetic races and customs. Since homogeneity is so important in the team-play of an army, he would not normally welcome any further outside units, even temporarily; but the crisis of the winter of 1917–18 had necessarily imposed a larger hospitality.

In mid-December Haig approached Pershing with a plan. Our battalions or regiments under their own flag were to be attached, one to a British brigade, for trench training purposes. At the same time our division and brigade commands would be learning their parts in co-operation with British commands which had had three years' combat experience. As soon as an American division staff had been organized and indoctrinated by actual contact with the enemy, our regiments would be withdrawn into American divisions under their own command and assigned to the American Army. By this method the Americans would become more promptly available for action against the series of German offensives which was anticipated.

ROBERTSON REBUFFS HAIG

At first, Pershing found the plan unacceptable, his reasons being: difficulties with the French, the American desire to be self-contained, and that the training of staff was required before that of units.[5] However, on December 27, when he and Haig met as soldier to soldier at Haig's headquarters, Haig was able to report to the British War Office that they had come to a practical understanding. Since the British brigades were organized in transport and supply for twelve battalions, and were down to nine, we need send at the start only officers and men, without their division trains; the British would feed them. This American reinforcement to the British army would be brought over by British shipping, in addition to Pershing's own twenty-four division program. Haig was sure that the British could care for 2,000 Americans daily at Havre, while the Southampton route could be further developed.

But Sir William Robertson, British Chief of Staff, consid-

ered that Haig had exceeded his authority in these direct negotiations with Pershing. He insisted that if Britain was to supply the shipping, then the American battalions should become
a part of the British army. Sir William was a stubborn man,
who had risen from the ranks; and our stubborn Commander-
in-Chief came from Missouri! Sir William would not accept
the Haig plan; and Pershing would not accept Sir William's
plan.

Sir William, after an interview with Pershing in which
neither budged, reported in a memorandum to the British
War Cabinet that Pershing looked "older and rather tired, and
I doubt if he has yet an intelligent and considered view of his
task. . . . He himself is charged with all matters connected
with the Army in France, such as contracts for aircraft, provision of munitions, sea transport, etc., and is thus unable properly
to command and train his troops. . . . My general impression is
that America's power to help win the War—that is, to help us
defeat the Germans in battle—is a very weak reed to lean
upon." [6] Sir William was soon to be relieved as Chief of Staff,
but he exercised his power in full to the last.

THE FRENCH WANT THEIR SHARE OF AMERICANS

Meanwhile the Germans continued massing for their drive;
and the French were thinking that if the American soldiers
were to be fed into the British army the French army should
also have its share.

On January 3 Baker wrote to the President after a call from
the French Ambassador, who thought infiltration the best
means to protect our troops while they were learning fighting
conditions at the front:

"It seems to me entirely clear that if our regiments are in-
tegrated with either French or British Divisions the difficulty
of getting them back when we want them would be very great,
and that the ultimate effect of such a course would be practically to put our troops here and there in French and British
Divisions under the command of French and British Commanders, with a corresponding weakening of the forces under

General Pershing's command for independent operations. The disinterested ground urged by the French Ambassador, to the effect that it was for our good and was merely an accommodation on the part of the French, seems hardly to cover the whole case.

"I am assuming that we ought to rely upon General Pershing to decide this kind of question, as he is on the ground and sees the needs as they arise, and, of course, will desire to preserve the integrity of his own forces for independent operations unless the emergency becomes overruling."

PERSHING IN A MOOD TO YIELD

Two weeks passed, and the War Department had a surprise from our Commander-in-Chief, who, in the midst of alarms and appeals, had apparently become more apprehensive about the magnitude of the coming German offensive. His cable of January 13 gave the impression that he now favored accepting the Robertson proposal, which did not include building up our divisions in the manner recommended in the Haig proposal. In fact, Robertson rather dodged this point. I quote the essential parts of the cable: [7]

"General Robertson says in substance that he regards the situation as becoming very serious on the Western front and that Germans will undoubtedly exert every effort to win before our troops are able to play an important part in the War. Also that British will be unable to furnish many men even for draft. . . . He says further that even if the German attacks can be held, as is hoped, the British Divisions will become so exhausted in the process as to be fit for little employment afterwards. . . . He suggests that to bring over a given number of men completely equipped as divisions will be much greater task than to bring the same number of men as battalions and to transport . . . Then proposes that, in order to secure these infantry reinforcements, British Government are prepared to take risks as to their own supplies and provide sea transportation for these . . . without in any way interfering with present plans and arrangements for bringing our American troops. He proposes that we furnish for the above purpose

150 battalions to be distributed 3 battalions to each British division, so that they can retain their present strength of 12 battalions to each division. . . . But of course our battalions could be trained under our own officers. Later on, after serving with British divisions, if we so desired, they could be recalled for service with our own divisions. That everything would be done to meet our wishes in this and all other respects; although he believes it would not serve any useful purpose to put these units into British divisions for less than four or five months. He expressed himself as fully appreciating American sentiment regarding service under our own flag, but it was a question of doing that on the one hand or of Germany possibly establishing herself in a winning position on the other. The necessity of temporarily breaking up some of our divisions to meet this request was also discussed. . . .

"This whole question seems to me to be one of necessity, and we must consider the probability of strong German attacks in early spring and summer. While it would not be advisable in any way to alter our own program for bringing our divisions, yet the offer of the British to provide sea transportation for such extra men as we may be able to furnish for temporary service in their army would not interfere with that. . . .

"I would therefore recommend (1) that this request of the British Government be given serious consideration from the point of view of our national attitude regarding service in another army; (2) that it be regarded as a temporary measure to meet a probable emergency; (3) that as soon as possible the remaining troops of divisions thus temporarily broken up be brought over and the division reorganized; (4) that division, brigade, and regimental commanders and their staffs be sent over with their infantry for training with corresponding British units; (5) that the infantry be taken from those divisions that would not otherwise be transported until after June."

The following paragraph of Pershing's cable showed a change in the French attitude under the influence of Clemenceau:

"Have had a full and frank discussion of this question with the French as far as any such plan relates to them, and have stated that in my opinion, generally speaking, it would be a dangerous experiment on account of difference in language to put our regiments into French divisions for active work. They apparently hold the same view. M. Clemenceau gave his entire approval to the plan for such aiding of the British as above set forth. General Pétain also gave it his approval."

On January 19, Baker wrote to the President:

"The plan, you will recall, was worked out by General Pershing in conference with General Robertson, the British Chief of Staff, and had the approval of the French General Staff and of General Pershing.

"In short, the suggestion is that 150 battalions of United States troops be transported by the British, in their own tonnage, and assigned by them three battalions to each of their divisions, to enable them to keep their divisions at a strength of 12 rather than 9 battalions. General Pershing's stipulation is that these troops are to be transported by the British without interfering with or lessening the tonnage aid which they are to give us to carry out our own military program as agreed upon with General Bliss."

STILL MORE REARRANGEMENTS

Certainly our Staff at home and our Staff at G. H. Q. in France could agree on one point: the extra labor entailed by having Allies in the conduct of a war. The rearrangements necessary to meet the Robertson program appear in Baker's letter to the President, which continued:

"By taking 50 regiments practically equally from the Regular Army, the National Guard, and the National Army, no discrimination would be introduced into our own service. . . . These regiments would, of course, have to be armed by the British in order to co-operate with their forces. They would therefore take with them only their clothing equipment. The tonnage cargo requirements for the sustenance of these 50 regiments would be great if we had to arm and supply them. It would therefore not be practicable for us to send these troops [about 150,000 men], in addition to our own military program of 24 divisions, until after July 1. Meanwhile, if they are sent now they will be of material assistance to the British, will be trained with the British forces, and will make a substantial contribution on our part to the military strength of the Allies on the Western front. . . . As this project has the approval of General Pershing and of our own Staff, and is in the judgment of both the British and French General Staffs a wise course, I recommend that it be adopted. . . . When we select these regiments to send them abroad it will necessitate a reorganization of some of our own divisions and will leave a surplus of some division and brigade commanders, both in the Regular Army and in the National Guard, who will no doubt complain at the breaking up of their commands. We will endeavor to absorb these surplus officers by assigning the best of them in the places of men found physically disqualified or otherwise relieved for lack of military efficiency. Under all the circumstances, I think the military thing to do ought to be done, and if it meets with your approval I will send General Bliss, who arrived today in England, the cablegram attached hereto."

The cable to Bliss said that the proposal must include "the understanding, first, that the battalions may be recalled for service with our own divisions should it seem wise to do so; second, that the transportation of these troops shall not interfere with the assistance in tonnage to be provided by the British to carry out our own military program"—that is, the twenty-four division program for more than a million American soldiers in France by July 1, 1918.

THE REARRANGEMENTS ARE CANCELED

The President's letter of January 20, replying to Baker's of January 19, which I have quoted, said he was distinctly apprehensive lest the British, in their eagerness to reinforce their army with our battalions, should cut us off from the tonnage they had agreed to supply for our twenty-four division program.

The War Department continued for another two weeks its preparations to send the 150 battalions, when a cable from Pershing (January 30, 1918) left the plan for dispatching them, without their division officers and staff, so much paper in the files: [8]

"Your conclusion that the proposition to send infantry battalions for service with British divisions was recommended by me is erroneous. Have had the matter under consideration for some time and am convinced that the plan would be a grave mistake. . . . National sentiment in the United States against service under a foreign flag. . . . Such action by the United States would excite serious political opposition to the administration and to the United States in the conduct of the War. . . . Additional man-power on the Western front could be provided as quickly by some plan not involving amalgamation."

Pershing's counter-proposal was the same that Haig had made to him in December. Sir Joseph Maclay, British Director of Shipping, insisted he had no shipping to spare even for bringing over American battalions with their rifles and without their division trains; he had not enough to carry out the twenty-four division program. But the optimistic Lloyd George signed an agreement to bring over six additional American divisions to be assigned to the British. By this time Sir William Robertson was out of the War Office. In Sir Henry Wilson, the new Chief of Staff, Lloyd George had a man whose temperament was more akin to his own. Details as to how the divisions were to be trained with the British were left to Haig and Pershing. But even the resourceful British Premier could not materialize ships out of a conjurer's hat. He passed the question of transport on to Sir Joseph Maclay. Pershing did not hasten his negotiations with Haig at a time when British liners were being put at our service and the promise of the twenty-four division program, which meant soldiers for Pershing's own army, had passed into a more active stage of fulfilment. On March 11, ten days before the German offensive began, Pershing informed the War Department by cable of the conclusion of his arrangements with Haig, by which our divisions were to come as divisions at full strength and to be trained under the original Haig-Pershing plan of December.[9] The British were to supply us with machine-guns and mortars. We were to bring our motorized transport, but no animals, harness, or animal-drawn vehicles, with minor exceptions. Our artillery and ammunition trains were to be trained in our own area.

Now I turn to the development of the situation as the Allies saw it, as the Germans saw it, and then again as Pershing saw it, leading up to the day when the German army was to try to repeat the success of Caporetto, this time on the Western front.

On January 20, 1918, Bliss arrived in London on his way to his post with the Supreme War Council at Versailles. On the 22d Bliss began that series of illuminating letters and memoranda to Baker which form one of the treasures of war literature, not only for their historical value but also for their more distinctly personal qualities. (Before his death the General gave me permission to make excerpts from his letters; but I have been sparing in availing myself of the privilege. The immense store of his diaries and memorabilia awaits an adequate biographer.)

Bliss found that the inner circles of British opinion had been influenced by Major General Leonard Wood, who, in passing through London on his way to his tour of the front as a division commander, had talked most discouragingly of our home preparations. Lloyd George, Lord Reading, and the British army chiefs were all saying "the same thing" to Bliss:

"They want men and want them quickly. The proposal is, in a general way, for them to take our men simply with their rifles and the ammunition therefor and their clothing—the British to transport them and supply them in every way."

DISCUSSION—DELAY—ANXIETY AND FEAR

Writing to Baker on February 2 from Versailles, Bliss said that the Allies foresaw that the best they could do would be to hold the line in 1918, and that, without our prompt aid in man-power, even this would be endangered. He wrote, "I doubt if I could make anyone not present at the recent meeting of the Supreme War Council realize the anxiety and fear that pervade the minds of political and military men here."

Meanwhile, our people at home were doing without heat, munition factories were short of coal, and storms delayed and held up shipping; and in England a stricter food rationing was in force. The Supreme War Council, that clearing-house of Allied relations, was hearing warmer debates among the nations represented in the lobbies than it heard at its regular meetings, as it tried to resolve many minds into concerted action against the single mind of the German command directing all German energy to the final effort, while every Allied nation had its whispering gallery under the censorship and the Supreme War Council had one of its own.

Serbia not only sent in petitions to the Supreme War Council, but presented a huge memorandum to Baker to the effect that her soil was the logical jumping-off place for an Allied counter-offensive. Allenby's success in Palestine had renewed the hope of the "Easterners," whose faith had survived Gallipoli. It was argued that reinforcements for Allenby, who already had Jerusalem, would put Turkey out of the War, open the way for further support of Russia, and prevent Germany, which had invaded the Ukraine, from drawing on Russia's grain fields, herds, and oil wells, for bread, meat, fats, and fuel. Why not strike against the exposed flank of the Central Empires in the East when Ludendorff withdrew his divisions from the East to the West? This would serve the policy of Italy as well as of Greece and Serbia, who were calling for money and aid of all kinds. Lloyd George's imperialist imagination, as he bade Maclay find the shipping for the American divisions, was under the Eastern spell which called for more shipping to the Mediterranean. His own Chief of Staff was against his Eastern dream; so were the French staff; and so was Clemenceau, who was thinking of the safety of France before that of Serbia, and would spare no divisions for distant adventures.

Our country's territorial defense problem concerned the protection of the Panama Canal rather than the Suez. We had no territorial ambitions in the Mediterranean, or, indeed, anywhere in Europe. We simply wanted to win the War, bring peace back to the world, and have our soldiers at home again. There was no escape from the military logic of the situation. The President, Baker, Pershing, Foch, Haig, Pétain, and our staff at home and in France were "Westerners." Against all the extra shipping required, all the extra time needed to send troops to the East, and the long marches and lack of land transport, was set the speed with which the Germans on their interior line could send divisions over their military railroad system to meet any new emergency in the East. Hindenburg and Ludendorff would have welcomed such an opportunity to beat the Allies in detail. But they, too, were Westerners in that they had brought all their strength to bear for a decision on the Western front. The victor there could easily mop up any remaining opposition elsewhere. And the War was to be won on the Western front.

Lloyd George, whose nature revolted from all forms of passivity, sought for some escape from the military fact from which there could be no escape: the offensive was with the Germans. The British and French armies could only strive to learn the point of the German attack before it came. Ludendorff, who had become the tactical master of the coming campaign, with Hindenburg sitting in council, had no illusions. His mind was on the U-boats' part as well as the army's. Material for submarines had priority; mechanics to build them were withdrawn from the front.[10]

"The question was: what will be the rate of submarines in the spring of 1918? Will the submarines, even if they have been unable to damage England decisively, have so far reduced tonnage that the new American troops cannot come over in a short time and will they be able to strike at American transports while engaged generally in destroying hostile tonnage? . . . I felt obliged to count on new American formations beginning to arrive in the spring of 1918."

He considered that Austria-Hungary could not hold out much longer. She had lost 1,800,000 in killed, wounded, and

prisoners. Only her army held her many-jointed empire together; and it must have victory soon or there would be disso-
lution.

"The condition of our Allies and of ourselves and that of
the army all called for an attack that would bring about an
early decision. . . . Delay could only serve the enemy, since
he was expecting reinforcements. The crown of success was an
operation in which we could bring to bear the whole of our
superiority. It was our great object. If we did not succeed at
the first attack, we should have to do so at the next; by then,
indeed, the situation would have become less favorable—how
much less favorable would depend upon the rate of arrival and
value of the Americans and the losses which both sides sustained. . . . I was influenced by the two factors and by practical considerations, first among them being the weakness of
the enemy."

He decided against making his initial drive in the valley of
the Lys against the British in the North because "before the
middle of April its passability away from the roads was doubtful. That was very late in view of the Americans."

WOULD THE AMERICANS BE IN TIME?

For both the Allies and the Germans time was an essential
factor in the decisive race between life and death during the
early weeks of 1918, though these weeks are now little remembered as compared with the anxious days of early September,
1914, on the Marne. At the disposal of the Foreign Offices and
Army Staffs, and of Lloyd George and Clemenceau, were daily
confidential cablegrams which reflected the situation in the
United States. They knew of the Congressional investigations,
Chamberlain's attacks, the traffic congestion, the reported
shortage of clothing for the cantonments, the rising public dis-
trust of our war preparations, and the inadequacy of our own
shipping to get men and supplies to France. But if Britain
shared shipping would it bring men in time? The submarine
menace was not yet conquered. It still lay between Britain and
her army; between her and her supplies from the outside

world; between her and all the parts of her empire. Lord Beatty, Commander-in-Chief of the British Navy, reported to the British War Cabinet:

"Such large contingents of our naval forces are now absorbed in the regular duties of the anti-submarine campaign that we can no longer be certain of meeting the German fleet even on terms of equality. . . . So long as the enemy remains in his harbors he is in a position to operate on interior lines and with such forces as he may choose against our vitally important mercantile traffic with the Scandinavian countries. His interior position and the presence of his agents in neutral ports, from which convoys sail, facilitate the execution of surprise attacks with forces stronger than our opposing forces." [11]

British military opinion realized that the weary French army no longer had the resiliency it had shown on the Marne; and that after three years' fighting it had reached the stage—which the German army was to reach on that black day in August, 1918—where a few more blows might bring a collapse. What would Britain's position be then? She would need all her ships and men for her own protection. The British command, which had learned by costly experience how long it takes to build competent staffs, understood the problem our staff had in its big division; and how slowly our Army was forming in remote Lorraine, so far from our base. Those old in war were aware that those young in war must learn by experience. But had the American Army time to spare to get experience under its present system? Pershing seemed to be proceeding on the same principle of the slow building of a great force that the British had followed in building their New Army for 1916; but the crisis now confronting the Allies was just such a crisis as the British had faced in the "race to the sea" in 1914.

CULTIVATING THE AGGRESSIVE SPIRIT

During the first five months after his arrival in France Pershing had gone on undisturbed with his plan. His observations had convinced him that the Allies, after so many failures to "break through," had become too habited to trench warfare;

that the French, especially, had lost their aggressive spirit.[12] French soldiers, he learned, had been known not to use their rifles because Germans in the open sixty or seventy yards away were beyond the reach of hand-grenades. He foresaw that the American Army must strike the decisive offensive blow; it must be trained in the use of the rifle and in offensive open-warfare tactics. Any other procedure would have been out of keeping with American traditions. But the French, the British, the Germans believed in the offensive. It is an instinct of powerful races. It had carried British dominion to the ends of the earth; and brought the French and Germans into the race for colonies.

On Salisbury field and at Aldershot in 1914 I heard the same talk about the value of the rifle that I heard later in our training camps in Lorraine; and I saw it put in practice not only by the Canadians, who are our neighbors in western individualism and frontier marksmanship, and by the Australians, but by the British themselves, without being able to go through the trench line to open warfare. But one day—unless the War was to end in a stalemate—the breach must come.

I recall a delightful old colonel of the British Indian Army who had been with "Bobs" (Lord Roberts) on the march to Kandahar. He exclaimed: "What has happened to the offensive spirit of the British Army? Why are we sitting in trenches in face of the machine German soldiers? Wait until our Gurkhas [native Indian troops] arrive!" Those agile little fellows would leap over the trenches and have it out at close quarters with the Boches!

"But, sir," replied a young British officer who had been at Mons and in "the race to the sea" and had come out of the first battle of Ypres with half his battalion casualties, "I think you would find conditions in Flanders quite unusual and that we are doing all we can."

The British army had gone to Mons in an offensive spirit, and its regulars, with veteran fatalism, had doggedly held their ground and stayed the enemy's advance by their rifle fire on their retreat. France, on the thirteenth day of mobilization in

August, 1914, with more men at the front than the Germans
—an advantage that must soon pass—had made her ill-fated
advance into Lorraine. Russia also took the offensive at the
outset; and so did Italy and Rumania upon their entry into
the War. The French made a major offensive in Champagne in
1915, joined in the initial attacks of the Somme in 1916,
and, after recovering Douaumont, suffered the disaster of the
spring offensive of 1917. Britain's New Army had the aggressive
drilled into its bones. It was conceived and trained for the decisive final blow; in that spirit it had begun the long Battle of the
Somme in 1916, and had continued its hammering in the still
longer battle of Passchendaele during the summer and autumn
of 1917. In our Civil War, Lee practised the counter-offensive
against superior numbers. All great commanders of all time
have championed the offensive. Each in his turn, they have reiterated it as if it were a new discovery, in order to impress
their commanders and soldiers with its importance. In writing
of his plans for his offensive in 1918, Ludendorff, who had become the tactical sponsor for the coming German campaign in
the West, said: [13]

"The attack is the strongest form of combat; it alone is decisive; military history proves it on every page. It is the symbol
of superiority."

Pershing would also drill the offensive spirit into the very
bones of his army, and he did it magnificently. Every American soldier must go into action with the conviction that he
would be the master of the enemy. As long as the Allied trench
wall held, Pershing was as secure as if he were on the parade
ground at West Point, applying the Military Academy's thoroughness in forming his new army for a victorious Somme. He
seemed to divine that the trench wall would hold. He went
on with his sturdy ploughing, sending in his requisitions by
cable, and writing an occasional letter to Baker. On November
13 he wrote that Pétain had arranged for the Americans to
have a sector on the side of the Saint-Mihiel salient. This sector, being sunk at a sharp angle into the trench line, would
favor his eventual offensive operations and preclude a German

offensive on an extensive scale. On January 26 he wrote that
Joffre told him it would be a mistake for us to assign our regi-
ments to the British. Joffre held to his principle stated to the
War College: "It is bad to mix armies."

On February 24 Pershing wrote to Baker that officers required so much experience and practice that training troops
took a long time. This was particularly true of higher officers
and staff officers, who must be masters of so much detail which
could be learned thoroughly and finally only in the front lines.

PERSHING PLAYS A LONE HAND

Pershing was applying the tradition of the conscientious post
commander in the old days on the plains, in overseeing the
labors of his officers on trial at their new tasks. No sooner had
he settled down to army business at his desk than the Indians
were making trouble again. Even the friendly Indians must be
watched, as Greeks bearing gifts.

Among the Allied "medicine-men" Lloyd George had the
tactical facility of Chief Joseph of the Nez Percés; and Clemenceau was another Sitting Bull. Sometimes the post commander
faced them in the same conference with the fighting chiefs of
the Allies—Foch, Pétain, Haig, Robertson, and Wilson—who
were all on the warpath against Chiefs Hindenburg and Ludendorff. Again, he met the Allied fighting chiefs individually
and in groups. Pétain seems to have been generally a good Indian, but all the others were forever reappearing at the stock-
ade gate with some fresh proposal in a new disguise, which
aimed at scattering his garrison. Armies are essentially nation-
alist, their commanders the high priests of nationalism.

"Pershing with his tight-lipped smile kept putting things
off," said Clemenceau.[14] The Pershing smile—that smile which
had its tradition, too, in the old poker-playing frontier posts
—seemed to irritate the Tiger, who had at last met a man who
could be as stubborn as himself. The smile seemed to be agreeable to a proposal, only to be qualified with Pershing's remark
that he would "think it over." Normally, the American
Commander-in-Chief, who was such a good listener, bore him-

self with the observant calm that he had shown in dealing with the Moro chiefs. At the same time he saw every button on Clemenceau's coat, as he would see that of every soldier on inspection. Occasionally, however, as the medicine-men spun webs of artful language—an art at which he had less talent than they—he would bang the table with his fist, and employ short and simple swear-words, reminding them that they had better not tempt the wrath of the Great White Father in Washington. He realized the power he represented, and so did they. They knew through their embassies and missions in Washington that the Great White Father did not bother Pershing with political Indian agents, but left entirely to him the post command as well as all relations with the Indian tribes.

FAILURE TO UTILIZE BLISS

Alone in France, among all those subtle and fair-spoken "medicine-men" and chiefs, that redoubtable figure of plodding determination labored on in the conviction that his would be the final task of licking Hindenburg and Ludendorff—medicine-men and fighting chiefs in one—and putting them back on the reservation to behave themselves better in future. There was no doubt about their attitude. They were hostiles. In their case there could be no negotiations, no quarter given. They knew how to make terrible medicine, which must be met in kind. And that great and canny post commander strained his eyes over the wagon trail of the plain, ever apprehensive lest some of Hindenburg's and Ludendorff's raiding braves— the U-boats—might have captured a supply train and a detachment of reinforcements. When the convoy arrived safely, he found that it did not bring all the supplies he wanted from that distant War Department. As his practised eye looked over the fresh batch of "shavetail" lieutenants and rookies, he saw that they had been improperly trained back in the barracks at home, and he had to take them in hand to teach them the very rudiments of Indian fighting.

Pershing's habit, and his clear sense of duty, made it impracticable for him to utilize Bliss in transferring some of the burden of negotiations from his heavily weighted shoulders, which he kept as erect as a West Point cadet's as an example in bearing to all his Army in dealing with either friendly or hostile Indians. As late as January 17, after Bliss had left Washington, Pershing wrote to Baker that he thought it better to retain Bliss, who knew the job, as Chief of Staff, and to appoint Major General Hunter Liggett to represent us on the Supreme War Council. For a time he thought that Bliss appeared to be inclined to turning over our man-power to recruit the British Army.[15] But that was in the period of the first acute apprehension after Caporetto, when it was feared that the Italian army might soon be out of the War and that the German and Austro-Hungarian armies would combine in an offensive against the British and French; and Pershing had reports that this might center in front of his own sector in Lorraine. For on November 13, 1917, Pershing, in view of Caporetto and the Russian collapse, wrote to Baker in the same strain as Bliss' memorandum of December 18 to Baker—the danger had become so grave that we could not wait until 1919 but must assist the Allies against the common enemy in 1918. On February 24, Pershing said that Bliss was very able, square as a die, and loyal to the core. Bliss thus stated his own conception of his relations to Pershing: [16]

"I do not propose that there shall be the slightest difference between him [Pershing] and myself. I discuss things freely and frankly with him in the privacy of his own house or my office, but when he has once decided on a course, I make it my own also, and so far as anyone else knows I surrender my judgment to his."

Bliss, "the mountain," knew the sign-language of Lloyd George and Clemenceau and Foch, just as well as his old classmate, Major General Hugh L. Scott, knew the sign-language of the real Red Indians. The medicine-men and chiefs personally liked him. He was articulate in council where many soldiers are often tongue-tied. He could say, "If we Allies remain so indifferent we may lose this War," in a way that brought harmony in place of discord. According to one observer:

"Bliss would have been the pillar of this or any other council, for he brought to the Alliance, where the members of every inter-Allied team always pulled different ways, what it needed most: rigid impartiality, even toward its own government. 'Very well, let Bliss arbitrate' (*'Eh bien, prenons Bliss comme juge de paix'*), Foch used to exclaim when a discussion got too heated; and Bliss listened like a sage and benevolent pachyderm. But once his mind was made up, he stuck his hoofs in the ground and was immovable. Even Foch dashed at him in vain." [17]

And meanwhile the German braves were doing their modern war-dance around the painted post, girding themselves for their attack on the settlements before the post commander could receive his reinforcements. They were [18]

"preparing battery positions, screening roads, constructing anti-aircraft shelters, and preparing gear for crossing the trenches, and finally to deploy in battle . . . dummy works on the fronts remote from attack. . . . It was necessary to bring up twenty to thirty batteries, about one hundred guns to each kilometer [eleven hundred yards] of front to be attacked. . . . These were, indeed, massed effects! . . . The barrage was practised with live ammunition, and the infantry trained to follow close behind it."

With infinite labor and pains Ludendorff schooled his battalions for driving through the trench lines and then for decisive warfare in the open.

By the middle of February the Allies knew definitely that the German concentration was to be on the inside curve of the Allied line between Champagne and Flanders. But on that long front Ludendorff might effect a surprise by deceiving the enemy as to the point of his main thrust. He might make it southward or eastward. It seemed logical that he would seek the joint between the French and British armies, and try to separate the two; and then, driving into the gap, spread it in the hope of turning the French back on the defense of Paris, and the British on the defense of the Channel ports.

The Allies ought to have a reserve army ready to prevent a breach wherever the attack came. This measure of preparedness was something as obvious to the civil as to the military mind. No soldier in any staff council would have contested it. The French army naturally had it in mind for their own front, and the British for theirs. But who would have it in mind for the whole? Who would think for the whole in such a crisis as a gap between the two armies? How could the many minds of the Supreme War Council be won to act as a single mind? The American representatives had the advantage of a detached view of the whole. Our country's borders were not under the cloud of the coming German offensive. The lightning from its burst would not set German battalions marching on our roads and German sentinels patrolling our streets as conquerors.

NO ALLIED RESERVE ARMY

Bliss became the spokesman of a unified command which the logic of the military situation might not win against the stiff fact of national interests. But the French would not for an instant consider that any other than a Frenchman should be entrusted with the fate of France. Lloyd George might favor the idea privately, but British public opinion, and the British army, in its experience of liaison in operations with the French army, were not yet ready to accept a French supreme commander.

Bliss' support of the plan for an Allied reserve had more immediate influence. The Council voted for the reserve and apportioned the divisions which were to be drawn to form it from the French, British, and Italian armies. Foch was chosen as its commander. He foresaw that inevitably the German plan, in case a first attack did not bring a decision, would follow this up with another, and yet another, keeping the advantage of surprise. He would reply with counter-offensives as well as with defensive action.[19]

Lloyd George might favor the Allied reserve on principle, but he yielded to Haig and his military advisers when, convinced that the German blow would be against the British front, they said that the British army could not spare a single division for the reserve. The British Premier, as the zero hour of national destiny drew nearer, was thinking of Britain, with an intact British army covering the defense of the Channel. Sacrifices without end Britain had made, but there might come a time when Britain must think of herself, or there would be no Britain. Clemenceau not only yielded to the conviction of Pétain, the French Commander-in-Chief, that the German attack would be against the French, who could not spare a single division for the reserve; he was thinking also of the defense of France if the British army should have to fall back to the Channel. And would Italy spare divisions if the French and British had none to spare? Not when the Italian appeal for coal had become so desperate that the British Secretary of State for War asked the American Secretary of War to come to London to consider how Italy could be satisfied.

And the American Army? After it was known that the German blow would be struck far from our own sector, why should not our four divisions in Lorraine become the Allied reserve? Baker's suggestion to Pershing on December 25 that we take up a position at the junction of the French and British armies represented a tactical arrangement that had occurred to others. Baker had assured Pershing that he did not press it "beyond whatever merit it has in your judgment." For Pershing to move his headquarters to Eastern France meant giving up his drill-ground in Lorraine; separating his army from his line of communications; being drawn closer into Allied relations. He did not consider his divisions yet ready for battle action. He had information that if Britain combed her depots of reserves she could largely increase her army at the front. Haig, indeed, had appealed months ago to Lloyd George to summon more men to the colors; but Lloyd George had replied that the limit had been reached.[20] The danger from the German drive could not be so apparent to the preoccupied Pershing in his isolation as it was to the Allied commanders. It had been foreseen for late February, and then early March, and was so long in coming that even the fears of the French and British had been lulled. Baker had not pressed his suggestion again, since Pershing's judgment was against it. Meanwhile, the Allied whispering galleries had an idea that the reserve actually existed. Warning had been sent to all the Allied censorships that no mention must be made of the size, location, and composition of that reserve—which actually consisted of one Ferdinand Foch, a bow-legged little French general aged sixty-six, and his faithful right-hand man, General Weygand, with their orderlies.

BAKER SEES BROKEN BATTALIONS AND REFUGEES

But I shall now continue my journey with the Secretary of War on the first day of the first German offensive of 1918. As we passed the junction of the British and French armies, we were riding over the same roads that had seen the retreat of the British army in 1914 before the advance of von Kluck's right wing. Soon gun-blasts nearby, above the vicious undertone of rifle and machine-gun fire, drowned the even roar of the fifty-mile front. If Baker had been in an airplane he might have seen, through the smoke and soil sprays of shell-bursts, the laboring ants of the German infantry advancing behind their shield of rolling barrages; but even on the earth our Secretary of War, who had never before seen war, now had a close view of a great army hard pressed in action. Reserves, ammunition, and empty ambulances were moving forward; the ambulances heavy with wounded who could not walk were moving to the rear. The "walking wounded" were working their way out of the arena where the German attack had flashed its lightnings out of the morning mist into Gough's men. The Germans, as a part of their long-planned dramatic surprise, would strike enemy morale in the rear while they drove their legions against his front line. They had started a bombardment of Paris with a gun that had a range of seventy-five miles.

The refugees were on the road again. Early in the War, from Belgium to Switzerland, their processions in flight before the enemy had become familiar back of the Allied battle-line. They were out of place in the military zone, in the way of the fighters in the gladiatorial ring. Their only usefulness to the army consisted in paying taxes, growing food, making munitions, and bringing up their male children to become healthy recruits when they should be old enough to join the colors. So they were sent south to wait until peace, in victory or defeat, should allow them to return to their homes. The picture of their unconcerted individualism, their unkempt and nondescript civilian attire in the presence of military precision and uniform garb, their helplessness, the quiet stoicism of their relief that at least they could get their children out of the zone of fire—all this had become a memory in the long era of trench warfare which held the growling and wrestling armies practically stationary. Those whom we passed on this March day in 1918 had returned to their homes after the German retreat to the Hindenburg Line a year ago; some of them not to ruined homes but to the new houses which American reconstruction units had built. Seed and animals had been provided for them. They had dug up dud shells and shell fragments, leveled their shell-torn fields, begun to look forward to green spring and harvest and to life going on as it had in the past. Now the storm had driven them out again; the shells were rending their new homes. There was nothing for them to do but to keep on going and get out of the way of the ambulances and the ammunition wagons.

It was inconceivable that two men on such a journey as we were making should not talk of what we saw; or that, in the face of such evidence, our talk should fail to congeal into the stark, cold realization that not large bank accounts nor material resources, but courage, skill, weapons, and human willpower were what really stood between our safety in a motorcar, beyond the range of shellfire, and our becoming human leaves driven by war's storm.

The towers of Amiens Cathedral appeared in the afternoon light above the war traffic around the town. If the Germans reached Amiens, the focal railroad point that was the capital of the British army in France, then, in the battle of movement in the open, they would not have much farther to go before it would be downhill to the sea.

As Baker went on board the cross-Channel boat, some Australian soldiers, who were on their way to leave in England, received the order to return over the gang-plank just as it was about to be raised. They were not to see Blighty this time. Some of them would never see it again. They received the orders with the fatalism of veterans. They did not step lightly off the boat—they just stepped, gears grudgingly reversed. They were dependable, war-seasoned men who knew their part when they faced the enemy.

The news was bad; but surely it would be better tomorrow. The past history of offensives on the Western front had been that the great gain was effected on the first day; there was less gain on the second; by the third, momentum was lost; and then the communiqués of the attackers announced that "we are consolidating our gains." But this time the precedent had been broken. Saturday morning's report of the second day, and then Sunday morning's of the third day, told of more towns taken, towns which the British had fought so sturdily to win at such heavy costs, and of the further progress of the threatening line on the map toward Amiens.

A GLOOMY SUNDAY IN LONDON

On Sunday Baker saw London at its grimmest. Nearly four years earlier, the bulletins of the retreat of the British regulars had been a shock to England, soon followed by the victory of the Marne. Then, underlying the suspense of the first and second battles of Ypres, and of Verdun, was the confidence that the British New Army, then forming, would throw its weight in the balance and assure eventual victory. Then later, America had come in as an offset to the collapse of Russia and the unrestricted submarine warfare. The British had more readily

endured stricter food-rationing as the British New Army began its Flanders offensive in the summer of 1917; and they had
in the capture of Jerusalem some compensation for the Austro-
German offensive from the Alps to the Piave. But now, in the
spring of 1918, the entire power of the German army was concentrated against one part of the British line in France and
was making these ominous gains.

Our own people, who had become used to the Allied wall
as a fixture on the map, now saw it caving in. It was the British
and the French armies that were yielding this time, and the
arena was not Russia, Rumania, or Italy, but France, where
we had an army of our own. Our newspapers reported that
shells from the long-range gun had not disturbed the Palm
Sunday crowds. But three days later they announced that it
had killed seventy-five and wounded ninety in a Good Friday
service in a Paris church; for the censors thought the truth
might put rage into the hearts of the Allied fighters. The
Kaiser was quoted as saying that the Lord had "gloriously
aided" and that "we shall win everything." Ludendorff reported the capture of 45,000 prisoners and 600 guns. London
dispatches estimated that three million Germans were now
massed on the Western front. McAdoo said that the next Liberty Loan would be for three billion dollars. Indignant senators criticized War Department delays. Senator Lodge said a
year had been lost; it was time our public knew the truth.

Roye fell; the Germans were near Albert. Practically all the
old battlefield of the Somme had been lost. But more serious
than public reports were the unpublished official bulletins.
For the British and French armies had lost contact. On the
23rd Pétain told Haig at Ducy that contact would be re-estab-
lished. On the 24th, however, the situation had become so much
worse that Pétain instructed his commanders that it was "essential
that the armature of the French armies, taken as a whole, be
solidly maintained; in particular the Reserve group of [French]
armies must not be cut off from the remainder of our forces. This
being assured, maintain contact with the British if possible." [21]
Haig said, "The British army will have to fight falling back

slowly and covering the Channel ports." Meanwhile, people in America were scanning each fresh newspaper edition for news that our troops were in the battle.

The thorough policy of preparation, so often associated with Fabius and McClellan, may mean in peace such a preparedness to the last button and cartridge as enabled von Moltke to win his speedy victories over the Austrians and the French. Even in war it is often right; and its value, like the value of any military policy, is best judged by the result, which in the World War was victory for the Allies. If Grant, who drove forward from Fort Henry to Fort Donelson, had been mired in the mud before fortifications he could not reduce, he might have been regarded as stupid and foolhardy. Yet there is always an appeal in vision grounded in keen perception of opportunity, in not underestimating your own troops, and in a daring initiative and imaginative leadership that puts fortune to the touch.

IF WE HAD HAD A CHANCE TO FIGHT!

Now this narrative will take a speculative turn which has become irresistible to the author. Suppose the Allied reserve had consisted of our four divisions then in France! Suppose they had been moving forward to the front on the roads back of the junction of the British and French armies, instead of three hundred miles away in Lorraine! They would have been in action not as a part of either army, but as an American corps—an integral American force as large as the original British Expeditionary Force at Mons; larger than the five German divisions that put Prussian stiffness into the Austrian backbone at Caporetto; larger than either Meade's or Lee's army at Gettysburg; larger than Grant's at the beginning of his Wilderness campaign, and twice Lee's against him.

Blood and iron! Would these divisions fight? No one who knew their officers and men, many of them the early and eager volunteers of the preceding April and May, who had drilled at the elbows of veteran Regulars, but would give a stare of amazement, of sheer silent disgust, at any low, weasel-minded

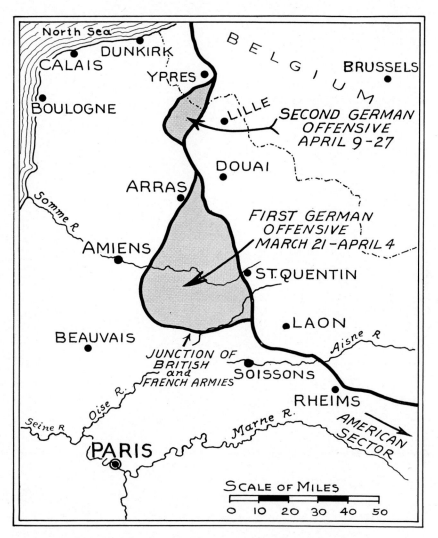

North Sea

CALAIS

DUNKIRK

BOULOGNE

B E L G I U M

BRUSSELS

YPRES

LILLE

SECOND GERMAN
OFFENSIVE
APRIL 9-27

DOUAI

ARRAS

FIRST GERMAN
OFFENSIVE
MARCH 21 – APRIL 4

Somme R.

AMIENS

ST. QUENTIN

BEAUVAIS

LAON

Aisne R.

JUNCTION OF
BRITISH
and
FRENCH ARMIES

SOISSONS

Oise R.

RHEIMS

Seine R.

Marne R.

AMERICAN
SECTOR

PARIS

SCALE OF MILES

0 10 20 30 40 50

THE FIRST AND SECOND GERMAN OFFENSIVES OF 1918

pessimist who could ask such a question. Will a bull-terrier fight when another terrier nips him?

The 1st was number one of our Regular divisions, with the haughtiness of priority to live up to; the 2nd had its rival brigades of Regulars and hard-boiled Marines; the 26th, National Guard, carried the honor of New England; and the 42nd, National Guard of many States, had infantry regiments from Ohio, Iowa, New York, and Alabama. Would they fight? They had been trained as the pioneer divisions directly under the eye of the great and severe post commander who had never left them free of reminders of how a valiant soldier ought to carry himself. The 1st had been nine months in France; the 2nd, six months; and the 26th and 42nd, five months—or longer than the Canadians and Australians before they were in violent action. Under the intensive régime to which they had so loyally responded, they had had from three to four times as many hours of daily training as Regulars in peace-time. The eyes of the world would have been upon our soldiers in that arena, on these the latest initiates to submit to its test. Rival division would have been in competition with rival division, all proving themselves in common action with British and French veterans. They would have faced an occasion that inspired them to keep faith with a resolution to win or die.

I can see how such riders of our military past as Francis Marion, Sheridan, Stuart, Pleasanton, Forrest, and young Merritt would have risen in their stirrups as fortune spread wide the gate to a soldier's golden chance. I can imagine Washington, who made his hazard in crossing the Delaware, fired with the spirit of his youth on the wilderness frontier; Grant, silent, unassuming, even unmilitary-appearing, as he stood beside the road, considering a nod sufficient for the quick mind of Sherman, as he looked toward the front; and Lee in like manner nodding to "Stonewall" Jackson as if no further instructions were needed as soldier glance met soldier glance in mutual understanding.

These four divisions, if they had wanted a further spur to

give the answer there on a European battlefield to European flings that we were too proud to fight, might have looked back to the example of George Rogers Clark fording icy streams to surprise the garrison at Vincennes; or "Mad Anthony" Wayne at Stony Point; or Campbell at King's Mountain; or Winfield Scott—not the Scott of seventy-five at the outbreak of the Civil War, but the Scott of twenty-eight at Lundy's Lane, and of sixty-one, when, against the advice of his staff, he proceeded to storm the pass at Cerro Gordo; or the Mississippi Rifles at Buena Vista; the Federal charges at Fredericksburg; Jackson at Chancellorsville; Warren calling the raw regiment up to the defense of Little Round Top; Pickett's Charge; Hancock crying "Stop them!" as he rode along the ridge; and that little band that stormed San Juan Hill.

All my war experience convinces me that our four divisions would have kept on going until they had closed the gap or been dissolved into the German lines. And I may add, in all respect for the preferable caution of "Heads I win and tails you lose," that their success may be safely assumed from that of the French reserve divisions whom Foch sent on the mission that might have been ours. Since the Germans had broken through the trench system, we would have had real open warfare, the opportunity to use our rifles in pitched battle.

Ludendorff and all his masterful staff officers would not have had to wait on the reports of their intelligence section as to when the American reinforcements would make their presence felt; and the subtle, whispering, even telepathic communication that passes through armies and peoples, playing upon the delicately tuned strings of morale, would have had word of the metal of which American soldiers are made. Nor would our action on that day have been camouflaged, as our last action of the War was, in the mists of the prolonged battle of the Meuse-Argonne; it is even possible that the Meuse-Argonne need never have been fought at all—or at least that it would have come earlier than it did. And if Private Baker of Jeb Stuart's cavalry had been still living, surely he would have forgiven the smallest and most studious of his sons for making that suggestion to a military man, if he did not press it beyond its merits in the judgment of that sound and thorough Commander-in-Chief.

The venturesome side of my undisciplined spirit having indulged in this outburst solely from personal inclination and judgment, I shall now strive to exclude further speculation from this narrative, which I resume with reference to what actually did happen.

XXV

UNIFIED COMMAND

NEVER had the presence of an American in London been so important to Britain or the United States as that of Baker in those perilous days of the fourth week in March, 1918. The preservation of the integrity of the A. E. F. had become endangered by the fact that we were not fighting on the battle-line as an integral force. Before our big divisions could be withdrawn from the trenches in Lorraine and brought to Picardy, the British and French armies might be completely separated. The German attack having been directed against the British, and having all but destroyed Gough's army, it was the British who at present had the acute need of our man-power. American reinforcements for the British might be fighting with their army, which had its back to the sea, while the A. E. F. might be fighting with the French army, which had its back to Paris. Preceding the personal appeal to Baker after his arrival in London, Lord Derby had sent a cablegram to Lord Reading, now British Ambassador in Washington: [1]

"You should explain to the President that we are engaged in what may well prove to be decisive battle of the war. The Germans are concentrating the greater part of their available forces against the British front and are pushing their attacks with the greatest determination. We have every hope of checking them, but our losses have been very heavy and will be heavier. This is only the beginning of the campaign of 1918 and we have to look to the future. In the present state of our man-power resources we cannot keep our divisions supplied with drafts for more than a short time at the present rate of loss, and we shall be helpless to assist our Allies if, as is very probable, the enemy turn against them later. We have the divisional cadres ready with all necessary services, and what we require is men to help us keep them filled. You should appeal to the President to drop all questions of interpretations of past agreements and send over infantry as fast as possible without transport or other incumbrances. The situation is undoubtedly critical and if America delays now she may be too late."

Our divisions in America were three thousand miles from the battle-line; Pershing's, only three hundred. Baker, upon his arrival in London, had at once telegraphed to Pershing suggesting that he consult with Pétain as to how the A. E. F. could be of the most service. But Pershing had already seen Pétain before he received the telegram. Pétain asked him to take over trench sectors in Lorraine, relieving French divisions for the battle-line.[2]

Baker's busy time in London included attention to one of the original objects of his visit, a problem which the advance of the German avalanche had made even more acute: Italy's demand for rolling stock and aid, which had interfered with the A. E. F.'s supply system. Before the offensive began Bliss had gone to Italy on a hasty trip to ascertain the actual facts of the Italian situation. Baker wrote from London to Bliss, who should be back in Paris the morning the letter arrived:

"Of course it is entirely possible for us to send over cars and engines, and we are doing it, but they become a part of the common stock and are distributed by the French railroad management so that there is no assurance that even our own cars will be available for our own transportation of supplies and subsistence; yet without such an assurance an entirely new element of hazard is brought into the proposed large numerical increase in our Expeditionary Force."

Uncertain how far the German drive against the British might go, and uncertain but that the next drive might be against the French line, the French would be even more avaricious of rolling stock. Moreover, they might shut off European supplies upon which our Army was largely dependent.

On March 26 Secretary of State Lansing sent a cablegram through Ambassador Page, saying:

"I am desired by the President to request you to ask the Secretary of War if he does not consider it would be wise and have a beneficial moral effect for him to return to France at once."

But the grave bulletins showing the continued success of the Germans had already sent Baker to Paris before the cablegram was received. Bliss met him at Boulogne, bringing all the latest information from the Supreme War Council as well as from Italy. The threat of German victory on the Western front had more than ever bound up Italy's fate with that of the Allies. Their defeat would leave her helpless in peace negotiations with Germany. She must now depend upon her resources and man-power against an Austrian offensive. Bliss' hopeful thought in the crisis was that it would bring unified command, which he had so steadily advocated.

DISASTER TAKES A HAND IN HIGH POLITICS

I have made a point of not quoting letters that Baker wrote after the War; but one to Bliss on October 24, 1922, is a warrantable exception to the rule. Baker kept no diary. His memoranda and letters never indulged in personal matters or political gossip. On his trip abroad he went his way from conference to conference, apparently no more impressed by meeting famous generals and statesmen with whom he had business to transact than by the run of callers at his office as Mayor of Cleveland. This letter to Bliss is a distinctive document about his first trip to Europe in that he mentions where he dined. So far as the written records go, he might have traveled dinnerless from Paris to the ports, to headquarters, and to London.

"I recall very well the interview at the White House after your return in 1917, and the attitude of the President on the subject of single command. From that time, he and I discussed the subject several times, and with his permission I brought it up more or less casually with British military representatives in Washington. When I went to Europe in March, 1918, you will recall that you and I discussed the question at Versailles before the big drive began. I went to England and had dinner at Ambassador Page's house with Mr. Lloyd George, Sir Henry Wilson, and others. The big drive was then on, and at the dinner table that night the question of unified command came up, Mr. Lloyd George stating as a comment upon the breach made between the British and French lines by the Germans: 'This means a unified command.' Admiral Sims, who was present, remarked: 'Why could you not have done that months ago?' To this, Mr. Lloyd George responded that no British Government which had proposed putting the British army under a French commander prior to that time could have remained in power. I expressed delight at the idea of unified command and told him that President Wilson had shared it from the beginning, but had felt that until our own military efforts were more formidable we had no right to urge it on his attention."

Great as was their potentiality, "our military efforts" were certainly not "formidable" as yet. It would have been a mistake to impress unified command artificially from the top. It must come as the expression of the common need, backed by conviction which would support it through vicissitudes and under a commander whose fitness was generally accepted. If it had been established early in the War a costly failure of a grand offensive to break through the trench lines would have led to recriminations between the Allies. One Ally would have cried out over the sacrifice of lives to the incompetency of a general of a foreign nation, and in turn been charged with not having given him the loyal support that would have insured success. The ensuing rupture might have made it impossible ever to bring the armies again under a single head.

When Haig learned that Pétain had concluded that the French army must protect itself, he sent for Sir Henry Wilson, the British Chief of Staff, to come to France. The next day, the 25th—the day Baker left London—Haig took a decisive step. He gave General Weygand, who was Foch's Chief of Staff of the paper inter-Allied reserve army, a note asking for at least twenty French divisions "astride the Somme, west of

Amiens," to operate against the flank of the German attack on the British army. And Haig further said (as I have already mentioned), "The British army will have to fight falling back slowly and covering the Channel ports." In other words, either aid must come from the French or the separation of the two armies must become an accepted fact in future action. If the French were to fend for themselves, then the British must do the same, and the Italians, and the Americans in turn. Thus in three days new German battle tactics seemed to have blasted the aims of the House Mission for co-ordination, the concert of Rapallo, all the resolutions and labors of all the nations represented in the Supreme War Council to pool the Allies' men, money, munitions, and shipping in a common cause on that old principle of hanging together or hanging separately, which held the thirteen colonies together in the Revolution. Indeed, the German plan of striking the joint of the armies was so far fully justified. German policy, which had cut off Russia from the Allies, reduced Rumania and Serbia to quiescence, and sent Italy back to the Piave, was well on its way to achieve the separation of France and Britain before Americans could arrive on the scene in force.

Hindenburg wrote: [3]

"We must aim at a great and if possible surprise blow. If we did not succeed in breaking the enemy resistance at one stroke, this first blow must be followed by others at different points of the enemy lines until our goal was reached. . . . We had a new enemy, economically the most powerful in the world, an enemy possessing everything required for the hostile operations, reviving the hopes of all our foes and saving them from collapse while preparing mighty forces. It was the United States of America, and her advent was perilously near. Would she appear in time to snatch the victor's laurels from our brows? That, and that only, was the decisive question! I believed I could answer it in the negative."

The Germans had effected the surprise blow by sudden and unperceived concentration against Gough's army. But counting total numbers on each side of the trench line from Switzerland to the Channel, they had theoretically no advantage in either men or material adequate to insure a decisive victory. Under the single Hindenburg-Ludendorff mind against armies whose team-play had been broken, they had established a vast superiority in force over part of the British sector. They had the advantage of an army which was able to strike the enemy's army in detail in the old days of pitched battles. Another favoring factor was their faith in Hindenburg as the father of victory. As he expressed it:

"What was there that enabled us to hope for one or more real victories such as our enemies had always failed to secure hitherto? It is easy to give an answer, but difficult to explain it. The answer is the word 'confidence.' "

Hindenburg had reason to be confident on the day Pétain refused to part with his divisions to support Haig; reason to think that if no aid came to the British, the Germans might take Amiens. According to Foch:

"Each of the two commanders-in-chief found himself faced by the responsibility he owed his country. Each was concerned most of all with preserving and maintaining his own army. . . . As opposed to a single German battle, two distinct battles were being fought by the Allies: a British battle for the ports, and a French battle for Paris." [4]

The talk between Foch and Clemenceau on the 25th has been interpreted by both in their reminiscences; but the determining factor in history is that on the afternoon of March 26th Clemenceau, Foch, Pétain, Haig, Lord Milner, and Wilson, Chief of the British Staff, were in council in the garden of the town hall at Doullens, north of Amiens, over the monstrous fact of a gap of twelve miles between the two armies. All agreed that Amiens must be saved; and this could be done only by common action. At first it was suggested that Foch co-ordinate the forces around Amiens; but Haig would broaden his part to include all British and French forces in France and Belgium.[5] Clemenceau and Milner signed the following agreement:

"General Foch is charged by the British and French governments with co-ordinating the action of the Allied armies on the Western front. To this end he will come to an understanding with the commanders-in-chief, who are requested to furnish him with all necessary information."

This was far from actual supreme command. Foch could not give orders. Compliance with his direction of troop movements was subject to the consent of Haig and Pétain. His authority lay in his lucid expositions, convincing them of the soundness of his conceptions, and in his prestige as Professor Foch, author of "The Principles of War," the Foch of the Marne and Ypres. Pershing was not at this conference, since no American soldiers were near Amiens except the 6th Engineers, who were engaged in repairing railroad lines, and who dropped tools for rifles.

Upon Baker's arrival in Paris he was met by Pershing. Our Commander-in-Chief now had reasons for serious concern. His drill-ground and his great vision of the American Army and its extensive line of communications were imperiled.

"I'm for unified command and for Foch!" he said, as he pointed at the map showing the line the German advance had reached according to the latest reports.[6]

Baker was sending daily reports to the President. He reassured Lloyd George that all our divisions were at Pétain's disposal. Haig, having been driven out of portions of his trench system in the Amiens region, must construct new defenses in the rear. Baker telegraphed Lloyd George that three full regiments of engineers had been sent to Haig, and that

"others will go as soon as transportation can be found for them. The question of preferential treatment of infantry from the United States cannot affect the present situation but will be treated as the needs of the situation require. Meanwhile the infantry of the first six divisions to be brought by the British can of course be brought first."

That is, in this emergency, divisions for our own twenty-four division program were to yield precedence to the six divisions to be assigned to the British. On the same day (the

27th) that Foch took over direction of the battle, the anxious military representatives of the Supreme War Council had adopted a resolution that

"the new situation requires new decisions. . . . It is highly desirable that the American government should assist the Allied armies as soon as possible by permitting, in principle, the temporary service of American units in Allied Army corps and divisions. Such reinforcements must however be obtained from other units than those American units which are now operating with the French. . . .

"The military representatives are of the opinion that, from the present time, in execution of the foregoing, and until otherwise directed by the Supreme War Council, only American infantry and machine-gun units, organized as that government may decide, be brought to France, and that all agreements and conventions made in conflict with this decision be modified accordingly." [7]

Bliss hastened from Versailles to Baker in Paris with the resolution the moment it was passed. As soon as Baker had read it he sent a cable to the President in which he said that the paragraph which

"postpones the organization and training of complete American divisions as parts of an American Army ought to be conceded only in view of the present critical situation and continued only so long as that situation necessarily demands it. The question of replacements will continue to embarrass the British and French governments, and efforts to satisfy that need by retaining American units assigned to them must be anticipated. But we must keep in mind the formation of an American Army, while at the same time we must not seem to sacrifice joint efficiency at a critical moment to that object. Therefore I recommend that you express your approval of the joint note in the following sense:

"The purpose of the American Government is to render the fullest co-operation and aid, and therefore the recommendation of the military representatives with regard to the preferential transportation of American infantry and machine-gun units in the present emergency is approved. Such units when transported will be under the direction of the Commander-in-Chief of the American Expeditionary Forces and will be assigned for training and use by him in his discretion. He will use these and all other military forces of the United States under his command in such manner as to render the greatest military assistance, keeping in mind always the determination of this government to have its various military forces collected, as speedily as their training and the military situation will permit, into an independent American Army, acting in concert with the armies of Great Britain and France, and all arrangements made by him for their temporary training and service will be made with that end in view." [8]

This answer was received from Washington:

"The President concurs in the joint note of the Permanent Military Representatives of the Supreme War Council in the sense formulated in your number 67 March 28th and wishes you to regard yourself as authorized to decide questions of immediate co-operation or replacement." [9]

We were to supply 120,000 infantry and machine-gun personnel to be brought over in April. Baker made it clear that these were to serve with the British or French only until the emergency was over. He would not commit himself to continue the program beyond the month of April.

Now I return to the subject of unified command. Already, on the 27th, Baker had cabled the President announcing that the Foch "arrangement was everywhere regarded as most happy and will probably mean a supreme command for the rest of the War." The next day, the 28th, he cabled: "General Pershing is with General Foch today. On his return I will send you real situation with regard to supreme commander. No announcement has been permitted on the subject and some confusion exists as to just what has been done"—in the fog of war where Foch under the faint authority he had received was making his dispositions which had already closed the gap between the two armies but not yet stayed German progress toward Amiens.

Thus far the Allied peoples had had no word that the American Army was to take any part in the action, although any plan in this respect might be concealed for strategic purposes. Assurance of American support from Washington and our people, three thousand miles away, was an empty formality in the morning papers from Rome to London, where the truth could not be denied to readers of the communiqués. It was clear for them, no less than for Baker and Pershing on the map in Pershing's Paris headquarters. And deep in the minds of leaders and the thoughtful was sunk the fact that so long had both sides fought, and such was their weariness, that the moment might come when just a little more pressure, just one more blow, might turn the balance between the will to continue the fight and demoralization. The bent sword might suddenly break.

It would be no assurance to the Allied peoples or armies, especially the armies, to say that our divisions were taking over quiet sectors to relieve French divisions for combat. Rather it would confirm the intimations of the whispering galleries of London, Paris, and Rome, that little real military aid might be expected from America. European nationalistic reasoning, applying itself to American isolation, might privately wonder why America should sacrifice the lives of her youth in a distant quarrel: it would be quite in order for her to make peace when she saw that she was on the losing side.

A declaration from the President himself, or from all the members of the Cabinet, and resolutions by the Congress could not meet the occasion. It was not in order for a Secretary of War, who did not obtrude his personality, to sound bold phrases or pæans of encouragement to the Allied battle-line which wanted to hear from a soldier that soldiers were coming to stiffen it in an unequal struggle. On the 26th, at Foch's headquarters, Pershing said to Foch:

"I am come to say to you that the American people would hold it a great honor for our troops if they were engaged in the present battle. I ask it of you in my name and in that of the American people. There is at this moment no other question than that of fighting. Infantry, artillery, aviation—all that we have are yours to dispose of them as you will. Others are coming, which are as numerous as will be necessary. I have

come to say to you that the American people would be proud
to be engaged in the greatest battle in history."

Since the "Lafayette, we are here!" of July 4, 1917, which
had been credited to a man who was not a phrase-maker, Pershing had become an uncommunicative and vague figure at the
head of a vague army, cautious in counsel to the Allied leaders,
never brilliant, deliberate in forming judgments and making
decisions, and stubborn when once convictions were formed.
To have said "Lafayette, we are here" on March 28, 1918,
would have meant a free play in the Allied whispering galleries of "We have heard you were. What are you going to do?
Keep at your exercises in your training camps? Occupy your
quiet trenches?" Pershing's announcement held a fire and emotion that came as a surprise to some of the Allied leaders when
he broke his silence in behalf of the vanguard of our soldiers
in France and of the power of his country, which, as its spokesman, he irrevocably committed to the armed support of the
Allies. We were with our companions in arms to the bitter end.

His words carried the greatest thrill to the Allies since our
entry into the War. They added their support to the incentive
of the Allied reserves going into action in the battle area past
the retreating refugees; and his placing our Army at Foch's
disposition had the authority of expert advocacy. The next day
Bliss was with Foch, coming at Foch's request. Foch reports
that the soldier-philosopher spoke with that bluntness he could
summon to fit a situation:

"We have come over here to get ourselves killed; if you want to
use us, what are you waiting for?" [10]

Now that Pershing had spoken, Baker sent this cablegram to
the President:

"I have just been shown a copy of a message from Lloyd
George to you with regard to General Foch and American
troops. The situation seems to be that Lloyd George is personally in favor of a Supreme Commander but fears British
opinion will be the other way because such a Commander
could sacrifice the Channel ports to the defense of Paris. The

General Headquarters A. E. F.

March 30th, 1918.

No. 1004-R
Dated: March 29th.

PERSHING

    AMEXFORCE HAEF

      Transmit following message to General
Foch: "May I not convey to you my sincere? congratulations on your new authority question
Such unity of command is a most hopeful augury
of ultimate success. We are following with profound interest the bold and brilliant action of
your forces. Woodrow Wilson". March

                        McCain

C of S

I was in Paris when this was received and discussed unity of command and cabled President - recommending that the cable be + clear - non an Pershing + Parker

Dear Mr. Secretary:
  This message rather
indicates the President's view
of the new arrangement.
I have just received it.
       J. J. P.

WHEN UNITY OF COMMAND WAS ESTABLISHED
UNDER FOCH

arrangement therefore is that General Foch is to be supreme enough to co-ordinate but without being called Supreme Commander. General Pershing will of course act under General Foch, as Pétain and Haig have already agreed to do. I venture to suggest that in replying to that part of Lloyd George's message you might go further than he asks and say that you are willing to accept a general supreme command whenever the French and British are. Perhaps the relative smallness of our present force and our having no immediate defensive object in France would make it unwise for us to urge the point, though the present events would seem to have demonstrated the need. The second part of Lloyd George's message is covered by joint note of Versailles conference about which I wired you two days ago. General Pershing's prompt and fine action with regard to the use of our troops and facilities here in the emergency has won enthusiastic commendation from French and British. Our First Division will shortly be withdrawn from trenches and used in battle." [11]

The allusion to our having no immediate defensive object in France reflected British concern over the safety of the Channel ports and French concern over the safety of Paris, and the importance, so evident to one who had the feel of the situation, of not overplaying our hand. The last sentence carried assurance stronger than diplomatic representations. Our First Division was to become a part of the Allied reserve in the battle area.

A few hours before he received Baker's final cablegram, the President had sent a cable to Lloyd George and Clemenceau advocating unified command, and the following cable to Foch:

"May I not convey to you my sincere congratulations on your new authority? Such unity of command is a most hopeful augury of ultimate success. We are following with profound interest the bold and brilliant action of your forces." [12]

The value of a single mind against the single German mind, a single battle against a single battle, had been demonstrated in military action. By April 1 the first German offensive had run down in extending itself over the shell-pitted old Somme battlefield, with its broken roads and flattened towns and villages. The German soldiers, who had been so thoroughly drilled and so skilfully blooded to press their attacks, sought rest on the cold, damp ground only to have their remaining strength refrigerated out of their weary bodies and their remaining will-power out of their dazed brains.

On April 3 another conference of the statesmen and generals, including Pershing, took place at Beauvais. They adopted this resolution:

"General Foch is charged by the British, French, and American governments with the co-ordination of the action of the Allied armies on the Western front. To this end all powers necessary to secure effective realization are conferred on him. The British, French, and American governments for this purpose entrust to General Foch the strategic direction of military operations. The commanders-in-chief of the British, French, and American armies have full control of the tactical employment of their forces. Each commander-in-chief will have the right of appeal."

The last sentence attached a string to the authority of supreme command which the French might pull to save Paris, the British to save the Channel ports, or Pershing to preserve the integrity of his army. Nationalism made an immense concession to a common cause even with this limitation, which was the only safeguard lest Foch, a Frenchman who would think of France first in a final crisis, should sacrifice the interests of her Allies to save his motherland.

Where would the enemy strike his next blow? To the civil mind it might seem that obviously it would come in the Amiens region where he had already broken through the trench line. But this would be the most impracticable place. To the rear of his new line stretched a desert without shelter. The enormous amount of material for another offensive would have to be transported over shell-torn fields and roads. Here the British had built new trench systems and had their backs to intact roads and an established transportation system; and here was their concentration of reserves which they could not move to meet another attack until the Germans should have disclosed the point of their next concentration.

A cable from March, now Chief of Staff, to Pershing carried assurance for Foch, on the same day that he was formally chosen Generalissimo, that we had more than a million men in training to draw upon, if he could hold the enemy until they arrived; and for Pershing that soon he would not be feeling so lonely in France as he felt at present with three hundred thousand men.[13] March had word that, counting the 60,000 that British ships would transport in addition to the capacity of our own ships, "120,000 American troops could be embarked in April and rather more the following months."

As an offset to the misfortunes of the British army, submarine sinkings had decreased, thanks to the steady success of the depth bombs and other counter-measures, while the crisis on land had inclined the British to spare shipping for us. The *Leviathan* could now make direct trips to Brest.

TO MEET THE NEXT OFFENSIVE

Lord Reading appealed to the President to send over 120,000 infantry and machine-gun personnel a month for three months to the British army, which would give Haig a total of 360,000 American troops; but, contrary to reports, the President did not agree to this, although he asked for a maximum of troop tonnage. Baker had not agreed to it; and the President told Reading that he would take no further action in the matter until Baker returned from France.[14]

The Somme offensive over, the President again reminded Baker of the importance of going to Italy. So many disillusionments in the way of Allied reverses had come to the White House that it was not surprising that the President should be concerned about Italy's morale when we had yet sent no troops to Italy, even to "show the flag." Baker visited the Italian front and Rome in a hurried tour; and the Italian army and people had the assurance that we were just as much the ally of Italy as of France.

Upon his return to Paris, before sailing home, Baker accepted an invitation for the only public ceremony he attended in France: the municipal celebration at the Hôtel de Ville in Paris of the first anniversary of our entry into the War. It had been a long year since April 6, 1917, when the Allies thought they would need only our financial and commercial aid; a long year since Baker had begun spending two billions of dollars without authority of the Congress, and had told the War College he wanted plans not for a million but for a million and a half men; since Senator Martin had said to Major Pierce, "Good Lord! You aren't going to send soldiers over there, are you?" In that long year the once-mighty Russian empire had turned Bolshevist, the Italian army had been driven back to the Piave, the British had lost their old Somme battlefield, and the only good news by land had been the capture of Jerusalem.

On his trip to Europe the Secretary of War had seen much and learned much, had realized the truth of Clausewitz's saying that

"war is the province of uncertainty. Three-fourths of those things upon which action in war must be calculated are hidden more or less in the clouds of great uncertainty. Here, then, above all else, a fine and penetrating mind is called for, to grope out the truth by the touch of its judgment."

As Baker left Paris he knew that our 1st Division was on the way to the region of Beauvais behind the left flank of the French army, near the British right. If the next German drive were to be in the Montdidier region, as many military prophets foresaw, then the 1st would see violent action. But Hindenburg and Ludendorff had chosen to strike the British army, which had seemed badly shaken by the German onslaught. Perhaps their decision to make their first offensive against the British rather than the French army, because it was the professional army, was fortunate for the Allies. The French was the wearier of the two armies; and in the estimate of the chances Hindenburg and Ludendorff seem to have overlooked the tradition of "the thin red line" and British tenacity. The valley of the Lys lay nearer the sea than Amiens, near Calais on the English Channel itself. In that mighty struggle, in the cruelest cockpit of the War, the British, who had already yielded the gains they had won step by step on the Somme, were to lose Armentières and Kemmel, points which they had held all through the War. Baker experienced quite as much suspense when, on his return voyage, he read the wireless reports of the second German offensive, as he had earlier when he had been in France and England during the first one. Upon his return he received a highly historic letter from Bliss which Bliss began on the 10th, and which was a bulletin from day to day of the progress of the battle. On the 11th Haig issued his famous "backs to the wall" call to his troops:

"Every position must be held to the last man; there must be no retirement. With our backs to the wall, and believing in the justice of our cause, each one of us must fight to the end."

Foch had concentrated reserves at Amiens, fearing to uncover it lest the Germans should make a third attack in that region. On the night of the 11th Haig informed Foch that his British reserves might not be sufficient. He appealed to Foch to send French divisions to the battle-ground. Bliss wrote that at six on the evening of the 11th Foch had telephoned him asking his concurrence and Pershing's before he put our 1st Division into the battle. Foch wanted to know whether the 1st was ready to go, and whether it was completely at his disposition. He understood that General Bullard, who commanded the 1st, had been ill. Would another officer be designated in his place? Foch expressed his concern that the commander of the 1st should be familiar with his troops. Bliss telephoned Foch that he had telegraphed Pershing, who had sole charge of the dispositions of the American Army, to communicate direct with Foch.

The next day, the 12th, at noon, Bliss recorded that he had just received another urgent message from Foch in which he said that he had heard nothing from Pershing in answer to his message of the previous evening. He begged Bliss to get an immediate answer. Bliss telegraphed again to Pershing, but remained uncertain whether either of the messages would reach Pershing, who had gone to oversee the induction of an American division into the trenches in Lorraine. Apparently, no one at his headquarters had authority to act in his place during his absence.

At 3.30 P. M. on the 12th, Bliss received a copy of a message from Pershing to Foch in which Pershing said that Bullard, who had been temporarily incapacitated, was on his way back to his command:

"Upon his arrival and upon the completion of the brief program of instruction in open warfare, there is no reason why this division should not take its place actively wherever you desire to place it. In case you consider it urgent, division can go in at once."

Later, the 1st went into the Cantigny sector, where it made an offensive of its own at the end of May. No American divisions served against either the first or the second German offensive; but a great opportunity came to the 2nd at Château-Thierry against the third. Upon his return to Washington Baker had the good news that the second offensive was being held. Although so many affairs awaited his attention that he had no time to read *Harvey's Weekly,* it may be noted that Colonel Harvey welcomed Baker's homecoming in a characteristic paragraph:

"Those who heard our nobby little Secretary of War jumble facts and figures into an oratorical effort when he attempted to defend his administration before the Senate Committee, can readily visualize his breathless haste in recounting to the British leaders America's unprecedented accomplishments. . . . Our little chattering ex-Pacifist."

XXVI

BACK AT HIS DESK

A NEW chief military adviser, Major General Peyton C. March, came in from the door at the right with the daily basket of papers. March had long been a conspicuous officer in the Army, and it might be well here to tell something about him. His branch of the service had been the light artillery, the field guns that keep close to the infantry, the guns of "Forward the guns!" of old-time battle tradition, the mobile guns behind foam-flecked horses, that unlimbered with an acrobatic precision to steady a wavering battle-line with the welcome scream of their shells over the infantry's heads. Young Captain March had commanded the famous Astor battery in the Spanish War. With Pershing, Crowder, Kuhn, Morrison, and other American attachés, he had seen great armies in action in the Russo-Japanese War.

I recall how, on a hot day, March and I climbed a ridge in Manchuria to look down, as from a gallery, upon the battle of Liao-yang on the plain at our feet, while the Japanese pressed their charges. It was the first great battle with the artillery of the period. There were more guns in action than Grant and Lee together ever had; twice as many men on the Japanese side as there had been in both armies in the Wilderness, and more than twice as many as at Gettysburg.

"To think that I should live to see this!" said March, as he chose a seat on a rock and glued his glasses to his eyes. All those flashing guns made an artillerist's paradise, a paradise for any professional soldier observer. March remained as immovable as the rock under him. When I made a remark he remained mute, evidently unaware that I had spoken.

The plan of the battle was as clearly plotted in living lines of action as ink lines on white paper. At our feet were the two main bodies, the Russians with an unfordable river in their rear, the Japanese front of attack disappearing into the mists of shell-bursts on the plain. The river ran approximately east and west through the city of Liao-yang, where it was crossed at approximately right angles by the railroad by which the Russians must make their retreat.

Across the river a separate battle raged as the Russian reserves formed in resistance to Kuroki's corps, which had slyly and skilfully laid its pontoons and crossed the river over night. Kuroki's battle-line was attacking the hills parallel to the railroad. If Kuroki's shells reached the railroad before the main Russian force had made good its withdrawal, there might be a decisive victory. When March became eye-weary at last and lowered his glasses, I remarked:

"It looks as if the Russians were bagged. There may be another Sedan."

"When one hundred and fifty thousand men want to get past fifty thousand, they'll go," March replied.

At that, he had bitten off his words and given me that decisive March look with which so many people who had business in the Chief of Staff's office, and who learned to be brief about it, were to become familiar. The Russian main body lost only a small number of prisoners in its withdrawal.

March's recall from France to Washington meant that he had to give up the command of a forming artillery force which was to be ten times as powerful in the Meuse-Argonne as that of both armies at Liao-yang. He would have directed this terrible orchestra from a headquarters well back of the lines; but the old tradition prevailed in the minds of soldiers as well as the public: being in France meant being at the front. Sitting at a desk at headquarters in France and reviewing troops back of the battle-lines—that was action; whereas sitting at a desk in Washington and reviewing troops in training camps had the look of inaction. None the less, the professional attainments and military organizing capacity of any Regular who was over thirty, unless he was a master of troop movements and of battle tactics, might be quite as valuable at home as they would be in France.

March received high recognition in being given the irksome and titanic task of military co-ordinator of the whole, who must speak the language of the soldier to the soldier and also to our industrial war leaders. The measure of his service at home would be registered in results in France. There could be no glory for him in success, no cheers as the leader of victory parades.

On the way back his ship passed that of Baker bound for France. When he came to his desk on March 4, the organizer went immediately into action. The spurs were in the flanks of the war steeds of democracy that had been trained to harness. He said that he had not wanted the job, but now that he had it he proposed to conduct it according to his own ideas.[1] Those who knew March's strong character knew that he would; while they foresaw that a much larger company of men were now to become familiar with the March personality. To Major General W. S. Graves, his assistant Chief of Staff, he said: "I'll keep you on this for four months, and then you go to France." Graves understood what a busy time he would have before he received his reward. Invitations to dinner that awaited March on his arrival were dismissed with the laconic remark through an aide that we were at war and the Chief of Staff had no time for social engagements.

The Chief of Staff's office and that of his assistants were alight late that first night after he took charge as they were to be every night until the Armistice. It was "Yes" and "No" very quickly at the Chief of Staff's desk. His tirelessness matched Baker's with a sixteen-hour day; and he expected all under him to be as tireless as he. The cablegrams from the Chief of Staff to the A. E. F. now had a more explicit, definite and sometimes abrupt tone; it is possible to draw a line among the documents at the point where the March régime began. He gave and wanted definite information "in order to have the greatest co-operation at home and abroad." [2]

Baker wrote to Bliss on April 29 about March: "I find his

judgment quick and sure, and he seems to have the ability to inform his judgment by a study of details, which is rather rare in so quick a mind." Two strong men, Pershing and March, of such different characters, were now in touch at the ends of the cable, and the part of Baker was how to make the most of their strength in a common purpose. Happily, March arrived at the time of the outset of our heavy troop movement, which required most expert and sure direction to prevent confusion. Baker had said that he would make no actual Chief of Staff until he had found his man. March proved to be the man, and soon shared with Pershing and Bliss the honor of having on his shoulders the four stars of a General, without the prefix of Brigadier or Major. Either Cromwell or Alva would have welcomed a March, who was all soldier, a keen, slashing, dextrous blade, whose philosophy of war was mixed with no daydreams and tolerated no conventional excuses. In cutting away human "dead wood" he did not hesitate to draw blood. To him war was war, and his part that of a servant of the democracy in the task assigned to him.

WE ENTER THE DOMAIN OF WAR HATE

Through the door on the left Baker was learning what the mood of the country had become during his absence as the result of the suspense and the threat of the two German offensives. Our strengthened determination, after the stern winter, had whetted our rancor against the enemy and our suspicion of alien sabotage and plots. The era of spy-hunting and one-hundred-percent Americanism had begun in earnest. It aided in establishing proper safeguards; but their application must be accompanied by discretion that would not defeat its object. The sifting of all the contributed information, which might reveal quite unsuspected persons as German agents or sympathizers, or falsely accuse perfectly innocent persons, was the thankless task of the Intelligence Section, under Colonel Ralph H. Van Deman, which had at its disposal all manner of experts in the reading of secret ciphers in every language spoken in the United States, in all racial psychologies and customs, and

listed everyone accused of defeatism or having a reputation for
pro-German or anti-war sympathies from the Reds of the lumber and mining camps and the back alleys to those of more important position who might give lip-service to patriotism but
secretly be in the service of the enemy. Volunteers in counter-
espionage sometimes interfered with official investigations by
giving the suspected person a warning that he was under surveillance.

Confidential cablegrams reported information on both sides
of the water as to suspects, and there were warnings from this
side to the G. H. Q. of the A. E. F. about persons who had
slipped through the State Department with passports, but
should be apprehended on the other side. A passport could not
be refused to one quite eminent man, since there was "nothing
on him," yet his pro-German financial interests and his pre-
War associations made it advisable that an eye be kept on him
in Europe. The British and French intelligence sections
warned us of people whom they suspected; and in turn we
warned them of people whom we suspected. The deeper we
were in the War, and the larger the loss of personal liberty,
the readier were the mass of the people for stringent measures.

As a part of March's program of co-ordination, and one of
the results of Baker's trip abroad, March kept Pershing informed by bulletins of the state of public opinion at home.
This opinion, on one subject, is reflected in the cable of May
14, which I give as it was deciphered by the cable operator: [3]

"German propaganda never busier in United States than
now. Headquarters said to be in Spain and working to dis-
credit United States Government in Mexico, Central, South
America where the book 'The Vampire of the Continent' has
recently appeared. Germans spending millions of dollars to
spread discontent especially among negroes. Unrest in industrial plants particularly stimulated. Vicious attacks made whenever possible on Wilson and others high in Allied Governments.
Congress given enormous aid to authorities dealing with this
in passing much debated (?) Sedition Act, which confers drastic powers. Wilful spreading of false reports, incitement to

disloyalty, opposing cause of United States by word or act, among things heavily punished, and giving wide scope. Control of mills made still more powerful in the vicinity than heretofore for opposing propaganda of all kinds. Said that the numerous Pacifist and obstructive societies having their headquarters in New York are much depressed and think likely they will have to go out of business and in any event see their activities much curtailed."

Already on April 12 the Congress had amended Section 4067 of the Revised Statutes, which gave the President the power to apprehend, restrain, secure, and remove alien enemies, so as to apply to women. This seemed very important, since it had been demanded by patriotic women after the War had shown how peculiarly gifted women were for propaganda and espionage. The Congress, which had been so reluctant to go further than Section 4067, when it passed the Trading-with-the-Enemy Act on October 2, 1917, followed the Sabotage Act of April 20, 1918, with the Espionage Act of May 6, 1918—clearly the repercussion of the first and second German offensives. The Espionage Act, which would have brought such an outcry of protest six months before, gave the President astonishing powers if he cared to use them. On May 20 March's bulletin of information to the A. E. F. reported: [4]

"New sedition laws give government enlarged drastic powers dealing with all kinds disloyalty, give satisfaction to most, but certain elements of press find it too extreme and source of danger. Colonel Roosevelt in his *Kansas City Star* editorial says, 'President should be supported or opposed to degree warranted by his good conduct or bad, his efficiency or inefficiency in serving nation as a whole. Absolutely necessary should be full liberty tell truth about his acts, as necessary to blame him when he does wrong as to praise him when he does right. Any other attitude base and servile. Administration shows itself anxious to punish newspapers which uphold the War but told truth about Administration's failure to conduct it efficiently. Failed to proceed against various powerful newspapers which opposed the War or attacked Allies, or directly or indirectly aided Germany, as these papers upheld Administration and defended inefficiency. Therefore no additional power should be given Administration to deal with papers for criticizing Administration.' "

On June 15 the Espionage Act was to be further amended and strengthened in order to prevent the advocacy of defeatism or the practice of sedition in any form. One of the dangerous sources of anti-war sentiment had been the foreign-language newspapers.

There was no suggestion of suppressing *Harvey's Weekly* in which, in the issue of May 4, Colonel Harvey made a second comment, in a language that was not alien, on Baker's return to America:

"He has not now any clearer comprehension of the real condition of the world's affairs than he had when he went away. He is still a pacifist waging academic warfare in an academic way . . . twittering, twittering day in and day out about things past and things to come with as little heed for the horrifying present as a grasshopper. . . . Nothing but piffle, piddling pacifist piffle, from an American Secretary of War. . . . Smiling Mr. Baker descends upon Washington like a cloud of poison gas and the wheels begin to slacken . . . shockingly and dangerously unfit for his job . . . our gentle, propitiatory Secretary of War."

The reference to German propaganda in Mexico in the cablegram of May 14 is worth mention in passing; for German incitation was apparently responsible for the frequent alarms that came to the War Department of the gathering of Mexican bands on the border. This required that we keep a considerable force on patrol, which represented about the most miserable duty that could fall to the lot of the American soldier in 1918 while his comrades were going to the real front. The possibility of war with Mexico, if not a major problem, was not the least of our minor problems, when we were straining to get man-power and supplies to France. Now that we were at war with Germany, anything she could do to make us trouble in any quarter became quite in order, nefarious though it may have seemed at the time.

Baker's own views about alien sedition within our borders had not changed. He would be as severe with the guilty as with slackers who posed as conscientious objectors. But the Intelligence Section, in seeking out the real offenders, must avoid inciting indifference or sabotage by too drastic action in doubtful cases which might be more subject to influence by keeping the steel encased in a velvet glove.

MOBBED—BUT A LIBERTY BOND IN HIS POCKET

The same Secretary of War who quietly remarked that the way to win the War was to kill as many enemy soldiers as we could as fast as we could, could say at the same time in one of his letters to Bliss:

"The spirit of the country seems unusually good, but there is a growing frenzy of suspicion and hostility toward disloyalty. I am afraid we are going to have a good many instances of people roughly treated on very slight evidence of disloyalty. Already a number of men and some women have been 'tarred and feathered,' and a portion of the press is urging with great vehemence more strenuous efforts at detection and punishment. This usually takes the form of advocating 'drum-head courts-martial' and 'being stood up against a wall and shot,' which are perhaps none too bad for real traitors, but are very suggestive of summary discipline to arouse mob spirit, which unhappily does not take time to weigh evidence.

"In Cleveland a few days ago a foreign-looking man got into a street car and taking a seat noticed pasted in the window next to him a Liberty Loan poster, which he immediately tore down, tore into small bits, and stamped under his feet. The people in the car surged around him with the demand that he be lynched, when a secret service man showed his badge and placed him under arrest, taking him in a car to the police station, where he was searched and found to have two Liberty Bonds in his pocket and to be a non-English-speaking Pole. When an interpreter was procured it was discovered that the circular which he had destroyed had had on it a picture of the German Emperor, which had so infuriated the fellow that he destroyed the circular to show his vehement hatred of the common enemy. As he was unable to speak a single word of English he would undoubtedly have been hanged but for the intervention and entirely accidental presence of the secret service agent.

"I am afraid the grave danger in this sort of thing, apart from its injustice, is that the German Government will adopt retaliatory measures. While the Government of the United States is not only not responsible for these things, but very zealously trying to prevent them, the German Government draws no fine distinctions."

When the draft men of the 77th, or "Melting Pot," Division had been only six weeks in camp, word reached the War Department that there was much pacifist and even disloyal sentiment among the draftees. The contrary report of General J. Franklin Bell was supported by the extraordinary number of subscriptions to the Second Liberty Loan among the men, as well as by their commander's report of their willingness to learn the soldier's routine which was so new to them. Baker's cure for disloyalty lay in the spirit and manner of the draft, which conscripted service and then developed the homogeneous spirit—the gang spirit, if you will—in companies and battalions. In their ranks were members of all the races of the Teutonic allies, as well as the other races of Europe, speaking a dozen different languages in the same division. Lessons in English had been made a part of their training in order to prepare them for citizenship.

It must be borne in mind that the Germans whom Baker would kill as fast as we could to hasten the end of the War were in the German army; and he would make fighting soldiers against the enemy out of those among us who might normally have blood sympathy with races in the enemy ranks. The draft brought the men in; but their will to combat was something that was not to be impressed upon them, but that they must express. Parents of foreign birth had their first argument for loyalty in the fact that their sons were in the War sharing its dangers; and the final argument to develop their will to victory when the lists of casualties began coming in. It was after

the third German offensive, after Château-Thierry, when our
men had made their stand on the Paris road, that the Congress
strengthened the Espionage Act by the amendment of June
fifteenth.

But a proper complement of the disciplinary action against
aliens, which may have served better to imbue them with
patriotism, was the bent given to our Fourth of July celebration in our second year in the War. The Committee on Public
Information arranged that it should be in honor of the foreign-
born Americans. On the nation's natal day, Americans of the
old stock, Pilgrim Fathers, early Virginians, covered-wagon set-
tlers, and forty-niners, yielded the places of honor to the late
comers to whom war was their opportunity to prove their faith
as members of the national family in good standing. On the
occasion of the pilgrimage to Mount Vernon, President Wilson
spoke there in the spirit of the occasion, pledging the country's
patriotism anew at that patriotic shrine. When we were worry-
ing about whether we could send men fast enough to hold the
Germans in the summer of 1918, we were certain that we not
only had enough soldiers if there were ships to transport them,
but that they would fight out of conviction.

A NEW CHIEF OF ORDNANCE

Having followed one subject through a certain phase for the
sake of continuity, I now turn to another. Upon his return
from Europe Baker was to learn how far the progress of the
production of material was fulfilling the promise of the plan
of a year ago. The soldier-cities had now become established
institutions. Senators were airing no complaints from constituents about clothing, or hospital facilities, or about sending
our men without arms against the enemy. Even Colonel
Harvey admitted that rifles were coming in sufficient quantities from the factories, as Frank A. Scott had promised that
they would. Baker wrote to Bliss on April twenty-ninth:

"In the same way the machine-gun controversy seems now
to be a thing of the past, since the Browning light gun is already

in quantity production and the heavy gun is beginning to be produced from machine tools; and there is a certainty of an adequate supply of these weapons, particularly in view of the fact that we will be accumulating them while our machine-gun units are associated with British and French troops. During such time they will of course have to use the machine-guns and ammunition of the armies with which they are placed."

In spite of the drain of the two German offensives, the French were confident that they could supply artillery for all the troops we could send. But Baker found that a thorough "examination of the Ordnance Department was in order," as he wrote to Bliss. The reorganization of the Ordnance Department in December and January before Baker left for Europe had been one of the examples which proved that reorganization may not in itself mean progress. Again the answer was "the right man." In line with Baker's original plan to profit by the experience of chiefs trained in France to direct affairs at home was his summoning of Brigadier General Clarence C. Williams, Chief Ordnance officer of the A. E. F., from France to become Chief of Ordnance in Washington. But instead of the cramped quarters that Williams had left when he went abroad with Pershing's pioneer staff, he found spacious offices in one of the War Emergency buildings. But the control system of his predecessor (Crozier's successor), which looked well on paper, had been most harassing in its execution to the steel-makers who had undertaken that new and tremendous task of making guns. Their labors had been subject to delays due to changes of program by the A. E. F. and in receiving designs from Europe, and to the inevitable effect of the assurance that the French, who were not interested in our home program, could supply us with ample artillery if we would only feed their plants with material. Nevertheless, our dependence for any branch of arms upon another nation had not become more pleasant since the German offensives began. Laymen could hardly be expected to realize the length of time required to produce a gun, when this was not realized by many professional soldiers. Upon our entry into the War our two private steel plants which specialized in ordnance had contracts for guns with the British government which they must complete. Aside from this, practically all their capacity for forgings was obligated to the Allies, whose needs must have priority. We had therefore to build new plants to meet our own program.

The British had to wait until the Somme, nearly two years after Britain's entry into the War, before they had sufficient artillery for a great offensive; the French, who had entered the War short of mobile heavy artillery, had waited a year for sufficient .155's; and the Germans had taken many months to build the big Bertha which bombarded Paris, and longer to build the submarines for their submarine campaign of February, 1917. Before the War, Britain, France, and Germany had trained mechanics in their great private plants, under government support, which supplied, aside from the home market, a world market in which we could not compete. During the thirty-three months since the War began they had been training additional forces of skilled labor. Williams brought to the Ordnance Department an experience in France, a breadth of mind, executive ability, and understanding of the dollar-a-year man's effort which were most salutary.

TANKS NOT SO EASY TO MAKE

A French proposal for an American tank plant in France had been hampered by the difficulties in Allied relations, by priorities, the shortage of shipping, and the disorganization ensuing on the Italian disaster and the German offensives on the Western front. Our home tank program was behind the optimistic promise of the spring and summer of 1917, based on the conviction that our resources in steel manufacture peculiarly fitted us for the fabrication of tanks, which were the war-offspring of the American caterpillar tractor. The land of mass-production would surely excel in the mass-production of tanks. Our national pioneering confidence, in the tradition of our national expansion and as the proper complement of our national competence and size, overlooked the fact of the many months it took to make the corporal's guard of primitive tanks which gave the Germans a psychological surprise in the Battle of the Somme. Tanks had performed no marvels in assisting the British infantry and the standardized arms in taking a limited objective, but they had been promising enough to warrant building sufficient numbers for a more extensive test. The Germans saw that the tanks might have value, but concluded, at the time, that the material and labor for their production might better go into less experimental channels and, anyhow, until they captured a model which they could improve and reproduce. After the first trial of the tanks it was more than a year before the British and French had them in numbers. By the winter of 1917–18 they had incontestably proved their value; and it was clear that Pershing could not have too many of them for the offensive of the integral army of his giant vision.

THE SO-CALLED "WAR CABINET"

It is small wonder that Baker, soon after his return from abroad, said in a letter to Bliss, "A free half-hour with me is as rare as a circus day to a schoolboy." The meetings of the new "War Cabinet" did not take much of his time. This seems to have been started, while Baker was in Europe, apparently as a sop to those who had been demanding a coalition cabinet. It included, with the regular Cabinet members, the fuel and food administrators and the chairmen of the War Industries Board, the War Trade Board, and the Shipping Board. In Baker's absence, the Assistant Secretary of War attended the first meeting, when photographs were made of all present with the President. There seem to have been few more meetings; but the purpose of the War Cabinet, except as a general conference, remains vague to me in spite of all the documents I have read. Meanwhile, the regular meetings of the official Cabinet continued, each member performing his regular duties, while Baker continued to run the War Department.

McAdoo had a kingdom of his own in the railroads and Treasury. The other Cabinet members who were associated in the Council of National Defense and who were most free to aid Baker in his problems were Lane, Houston, and Wilson. As there was less war activity in the Interior Department, Lane gave a great deal of time to War Department problems. Houston remained a bulwark. Although as Secretary of Agriculture he was responsible for food production—Hoover looked after food control—Houston's historical knowledge of war and his expert knowledge of economics were of large service to Baker. Secretary of Labor Wilson had close relations with the War Department in labor problems. The sound basis of co-operation between Daniels of the Navy and Baker met the new emergencies of 1918 with the same spirit as in 1917. Secretary William C. Redfield, of the Department of Commerce, at a time when war-commerce had become almost the only commerce, strengthened the Bureau of Standards as an invaluable adjunct. All this has no object except to state that the whispering gallery was mistaken in thinking that the unofficial "War Cabinet" had supplanted the official Cabinet.

A SUBJECT THAT WOULD NOT DOWN

After Baker's vivid experience of Allied relations in France, a new crop of Allied difficulties formed a part of the accretion of problems on his desk which he could consider in the light of his observations abroad. That ghost of the integral army, which would not down, had been haunting the White House. The President had given no encouragement to Lord Reading that we would continue for three months the program of 120,-000 infantry a month to be trained with the British. It had even been reported back to Washington that Baker had agreed to this with British representatives in Paris. Baker had a transcript of his talk at the conference cabled to him. It showed that he had not so agreed. Baker at once gave Lord Reading what came to be known as the "Baker memorandum."

By this we agreed to go on shipping infantry and machine-gun personnel at the rate of 120,000 a month in April, May, and June, if the British supplied enough additional shipping. "The troops when transported will be under the direction of General Pershing, assigned for training and use with British,

THE PLANT WE CREATED FOR BUILDING SHIPS AT HOG ISLAND

French, and American divisions as exigencies require from time to time . . . but it is also understood that this statement is not to be regarded as a commitment from which the United States Government is not free to depart when exigencies no longer require it." Even then Baker stipulated that it was not to interfere with "carrying small numbers of personnel for other arms or as replacements for our own divisions."

Baker wrote to Bliss on April twenty-ninth:

"I had the very strong feeling that we ought to adhere to the recommendation of the Permanent Military Representatives, shipping both in British and American controlled tonnage infantry and machine-gun units until the situation in Europe so alters as to justify a diversion of a part of the tonnage to other uses; but I did not believe and do not believe that our action in this matter should be made the basis of a binding agreement which would authorize the British Government to regard itself as justified in keeping watch over our movements and complaining of our conduct if in its judgment our compliance with the recommendation of the Versailles conference was not absolute. In other words, I prefer to follow the recommendation of the Versailles conference as a matter of choice, rather than a matter of promise to Great Britain. . . . I am hopeful that the large shipments of American infantry and machine-gun units will really and in fact prove a substantial aid in the battles of this summer, even if the present great battle should come to any sort of temporary halt."

Lloyd George's reply on the same day that Reading transmitted Baker's memorandum to him was that "we accept Secretary Baker's memorandum as it stands. Pershing is here [in London] and arranging details with the War Office." Pershing, ambassador on the move as well as general in command, made what was known as the Pershing-Milner agreement with Lord Milner, by this time British Secretary of State for War. This was practically the same as the offer that Haig had made four months previously. Six divisions were to be trained with the British. On April 29, after the second German offensive had been stopped and the British were apparently secure in their lines in Flanders, Pershing, relentlessly pursuing his object in and out of crises, had the principle of the mobilization of all American divisions into an American Army at the earliest practicable moment accepted at the Abbéville conference, at which Clemenceau, Milner, Foch, Haig, and Wilson, Chief of the British Staff, were present.

By this time it should have become clear to all concerned, premiers, war ministers, ambassadors, members of Allied missions and generals, that the President and the War Department consistently supported Pershing. There was no other course in principle or in policy. At the first sign of any other a dangerous train of intrigue and confusion would have been started. It would have been an advantage if every day, while the Chief of Staff had his basketful of papers on Baker's desk, Baker might have had a talk with Pershing over the long-distance telephone; but the trans-Atlantic telephone was not yet in operation. Well might General Bliss write to Baker, in expressing the disadvantage of making war so far away from home, that "any of my colleagues among the military representatives on the Supreme War Council can and does pick up his desk telephone in the morning of any day and talk freely with the prime minister of his country and receive his instructions as to whether or not to pass on the consideration of any particular question." [5]

FOCH PRESENTS A GLOOMY PICTURE

Lest we should not be fully aware of the crisis, Ambassador Jusserand, a year after the departure for France of Joffre, who had said we need never send over more than 500,000 men to France, brought to Baker the appeal of Foch, as the new Generalissimo, written on May 2nd. I quote the translation as delivered to Baker:

"It is in fact necessary to well understand that the characteristic of the last enemy offensive has been to cause losses in infantry and machine-guns out of all comparison with such losses as occurred during the last three years of the War. The British army's losses in infantry have surpassed in an unexpected measure all those which had been previously suffered. It is the same with the French proportionately to the part they have borne in the battle. And it is inevitable that, in the coming weeks, the infantry losses will go on increasing. The troops which must be recuperated without a moment's loss are therefore infantrymen and machine-gunners; the more so that the resources in infantry and machine-gunners which the Germans have still in their depots are estimated at between 500,000 and 600,000 men; while the British depots are almost empty, and the French ones will remain without resources until August next. . . .

"After the enormous losses which it has suffered with splendid valor, the British army has just had ten of its divisions suppressed, and in order to definitively stop the German armies, it is not enough to replace them: new forces in *infantry* and machine-gunners are necessary to us *without any delay*. . . .

"In my conscience, I deem it of absolute necessity that there arrive monthly from America in France, during at least the months of May, June and July, by right of priority, 120,000 American infantrymen and machine-gunners. I even consider that, if tonnage allows it, as we have been led to understand it may, it would be highly desirable that this number be surpassed. . . ."

And the answer was that we would give Foch three times 120,000 in May, if we could get the ships. Mr. Randolph, the veteran clerk, thought Mr. Baker had been very wise to have so many soldiers ready. You could not have too many soldiers to win a war; and you always needed more than you had estimated at the start. Soon the long casualty lists would be coming in. The Adjutant General's office was already preparing for them. And the dispatches had become very exciting of late, as they had been in McClellan's Peninsular campaign and from Fredericksburg to Chancellorsville.

But were we training our men properly in the home camps and cantonments? The changes in tactics no less than in arms were a moving picture. The British and the French had sent to us sets of instructors who disagreed with each other and who were told they were wrong by instructors who arrived a few weeks later; and Pershing had sent home officers and instructors as he labored to keep abreast of the changes.

A letter on the subject from M. André Tardieu, High Commissioner of France, lay on Baker's desk the day he arrived home. Six months ago M. Tardieu had written of the tremendous power of the French army, which we need assist with only the final kick to insure victory; and he had been planning a Franco-American shipping company lest Britain have France and America at her mercy in world commerce-carrying after the War. M. Tardieu had now taken us into the Allied family so completely that he talked to us with a candor which the head of the French mission would have hardly essayed at the time we were asked "to show the flag." His letter was quite peremptory; the kind that would have led our great post commander abroad to stiff language in further conviction that not all the hostile Indians were on the other side of the trenches. The reform in training upon which all authorities had agreed had been delayed in a manner that might prove very costly. Would Baker speed it up? He had the man for the purpose in March. Biddle, the former Chief of Staff, had held up the training plans of the expert Major General John F. Morrison, which were now put in effect. But, as Mr. Randolph well knew, not only had no army ever had enough men, but its recruits had never been well enough trained.

XXVII

AVIATION—THE RECKONING

ENEMY success in France, in the spring of 1918, pitched in a high key the stern chorus of inquiry from the Congress, the press, and the people. What had become of our seven-hundred-million-dollar aircraft program? Those clouds of planes that we had ordered and appropriated for—why weren't they driving the German planes to earth and bombing the Germans out of their trenches? All doubt as to what would be the subject of our great war scandal had been set at rest: it was aviation. As reflecting public agitation at its height, I quote one of the cable news bulletins from the office of March, the Chief of Staff, for the information of the A. E. F. on May 9, 1918: [1]

"Borglum made second scathing report expenditure near billion dollars has had small result due to colossal profiteering, calling for criminal investigation members aeroplane board. Says no proper judicial inquiry has been made. Attempt in Senate by Hitchcock to minimize work. Movement to start strict investigation. Aeronautical Society charges gross carelessness of Signal Corps; says Aircraft Board has abandoned hope large supplies aeroplanes for 1919; recruiting and training men for flying slowed down for this reason. Press generally calls for investigation, startled by hints of criminality."

I quote a succeeding bulletin of five days later, on May 14: [2]

"Country's indignation over aeroplane situation crystallizing into action. Opinion is divided. Three different investigations will be made. Attorney General ordered by President make one. Senate Military Committee decided conduct its own. House Military Committee examined officials who have carried out plan, and is satisfied Borglum's graft and inefficiency untrue. Squier asked for military inquiry. L. Snowden Marshall

ordered by President make official investigation to check up
Borglum. Neither report made public. Borglum's letters message to President published. Borglum responded with open
letter saying 'Charts of reconstruction of aviation organization
fill me with definite alarm.' He charges attempt by officials to
block investigation. President published letters denying Borglum given sweeping powers as official investigator."

And a third one, ten days later, May 24: [3]

"Appointment Hughes to Aero investigation regarded as
meeting same national desire non-partisan action. It shows
broad-mindedness of executive, says *Pittsburgh Post,* determination to allow no partisan consideration stand in the way of
drafting the competent. . . . We shall get at truth, is decision *Louisville Courier-Journal,* recalling Hughes' work in
other investigations."

I have already written of the backwardness of our civil aviation upon our entry into the War; of our lack of facilities for
manufacture; of how military secrecy had kept from us valuable information about the progress of aviation engines and
equipment on the European front; and how the revelation of
our lack of any modern planes had given Baker a convincing
argument, which won a comparatively liberal appropriation in
1916 from the Congress for aviation. In no branch of warfare
had we more to learn, and in none, except guns, were we so
ill prepared for rapid production as in this, the latest and most
rapidly changing. In none had controversy raged so actively
over the merits of types; in none had the adoption of a type
been followed so quickly by its rejection in practice. Upon our
entry into the War home factories set to work upon the Gnome
engine, but soon after the A. E. F.'s pioneer staff arrived in
France we had word that it had become obsolete; and all that
had been done was wasted. The A. E. F.'s own aviation
program contemplated 672 planes to every 100,000 rifles, nearly
double the 374 of the French and more than double the 294
of the British. We were to train 4,000 aviators a month. Where
were we to get the instructors? Training planes, hangars, avia-

tion fields must be built before we began making planes for the front.

However, Pershing's program, which represented more than his expectations, was modest compared with the request of M. Ribot, then Premier of France, that we send overseas two thousand planes a month in the first six months of 1918. At the time the French army's total of planes of all types was seventeen hundred; and I may mention incidentally that as late as July 30, 1918, the total air force of our Allies—who were close to the front and had had more than three years of war in which to develop production—was 5,288 airplanes and 764 balloons, while the total German air force was 3,309 planes and 194 balloons.

I have told how our people in the full tide of American imagination became so captivated by the possibilities of aviation and so sure of our capacity for rapid production that the Congress responded with an immense appropriation to carry out the colossal dream of the Ribot program. Since the fine tooling of European engines required so long a process by highly experienced and deft technical labor, we designed the Liberty motor with a promptness and under reported circumstances which further thrilled our national confidence. We must have mass-production; but standardized mass-production of machines was only in its early stages—an advance which had been much exploited in the making of automobiles, whose engines seemed to the layman to be much the same as airplane engines. Many rich purchasers of cars still preferred the foreign makes, before the accuracy of standardized machine-production had proved itself superior to that of hand-tooling; and it is worth repeating that one of our great automobile manufacturers, as late as early 1928, took more than a year to prepare his plant for the mass-production of a low-priced car.

The Aircraft Board had been created by the nation in sky-blue optimism to perform an industrial miracle. The Board gallantly essayed the task, under all the handicaps I have mentioned, in what was to be one of the most astounding chapters of the War. Our manufacturers were nearly ready to begin the production of the eight-cylinder Liberty on July 13, when, a month after Pershing's arrival in Paris, he called for a twelve-cylinder, which was more difficult of production and required that the manufacturers develop and build new machinery. Ten months later the experts of the A. E. F. were again asking for the production of the eight.[4]

Between September 4, 1917, and February 9, 1918, the Packard Company, in taking the new motor through its growing pains, made over a thousand changes, and the Ford Company, by March 21, 1918, nearly a thousand. Whereupon Ford wrote that the succession of changes "raises havoc with the morale of our sub-contractors," and "we are going to shut our eyes and produce as we stand equipped today." [5] Meanwhile, aside from the enormous calls of the A. E. F., the Allies had asked for their share of Liberties. Britain and Italy wanted more by the spring of 1918 than either had planes at the front; the Ordnance Department wanted one thousand for tanks, and the Navy seven thousand for heavy sea-planes.[6]

THE FOUR—THE NINE—THEN THE FOUR AGAIN

What type of plane were we to build to be driven by our engines? Our first plan was to reproduce the European models which the experts of the A. E. F. recommended. The Curtiss Company's draftsmen had completed their work, material had been collected, organization formed, and they were just beginning construction of the single-seater Spad day scouting and day bombing machine, when Colonel R. C. Bolling, of our technical mission abroad, sent word on November 8, 1918, from the A. E. F., that single-seaters had become obsolete. Colonel E. A. Deeds of the Aircraft Board suggested that we continue building Spad bodies here for engines to be installed in Europe, but Pershing answered on December 15, "United States should leave production single-seater fighter to Europe." The Curtiss Company had to cast aside the old model and prepare to produce the new.[7]

Colonel Rees of the British Mission had said in June, 1917, that the two-seater Haviland was the latest word in the day fighter and bomber. We planned to make eight thousand, supported by the recommendation of the Bolling Mission. It was four months from the time the type was accepted before a model was received in America. Then came the controversy between the Haviland-4 and the Haviland-9; the British found upon trying the four that it was not so good as the nine; we had better make the nine. While we waited for designs of the nine across three thousand miles of sea we went on with the four in order to achieve production of some kind of bombing plane.

The design of a new plane, which the Allies could have in the hands of their own makers instantly, must come by mail or messenger to America. The ship that bore a model might be sunk by a submarine. The Allies did not always have a model of the latest type to spare, or they delayed until a more improved one could be sent. The Aircraft Production Board waited for four months for a model of the Bristol plane after it had been recommended by the A. E. F. Then the British drawings which accompanied the plane were half in British measurements and half in metric, and the details about equipment were missing. When we had built a Bristol it was not up to expectations. Finally, after six million dollars had been spent preparing for its manufacture, we had to abandon it because it could not carry our twelve-cylinder Liberty engine.

Next in order were night bombing planes which, in our air dream, were to blast the Germans out of their trenches. Our little band of experts who had to learn so quickly all the European experience of three years, as they went from hangar to hangar abroad, were gleaning information from the experiments of the British with the Handley-Page and the French with the Letort, while the Italians had the Caproni and the Russians had the Sikorsky. No would-be purchaser of an automobile could ever have been more confused between the makes of cars in the early experimental stage of automobiling than were our Allies in the choice of night bombing planes. At first, the Caproni was not supposed to be in the running, but the Italians were enterprising enough to send a monster Caproni biplane and triplane to America. Their flight over Hampton

Roads in September, 1917, had been a sensation, making us still more air-minded.

After conflicting cables through the summer and fall of 1917 came the cable from the A. E. F. on November 10, "Advise concentrate your efforts on Caproni without regard to Handley-Page because not in position to send Handley-Page machine and preferable adopt one type night bomber."

The British, French, and Italians were each concentrating on one of their own national design, while we had been blown hither and thither by prolonged and contradictory advice in our professional search for perfectionism. On November 22 came another cable: "Recommend withhold further consideration of Caproni until we obtain complete drawings from Caproni or elsewhere designed for Liberty engine making substantial advance over Handley-Page." [8] Mass-production of a plane built for another type of engine involved its suitability to the Liberty engine of mass-production. Yet it was not in order to say aloud, "Why in the devil don't these fellows 'over there' settle on something and stick to it?"

Meanwhile, the Aircraft Board had set to work on the Handley-Page as soon as the British secret service released the plans. In mid-October, however, a new design arrived canceling the first. This was well under way when some three months later, at the end of December, 1917, it was canceled by the substitution of a third design.

Brigadier General Foulois, in the middle of February, 1918, sent over from the A. E. F. detailed instructions about equipment that meant further delay; for plane and engine itself were only the body that had to be clothed; a list of the equipment in detail would take a page of this book. From British experience we were learning that aluminum washers should replace steel; air pressure was being used for the gasoline system, and cables for the interplane bracings instead of streamline wires, and so on. Another change might come with the next mail or by cable the next day. The minute modifications for airplanes were peculiarly subject to garbling by cable. I will give an example that is before me in the files of cables sent to the A. E. F.: [9]

"For Air Service: With reference to your 404 paragraph 7: Your cable giving bombs required per plane seems enormously excessive to Allied Commission and experienced foreign fliers here. Urge you check against actual practice at the front. . . . For example confidential data aerial bombs brought back by House Commission and designs of planes verifies fact D. H.-4 only supposed to carry four 112-pound bombs or equal; N. H.-9 two 111 and one 230 or fourteen 20-pound; Handley-Page sixteen 111-pound: based on our plane program sent you, in order to follow your bomb requirements per plane type means probable change design, speed, and characteristics of D. H.-4 and D. H.-9 plane. Urge you cable immediately revised exact bomb requirements each type plane and base it on type of bomb we have developed and can produce, as described in detail, our 590."

MOST FICKLE AND MOST TECHNICAL

The first part of this cable is a reminder that in aviation, as in all other activities, the War Department was baffled by a confusion of advice from the Allied missions in Washington at the same time that the A. E. F was being baffled by its own and Allied experts; only the conflict in advice never ceased to be greater in aviation than any other branch. If the preceding cable proves hard reading for the average layman, it is simple compared with the following cable, which I quote, not as pastime reading but as a concrete documentary example of the difficulties of aviation production in the United States in 1917–18:

"For Air Service. At meeting of Inter-Allied Committee of Aircraft Production Board following resolution was passed and it was decided that representatives of Allies should each transmit it at once to their governments with request for immediate action. Begin. Production of acetone and similar substances is insufficient to meet the requirements of Allies for manufacture of explosives and also for manufacture of airplane dope. Resolved to ask Inter-Allied Committee in Paris to consider and if possible to recommend adoption of nitro-cellulose dopes such as (?) titanine. End. An immediate investigation at the front should be made of British battle planes using (?) only nitro-cellulose dope. Cormack states English battle planes use either nitrate (?) or acetate dopes indiscriminately, depending on supply available (?). An immediate cable is necessary so we can determine if titanine formula can be adopted for our battle planes. If not, United States cannot supply necessary quantity of acetone for English explosives. It must be clearly understood that total production of acetone in this country is barely sufficient to furnish English explosive requirements and none will be available before July 1st to make acetone dope if English requirements are met. Teeple (?) and Whitaker, greatest chemical experts in this country, are permanently on our staff investigating substitutes."

Acetone was the "dope" absolutely essential for coating the cloth which was then used in covering the wings of planes. Shortage in acetic, anhydride, and glacial acetic acids, cellulose acetate, acetate of lime, and methethyleketone might not mean much to the man who flew the plane, but were of vital importance if he was not to go aloft in what he would call a "flying coffin." With every plant in the world running full capacity to meet Allied needs against Germany, who was the mistress of chemical production before the War, American scientific industry labored to develop all manner of new sources of production: acetate of lime, for example, from the black liquor of our pulp mills, sawmill waste, cottonseed hulls, and blighted corn. If we were to have the three million gallons of castor oil for our mass-production of Liberty motors, there must be an enormously increased crop of castor beans. Castor-bean seeds had been rushed by a special ship from Bombay. We planted 100,000 acres in the United States and the West Indies. There must be also a standardized mineral lubricant, when there were twenty-two kinds in the market. Half a million dollars' worth of planes were ruined at Kelly Field for want of satisfactory oil in that pioneering period of aviation.

To the minds of the Allies, priority for material for their armies, which were already fighting while our own Army was forming, particularly applied to aircraft production, since our mass-production aircraft program might prove to be the most visionary of our projects. Until our entry into the War linen had been the only practicable covering for the wings of planes. It alone had sufficient lightness, strength, affinity for "dope," and resistance to tearing by bullets. We should need 1,500,000 yards of linen for 1917, 10,000,000 yards for 1918. The Russian supply had been cut off; there were strikes in Ireland, the other chief source, and such a shortage that the British government had taken over the whole supply for allocation to its own and Allied planes. Britain assigned us enough to start our program; and then, as the land that manufactures fine cotton, she sent us 40,000 yards of cotton substitute which we found would not do at all. Our useful Bureau of Standards had been working on a cotton substitute for a year; and Albert Tilt, an American textile expert, with all experts of the textile industry at his service, produced, after five months' experiment, a cotton fabric that was smooth, taut, and waterproof, and "took the dope" well. So we were no longer dependent on Irish linen.

THE I. W. W. AND AIRPLANE PROPELLERS

But in one essential material for airplanes in those days we had as much of a monopoly as the British had in linen. Spruce from the moist Cascade range of our Pacific Northwest was the only practicable wood for propellers. Soon after our entry into the War aviation experts from the Allied missions joined representatives of the lumber committee of the Council of National Defense which had gone to the Northwest to encourage production.

All but fourteen per cent of a giant tree remained where it fell; and then only four and one-half per cent proved to be of acceptable quality after sawing at the mill. The local lumber interests had enjoyed rich bounty as the Allied governments competed for their best timber at $2.50 a thousand feet. High days had come to the I. W. W., whose incentive to fomenting labor unrest was not related to war but sprang from hostility to Capital. The government supported the organization of the Loyal Legion of Loggers and Lumbermen as a corrective of the I. W. W. We built loggers' camps, laid spur tracks to the hitherto inaccessible mountain sides where we took the heart of the trees; and we built drying kilns and a mill that covered five acres. All this represented another drain on our material and energy.

Colonel Brice L. Disque, who was sent to report on the labor crisis, found the I. W. W. hampering production by "drawing water from boilers and then firing to white heat, placing emery powder in borings and cylinders," and "cutting fine spruce logs into short lengths." Disque recommended sending in troops. So we sent troops from Vancouver barracks until 14,000 were in this service, and the lumbermen's demand for an eight-hour day was recognized with the velvet touch of the glove that covered war's steel hand.

The Allies need no longer worry lest they might not get enough spruce for their own planes, and we found that we could use fir as well as spruce for the propellers. Special trains with priority bore the timber from the mills for fashioning in the East. In August, 1917, there were 200,000 feet of spruce cut, and in March, 1918, after the airplane scandal had started, we shipped nine million feet of spruce and three million of fir; and in April, when the airplane scandal was well under way, we shipped eleven million feet of spruce and five million of fir. The lumber production, which had been the chief cause of alarm, was, in spite of the I. W. W., a simple business compared with building the planes themselves.

Happily, the aviation experts did not decide, the day after the five-acre sawmill had been completed, that spruce had become obsolete for propellers, which hereafter must be made of some wood that grew in Kamchatka or two thousand miles up the Amazon; or that linen and cotton had become obsolete as a covering for airplane wings, which must hereafter be made of piña cloth from the Philippines or woven from Icelandic moss; which is not saying that, if our aviators were at a disadvantage in equipment compared with the Germans, they ought not to have the new material, or that the A. E. F. was entitled to expect a thousand propellers of the Amazonian wood to be cut, kiln-dried, shaped, and in France a week after the requisition was received.

THE SPOILED ACES OF FLIGHT

Next to the efforts of the friendly Indians to kidnap Pershing's battalions, and the birth-pangs and subsequent distempers of the S. O. S., the great post commander faced no problem more troublesome than aviation, which had the most invulnerable defense mechanism to excuse mistakes and vacillating policy of any branch of the service. Every whim of the ace flier was law to the ground force of the flying field, which had Milord's steed ready for him to mount before he rode forth to the tournament of the skies; and his bath and pleasant quarters awaiting him on his return. Yet by the third year of the War the flier had lost some of his glamour at the front. It had been found that the ability to fly was not uncommon; that there was no end of volunteers for aviation, though there seemed never to be enough common soldiers. Mortality among the fliers was not much higher than among the men who went over the top again and again. Aces had their names emblazoned in the communiqués, while the surviving officer of a veteran battalion which took its objective was not mentioned. Ascending, well-groomed and well-fed, to death in a plane seemed quite as pleasant as going over the top from filthy trenches, to be mashed up in No Man's Land among putrid corpses.

Pershing expressed the opinion of the men at the front as a whole in a cable of November 27, 1917: [10]

"For the reason that flying duty in aviation section is no more hazardous than duty with other combat troops, and involves nothing like the hardships endured by troops that occupy the trenches, repeal is recommended as early as possible of laws providing increased rank and pay for qualifications as Junior Military Aviators, Junior Military Aeronauts, and for any other increased pay for engaging in aerial flights. Such laws are productive of improper balance in rank and pay and result in injustice to other arms; and are no longer necessary in order to get personnel, as was the case when passed and aviation was in an experimental stage. General Foulois in full accord with recommendation."

The repeal of the law was immediately recommended by the War Department.[11] Pershing was never more scathing than in his comments on the aviation branch, especially on an inspection of its quarters in Paris. I recall the occasion when he had before him an aviation board—still another aviation board—which began a controversy over designs and policy in his presence.

"I did not bring you here to have you argue, but to tell me as experts what you want," he said. "You return to council and keep at it until you have a definite recommendation."

His attitude would have been appreciated by the Aircraft Board at home which was trying to keep up with the A. E. F.'s aerial changes of mind. In no war activity, however, would civilian interference with professional control have been so much criticized as in aviation. Pershing himself did not pretend to understand aviation technique. No major general did. Pershing favored the idea of a Regular superior in aviation, as in all other branches. His concern in this respect was early expressed in a cable, July 28, 1917, in which he said that he should like a Regular officer from home because he had military experience to replace Major R. C. Bolling, a lawyer who had been sent early to France as the head of our aviation commission because of knowledge and experience he had gained as a pioneer in aviation development.[12] (Later, Bolling, then a colonel, was killed in the first German offensive of 1918 while on a tour of inspection of the British front.) Pershing thought that Colonel William Mitchell would do well handling aviation instruction or in charge of tactical aviation later on. Another factor, incident to the novelty of aviation as late as 1918, was that no officer with enough rank for high aviation command was able to qualify as an aviator. The young fliers resented being under command of a man who himself did not know how to fly, no matter how much military experience he had had with infantry or artillery.

It was because of his association with aviation, his faith in it, and his distinction in the field of kindred technical knowledge, which had been recognized the world over, that Major General George O. Squier had been made army head of the great aviation program. At his service and that of the Aircraft Board were all the talent and manufacturing resources of the land, with plenty of money to spend. Having given them a free hand, the people dismissed the subject with no realization that they were attempting not only the improbable but the impossible.

It was one of the anomalies of the Senate Committee investigation of the War Department in December, 1917, and January, 1918, that it had paid little attention to the progress of the aircraft program in comparison with that of guns, rifles, clothing, and rolling kitchens. The enormous activities of the Aircraft Board received an amount of publicity that impressed the public imagination with the conviction that all was going well. Even when Coffin and Deeds said the aircraft program was two months behind schedule, there was no public criticism.

A SCULPTOR TURNS INVESTIGATOR

But Gutzon Borglum had already started on his secret personal investigation and was laying the powder train from Washington to factories and flying fields for a widespread explosion. Borglum, a sculptor, had none of the timidity of Baker, or Pershing, or the senators, in the presence of the aviation experts. It may be remembered that he entered this narrative just before our declaration of war in a letter to Baker in which he explained his ambition to perform another by no means small task, that of a mutual friend bringing the President and General Leonard Wood into harmony.

He had been very active in his interest in war, and it was through Baker that he received a note signed by the President. With this as his authority he appeared in the offices of the busy chiefs of aviation administration and aircraft production.

A note from the man who was not only Commander-in-Chief of the Army and Navy but also the nation's chief executive, then at the height of his prestige and having unprecedented personal power in world affairs, opened all doors to Borglum; and he assumed the rôle of an investigator who called for all manner of reports to be prepared for him. It was not for the aircraft people to ask: "Why a sculptor for this job?" There was the President's signature, and indeed Borglum's attitude implied that he had become the keeper of their reputations.

The first reference in Baker's files to Borglum's enterprise is in Baker's letter to the President, January 2, 1918, returning a letter which Borglum wrote to the President:

"Some of the statements made in Mr. Borglum's letter are difficult to accept. . . . And yet I never feel it safe to rely on any situation so long as there is one upright, responsible doubter. . . . I have attached to my own office here Mr. Stanley King, a capable, upright, and disinterested business man. Would it not be wise to have Mr. Borglum urged to come to Washington, talk freely with me, let me associate Mr. King with him, and give them an absolutely free hand to investigate every suggestion which Mr. Borglum can make, for the purpose of reporting directly to you, or to you through me, so that on the basis of such an immediate and thoroughgoing inquiry we can remedy what is wrong or set right any unjustified apprehensions?"

But Borglum was in no mood to have Stanley King associated with him. Meanwhile, Baker had passed the word that the Signal Corps and Aircraft Board need not turn their files over to a man who had no authority to ask for them. To make this a precedent might leave busy men with no time to spare from their work for interviews with personal investigators. On January 21 Baker wrote to the President: "Today I learn that Mr. Borglum has been seeing a large number of people, exhibiting to some of them, at least, the letter signed by you, and making seemingly irresponsible statements about the Aircraft Board and the aircraft program." Baker mentioned allegations brought to him that Borglum was looking for suitable men to

MANY APPEALS TO THE NATION

replace the present Aircraft Board and proposing to organize an aircraft production company; and suggested that the President ask Borglum to return the letter.

On February 1 Baker wrote to the President:

"I do not know what steps have been taken in the Borglum matter since you last spoke to me about it, at which time you told me you planned to write him a letter. I have heard that he has filed a report with you, but I have not seen a copy of it. As you know, Mr. Eugene Meyer, Jr., has been acting for me as liaison officer with the Aircraft Board. He has attended sessions of the Board, is familiarizing himself with its affairs, and his presence there is welcomed by the members of the Board.

"Would it not be wise to submit the Borglum report to Mr. Meyer for a critical analysis and, so soon as he shall have gone over it, assuring himself of the portions of it which do recount substantial things and separating out those which are merely speculations based upon insufficient or erroneous data, to have a meeting with Mr. Borglum at which Mr. Coffin, Mr. Meyer, and I could be present?"

WOULD SEIZE ALL FACTORIES

Borglum's report was sent to Baker by the President, and Baker called in General Squier and Mr. Meyer to go over it. Borglum had made most serious charges against Colonel Deeds of the Aircraft Board. Deeds had already been questioned by the Senate Committee on Military Affairs in its hearings, which had found his answers satisfactory. When he accepted a commission in the National Army he had made a report to Secretary Baker and the Aircraft Board detailing all his business connections and announcing his resignation from all interests which would be in any way related to aircraft production. Baker wrote to the President:

"Mr. Meyer points out that Mr. Borglum's report is really a repetition of much of the comment which has been going around in a more or less suppressed way about Colonel Deeds. A few days ago a New York *World* reporter came here with a skeleton of the same story. I turned him over at once to

General Squier, and he has written me that he went through all of the facts with General Squier and is satisfied that there is nothing in the story.

"In the meantime, in order not to take any chances in the case, I had the whole matter brought to the attention of the Inspector General of the Army with directions to follow the thing through, and leave no possibility unexamined.

"The villainy attributed to Deeds is too monumental to be believed, and I suspect that Mr. Borglum has no further information on that subject than the New York *World* reporter had, which turned out to be without substance. However, I concur in Mr. Meyer's recommendation that a thoroughgoing inquiry be made into the matter, and a record established, for the protection of both the Department and Colonel Deeds, and I am asking Mr. Meyer to undertake this inquiry.

"The last suggestion of Mr. Borglum—that the government seize all airplane factories, proceeding itself with the manufacturing of aircraft—would not, in Mr. Meyer's judgment or in mine, produce any better results than we are now getting."

Government control of manufactures had been wholly against the policy of the War Department and the War Industries Board, and the seizure of many thousands of private manufacturing establishments would hardly be in the same category as government control of the railroads. There ought to be more centralized direction of aircraft production for the same reason that Willard and Baruch had called for it in the War Industries Board; but this must wait upon the passage of the bill which Baker had drafted, and which when passed was to be known as the Overman Act. The purpose of the Overman Act, however, was to relieve industry of governmental influence and red tape.

Meanwhile, the A. E. F. waited for those American airplanes whose production had been subject to all the changes of specifications. If we were to have an American Army we must have American planes. The Italian disaster had heavily depleted Italian aircraft. The German offensive was coming. After the backing and filling about specifications and all the changes of equipment, this warning was cabled to the A. E. F. on January 26: "De Haviland-4 just barely in production. Schedule will fall below estimates previously given you." Back came the reply that as the French and Italians could not keep their contracts to supply us with battle planes we must hasten shipments from America.

Then the Aircraft Board gave orders to ship four De Haviland-4's from Dayton to France. Unhappily, only one was actually shipped, since the other three did not pass muster on their final trial. The Committee on Public Information issued a statement on the authority of the War Department that American battle planes were on the way to France. The press celebrated the announcement with front-page headlines, which were soon followed with larger headlines over an Associated Press dispatch from France, to which the censor was a party, saying that German planes were coming and going at will over the American lines. Naturally, people concluded that Pershing had allowed this to pass only as a desperate means of going outside official channels to reach home with the truth. The dispatch certainly stretched propagandist license. At the time it was sent, our aviators, flying French machines, seemed to be (according to my own frequent observations) holding their own on our front, and there were more Allied than German planes in the air along the whole front. Our staff at G. H. Q. had not been happy in reading the glowing accounts of our aviation program in the American press up to the very moment of the sudden turn of public emotion to doubt and then to disillusionment.

On February 28, just as Baker was sailing for France, Pershing sent this cable: [13]

"Newspaper clipping from United States received here to effect that United States has thousands of fliers in France and that thousands of American aeroplanes are flying above the American forces in Europe today. As a matter of fact there is not today a single American-made plane in Europe. In my opinion the result of such bombastic claims in the American press has had the effect of materially stiffening German production. Some sane statement might be given to the press at home to counteract these exaggerations. These statements are grossly exaggerated and are extremely detrimental to the future efficiency and expectations of the Air Service American Expeditionary Forces. Emphatically protest against newspaper publicity of this nature and urgently recommend drastic steps be taken to stop publication of such articles. One clipping in question is being returned by mail today. Suggest this matter be brought to the attention of Mr. Howard Coffin."

We had no censorship at home such as Pershing had in the A. E. F. Pershing's indignation, in his own labors to bring his experts to a definite program, was as natural as the interest of our own people to hear of battle action by our Army in Europe, and as natural as our aircraft chiefs' ambition at home to satisfy public expectations while they restrained any open expression of their irritation with all those changes of specifications from the A. E. F. As for "stiffening German production," this was just routine propaganda by the Intelligence Section. The Germans were producing all war material to the limit of their power, for a decision early in 1918, which was their only hope of victory.

FROM OPTIMISM TO SKEPTICISM

With criticism of results becoming widespread, and the insinuations of the whispering gallery more open, Chairman Coffin of the Aircraft Board called for a complete investigation. Benedict Crowell, acting Secretary of War, appointed L. Snowden Marshall, E. H. Wells, and Gavin McNab as an investigation committee, while Walter S. Gifford was to act in the same capacity in the Council of National Defense. The press stated that Congressmen were aghast over the apparent complete breakdown of our aviation program.

On March 21 and 22, Borglum put the match to his train of powder in two newspaper articles which charged all manner of inefficiency, corruption, and criminality. The Senate became a forum of indignation and of resolutions, in which aeronautical societies joined. To counter the attacks on the administration a zealous member of the Committee on Public

Information rushed out some pictures with captions showing battle planes which were completed; unfortunately, these were training and not battle planes—he did not know the difference between the two. His error was exploited through the land at the moment when the Germans threatened Amiens, Marshal Foch took command of the Allies, and Pershing put all he had—troops, guns, and also aviation—at Foch's disposition.

The "so-called Liberty motor," which had been the wonder product of our mechanical genius, was now also proclaimed by senators and in the press as a failure. W. A. Morgan, former vice-president of the Curtiss Company, declared it had been a mistake to give up the single-seater plane, and no member of the Aircraft Board or the Signal Corps, so well disciplined was their loyalty to the dominating idea of the infallibility of the A. E. F., mentioned that it had been abandoned on the recommendations of the A. E. F.

With the newspapers begging the members to relieve the public suspense, the Senate investigating committee hastened its findings, in which the majority report said that the aircraft program had been a "substantial failure," and the minority that America "might be justly proud of its achievements." This left the nation in no wise less discouraged or perplexed as the bulletins of the Germans' successes in their second offensive were arriving and Baker was on his way home to find awaiting him his most serious problem, the aircraft situation.

A NEW ART IN OUR COUNTRY

On Baker's desk was the report (April 12) of the Marshall-Wells-McNab committee appointed by Acting Secretary Crowell to ascertain the causes of delay in deliveries and the inherent faults of the organization. "A new art in our country. . . . Few men of any experience whatever in aviation or with any advanced scientific knowledge of the subject. . . . There fell upon this quite minor division [the Signal Corps] of the service a tremendous burden for which it was ill equipped. . . ." And in prevision for the future, which was to know such violent controversies on the subject, it was suggested that "eventually it will be desirable to make of the aircraft service a separate department entirely distinct from the Army and Navy."

For present purposes there were inherent faults in the organization calling for "prompt and decisive action." The remedy was that of one mind in place of many minds. As Gavin McNab put it in his comment appended to the report:

"The law is unworkable. It provides a deliberative advisory body without authority or executive power. . . . Deliberation has been out of proportion to production. There has been too much authority without ability, and too much ability without authority. It is difficult to translate thought into action and action into machinery, but this is impossible with executive authority paralyzed by large advisory councils."

The Committee recommended a civilian administrator of production who should be "of broad industrial experience, a business man accustomed to doing big things in a big way, and he should be clothed with absolutely dictatorial powers. . . . He should have control of the Equipment Division of the Signal Corps."

The law creating the Aircraft Board with its advisory functions had been passed by the Congress at a time of public and Congressional jealousy of centralization, and when the War Industries Board of civilians was under fire for assuming too much authority. This attitude had been particularly sensitive about aircraft, as I have already mentioned. No dollar-a-year man must meddle with the Signal Corps in its expert business.

To overcome the proven defect of the law, Baker again applied extra-legal executive action in a drafted plan of reorganization along the lines of the Marshall-Wells-McNab committee's recommendations. He sought the one man, and a man who had one mind. The Committee's report said:

"The administrator should have no connection or interest in any concern in any way connected with aviation or the production of airplanes; but he should not be limited in securing assistants from concerns so engaged. The reason for this latter provision is that the number of men available for this service is extremely limited, and practically all of them have connections with manufacturing concerns engaged in airplane work."

One captain of industry, John D. Ryan, President of the Anaconda Copper Company, certainly had no relation to airplane production. He had been on Baker's list of possible successors to Daniel Willard as Chairman of the War Industries Board. A certain interview had not lessened Baker's high opinion of him. On this occasion H. P. Davison and Ryan had gone to Baker with a plan for extension of the power of the Red Cross. Baker proceeded to show how completely the plan conflicted with sound policy. After leaving Baker's office Ryan remarked: "That's one of the worst lickings I ever had. I'll never go to a man again until I've mastered my subject." [14]

ONE MAN—ONE MIND—TAKES CHARGE

With Baker's recommendations before him, President Wilson announced on April 29 that Ryan would henceforth be in charge of all aircraft production and equipment. Major General William L. Kenly, who had just returned from France, would be head of the division of military aeronautics, which had charge of training and the military side of aircraft. Squier would give all his attention to the Signal Corps. There was no public or Congressional demur to this extra-legal action, which would have brought an outburst of condemnation of its imperialism a year ago. Thus the evolution of democracy toward war autocracy continued, speeded by the bad news from France. It was henceforth to be the President to Baker and Baker to Ryan in aviation. Baker said in his letter of April 28th to Eugene Meyer, Jr.:

"I had intended asking you to come in and talk with me both about the reorganization which has been effected, and about your own activities by reason of the reorganization; but, of course, your sensitive judgment has seen quickly the situation created. I think now that it would be better if Mr. Ryan were given a free hand, and direct avenues of information were established between that section and me; and so for the present I shall not ask you to interest yourself in the matter as you have been doing so helpfully in the past."

Coffin, father of industrial preparedness, and Squier, whose imagination had joined Coffin's in visualizing the mighty part aviation should play for America, and Colonel Deeds and Colonel Waldron, as has been so often the fate of pioneers, had to leave to their successor the realization of their dreams just as production in quantity was about to begin. If they had been war-wise, as Mr. Randolph could have told them, they would have chosen "Yes" jobs on our entry into the War. But they had put upon themselves the worst of impossible tasks in which they had to say "No" to the patriotic manufacturers of incubators, birdcages, and washing-machines, who thought that their plants were fitted to make airplane engines, and No to all the novel types of airplanes which included those propelled by suction and the versatile Borglum's.

Baker wrote to Bliss on April 29:

"I had known for some time that the importation of the advertising methods of American private business into a government department would lead to unfortunate disappointments of too florid expectations, but I confess I do not know how the American mind could have been sufficiently aroused to the need of great effort in aircraft by any other process. And while I regret that public expectation was whetted to too great a degree, I nevertheless think that the progress made in aircraft development has been remarkable, and the industrial facilities created for the quantity production of aircraft will, I am satisfied, in a short time produce a real result."

"NO MORE CHANGES—GO AHEAD!"

Ryan had the authority, to be confirmed by the Overman Act, which his predecessors lacked and could not achieve by executive action in council. He called the experts, foreign and American, together. They agreed that the Liberty motor, now being made in numbers and with quantity production in sight, was satisfactory. Then in Detroit, where the large majority of the factories were located, he summoned the makers and said: "No more changes. Go ahead!" [15]

Then Ryan inspected all the factories which had undertaken production, and weeded out the incapables. He paid tribute to the spade-work of his predecessors. The dissatisfaction, he found, had been largely caused by representations beyond the possibility of performance. "There has been no such delay with the work, nor anything like such incapacity of those in charge, as have been intimated in some of the criticisms of the accomplishments, or lack of them, in production." By doing it in a big way Ryan was not making a big task difficult.

"After Ryan took charge I had no more trouble about aircraft," Baker said.[16]

However, while Ryan was proceeding with full authority from the Secretary, Gutzon Borglum, on April 29, sounded the call for a criminal investigation, which was voiced in the Senate the next day. Those guilty of past errors must be brought to the bar. The Marshall-Wells-McNab committee had favored an investigation because of Borglum's grave charges, but thought they would not be sustained. "The impression that has been left in our minds of the personnel of government officials and contractors engaged in this work is that they are honest, patriotic, and zealous." The committee had no power to summon witnesses and produce papers. Baker wrote to the President on May 3:

"I feel that the situation is one of enough gravity to require prompt and adequate action. I have hesitated whether to advise having the whole matter placed in the hands of the Attorney General and investigated through a grand jury, or the formulation of a Court of Inquiry through War Department channels. I believe it would be possible to constitute such a Court so as to command public confidence, and it would have full power to summon witnesses and compel testimony, and upon the basis of its findings punishment could be made to follow by immediate court-martial of all persons found guilty of any offense, so far as such persons are connected with the Military Establishment; and civilians could then be brought before grand juries for indictment and punishment.

"I am having the Borglum reports to you carefully digested by a member of the Judge Advocate General's Corps, so as to extract in the form of a précis the sort of instructions which could be given to such a Court if one were assembled. I am anxious to seek the most convincing method of showing that the War Department is as anxious as anybody else to discover and punish wrong-doers."

The President decided in favor of an investigation by the Department of Justice in charge of Assistant Attorney General William D. Frierson. Baker, writing to Attorney General Gregory on May 7, turned over all reports and papers and the Judge Advocate General's digest.

"It may be that you will determine that the proper investigation of this subject requires the use of a body authorized by law to summon witnesses and compel testimony and the production of books and papers. Should you determine that you do desire to have such a body, the President is authorized under the Articles of War to create a Military Board, which can examine into all charges and accusations made with reference to any matter or thing in which the War Department is concerned, or any charge against any military officer or accusation against any civilian employee of the War Department in connection with his conduct regarding any matter concerning the War Department, and any accusation or charge against the Aircraft Board. Should the President appoint such a Board as this at the instance of the War Department, it might be thought that since a bureau of the War Department was itself under inquiry the tribunal would not be sufficiently detached to conform to the existing circumstances. It is within the power of the Secretary of War to commission civilians for military service, and I will be very glad to ask the President to commission any civilians whom you might desire and constitute them into such a Board so that you could have their services and at the same time have them clothed with the authority of the military law in the matter of the powers to summon witnesses and compel testimony."

On May 8 Baker wrote to the Attorney General:

"I am also placing in your hands a very extraordinary document in book form, being a confidential report to the Military Intelligence Section of the War College Division, which has just been brought to me, covering a variety of activities on the part of Mr. Borglum and containing, I believe, the contents in full of the so-called Mix papers. This I am sending in order that you or Mr. Frierson may have a complete view of the situation. Whether or not Mr. Borglum in these transactions was guilty of any sort of wrong-doing I do not undertake to judge, chiefly because that question is one of the issues involved in the inquiry which you are instituting, and secondly because, no matter how much wrong-doing Mr. Borglum may have been guilty of, the fundamental question is whether persons directly associated with the War Department and aircraft production have been guilty of wrong-doing, and I do not desire to have any sort of reflections upon the balance of good faith of Mr. Borglum to act as a shield for any other person whose conduct is open to criticism. In other words, whether Mr. Borglum is personally trustworthy or not makes no difference if the accusations which he makes are susceptible of any sort of proof."

Not even that other sculptor Michelangelo, who was also a statesman, had ever taken so sensational part in his country's affairs as Borglum. Never had a President written a letter of introduction which had been more liberally used. The Senate Committee was not satisfied to leave the affair to the Attorney General. Senator Chamberlain said the Senate would go on with its own investigation. The President published to the country sworn statements intimating that Borglum was seeking personal profit out of the aircraft situation and had stated he could do anything he wished with the President through his personal friendship. Borglum branded the President's statement as a "scurrilous frame-up." All this was interesting to the Allied missions and choice fare for the whispering gallery.

Then the President met the Senate objection to his Attorney General as an investigator by a dramatic stroke in asking

Charles E. Hughes to accept full power to co-operate with the Department of Justice. The former investigator of the insurance companies, former Governor of New York, former Justice of the United States Supreme Court, and Republican candidate for the Presidency against Wilson in the late Presidential election, and future Chief Justice, who had been modestly doing his bit with the draft boards, accepted this war duty. Even Senator Chamberlain was now willing to give up the senatorial investigation. Justice Hughes' report, on the basis of the examination of two hundred and eighty witnesses and seventeen hundred pages of testimony, did not appear until two weeks before the Armistice. In brief, Justice Hughes' conclusions were practically the same as those of the Marshall Committee.

Meanwhile, the country, being satisfied that Hughes would do justice, concluded not to bother further with water that had passed over the millwheel, and went on with the business of winning the War. More to the point in this respect than the investigation were the orders Baker had ready for the President to sign as soon as the Overman Act was passed on May twenty-first. This left Ryan's authority and Kenly's no longer based on executive extra-legality. On May 17 the Packard and the Lincoln companies had telegraphed to the President announcing "the completion and shipment of the first thousand Liberty engines." Since a plane occupied a great deal of cargo space and required very careful handling in shipment, Ryan had decided to concentrate on the manufacture of Liberties and on supplying material for the building and assembling of planes abroad.

MORE POWER IN FEWER HANDS

To enable us to do our own part better in saving the world from Kaiserism our democracy had to waive legislative rights which are the fundamental safeguard against autocracy. Compared with the European systems, in which a vote of no confidence by the national legislature brings an immediate change of government, our system may seem to be overloaded with checks and balances and to respond too deliberately to the popular will; but the position of the President in our system is such that the Overman Act, approved on May 20, 1918, could confer on him war-powers greater than those of Lloyd George or Clemenceau. Advocates of centralization through an agency similar to the British War Cabinet now saw it established in a single man. The Act, which would remain in force until six months after the end of the War, was brief for the very reason that it gave him such complete powers.

"The President is hereby authorized to make such redistribution of functions among executive agencies as he may deem necessary, including any functions, duties, and powers hitherto by law conferred upon any executive department, commission, bureau, agency, office, or officer, in such manner as in his judgment shall seem best fitted to carry out the purposes of this Act, and to this end is authorized to make such regulations and to issue such orders as he may deem necessary." (Orders, of course, for the most efficient prosecution of the War.)

Authority to change and transfer personnel was also granted to the President. At his complete disposal were all the war funds from the Liberty Loans and the heavy war taxes whose direct application was being felt by citizens at every turn. Thus had the Congress made the final concession—although a year earlier it had been still so jealous of its peace-time authority that it had taken three months to pass the first emergency appropriation bill, and in this had still held to the rule of appropriating specific sums for specific purposes. Those legislative warriors on the Hill, who had fought many battles with the Chief Executive, had created a dictatorship in the White House; and, to make sure there were no limitations, Section 6 stated that "all laws or parts of laws conflicting with the provisions of this Act are to the extent of such conflict suspended while this Act is in force."

That is, the Congress said, "Yours is now the power you asked for in order to win the War." But it added, "Yours is also the responsibility, for which you will be held accountable," as stated in these words in the Act itself: "which regulations and orders shall be in writing and shall be filed with the head of the department affected and constitute a public record." And finally, that "the authority by this Act granted shall be exercised only in matters relating to the conduct of the present war."

Here were the text and the guide for future Congressional investigations as to the way this present war had been conducted, whether honestly and efficiently for the good of the whole, or for political or other ulterior ends. On his part, the Secretary of War, who had had the draft bill ready for submittal to the War Congress, now had in writing the orders creating the aircraft autocracy ready for instant promulgation when the Overman Act should be signed.

Of all the chiefs whom the President as supreme chief delegated to act for him, the most important would be the so-called "dictator" over the heads of corporations large and small, over factories and plants employing workers by the thousands or by the tens, over all the industries which were making munitions and supplies, and over the production of the raw material from which these were fashioned. A year earlier our business men would have objected strongly if Bernard Baruch had been made Chairman of the War Industries Board, and especially if he had been given so much authority as he now received under the Overman Act. Baruch was the son of a distinguished Southern surgeon, whose treatise on gunshot wounds had become a textbook for the armies of the Confederacy. Creative industry classified him as a speculator. An ardent admirer of Woodrow Wilson, he had been one of the original Wilson men in Wilson's campaign for the Presidency.

When the Advisory Commission of the Council of National Defense was formed in the autumn of 1916, the President had made Baruch the head of the Committee on Raw Materials, a subject with which he had become familiar in the wide range of his brilliant financial career. Actual contact with him in the pioneer and formative period, and through the torrid heat of the Washington summer of 1917 and the blizzardous winter of congested traffic and unfilled orders, had revised his colleagues' opinions of him. "Barney was all right." He was as keen and single-minded in his country's business as he had been in making his fortune. Tall, personable, with his prematurely white hair, the man who "had met the best of them in the battle of Wall Street," had a flair, a facility, a resourcefulness in any situation, an unconquerable optimism, and a store of volatile and inexhaustible vitality which had survived the many casualties on the front line of industrial preparation and procurement.

He would say to volunteers who had suggestions for improving some part of the war industrial organization, "Look over what we are doing in that line and if you find that you can do it better, go ahead!" [1] Thus the volunteer either made a definite contribution, or went home realizing the difficulties of the problem instead of being disgruntled. Baruch's idea, as he put it, was not "to knock people but to get on with everybody so as to get the best out of them." When Daniel Willard resigned as chairman of the War Industries Board, and Baruch succeeded the "first citizen of America" (as Baruch called Willard), the time had come for a single front-seat driver in industrial procurement. Baruch was the personal choice of the President, who had implicit faith in "Doctor Facts," as the President called

him.[2] On his part, Baruch regarded the President as the greatest man in the world. Time had shown that Baruch had a certain advantage in being an outsider to all leaders of creative
industry, who might be unable to unite on a chief from their
own world. Other factors favored his appointment. He was a
close friend of McAdoo, the ruler of finance and the railroads,
which were so intimately connected with procurement. He had
ready access to the President, who trusted his judgment. In an
era of ample funds and office space, Baruch had what Willard
had sought in vain—power over the machine which Frank A.
Scott had assembled from such diverse parts in the chaotic early
days of the War. The new dictator was too wise to make any
radical changes. He had trained lieutenants in his associates.
His part was to develop better team-play and put more drive
into our industrial program. In the course of tightening the
organization he brought in, as head of the new division of Planning and Statistics, Dr. Edwin F. Gay, who had been doing
similar work for the Shipping Board and War Trade Board.

The national alarm, after the German drives, was drafting
not only more registrants to fill vacant places in cantonments,
but also men of prestige and experience, whose assignment
to key positions in war-work gave the people further assurance.
Charles M. Schwab had been made Director General of the
Emergency Fleet Corporation of which Charles Piez remained
the manager. We were fabricating steel ships in four great yards;
and Schwab knew steel and big business. Hurley had called in
P. A. S. Franklin, a practical shipping man.

THAT REDOUBTABLE MILITARY ADVISER

Now, for our home opposition to the team-mind of Hindenburg and Ludendorff on the Western front, we had one mind
in the War Industries, the War Trade, and Shipping Boards;
one mind in transportation, in aircraft production, in agricul-
tural production, in fuel and food administration—and that
very decisive mind of March in the Chief of Staff's office.

There was the March look—and the March grin. After the
look's probing rapier-thrust at the man before him came the de-

cision. Buts, ifs, and ands were not in March's vocabulary. The conventional amenities, which ease friction among men, did not occupy much of his time when the nation had a war on its hands. He would be harder on a Regular than on a reserve officer. The Regular ought to know better. His country had trained him for war; and he had no excuse if he did not either reach the enemy trenches or leave his body hanging on the barbed wire.

"Send him to the Philippines!" This was not just a threat from March. It immediately became an order, a vivid warning to any other weary man who nodded at his work. Mr. Randolph might well wonder how March would have got on with Stanton as Secretary of War; but there could be no doubt that the Chief of Staff kept things humming.

War Department gossip, as I have heard it retold, sometimes expressed curiosity as to how many tennis balls March burst in the early morning game which was his only relaxation and exercise in fortifying himself for his day at his desk, where anybody who he considered had real business with him would find him from eight until midnight—though callers, in face of the March look, never remained there overlong. Senators, who are accustomed to have official doors open at their approach, were met by an aide of the Chief of Staff, who asked them to explain their errands. Then they were turned over to someone in charge of personnel or whatever other subject they were interested in. They might well see in March the personification of the war devil to whom they had had to surrender constitutional powers and the privileges of senatorial tradition. Lest the Congressmen should lack information, March had a room fitted with charts and maps, where an officer, in the strict confidence of an "executive session," explained war plans and progress—which very often appeared in the newspapers the next day. March's strategic plan of identifying the author of the leak, if not agreeable to the victim, was entirely successful.

Baker seemed to understand both his chief at home and his chief in France; and in turn both learned to understand him, while, in common with General Scott, his first Chief of Staff, they sought to instruct him in true military principles. March himself, in a lecture to the War College afterward, spoke of "the education of a Secretary of War"; and Baker said from the same rostrum: [3]

"I learned . . . from General March that when the moment comes to strike, a vigor and intolerance of position that amounts to ruthlessness may be necessary. I used to say to General March that he wasted a substantial part of my time, and he would ask how; and I would tell him that I had to go around with a cruse of oil and a bandage to fix up the wounds which he had made. These seemed unnecessary in the day's work, and if I could abandon the oil and bandage, I could probably devote more time to my own job; but he would go out and make more wounds."

A college graduate before he went to West Point, thoroughly grounded in military history and principles, March seems to have learned from his training and his experience that the business of a soldier is to be a soldier to the limit when war comes, and that the supreme quality in a soldier should be decision. War was action, and procrastination an unforgivable failing. "Nine times out of ten," said Baruch, "his decisions were right." [4] This is a high percentage. Great executives regard five out of six or three out of four as a high average; and two out of three as enough for success. Other industrial leaders, I found, agreed with this view. Not only did March sink the spurs into the army steeds, but he was not loth to prick the industrial steeds who were not under his authority.

"He never let up on us," said Hurley of the Shipping Board.[5] Other industrial leaders with whom I have talked all agreed that March never failed to remind them that the nation should have no thought except to meet the calls of the A. E. F.

If Baker had not also been prompt in decisions March might have found the education of a Secretary of War still more troublesome. There was a No mightier even than March's: Baker's quiet No, which could be as final as a military "Goddam' it, No!"—and beyond that the No of the President, and beyond this the potential No of the people who had bestowed so much authority in few hands so as to have all the hateful war dictatorships over by hastening the end of the War. There was the Secretary's chuckle to match March's grin, and to match Pershing's stubborn earnestness in keeping to his furrow and his receptive smile to Allied statesmen and generals before he said he would think the matter over.

Be it a No or a Yes from the Secretary, its promptness was gratifying to March. Now he knew where he stood; that question was settled.

According to various interpretations of the March grin, it might be taken as appreciation of a joke; or an intimation that he saw through a suggestion and it did not wash; or the prospect pleased him, and so, "Go ahead"; or he was administering a dose of medicine—or taking one himself.

BUT THE SOLDIERS CONTINUED TO SING

Soon after March had become Chief of Staff he applied his usual incisive method of familiarizing himself with home organization and personnel in his first talk with Raymond Fosdick, who was at the head of all the arrangements for the entertainment and recreation of our soldiers from the Pacific Coast to the trenches. March wanted to know what the singing instruction in the camps and cantonments had to do with winning the War.[6] It happened that this point had been discussed by Baker on the occasion of the first National Community Song Day in Washington at a time when March was busy training our artillery in France.[7]

"I do not know whether history records it, but I imagine that the Song of Deborah was sung by the people of Israel until the days of the Maccabees, for it not only embodied the highest inspiration of the military and moral ideals of a great people, but it was the top pitch of their enthusiasm. . . . I remember that I once heard (these things come back like pages from a scrap-book) how some ancient king planned to send his army against an adversary, and in advance he sent an ambassador, or messenger; and the ambassador came back and said, 'Your Majesty, these people cannot be overcome. They sing as they fight!' Our Army in France will sing because of the helpfulness of song. There are emotions which find no other mode of expression. They will sing because their cause is just and they know it. They will sing because they are the sons of a free people."

Once the Chief of Staff understood that the instruction was designed to build up military morale, all doubt on the subject was cleared from his mind. There was comforting reassurance in the singular heartiness of "Hail! Hail! The Gang's All Here!" which I heard our men singing as they advanced along the Paris road to meet the Germans advancing from Château-Thierry.

Many Regular officers thought that it was a mistake to have so large a civil organization as that of Training Camp Activities co-operating with the Army without being directly subject to its discipline. Indeed, many of the leaders of the various welfare societies, who had found it so difficult to harmonize social and religious differences, concluded, in the light of their World War experience, that in any future war the Army had better take charge of all welfare work.

Sometimes March's system in drawing out a man displayed a certain teasing quality. This was in play now as he asked Fosdick why he did not take rank in the Army.

"How about making you a colonel?"

"No!"

"A brigadier general?"

"No!"

Of course the suggestion was not serious. March was rigidly opposed to placing eagles or stars on the shoulders of civilians, however worthy, in any such free-handed manner.

"In my work," Fosdick told the Chief of Staff, "I must frequently talk with privates, if I am to understand their feelings and needs; and they will be more approachable if I am not an officer."

March grinned. He had Fosdick placed: and Fosdick soon had March placed—admiring him for his outspokenness and his driving power in forwarding supplies for the welfare work in France, when the growth of our Army in France was out of proportion to huts, canteens, and other facilities.

In the late gatherings in the Secretary's office, after the day's work was over, March could be as pungent as Bliss, if not so philosophical. One night, all who were present took the regular intelligence test for soldiers. March passed with 100%, and Baker was not far behind him; though the others who did not do so well insisted that this was a poor method of judging real intelligence. In place of Ralph Hayes, who had gone to a training camp, Stanley King had become private secretary. King, a tall, thoroughbred New England type, had come with the early group of the dollar-a-year men. A lawyer and an employer of labor, he had a singular gift in dealing with labor. When he looked longshoremen, who were refusing to load ships for France, eye to eye, they responded to his personality as much as to his argument. He had been on various labor adjustment Commissions—Arsenal and Navy Yard, Cantonment, and Harness and Saddlery; and alternated with Dr. Ernest M. Hopkins (later President of Dartmouth), and Felix Frankfurter in the direction of the Industrial Relations branch of the War Department. These three, with Lippmann and John R. McLane, composed that group which in many cases managed to keep industrial peace in war industry where other labor boards failed. Baker had found King so invaluable as an industrial adviser that he wanted him in continual association in his office. King was ready to be private secretary, or errand boy, or doorman, if it would help win the War.

"But you had better inquire about my references first," said King. "You hardly know me."

"I have the word of six men I trust that you are the man for the job." [8]

Then King placed before Baker a list of all the companies in which he owned stock. Some of the companies had war contracts, and King said he would sell his shares in these if Baker thought best. Anyhow, there was the list on paper for the files, and he did not want to be consulted about anything in which the stocks might be affected.[9]

King became guardian watchdog of the outer office and of the Secretary's time. Even visitors who came from the home town of Cleveland might have to state their business, as did the daily quota who came over with notes or to repeat an oral reference to the War Department from private secretary Tumulty. King stood up to March.

"I see that you have been taking this order direct to the Secretary," March said to him once. "Don't you know that such things should come through me?"

"Nobody knows about it but the Secretary and you and me. Who is going to tell the Congress?" As he was not in uniform King could talk back in that way to the four stars on March's shoulders. When the issue was brought to Baker, and he said King was right, March grinned. That point was settled.

At night, after sixteen hours' mental strain, when they met in the relaxed mood of the circle around the Secretary's desk, in which rank and station were not so important as a good story, differences were forgotten; even promotions were almost forgotten.

PERSHING, MARCH, AND PROMOTIONS

Pershing had cabled on January 29, 1918: [10]

"We are caused embarrassment by fact that officers are being promoted in the United States to grades of captains and above and are then sent to France where they serve with officers of their own arm or corps of equal or greater experience who have failed to get promotion owing to the fact that they are in France. Policy here is to hold back on promotions, especially in higher grades for present."

On April 23 he wrote to Baker that failure to promote many of his subordinates had placed him in a trying position, and was proving very bad for morale. He complained that some colonels who were serving at home had received brigadierships although they were juniors to men who were doing good work in France.[11] He cabled on April 27: [12]

"It is urgently urged that the tasks before us make it imperative that promotions be just and fair, and that special cases of promotion of juniors be made only for exceptional efficiency with troops in active service here. It is observed that 25 brigadier generals were promoted and that only 17 recommendations were called for from here. Reference to promotion of brigadiers to rank of major general, consider General Traub the best brigade commander in this command and believe him superior to most of the present major generals. It is requested that the above views be brought to the attention of the Secretary of War without delay, and that confirmation be suspended until an additional list of deserving officers on duty here whose names were not considered for reasons stated can be submitted."

At the time Pershing sent this cable, about two-thirds of the Americans in army uniforms were in the United States; so the colonels at home were thinking that they were by no means receiving an unfair share of brigadierships. March, in answer to this cable, reminded Pershing who was Chief of Staff: [13]

"Your 954 has been shown the Secretary of War, who directs you be informed accordingly as follows: The American Expeditionary Force is only a part of the American Army and whatever promotions to the grade of major general and brigadier general are necessary will be made by him from the entire Army. You were directed to submit recommendations, as were other general officers. These instructions did not limit your recommendations in any way. Your recommendations are regarded as especially valuable as far as they are limited to the American Expeditionary Force, but the efficiency of senior officers at home is determined by what they accomplish here, based upon specific reports of inspectors and division commanders. The Secretary of War demands the utmost efficiency in his generals and is going to get it, regardless of rank and appointments. There will be no change in the nominations already sent to the Senate."

Later, Baker wrote this note underneath the copy of the foregoing cable that is in his files: "An excellent illustration of the way *not* to send a message. March's manners were not always considerate, but he did get results."

In a letter of May 13, Baker wrote to Pershing:

"Clearly, we must rely upon your judgment in promotion of men who are with the American Expeditionary Force, and in the nominations which were sent to the Senate our thought was to do so. But at the same time there is a very large number of officers here in the United States, many of whom are doing excellent work under the great handicap of being denied, for the present at least, the opportunity to go to Europe where of course all officers of spirit want to be. If we were to limit promotions to the men who are in France, and exclude those who are in this country, it would have a most damaging effect upon the spirit and hopes of the men here. I think there will be no difference of opinion among us in working out this policy, although of course it does have this apparently insuperable difficulty, namely, that we shall appoint some men to the rank of general officers here who will shortly thereafter be sent to you in France, and who when there will have rank greater than some of your own men; although if the two men had been before you for choice at the same time you might have preferred to have the man in France given the increased rank, rather than the one in the United States. I do not see how this can be avoided, but I hope its difficulties may be minimized."

To the Regulars promotion meant power, the reward of their profession, the proof that they were serving well. To those at home it was their only compensation for not being sent overseas. But the Regulars in France thought of themselves as at the front where the War would be won; they considered that honoring home soldiers at their expense was a poor way to encourage the martial spirit. The answer to that was that home morale also had to be kept up. What chance had Colonel Hines, who had become the one mind of our troop transport, or Major General David C. Shanks, who had built up the embarkation camps, of ever meeting the enemy in France? Because they and hundreds of others had become indispensable in home

SALVATION ARMY LASSIE
AT THE FRONT

POLICEWOMAN AND WOMAN
MAIL-WAGON DRIVER

GASSED

IN A DUG-OUT

organization, was this any proof that they could not lead a fighting unit capably? They had the bad luck. Were they to be marked by a further sacrifice?

The more officers we commissioned and the more colonels and generals we made, the more popular elevation became. Pershing, who had been jumped from major general to general without pausing on the intervening step of a lieutenant generalcy, said to one of his section chiefs one day: "How many colonels have I got to make to get this job done? Let me know, as I am in a hurry to have it finished." [14]

When the Regulars, the Guard, and the National Army were joined in the United States Army, the fever for promotions became epidemic among all the officers. Regulars were jealous of Regulars and of reserve officers who outranked them; and National Guardsmen wondered whether serving on the Mexican border had not been a handicap to advancement. Promotion meant good news for a proud wife, for parents, for members of your club. Reserve officers, who became misters again after the War, and did not want to be called captain or colonel then —and whose friends have forgotten whether they were privates, sergeants, lieutenants, or majors and remember only that they were in the War—saw the world as bright as the new metal tabs which they had just fastened on their shoulders. Now they knew they had made good, and all in their previous grade would have to salute them. Particularly radiant were the colonel who got his star and the brigadier general who had the additional star of a major general painted on his car. And it hurt to have to salute a fellow officer who formerly had been of your own rank.

But the dollar-a-year men had few worries about rank, unless they had taken commissions in the Army. Then they were as badly afflicted as the rest of us who were in uniform. Another bit of metal on their shoulders was not among the ambitions of all the ship-riveters, the powder-makers, and the women munition workers. Nor was it among the worries of the private soldiers, packed ten or eleven thousand strong on the *Leviathan,* or on other reconditioned German liners, or on British liners. It was enough for these khaki-clad tourists—the most popular we had ever sent abroad—that they would soon see France. They were man-power; infantry and machine-gun personnel for which all the Allied premiers, generals, and peoples were calling.

On May 11 Pershing reported to Baker that he now had eight of our big divisions complete in France.[15] The Secretary of War, who preferred to promise less rather than more than he could do, and who had said we should send over 120,000 men in the month of May, wrote to Bliss on May 31:

"We are finally beginning to feel some sense of confidence in the soundness with which our preparations are organized. The total number of American troops of all arms so far dispatched from America is 724,102. During the month of May alone we put on board transports 244,402 [double the number promised]. . . . Apparently with the assistance of British troop transports the question of getting the American army to France is soluble. . . . But the question of subsistence remains a serious concern. Roughly, we have estimated that to maintain an army of a million men in France will require the continuous employment of 2,500,000 deadweight tons of shipping, and we have at present in service only about 1,300,000 tons."

This was a compelling reason for our steel mills to hasten shapes to the yards, and for the riveters to set them in the hulls of ships, lest our Army in France go hungry. Meanwhile, we could rejoice that the submarine menace was rapidly subsiding. The sinkings of May, 1918, were only half of those of May, 1917. World construction had now overtaken world losses. But on May 31, when Baker wrote the letter, Paris seemed to be in danger; before the letter arrived, German soldiers might be billeted in the Tuileries. They had reached Château-Thierry in their third offensive; and against this offensive American troops were to have a part.

XXIX

TRIAL BY BATTLE

THE Commander-in-Chief's difficulties in forming an integral army were finally settled by the ancient and tried method of action, which is far simpler, more direct, and livelier than international negotiations. On May 28 the leash was slipped from the 1st, that pioneer Regular division so near to the heart of G. H. Q., which had favored it with choice officer personnel in its training.

Eight months, in which the Allies had suffered the Caporetto disaster and the first two German offensives on the Western front, had elapsed since Baker had written to Pershing on September 10, 1917, making a suggestion that might well be in order, so soon after our first contingent had arrived in France, to a Commander-in-Chief who belonged to that spirited branch of the service, the cavalry:

"I am especially concerned that our troops should not be engaged in actual fighting in France until they are there in such numbers and have made such thorough preparation that their first appearance will be encouraging both to their own morale and to the spirit of our people here. I think it goes without saying that the Germans will make a very special effort to strike swiftly and strongly against any part of the line which we undertake to defend, in order to be able to report to their people encouragingly about our participation and also with the object of discouraging our soldiers and our people as much as possible. I have no doubt this has all been present to your mind and I refer to it only because I want you to know that we will exercise all the patience necessary on this side and will not ask you to put your troops into action until in your own judgment both the time is opportune and the preparations are thoroughly adequate."

In this Baker was influenced by other reports confirming Pershing's cable on August 14, 1917, in which Pershing referred to confidential information he had received through the Russian intelligence service in Copenhagen.[1] Admiral von Tirpitz had set aside sixty-five submarines to attack American troop-ships and offered a reward of 200,000 marks to the commander of the first submarine who sank one. The German army, on its part, was said to be making a new shell-filler, prussic acid, for use against the Americans. "There have been other rumors to the effect that the Germans will try to affect the morale of our soldiers by employing new methods, as they did liquid fire and gas earlier in the War."

Incidentally, this was an illustration of the reputation the German army had established for its formidableness and its resourcefulness in surprises. But the Germans made no especially serious effort against us after our entry into the line in Lorraine, other than the usual trench raids, except in cases where our own activity stirred up reprisal, and in the local attack at Siècheprey. We had shown characteristic American ardor, endured the grilling vigil of the muddy Toul sector at the foot of Mont Sec, stirred up the Baccarat sector, met raids with raids in kind, all being as wearing on the nerves of restless young divisions as a general attack.

After the first German offensive was over, the 1st division had been transferred, as we know, to the battle area, where it was put in opposite Montdidier after the second German offensive had developed on the Flanders end of the British line. The 1st had now been ten months in France. The offensive that it was about to undertake was for a limited objective on a front too narrow for a break-through into open warfare. Its plan was made by the French staff, its conduct was under French guidance. Though it had the encouragement of all the prayers of the High Commands of both armies, after consulting all the oracles, the support of ample heavy artillery, and the presence of the Commander-in-Chief himself, yet our Staff, in this first venture, was apprehensive lest any details had been overlooked, as it pictured the effect on American, Allied, and German morale if the first American offensive should fail.

Pershing's canniness and thoroughness had their reward. In workmanlike manner, and with the aggressive spirit of the young army of the young nation in the presence of European veterans, it took the village of Cantigny. Our young officers and men who had come to France to fight showed how they could fight once they were off the leash. After all their careful schooling they were fast learning battle practice in battle action. Indeed, their conduct was as pleasant a surprise to some members of G. H. Q.'s training section, who thought it took three years to make an infantry soldier, as it was unpleasant to the Germans. In his cable to the War Department on June 1, Pershing said: [2]

"The 28th infantry under Colonel Hanson Ely made the attack supported by our artillery and several additional batteries of heavy guns specially sent to the sector for the purpose. . . . Our infantry reached its objective in schedule time and immediately organized its new position. . . . It was important in this first attack that we should succeed and that we should hold our ground, especially as the French had previously taken Cantigny twice and had each time been driven out by the Germans. Under my personal direction additional troops of the 18th and 26th were at once brought up to support the line. Five strong counter-attacks were made by the Germans, all of which were dissipated, leaving prisoners in our hands."

While his troops were learning fast in battle action, Pershing was learning what very excellent troops he had, although they had been trained for only nine months. Cantigny supplied him with a strong argument for his integral army. "This action illustrates the facility with which our officers and men learn, and emphasizes the importance of organizing our own Divisions and higher units as soon as circumstances permit. It is my firm conviction that our troops are the best in Europe and our staffs are the equals of any."

But the light of Cantigny in the news dispatches was obscured by the flashes of the guns of the third German offensive. This time Master Ludendorff had caught Master Foch napping, or Pétain or Pétain's subordinate napping, as you will. If Foch passes over this incident deftly in his memoirs he does not depart from the fashion of military reminiscences in encouraging his memory to fit facts to infallibility by the simple process of omission.

There had been considerable discussion at Foch's and the other headquarters and among the military representatives at the Supreme War Council as to the location of the third German drive. Nothing could be more thoroughly settled in the minds of Allied leaders than that one would come. For it was accepted that the offensive was still with the enemy.

THE GERMANS TAKE CHATEÂU-THIERRY

The second German drive, the battle of the Lys, had followed the first against Amiens within a week. The third had been long in the making, some five weeks, giving the Allies a breathing spell while the crowded transports were hurrying our man-power overseas. Haig thought the third would be in the Arras region, and once more against the British. Foch was inclined to the Montdidier-Noyon area, where our 1st was still in line at Cantigny, while the 2nd was on its way from the American sector in Lorraine to relieve the 1st.

The German battle-order expert at our G. H. Q., Major S. T. Hubbard, Jr., a reserve officer, had indeed, in studying the movements of German reserve divisions, penetrated the German designs weeks in advance of the actual attack, and repeated warnings were sent to Pétain's headquarters to look out for the Aisne sector. But what could a green American intelligence staff be expected to know about it? The warnings were unheeded. Foch was so convinced that the next offensive would not be east of Soissons that he sent battle-weary and depleted British divisions to hold a part of the Aisne line where, as he assured British G. H. Q., they would have rest "in a quiet

place on the Aisne." [3] So content was the French command of
that tranquil sector on the Aisne, which embraced the strategic
Chemin des Dames of bloody memory, that it had not made
airplane maps nor conducted trench raids for some weeks to
ascertain whether the German was storing any cards up his
sleeve on the other side of the line. Not until the evening of
May 27, a few hours before the avalanche was loosed, did the
French, through a captured prisoner, get any word of what was
impending, and then too late to summon any reserves of account in immediate support. Again Ludendorff had directed
painstaking German thoroughness to recovering the element of
surprise. His success was marvelous, even uncanny in modern
warfare. In spite of the many days that such a mobilization required, he had been able to gather for the attack forty divisions
and all their artillery, supply trains, and ammunition, without his enemy's knowledge.

Again the pins were moving on the maps of war offices and
on the pages of the morning papers. It seemed to be another
Caporetto, another "race to victory" in that third battle of the
Aisne. The Chemin des Dames was lost; and then Soissons,
which had been in French hands since the German retreat in
September, 1914. The French and the remnants of the weary
British could offer no resistance except on the Rheims flank.
Foch's reserves were far away in anticipation that the offensive
would come farther west. Gathering forty thousand prisoners,
four hundred guns, and supply depots on the way, the Germans
swept down the valley of the Vesle, over the river bluffs to the
banks of the Marne, and up the heights beyond Château-
Thierry on to a main road to Paris.

It was nothing less than a rout. Among the French soldiers
in disorganized retreat and along the lines of communication,
and among the people, I noted an attitude of nervous despair far
more ominous than their attitude when the German drive of
1914 was at full tide. Judging by the local impression, a little
more pressure from the enemy would bring the decision. My
conviction grew that it had been fortunate for the Allies that the
first two German offensives of 1918 had not been against the

French, who were now very near the breaking point which was to come to the German army August 8, 1918.

When the Germans had reached the Marne, our 2nd Division, which was on its way from Lorraine to relieve the 1st, was turned about and hurried by all available transportation toward the battle area. Up the road from Meaux to Château-Thierry, past the refugees with their household goods on their carts and leading their cows, past the detached French soldiers, came the Americans; and the sight of them brought from the hollow eyes of that disconsolate procession the deepest welcome that brave men can receive. My experience holds no more thrilling memory than that scene.

Facing the German line in the open fields and woods, one brigade of the 2nd deployed on the right side of the road and the other on the left. This brigade was to provide the second argument in simplifying negotiations for Pershing; but out of respect for chronology and in order to provide the background for its part and that of other American divisions, I shall consider now the effects of the third German offensive on Allied plans. It summoned the premiers again into the gravest council since that of Rapallo, just as the 2nd went into action across the Paris road and the green uniforms and heavy helmets of the Germans were nearer Paris than they had been since early September, 1914. Not only was the 2nd in position, but machine-gunners of our 3rd, a division which had been in France a bare two months, had been hurried through the tide of French refugees from its training area in the American sector in time to harry the Germans on the other side of the river and secure the bridgehead at Château-Thierry.

FOCH'S APPEAL TO PRESIDENT WILSON

In this crisis the Allied leaders had an advantage lacking in the crisis after the Caporetto disaster, in the Supreme War Council's established machinery for common action and in an actual generalissimo who had actual reserves at his command, including the two American divisions whose alacrity had been so consoling since they had been given the word. At the moment there were already 650,000 Americans arrived in France, not to mention the packed transports on the way; and, two weeks later, Pershing could report to the War Department seven hundred and thirteen thousand.

There was one subject on which all the Allied generals could always agree, and all generals of all time had ever agreed: the need of more troops. Upon this point all Allied premiers also could always agree, except the premiers of the countries who were to provide the reinforcements from a war-exhausted nation. Now, supported by Foch's recommendation, Premiers Lloyd George, Clemenceau, and Orlando, for Britain, France and Italy, appealed to President Wilson to send an American army overseas, which was then stated as three millions, but would have amounted to five millions.

"He [Foch] places the total American force required for this [ultimate victory] at no less than 100 divisions, and urges the continuous raising of fresh American levies, which in his opinion should not be less than 300,000 a month, with a view to establishing a total American force of 100 divisions at as early a date as this possibly can be done." [4]

After Cantigny and the 2nd's stand on the Paris road, Pershing's figure had great stature at this gathering, which wondered whether its next meeting might not be to the rear of Paris with the footsteps of German officers again resounding on the hardwood floors of the Palace of Versailles. Pershing was not now subject to pressure to put in his men as replacements among the French and British, but only to bear a hand to have America hurry on board the British and American transports all the men they could carry. His worries lest our troops who were with the British might be swallowed by the British army were at an end, when it was the capital of France, and not the Channel ports, which was being threatened by the third German offensive. Foch decided that our divisions, which had been arriving so rapidly behind the British line and had been given such intensive training, were available as divisions on the French front. On June 3, after Pershing attended the meeting of the Supreme War Council, he said in a cable in which he supported the call for 100 American divisions: [5]

"Consider military situation very grave. . . . Our 2nd Division entire is fighting north of Château-Thierry and has done exceedingly well. It is General Foch's plan to take the divisions from behind the British lines as needed and use them with French artillery in Lorraine to replace French divisions for the battle. . . . The attitude of the Supreme War Council since Saturday has been one of depression."

And in evidence of the change of attitude by the Allies on the subject of independent American divisions, this further paragraph in Pershing's cablegram is important:

"The utmost endeavor should be made to keep up a constant flow of personnel to the full capacity of tonnage, and I very strongly urge that divisions be organized as rapidly as possible and be sent over entire after July, and also that auxiliary troops of all kinds be shipped in due proportion. It should be most fully realized at home that the time has come for us to take up the brunt of the war, and that France and England are not going to be able to keep their armies at present strength very much longer."

He was also concerned that, on their part, the French and British should at once utilize their 1919 drafts, which "still lack a month or so of completing their training. . . . It might be wise to request the respective ambassadors to urge their governments to put in every available man to meet this crisis and hold until our troops can be felt." He had reports that our progress in artillery at home was very far behind, and "as it is unlikely that France will be able to do more than meet her own requirements from now on," he urged an access of home effort. This alarm might be warranted if future German offensives were to continue to capture Allied artillery at the rate they had been capturing it. On June 7 Pershing became apprehensive about Russia: "There seems to be real danger that Germany may recruit her man-power from Russian peasants,"

CABLE COMPANY:

Received at the War Department

Washington – June 4, 1918.

No. B 3 CO

From ....Paris......................................

8:22 A. ....M.

To............The Adjutant General,..................
....Washington.

Copies furnished as noted:

Number 1235.   Personal and confidential.

For the Chief of Staff and Secretary of War.

Paragraph 1.   Consider military situation very
grave. The French line gave way before what was thought to be
a secondary attack and the 8 divisions that occupied that front
have lost practically all their materiel and a large percentage
of their personnel, although actual number of men and guns are
yet unknown. The German advance seems to be stopped for the time
being. The railroads in the areas they have taken are not
available for their use principally because of the destruction of
the tunnel at Vauxaillon. As already reported, the infantry of
our third division is being used in Lorraine and the 5th along
the Marne. Our 2d division entire is fighting northeast of
Chateau-Thierry and has done exceedingly well. It is General
Foch's plan to take the divisions from behind the British attacking line as needed and use them with French artillery in Lorraine
to replace French divisions for the battle.

Paragraph 2. The attitude of the Supreme War
Council which has been in session since Saturday is one of
depression. The Prime Minister and General Foch appeal most
urgently for trained or even untrained men, and notwithstanding
my representations that the number of trained infantry in
United States would be practically exhausted by the middle of

CONFIDENTIAL

Form No. 685—A.G.O
Ed. May 14-18—10,000.

PERSHING'S GRAVE CABLEGRAM AFTER THE GERMANS HAD
TAKEN CHATEAU-THIERRY

he cabled, "unless Allied powers can counteract German influence." [6]

In a postscript to a letter on June 1 to Baker, for which the
courier waited, Bliss wrote: "I am just informed that the
French government is packing up papers preparing for possible
removal from Paris." Clemenceau, from the tribune of the
Chamber of Deputies on June 4, spoke his defiant "I fight in
front of Paris; I fight at Paris; I fight behind Paris"; and President Poincaré, who had once before evacuated Paris, became
stubborn in face of suggestions that he do so again.

PREPARING TO EVACUATE PARIS

On June 10 Pershing sent the following cable to the War
Department: [7]

"Since the last successful offensive by the Germans against
the French north of the Marne, the possibility of losing Paris
has become apparent, and has brought out many conjectures
as to its effect upon the French people. A few French officers
think that it would cause the fall of the present Ministry and
its replacement by a Ministry in favor of peace. I have discreetly discussed the subject with M. Clemenceau and General
Foch and presented to them unfortunate position in which
the Allies of France would find themselves in such eventuality.
Both gave strong assurances that French would continue to the
end. M. Clemenceau told me that this conclusion had been
reached between him and Mr. Lloyd George. A determined
effort will be made by the Allies to save Paris, but if it should
be lost the present French government and the military will
do everything to keep France in the War. In conclusion, the
consensus of French opinion, in which I concur, is that the
French people will hold the ideals for which the Allies are fighting above any temporary loss of territory, and that the country
will stand firmly by the coalition."

With our divisions now so widely scattered in France, the
prospect of such a disaster as the loss of Paris and a general
Allied retreat was one of the "very confidential" matters not
secretly cheering to the War Department. It would take us some

time to send the 100 divisions—or 5,000,000 men—to France, although we had still more than a million in our training camps and 10,000,000 draftees registered. That 100-division program, which will be taken up later as a separate subject, succeeded the integral army issue as Pershing's worry.

I continue on the present subject.

The next day, June 11, Pershing sent a cable in which he said that "a battalion of our forces attacked the southern half of the Bois de Belleau. . . . The attack was entirely successful in gaining the objective." [8] This requires that we transfer our attention back to the brigade on the left of the Paris road before Château-Thierry.

It happened that this battalion belonged to the Marine brigade, and the action to which Pershing refers had begun six days previously. Our army staff, with all appreciation of the Marines' superb spirit, considered that marine training for landing parties, policing occupied ports, and operating as forces of pacification in backward countries, had not fitted their officers in the same way as those of the Army for army operations. Granting the soundness of the hypothesis, an influential factor to be considered is that here was the hour and it was met by the man.

HARBORD THE MAN FOR THE HOUR

Textbooks dwell on the man and the occasion, but the greater proof of him is in making as well as meeting the occasion. The commander of the Marine Brigade was Brigadier General James G. Harbord, who had been a major upon our entry into the War and had served on Pershing's pioneer staff. He could do a prodigious amount of work without ever being busy. At fifty-one army routine had not dimmed his initiative or his ability to keep his hands off details and the main essentials in view. He was not afraid of making decisions; even on the most tempting occasions he refused to follow the ancient custom of passing the buck. Nor was he one of the "Goddamners" who had to pound his desk with his fist to emphasize his vigorous and manly nature.

With a square jaw and lips that could form as thin a line as Pershing's own, he had twinkling and friendly eyes reflecting a sense of humor and human tolerance which were most helpful in taking a young organization through its initial trials. He knew Regular politics and how to protect his Chief from staff intrigues. In Pershing's absence he would act for him with a confidence and promptness which Pershing found acceptable. Early in 1918 Pershing had granted his wish for a combat command.

Harbord had another valuable qualification either for staff work or in the field, which soldiers sometimes overlook: he wrote clear, cogent, and excellent English which never left any doubt of his meaning. If no stenographer were at hand, he could type off an order or a letter on the little folding typewriter which he carried with him to the front. The other brigade of the 2nd being on the other side of the road, Harbord had a separate command of one-half of one of our big divisions, which war experience had shown to be the best-sized unit for tactical direction as a division. In his support he had Pershing's faith in him, while Colonel Preston Brown, the Chief of Staff of the Division (under Major General Omar Bundy), was one of the most brilliant of the Leavenworth men.

This time the action was not under French guidance. The Germans were occupying a wood called Belleau. Attacking a wood meant the ugliest kind of work, as every veteran of the War well knew. The Marines had come to France to fight— just that—as had the Regular brigade on the other side of the road, and the men of every National Guard and National Army brigade. All would fight in the same spirit, although with a degree of skill that varied with their training and experience.

Harbord took the men at their word. He unleashed the hounds, when it would have been the conventional thing, the evident counsel of wisdom, to dig deep trenches on the defensive. He not only attacked with a battalion, as Pershing reported, but he kept on attacking, foxhole to foxhole, rifle against rifle, machine-gun against machine-gun, grenade against grenade, and bayonet against bayonet—losing foxholes and recovering them in that huggery-muggery among the tree trunks and brush and digging among the roots—but gaining, gaining, gaining.

We had proven ourselves eager in a catch-as-catch-can with German veterans. At a time when the Allies were gloomy over so dangerous a German victory, we had given proof that this war was our war in action. This carried more weight to our Allies in that crisis than all the talk about our war preparations or the hosts of soldiers we were sending across the Atlantic. Performance had taken the place of promise. British and French veterans, who were used to wood fighting, now accepted our soldiers as members in good standing in the Allied fraternity. But it is not necessary to quote from the universal Allied praise of the Belleau fighting; surely it will be recalled by all whose memories are old as the War. Legends quickly sprang up in the whispering galleries about how we fought like devils, like tigers, like red Indians, with our fists and naked to the waist, if unskilfully.

Hindenburg wrote about the third offensive and the American part: [9]

"Once more unexpected successes had filled us with fresh hopes and given us fresh objectives. . . . Now another factor was at work: the help of America. We had made the acquaintance of her first trained troops at Château-Thierry. They had attacked us there, and proved themselves clumsily but firmly led. They had taken our weak units by surprise, thanks to their numerical superiority."

Ludendorff said that we had attacked thinly held fronts in dense masses, and failed.[10] It is clear that neither Hindenburg nor Ludendorff relished the handwriting on the wall at Cantigny and Belleau Wood. And was the operation in the wood really unskilful, in the larger sense? The offensive again had its reward in more than the ground we gained. We took more prisoners than we lost, at the cost of fewer casualties than the enemy's. Beyond this, the effect upon our own people and the Allies resembled that of "Jackson standing like a stone wall" at Bull Run to the South, or Grant's "Unconditional Surren-

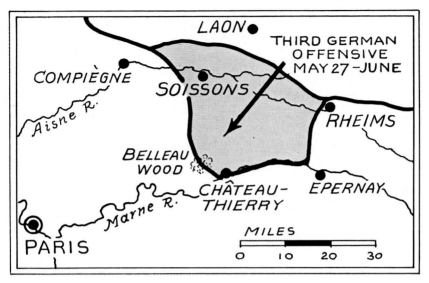

THE THIRD GERMAN OFFENSIVE

ON THE ROAD TO CHATEAU-THIERRY

der!" at Fort Donelson to the North. In these decisive spring months of 1918, the Allies, in their racial and national pride, wanted aid on the battle-line where national and individual fortunes were at stake. They might intrigue about the spoils once victory appeared in the offing; but their concern, when the house was on fire and burglars were on the grounds, was not whether the firemen and the policemen wore the buttons of the second or the third ward, just so they arrived on time.

Later, the brigade of the 2nd on the other side of the Paris road had its turn to show its mettle. A classic bit of Leavenworth planning by Colonels Brown, Upton, Conger, and Malone, which gave the Germans a complete surprise in a limited objective, took the village of Vaux and practically all the Germans in its cellars, with incredibly few casualties.

After these exhibitions by our Army, Allied military, political, and popular opinion was no longer seriously disputing the value of our own divisions under our own flag, if that was the best way to bring more American man-power to bear against the enemy.

We may now turn from the fighting overseas to affairs at home.

XXX

HEARTBREAKS

War is the mother of heartbreaks. No scientific planning of an army has ever been able to exclude them. In the World War they were so numerous that not even high rank always attracted attention to individual instances. Major General Leonard Wood, whose misfortune was so widely discussed, was not the only general who trained a division which he did not accompany to France; some division commanders had the worse misfortune of being sent home after they had reached the front.

The simple and easy method in a narrative of this kind is to give the name of the relieved commander as in command of a division one day and that of his successor the next day: "The 103rd Division (Smith) attacked Montmorency October 19," and then "The 103rd Division (Jones) again attacked Montmorency October 20." All that Smith himself may have known about the change is the order relieving him. His duty, in keeping with the Army code, is silence. As a soldier he obeys orders without asking their reason. Orders are presumably infallible. When he is relieved in the midst of action he must seal the cruel hurt deep in his heart. Yet, however exemplary his reticence, however uncomplaining his attitude, the officers and men of his division, who have seen their chief sent to the rear, are bound to indulge in gossip and conjectures, and these spread through the Army. In such a case, more than historical accuracy, fair play itself demands that all the documents available be examined.

Many of the men who trained divisions did greater service at home than they or their successors did in France. The greatness of the divisions lay in the divisions themselves. Many an officer, many a war leader, had given more and shown himself a stronger and abler man before prodigal effort wore him out, than did his successor who inherited the machine thus built.

No peace-time measure can foretell how officers will meet war's stern test. It finds weakness in the place of strength, and strength in place of weakness. It found a Grant in a clerk in a country store, a Stonewall Jackson in a professor at a military academy, a Hindenburg in an elderly retired general, a Napoleon in an out-at-the-heels artillery lieutenant, a Frederick the Great in a king's palace.

Six weeks after his arrival in France Pershing sent a cable, July 28, 1917,[1] saying that very few British and French division commanders were over forty-five or brigade commanders over forty. He wanted only general officers of physical and mental vigor sent overseas. Our division commanders, as the result of linear promotion in peace, were in the late fifties, and our brigadiers in the middle fifties. In his letter of September 10, 1917, Baker wrote to Pershing:

"In the matter of selecting corps and division commanders, I constantly feel that I ought to have your advice and judgment. You realize of course the difficulty of selecting division commanders out of our Army, made up as it is of very zealous and fine men but necessarily men who have had no experience in the sort of warfare now being waged, and few if any of them having even had the experience of actually commanding a division of troops in maneuvers. From all that you have said, supplemented by all I have learned elsewhere, the need for young and physically strong men is apparent, and I am perfectly willing to go any limit in meeting this requirement. It will of course necessitate passing over a substantial number of our older general officers who are very eager to go to France and who in their own idea and that of the country have certain right to be preferred. But their occupation here in the training of troops is, of course, a valuable contribution to the cause and, whenever I can feel sure in the selection of the younger man that he actually has the capacity to develop to a sufficient extent to justify his being preferred to a man of greater experience, I shall not hesitate. But most of these younger officers present problems of judgment and forecast, and your advice on the subject would be most helpful. At present I am planning to send practically all of the general officers to France for a visit to the front, so that they may come back to their training camps with actual knowledge of the conditions of present methods of warfare. After they have been to France, they are to call on me individually to report, and I hope in that way to have opportunity to make personal estimate of their vigor and alertness both of mind and body. In the meantime, you of course will see them all while they are in France, and I would be grateful if you would let me have an estimate of the impressions they make on you while they are actually at the scene of war and studying the conditions at the front."

OLD AND INACTIVE GENERALS

In a cablegram on November 10, 1917, Pershing repeated his previous view: [2]

"Earnestly request that only division commanders who have strong mental and physical vigor be sent here as observers. Division commanders who are in any way unable to stand continuous work actually in the trenches under conditions found on Western front are useless here. Consider it imposition on the Allies to send officers not fit in every particular. Of the major generals now in Europe following considered unfit: Clements, James Parker, Augustus P. Blocksom, John F. Morrison, William A. Mann, Hugh L. Scott, and probably Hunter Liggett of whom will report later. Their physical infirmities disqualify them to stand the cold, the discomfort, the continuous strain, and the nerve-racking bombardments. Recommend men mentioned be used at home and not assigned to fighting units."

Parker, Mann, and Blocksom would retire in a year. General Scott, who had been Chief of Staff before Bliss, and was in France on his return from Russia, was already retired. Pershing desired no generals of retiring age. In a letter to Baker on October 4, 1917, he included on his list of "unavailable" generals Swift, Plummer, Greene, Bartlett, J. Franklin Bell, who was an invalid, and Leonard Wood, who was physically unfit.

In a previous communication he had spoken of General Hunter Liggett as heavy and inactive, but he changed his mind about Liggett, whom he chose to organize the 1st Corps and afterwards to organize and direct the 1st Army, the highest command at Pershing's disposal.

In a prompt answer to Pershing's cables and letters, Baker clearly stated his attitude, which he did not change during the War. It rested with the Commander-in-Chief to refuse to receive any officer or to send home any officer he did not want. He had only to give the word and the War Department would issue the requisite orders. I quote Baker's cable, November 13: [3]

"Every effort will be made to send you suitable division commanders. In sending over those already gone it had been hoped they would be able to do the work until such time as the efficiency of the younger officers had been determined. You will be thoroughly supported in the relief of any officers that you care to relieve, and any recommendations made by you as to promotion or assignment will be given greatest weight. If you cannot make use of the officers behind the lines return them to the United States. Secretary of War desires particularly for you to understand that he will give full support to anything you may do or recommend in that regard."

Acting on this principle, Pershing cabled to the War Department on December 9 that he was going to relieve General William L. Sibert, Commander of the 1st Division, "in spite of his distinguished service in Panama" as an engineer.[4] "General Sibert is extremely deficient in those qualifications necessary for commander of troops in field." Pershing suggested that he be sent to command in Panama as "appropriate and not a reflection on him." Baker found other work of high importance for Sibert. He wrote to Bliss on May 31, 1918:

"We have made General Sibert Director of Gas, and are surrounding him with all the scattered agencies which heretofore have been at work on the offensive and defensive gas problems. He really seems to be the ideal man for this task. His scientific attainments give him the natural aptitude, and for some reason, fortunately, he has from the beginning taken a very deep interest in the use of gas, so that he has followed the progress of gas from the beginning of its use by the Germans."

Sibert was now working in an office in Washington. In command of a division during action he would have been out of the range of shell-fire at his wire center. In static warfare, where the men were simply facing the enemy, trench to trench across No Man's Land, he must obey a general order to visit the trenches twice a week; or he might go every day if he chose. Sibert was vigorous physically for his years and could have accomplished the trench inspection without losing his wind; but if, after having been trained as an engineer, he were more useful in making gas than in commanding a division, that was the service his country required of him in 1917–18. Yet his friends considered that he had been greatly wronged by the transfer, although he would not have been considered so if, in peace, he had been transferred to an engineering job for which he was better fitted than for the one he was doing.

Before Pershing's letter of October 4 was received, two of the men he mentioned in it as unavailable were already on their way overseas. Only a very rare passenger in peace-time had quite the distinction of a major general on a ship going to France in war-time. The following cable lists a most distinguished company: [5]

"Sailing of Division Commanders as follows: Commercial liners to Liverpool: Maj. Gen. Thomas N. Barry, Maj. Gen. Harry F. Hodges, and Maj. Gen. Henry C. Hodges, on *St. Paul,* Dec. 1st. Maj. Gen. Leonard Wood, Maj. Gen. Adelbert Cronkhite, and Maj. Gen. Charles J. Bailey, on *Adriatic,* Dec. 8th. Maj. Gen. Samuel D. Sturgis on *Manchuria,* Dec. 9th. On convoyed transports: Maj. Gen. J. Franklin Bell, Maj. Gen. Edward H. Plummer, Maj. Gen. Eben Swift, Maj. Gen. Henry T. Allen, Maj. Gen. Henry A. Greene, Maj. Gen. Harry C. Hale, on *George Washington,* Dec. 4th. Maj. Gen. Chase W. Kennedy and Maj. Gen. Joseph E. Kuhn on *Huron,* Dec. 4th. Maj. Gen. Francis H. French on *Covington,* Dec. 10th."

These commanders of divisions in training at home, who had served long and faithfully in the Regulars, were approaching the noon of their "day," when it was war that made their day. For wearing week on week they had been moulding the rookies into the force that was to gratify their soldierly ambition as they directed it in action. Since they would not be much under fire it was no reflection on their personal courage if they were relieved; but it meant professional humiliation that might embitter all their days.

Who was young and who was old among them was not to be judged by their ages. To apply the forty-year limit for brigade commanders would have excluded Harbord of Belleau Wood; to apply the forty-five-year limit for division commanders would have excluded Harbord and Major General Charles P. Summerall, who commanded our offensive of July 18, which turned the tide against the Germans. Hindenburg and Mackensen were close to threescore and ten. One man in the foregoing list, who was on the edge of sixty, received as high a tribute as Pershing could pay to a division commander; and others who were but slightly his juniors came through to the end with honor.

These did much better than most of those on the list of twelve younger men whom Pershing recommended by cable for promotion on November 27th, 1917: [6]

"Submit following for consideration as division commanders: Cameron, Langfitt, Holbrook, Buck, Muir, Duncan, Patrick, Menoher, Brewster, Lewis, Farnsworth, and Lassiter."

While the performance of certain ones of this group who received their promotions justified the highest expectations, others confirmed Pershing's remark in his letter of November 13 to Baker, that his impression of some of his fellow officers when they were young had not always been borne out now that they were older. For on this list were two whom he relieved with dramatic suddenness for incompetence, another whose shortcomings he realized in time, and another who was summoned before a medical board soon after he received his division. Yet another, whom Pershing later described in a separate cable as "the best brigade commander" in his command, proved to be a disappointment in command of a division.

Picking the right division commanders was even more difficult than picking the right chiefs for committees on the War Industries Board or the right chiefs for army bureaus and staff divisions in Washington. There was some reason in the policy of holding on to the tried old men until more efficient chiefs had been developed among the younger men.

"You must remember that he is an old man but a wise one," said Baker in the spring of 1917, "and we must help him along until we find a better." [7]

"He is a fine old officer," said Pershing in the spring of 1918, "and I must make him do for the present. If you think he can't see the forest for the trees, you ought to meet some of my narrow-minded ones." [8]

Regular to Regular, it was an awkward situation to overcome when promotions put an officer over his senior in the regular service—far more awkward than lifting number three over the head of number two to be number one in civil life, where number two might ease his disappointment by obtaining a job with another firm. On that list of major-general passengers were Wood, Bell, and Barry, who were all seniors to Pershing on the regular list; and in common with Pershing, as the result of service in the Philippines or the Spanish War, had been promoted over the heads of many seniors in order to put younger men in high positions in the Army.

THE PROBLEM OF LEONARD WOOD

Respected as they were in the service, Bell and Barry were not well known to the general public, being overshadowed by the fame of Wood, who had been the ranking major general for ten years. Wood was a brilliant speaker and spoke often. As you listened to one of his speeches it seemed a masterpiece of reasoning and appeal, but on analyzing the residue, in dissociation from his magnetism, it might prove disappointing. I sometimes wondered that one with his talents had not resigned from the Army and sought a political career in which he would not have been subject to the hierarchy of accident and linear promotion in the military service. In common with many public men he was unconscious of how freely he used his abundant gifts in winning support to gain his ends. His hostility to President Wilson was not concealed in his conversations. As one who knew him I might make allowances for Wood's "talking." But when, before a number of people, some strangers to him, he called President Wilson a rabbit, it was certain that this characterization by the senior major general of the Army would be carried to his Commander-in-Chief, the President of the United States, who might regard it as hardly in keeping with the code of Army conduct. Wood wrote "personal letters" in which he criticized the President very freely, and some of these were shown to the President.

I had several conversations with him in the winter of 1915–16, when I was home from the British front, and it seemed to me that the defects of his qualities had grown upon him.

An outcry rose from his legion of friends and admirers when he was sent to command the Southeastern Department at Charleston upon our entry into the War; and again when he was "exiled" from the Eastern seaboard to command the new 89th National Army Division at Camp Funston, Kansas. Yet there was supposed to be no better soldier material than the men of the Middle Western States, which had the highest average of draft men who passed the physical examination.

No sooner was he in London than reports were coming to Washington that he was talking very freely; one from Bliss in a letter to Baker; [9] another from our Embassy in London to the State Department. Singled out by his distinction at home he received much attention from Lloyd George, members of the War Cabinet, and those high in the British Staff, in the period of alarm over the coming German offensive, of Allied complaints at Pershing's procrastination, and of the resistance to Sir William Robertson's plan to use our man-power as replacements for the British army. Wood's lack of faith in our war administration was being expressed abroad at the time of the Congressional investigation at home and of the crisis in shipping and in traffic, when the railroads were snowbound. The British found confirmation of their fears in his statement that we could never be depended upon to have an effective force in France. All these repercussions I heard personally as I passed through London, returning to France from a mission in the United States. The only answer to make was that Wood was "talking," and that we had more than a million men in our training camps awaiting transport to France.

A BRITTLE MEETING BETWEEN PERSHING AND WOOD

British statesmen were asking why our ablest soldier was not being "used"; he ought to be kept abroad with our Army. In Paris he attracted almost as much attention as in London, and more than all the other touring American major generals together. At a time when there was so little news from the A. E. F., headlines at home flashed the word that Wood had already been in action in France and been wounded. What had actually happened was that while visiting a French school of automatic arms he was struck by a fragment of a mortar that was shattered by a premature detonation. He was the object of much sympathy at home at the same time that Senator Medill McCormick reported that Lloyd George had asked him that Wood be kept in France.

Since Pershing chose his officers, the power to retain Wood rested with Pershing. At Chaumont, the American Headquarters, the senior major general, with two stars on his shoulders, was ingratiating to his senior of the National Army, for whom the rank of general with four stars had been revived. Wood said to Pershing that he would tell the War Department it was treating him badly and should give him better support. To this Pershing replied vigorously that Wood would do nothing of the kind, and that the Commander-in-Chief in France could look after his own troubles.[10] Chiefs of Staff sections at Chaumont told me that Barry and Bell listened raptly to their lectures on the latest tactics at the front, but that Wood was inclined "to tell us instead of being told."

Wood, according to his biographer, wanted to accept a pressing invitation from the Italian High Command to visit Italy, but Baker's letter to the President on February 26 suggests that the invitation came at Wood's request:

"I enclose copies of two cablegrams received from General Bliss. The shorter one, you will observe, shows that the Italian Supreme Command based its request on General Wood's expressed desires. I have directed General Biddle to notify General Pershing that we have been informed of the statement of the Italian Supreme Command with regard to General Wood, but believe it important for him to return to this country as the other generals have done who have been sent to inspect the Western front; and therefore to make no change in his orders, which are for his immediate return to this country."

Wood also asked Pershing to be allowed to return to the United States by way of London, where he wanted to see St. Loe Strachey, editor of *The Spectator,* Sir Arthur Lee, his friend of Spanish War days, and Lloyd George.[11] Pershing ordered him home on the same ship with Bell from Bordeaux.

The reporters and his friends were on the lookout for Wood when he arrived in New York at the dramatic moment when the first German offensive was in the full tide of its threatening daily advance. A summons awaited him to appear before the Senate Military Affairs Committee in Washington, where the whispering gallery rejoiced in the prospect of hearing the truth from the man whom our Allies recognized as our ablest general and who was being wasted in this terrible crisis.

Wood appeared before the Senate Committee and turned the guns of his censure on the War Department. He presented disheartening pictures of the inadequacy of our preparations and the condition of our Army in France. We ought to have two million and a half men in training at home and two million and a half in France at once. As we had accommodations to train only a million and a half at home, and as he had complained of the quarters for them at Camp Funston and the lack of equipment, we should have to build accommodations for a million more as a further drain on our industrial resources as well as remove another million in man-power from industrial service. He did not raise his voice for man-power to build ships to transport the men we had ready to go to France. His criticism hardly encouraged the Allies to think we would build ships and be effective in France. He might have said in heartening our Allies in the crisis: "We have piled mistake on mistake, but the American people are aroused. This is their war now, and mismanagement cannot prevent them from bringing the full weight of their power to bear against the enemy."

To the War Department his attitude did not seem helpful at a period when the Overman Act, so greatly needed to remedy the weaknesses of war organization, awaited the approval of the Congress. Perhaps the senior major general of the Regular Army, who was out of favor at the White House, had succumbed to the failing of many other leaders by confusing the personal equation with the fortunes of the World War. Upon his return to his division, from which he had been absent for three months, he found how completely industrial America had equipped it and how rapidly intensive training turned American youth into seemly soldiers, which must have been a compensation to the division commander for his misfortunes.

HOW WOOD WAS DETACHED FROM HIS DIVISION

Even people who thought that Wood must accept the fate of his situation as the penalty for his opposition to the administration were aroused to indignation when he was relieved of the command of his division just as it was about to sail for France. It appeared as if he had been snatched off his transport.

While the pictures of nineteenth-century warfare give the impression that the general rode along the dusty road at the head of his troops so that he could have a good start in leading them in a charge, the modern custom for a commander of a division, which is larger than many of the famous armies of

WAR WORK AT HOME

WAR WORK AT THE FRONT

old, is not to precede his division to its destination when it is ordered to move. If he did, the man who is the head of the division would be away from the nerve-center upon which he depends for information by telephone and telegraph. Even behind the battle-front in France the rule prevailed that division headquarters waited until the first brigade was on the way.

Upon receiving word that his division was to start for France, Wood left entrainment to his second-in-command and went on to New York, the port of embarkation. Had he remained a day longer with his division he would have been there to receive the order "to remain at Camp Funston until the departure of the last unit of the 89th Division, when you will proceed to San Francisco, Cal., and assume command of the Western Department."

On June 6 Baker said in a letter to Pershing:

"Some three or four weeks ago General March and I in conference decided that General Wood should be detached from his division, as the time had about arrived for the 89th to sail. General March held the order up for a few days, and in the meantime the order went out to the 89th to entrain for Camp Merritt. At once, on receipt of the order, General Wood and his staff left for Camp Merritt, leaving his division to follow him. As soon as General March discovered that, he issued the order detaching General Wood. This was unfortunate, because it gave the appearance of our having practically waited until General Wood was ready to board his ship before making the order. As a matter of fact, however, his division will not all be entrained from Kansas until the ninth of the present month, and his speedy departure for Camp Merritt was hardly justified. As soon as the order was issued General Wood came to Washington and sought an interview with me. I of course saw him and he asked me to change the order."

Accepting the criticism that the War Department did not want to prolong the uproar that was bound to follow Wood's relief from his division does not imply that it delayed the order until he was at the transport's gangway to humiliate him. But Wood's friends saw this as the administration's revenge on him. They took it for granted that it was Baker rather than Pershing who did not want him in France. They denounced the report that Pershing had refused to have Wood as an attempt to pass the buck to Pershing. When the newspaper men questioned Baker, he refused to discuss the subject.[12] What was a Secretary of War for? To receive the buck. Wood, as he waited to see the Secretary, is described as pacing stormily up and down the corridor opposite the Secretary's office, which had known so many army heartbreaks, saying that he knew Pershing wanted him, and he would demand fair play.[13] Wood took Colonel Kilbourne into Baker's office as a witness to the interview, but left his aide outside, saying, according to Wood's biographer; "We had better not all go in. He will think we have come to kill him." [14]

Baker refused to change the order, and finally, in answer to Wood's pressing the question, replied that Pershing did not want him in France. Wood then went into the office of Major General W. S. Graves, Assistant Chief of Staff, an old friend, and sank down in a chair, appearing "utterly crushed." He doubted Baker's statement that Pershing did not want him; and he proposed to see Senator Warren, Pershing's father-in-law, and learn the truth about it. In reply to Wood's request for two or three days in Washington, Graves told him that he might have all the time he wished.[15]

WHY PERSHING DID NOT WANT WOOD

While Wood was in France Pershing had again definitely informed the War Department that he did not want Wood in the A. E. F. Pershing enclosed two envelopes in a letter written February 24, 1918, which he hoped would reach Baker before his departure for France. The memorandum in Envelope A included a list of generals whom Pershing found "unavailable" as division commanders. Since Wood had been originally an officer of the Medical Corps, Pershing thought that in relation to field command he should be considered in the same class as engineer officers. The contents of the second envelope, B, related exclusively to Wood. This is similar in substance and

tone to a letter to himself which General March published in
an article.[16] Pershing did not give me permission to use any
parts of his letters verbatim. (Happily for history's sake, Baker
granted to Pershing the free use of his personal letters for the
General's own invaluable individual narrative of the A. E. F.
by its Commander-in-Chief.) However, the usual custom of
paraphrase seems in order for Memorandum B, since the letter
to General March has been published and extenuating circumstances should be mentioned. It must be remembered that
both letters were written in the darkest hour of the A. E. F.'s
"Valley Forge," when Pershing had to look after such a mul-
titude of affairs and when troop movements were at a low ebb
from winter storms. The first German offensive was daily expected and many reports of Wood's critical attitude toward the
direction of the A. E. F. were reaching the ears of the
Commander-in-Chief.

Pershing reported that Wood had talked against the administration in Washington; his attitude was generally disloyal; he had created a bad impression of our high officers
among the Allies; was ambitious for notoriety; dragged his leg
in a more or less helpless manner; had spent little time in the
trenches; and that the new medical board which Baker had
appointed to examine general officers would find him incapacitated for active service. Pershing also mentioned that Wood
had just telephoned from Paris that Captain La Guardia of
the Signal Corps, a member of the Congress from New York,
and the Italian High Command had asked him to go to Italy,
but as he had visited all the other fronts, and had been so
long away from his division, Pershing had ordered him home.

The medical board in Washington, upon Wood's return,
found him physically fit. However, a medical board was not
expected to consider whether or not he would form a personal
faction to the embarrassment of Pershing in France, or whether
the Commander-in-Chief of the A. E. F. should receive subordinates whose loyalty he so evidently distrusted. Pershing
said personally that if Wood had been sent to France he would
have sent him back.[17]

Since Lincoln's relief of McClellan from the command of the Army of the Potomac did not arouse more controversy than the relief of Wood from command of the 89th Division, it is worth while to quote further Baker's letter of June 6, 1918, to Pershing, who did not include the passage in his memoirs, or indeed any reference to his attitude toward Wood. Baker wrote:

"I told him that I had sent all the Division Commanders over to France in order that they might inspect the modern method of war and in order that you might determine which of them could be most useful to you; that you had made me a list of the general officers whom you desired to have return and that his name was not on that list. He expressed some surprise at that, saying that Colonel McCoy had told him that you were very anxious to have General Wood for service under you. I told him I had not talked with Colonel McCoy on the subject and knew nothing of any such conversation. I then said to him: 'Frankness compels me to say, General Wood, that without at all discussing any reasons General Pershing may have for not including you in the list, if I were in his place I would come to the same conclusion upon very definite grounds of my own.' He asked me what those grounds were, and I said, 'Because it is very difficult, if not impossible, for you to be subordinate.' He asked me what I meant by that, and I told him that he had been my subordinate for two years and had been my most insubordinate subordinate. We had some further discussion of that, and he made some more or less irrelevant references to things about which I did not choose to inquire, and he then asked me whether he could see the President. I told him the President was his Commander-in-Chief and that I had no right to interfere in any way with such an interview, and that I would ask the President whether he cared to see General Wood. The President fixed a time when he would see him and spent half an hour with him, in which the subject of orders was not discussed beyond very earnest protestations of loyalty and good-will made by General Wood, and very earnest denials of all newspaper accounts of political activities and other unfriendly words on his part toward the President were entered. The President made no promises, and in that situation General Wood left Washington to return to Camp Funston to see the rest of his division entrain, and he is now there. I was greatly surprised to receive, yesterday, a letter from him, of which I enclose a copy, and I enclose a copy of my answer."

Now I interrupt this letter with a cable which Baker sent to Pershing on May 31:

"I am strongly inclined to think that it would be wise to let him [Wood] go to Italy when our first contingent of troops go there; but would prefer to have him secure this assignment on your recommendation rather than by my personal choice; so that I could tell him of your recommendation at the time I notify him of his selection. My idea would be to have him while in Italy a part of your general European command. Of course, he will not be sent to Italy or to France without your approval."

I continue with the part of Baker's letter which refers to Wood's desire to command our contingent in Italy:

"After General Wood had seen the President, the President asked me casually whether I thought any harm would be done by sending General Wood to Italy. I told him that it was obviously necessary to make any Italian contingent of our Army a part of your general command and that I was not willing to send General Wood there unless you wanted him; that if he was to go there I preferred to have him go on your recommendation, so that I could send for him and tell him that he went by your request; and that he would stay just as long as you wanted to keep him and not a minute longer. If you decide to use him in Italy I will tell him in very plain language that I have acquainted you with this Barry correspondence, and that his remaining in Europe will depend entirely upon your judgment; and that if you send him home I will not raise the slightest question as to the propriety of your doing so, or permit him to raise it."

But Pershing refused to have Wood in Italy.
Bell and Barry were both Pershing's seniors and had been

included in Pershing's list of "unavailables" in Envelope A. Pershing spoke of Bell's aggressiveness and loyalty, but his age and health were against him; and Pershing thought that Barry, although still vigorous, was too near retiring age and too far along in years to learn how to handle troops or to endure the strain at the front for any length of time. Both Bell and Barry, after their return from their tour of the A. E. F., passed the physical examination for general officers conducted by the medical board appointed for the purpose.

Naturally, when Bell and Barry were on their tour in France, a junior major general of Regulars did not like to tell these two seniors something that would break their hearts. It might be that the medical board would find Bell, at least, unfit; and it would be time enough for them to know the cruel truth when they received the orders from the War Department relieving them. Wood, however, forewarned both Barry and Bell that they were to share his fate.

THE CASES OF GENERALS BELL AND BARRY

In a letter to Baker written by Barry on June 3, Barry said that Wood, in passing through Chicago, had told him that Baker had said in the presence of Colonel Kilbourne that Pershing did not desire either Bell or Barry in France. Barry wanted to know if this were true and what reasons Pershing gave. On the day after Barry wrote his letter Wood wrote to Baker that he had gone over their interview with Barry and found Barry as surprised as himself at Pershing's attitude. Wood said he was now Pershing's junior (being a major general while Pershing was a general) and ready to serve under Pershing with the best that was in him.

Baker in his answer to Barry on June 6 continued to protect Pershing from the ill-will of his Army colleagues. Pershing was having troubles enough of his own. The Allies had just appealed to the President for 100 American divisions in France, and preparations were being made for the evacuation of Paris after the Château-Thierry offensive. Baker wrote to Barry:

"I enclose a copy of a letter received by me from General Wood and a copy of my reply. I am quite certain that in my conversation with him I said nothing about General Pershing's attitude toward either you or General Bell, though I do recall that, when he insisted upon his right as a major general of the Regular Army to go to France, I told him he was in like case with you and General Bell. He then said that neither of you had passed the physical examination, and I told him that General Bell had passed the physical examination and still did not go. It seems to me impossible that I said anything to him about you or General Bell, because I realized when I was talking with him that he would endeavor to make trouble out of anything I did say, and that he brought Colonel Kilbourne into my office as a witness.

"The fact with regard to General Pershing is quite simple. He has from the beginning insisted that division commanders ought to be very young men, and when the general officers from this side went over he expressed as to each of them who was sixty years of age or over a doubt as to the wisdom of their returning to Europe as division commanders. With regard to General Bell, he has been quite sick in Europe, and General Pershing expressed grave doubts as to the stability of his health; and when I talked with him in France about you, he spoke in the kindest terms of your zeal, your helpfulness, and his personal friendship for you; at the same time, however, expressing a doubt as to whether your strength was equal to the young man's duty required of a division commander under trench warfare conditions.

"So far as General Wood is concerned, I confess myself so mystified, and frankness compels me to say so disgusted, by his activities, that if I were making the decision for General Pershing I would decide against his going; and yet I regard this as a military question and I would not allow my personal feelings to control this decision."

Baker wrote to Wood on June 5:

"When, in our interview on May 27, you referred to the fact that, as the senior major general of the Regular Army, you were entitled to an opportunity in France, I told you that you were in no different case from General Bell and General Barry.

I do not recall having told you anything about General Pershing's advice with regard to those two officers. Whether I did or not, however, it seems to me that fine sensibilities would have required you to regard such a statement as personal, and I can see no reason for the use you made of it in talking with General Barry except to stir up in the ranking officers of the Army a critical attitude toward General Pershing as Commander-in-Chief of the American Expeditionary Force in France. This seems to me to be a significant instance of the indirect and insubordinate disposition on your part which I told you, in our interview, made it difficult to combine you with an organization of which you are not the head, with any expectation of harmonious co-operation.

"Since you refer to our conversation of May 27, I take the liberty of pointing out to you another incident in it which left an unpleasant impression on my mind. I refer to the suggestion made by you that, because you had protected General Pershing's personal reputation in some way in the Philippine Islands, he ought now to feel himself under the obligation to take a personal, rather than a military, view of the possibility of your service in France. This subject, however, you will remember, was not discussed, and the only reference to it was your own."

Wood replied protesting that he had never been insubordinate, that he had not represented that he had protected Pershing's reputation in the Philippines, and that his conversation with the Secretary was strictly official. Baker wrote to Wood on June 25:

"I have received your letter of the 22nd. The only part of it which seems to call for further comment is with reference to the statement in my letter of June 5 referring to your relations with General Pershing in the Philippine Islands. I am constrained to feel that you have forgotten what you said to me on that subject. My own recollection was refreshed and strengthened by the fact that the next day after your call upon me I learned from Mr. Tumulty, secretary to the President, that you had entered into the same discussion with him in great detail, covering much more fully with him than with me the incident to which you referred in our conversation.

"After I had written my letter to you of June 5, General J. Franklin Bell called upon me with regard to the promotion of one of his subordinates. In response to a direct question from me as to whether he had heard from you, he told me that he had, but that he did not desire to go into the matter. I requested, officially, a more complete answer to my question, and found that you had taken up with him by correspondence your recollection of our conversation, and had supplied him with written memoranda with regard to it, made by you and Colonel Kilbourne. However much you may have felt our conversation to have been official, it would seem that the circulation of that official conversation might properly have been left with me, since I am officially common superior of General Bell, General Barry, and yourself, and if I had desired the contents of the conversation brought to the attention of General Barry or General Bell, official channels for its communication were open."

Clearly these two minds did not meet. Wood had been properly silent to the newspapers, a silence that confirmed the impression that Baker was responsible for his disappointment. His friends were saying that the men of his division, when they learned that he was not to lead them to France, would show themselves lacking in spirit if they did not make a public demonstration demanding that the order relieving him be rescinded. This might have happened with a popular commander in the days of Andrew Jackson, or Scott and Taylor, and even in the days of Sheridan and Stonewall Jackson; but nowadays, when we thought of armies in terms of hundreds of thousands instead of tens of thousands, individualism was sunk in the whole of our military machine. Another "old man" had come; and "the gang" went on with the unpleasant job of winning the War with all speed. It was a great division and made a great record at Saint-Mihiel and in the Meuse-Argonne under Wood's able and beloved successor, Major General William Wright. And the precedent of McClellan held, in that

Wood became a candidate for President; although, unlike Mc-Clellan, he did not receive his party's nomination.

Bell had reason for a greater heartbreak than Barry in that he had won his brigadiership in the field in the Philippine rebellion while Barry had been on staff duty. Upon the outbreak of the Spanish War Bell had been a lieutenant of cavalry, very old for his rank. One day he told Major General Arthur MacArthur that he would swim a mile across an arm of the bay in the night and scout the Spanish trenches. Bell seemed a very talkative and rather boastful person. MacArthur dismissed the suggestion, but an old comrade of Bell's said, "Bell talks a lot, but he always does all he says he will do." Bell made the swim successfully.

THE CURTAIN ON BELL'S BRAVE CAREER

Later, after we were fighting the Filipinos, he would tie his pony at a safe distance, and crawl through the tall grass or jungle and return with most valuable information. Once when he rode up to MacArthur's headquarters after a scout and began talking, it was noticed that there was blood on his saddle. "You're wounded!"—as he had been, in the fleshy part of him next to the saddle. That gave Bell something more to talk about.

On his insistence that we were fighting the natives in an old-fashioned way, and that if he had a small force of picked men on native ponies he could go anywhere and lick anything he met, MacArthur granted his request and Bell was again as good as to his word. By his exploits in the Philippines he won the Medal of Honor from Congress, as well as his star. Eighteen years afterward he was no longer the tireless Bell of those days; but his spirit was the same. He had been the first Chief of Staff after Root had established the General Staff, had held many important commands, and now after he had fathered the melting-pot division, the 77th, he was not to go with it to the front in France. It could not be true that Pershing would keep him back. Baker was touched by his appeal, and in his letter to Pershing on June 6 wrote:

ARMY NURSES ARRIVING IN FRANCE

OVERFLOW OF GASSED MEN FROM A FIELD HOSPITAL

"Some days ago General Bell came down to see me. He is really a very heartbroken man about not being allowed to go back to Europe. He tells me that the doctors at the Rockefeller Institute have discharged him from observation. My own feeling about him is one of admiration for the work he did at Camp Upton. As you know, that camp was the hardest of all to build, because of the location; and the raw material which went to him to be trained was made up very largely of New York City boys who had been clerks in stores and had all the other frailties of physique which are likely to attend young men raised in a congested city. And yet General Bell made of them, so far as my observation goes, as fine a division as was made in any National Army camp, and in dealing with the disciplinary questions and questions of training he showed real genius.

"The General is an interminable talker but, curiously enough, he is a doer too, and I have a strong disposition to believe that you could use him in a training area to very great advantage. I am not urging it beyond pointing out the very remarkable work he did at Camp Upton which, of course, I had a better opportunity to see than you have, since you have been away during practically all of that time."

But Pershing could not see his way clear to change his mind about Bell.

EDWARDS AND THE YANKEE DIVISION

Another heartbreak, which attracted much attention in New England, was that of Major General Clarence Edwards, who had been Lawton's Chief of Staff in the Philippines, and at Root's and Taft's right hand in the Insular bureau. He had taken to France the 26th (Yankee) Division, which became very devoted to him, and had commanded it through all its actions until he was relieved in the last month of the War during the Meuse-Argonne battle. The only important references to him in the cables are first on July 18, 1918: [18] "I have ordered General Edwards to Rome and have placed General Treat in command of post in Paris. General Edwards has not demonstrated his ability to command a division. He will, I believe, fit well into the position assigned to him."

But Pershing cabled on the following day, July 19: [19] "In view of present conditions so much of my 1484 as refers to Major General Edwards is held in abeyance."

And finally, on October 11, 1918, during the battle of the Meuse-Argonne: [20]

"I request that the following officers be ordered to the States and assigned to duty training divisions or in command of training camps or other duty appropriate to their present ranks, which I recommend they retain. The major generals have had actual experience in handling troops in active operations. The others are not considered available for that duty but should be valuable to assist in training. Major Generals Clarence Edwards, John E. McMahon and Omar Bundy, and Brigadier Generals John D. Barrette, W. S. Scott and Charles H. Barth."

There was a heartbreak for the Marines, who hoped that they might have a full division of their own in France, when Pershing sent this cable on June 19, 1918: [21]

"Brigadier General Lejeune brings up subject of formation of Marine division for service here. Referring to my conversation with the Secretary of War on this subject, I am still of the opinion that the formation of such a unit is not desirable from the military standpoint. Our land forces must be homogeneous in every respect. Units and personnel must be interchangeable. Same uniform and equipment are necessary because of question of supply. Organization must be uniform throughout our units. Same system of promotion must prevail. While the Marines are splendid troops, their use as a separate division is inadvisable."

When a general whom Pershing had sent home stood before Baker's desk saying, "I want to know why I was relieved?", Baker replied that Pershing was in command in France; that any officer had a right to demand a court of inquiry and have his case investigated.[22] The general did not ask for the court.

(I may repeat here that being ordered back to the United

States often meant high tribute to officers who were needed to apply their experience in home organization.)

The A. E. F.'s own whispering gallery associated heartbreaks with Blois, the name of a town in the S. O. S. whither the misfits and war-fatigued of the advanced zone were ordered for a re-examination of their capacities before they received another assignment. Being "sent to Blois" often meant demotion to a lower rank. Tired generals had special consideration. They were given light duty which would enable them to rest without hurting their pride too much. Frequently the officer sent to Blois merely had been a square peg in a round hole, and was given a position for which he was fitted. Nor did Blois mean that Line officers would not serve with troops again. A well-known colonel, after his sentence to Blois by a division commander, reappeared at the front with another division and won his brigadiership by one of the most gallant examples of initiative in regimental action in the history of the A. E. F.

The public importance of heartbreaks among officers descended in ratio to rank from generals, who were numbered by hundreds, to lieutenants who were numbered by tens of thousands. Then there were the privates, who were numbered by millions. They must be the main concern of the War Department in its paternal rôle. Individual references to them appeared in the cables only when they became casualties. I quote from one requisition from the A. E. F. for quantity migration from the mass-production of the training camps:

"First, complete existing general organization and priority projects and add 50,000 replacements to those already requested. (This will require shipment of 325,000 men in addition to shipments already arranged for June and July.) Second, 6 complete army corps (36 divisions and army corps troops as per general organization project total 1,080,000), 114,000 Army troops, 293,000 Service of Supply troops, and 375,000 replacements. . . . For second half of September four divisions with proportion of Corps troops 120,000, 30,000 Service of Supply troops, and 25,000 replacements. Total 175,000. . . . It will be necessary to draft between June, 1918, and March, 1919, 1,552,000 men in order to complete in time the project as given in Subparagraph A."

I quote further for anyone who may be interested in the detail of four closely typed foolscap pages:

"E 410, 3 labor battalions; E 412, 6 labor battalions; E 461, 3 light railway battalions; E 462, 3 labor battalions; E 463, 2 light railway battalions; total Engineer Corps about 27,-000. . . . 1 shop company (paragraph 2 our cablegram 1167); L 213, 2 motor truck companies; L 461, 1 operating battalion; L 461, 1 construction and maintenance-of-way battalion; L 462, 1 light railway service battalion; L 211, 2 road battalions; L 212, 1 road-service battalion. Total about 5,700. . . . 2 railroad artillery repair shops; O 403, railhead ammunition service 158; O 404, 1 advance depot and repair shop; O 405, 1 automatic-weapon repair shop; . . . 20 railhead supply detachments organized as per courier cablegram 2, 3 officers, 100 soldiers . . . 7 bakery companies; Q 441, 7 graves registration sections, paragraph 7-A our cablegram 1367; Q 442, 2 fire companies; Q 443, 7 supply companies, paragraph 1 our cablegram 1238; Q 444, 23 units for hospital centers, courier cable 2; Q 446, 1 headquarters field battalion, conservation and reclamation service. . . . 18 sales commissary units; Q 451, 18 clothing units; detachment miscellaneous trades for last three items, see courier cable 2; total Quartermaster about 91,200. . . . Our replacement requirements are cabled separately."

XXXI

THE GREAT SOLDIER ODYSSEY

RETURNING now to the period of Pershing's gloomy cable of June 10, when the people were leaving Paris and preparations were being made for its official evacuation, we find Foch holding his divisions in reserve as he waited for the blow. It came promptly on June 14 after the third offensive, and its purpose was to burst the door to Paris wide open by a drive along the line from Noyon to Montdidier. This time Ludendorff did not catch Foch napping, and the French master appeared at his best against the German master. His French veterans, who realized the stake, rose to the occasion with the spirit they had shown in answer to Joffre's call in the first Marne when the War was young. The German gains were negligible. Once more Paris was safe and soon the danger which had prompted the packing up of official papers appeared as a nightmare long past in the swift drama of war.

Allied apprehension, which had been so acute in another quarter since Caporetto, gave way to relief and then to rejoicing. On June 15 the Austrians began a great offensive against the Italians. One wing of it broke down; the other put one hundred thousand men across the Piave. Providence was on the side of the Italians in unprecedentedly heavy rains, which made the shallow river a torrent. This bore down from the hills lumbermen's rafts, severing many of the Austrians' bridges and leaving them no alternative but retreating. By June 22 Venice was as safe as Paris. An army in success does not think in terms of dropping out of the War. Italy might begin to dream of her goal of Trieste again. The last of Austria's dreams was broken.

It was after the fourth German offensive had been stopped,

and after the repulse of the Austrians, that on June 25, 1918, Foch and Pershing sent this joint cable: [1]

"To achieve victory in 1919 it is necessary to have numerical superiority over the enemy, which can only be secured if we have in France 80 divisions by April, and 100 by July next."

The cable was "to be submitted to President Wilson." That is, it was a direct appeal to his Commander-in-Chief by our commander in France, and also a direct appeal by the generalissimo of the Allied armies—the spokesman in action of the unified command of which the President had been an advocate long before it was achieved.

Later, Pershing went even further than Foch. He favored 110 divisions. This would have meant more than a total of 5,000,000 men counting technical and Service of Supply troops. His first call in July, 1917, had been for a million for July, 1918, while he envisioned the possibility of two million for July, 1919.

Pershing had been a year away from the United States and so could not realize how deeply all the energy and resources of the nation had been drawn into war effort. In his many preoccupations it required the continuous play of great imagination for him to visualize the effect upon the home situation of his changing requisitions and plans, topped by this latest enormous demand.

In a letter of June 18, 1918—not received until after the Foch-Pershing dispatch of June 23, but written after the fourth German offensive had been stopped in its tracks—Pershing expressed his concern lest America should be left to fight the War practically alone the coming year. He feared that he might have to put some of his regiments into French divisions to give them courage, and he still dreaded lest the Germans recruit Russian man-power for their armies. He must have four hundred thousand men a month instead of three hundred thousand. Send him the hosts and a way would be found to supply them. Spain was an unexploited, virgin field for supplies. There need be no worry about food. There was plenty. He had to use strong words, he said, because the nation faced the most serious situation in its history. No matter about artillery. He could get it from the British if not from the French, and small arms, too. The animal question was on the way to solution by supplies from Europe. Facilities for evacuating cargo at the ports were being rapidly improved; and this a month before the congestion became so acute that it was proposed to send Goethals to France to find a means of relief. And Pershing would have our women put at work in the factories, not knowing that they were already there, engaged in all kinds of labor unfamiliar to them.

OUR FIRST MILLION MEN IN FRANCE

On July 1 Baker wrote to the President that 1,019,000 men had been embarked for France; double the number that the critics of eight months ago said we ought to have by midsummer, and equal to the number that had represented Pershing's extreme estimate a year ago. On July 4 the nation had this news in place of fireworks for its celebration of Independence Day, at the same time as the pilgrimage of the foreign-born citizens to Mount Vernon that I have mentioned. In a letter on July 6 to Pershing, who had been so solicitous that we should not reveal the number of men we had in France, Baker explained the reasons for his violation of military secrecy:

"There had been so much speculation about numbers that it seemed necessary to be frank and tell the facts. The American people are accustomed to demanding the facts, and there was some impatience manifested with the Department for its continued policy of silence on this subject. I realized when I made the statement that in all likelihood I should have to discontinue further reference to numbers, at least further specific references. The Germans, French, and British of course make no such announcements, and our Allies will not like to have us adopting a different course. There are doubtless good military reasons for not being very generous with information of this kind, which finds its way to the enemy and enables them to make more certain calculations. Still, if the rate of shipment which we have maintained for the last two or three months can be kept up for another six months, I am not very sure that exact news carried to Germany of the arrival of Americans in France might not be helpful to us rather than harmful. The German Government cannot fail to be impressed by this steady stream of fresh soldiers to the Western front.

"I was a little afraid that too enthusiastic comment might create a feeling of resentment on the part of our Allies. Their men, of course, have stood these attacks for a long time, and it would only be human if they resented the newcomers getting too much attention at the expense of organizations which are battle-scarred and have had their valor tested in great conflicts; and I have a little feared, too, that if our people here at home were fed too many stories of success they might get the notion that this great task is going to be easy for Americans, and so be ill-prepared for any reverse, no matter how slight, which might come. For that reason I have exercised a good deal of self-restraint in my own discussion with the newspapermen, and in such public addresses as I have made, have sought always to couple up the British and French with our American soldiers and to make the whole War a matter of common effort, rather than of our own national effort. This has been especially easy, because the spirit of America is now very high. The country is thoroughly unified and is waiting only to be shown how it can make further effective sacrifices and efforts. It occurs to me in this connection that it might be wise for you in your communiqués, from time to time, to refer to slight repulses suffered by our men; but of course I do not want our men to be repulsed merely to balance the news."

BAKER URGES OUR ARMY TO THE OFFENSIVE

And the son of Jeb Stuart's trooper, in a letter to Bliss on July 6—a year after the "Lafayette, we are here!" of the arrival of our first contingent in France—expressed his interest in aggressive action by the growing hosts of the A. E. F. He wrote:

"We have substantially a million and a half men in training here, all of them filled with ambition to leave for the front, so that for some months at least we are not likely to run short of at least partially trained men, and our supply program seems adequate up to the present time. . . .

WOMEN IN A MUNITION PLANT AT HOME

WOMEN TELEPHONE OPERATORS IN THE A. E. F.

"Now that American forces are going to France in real and weighty numbers, I am deeply hopeful that these fresh, high-spirited men will be used at the earliest possible moment for offensive operations on a large scale. I do not think it good for our men to put them on the defensive, nor do I think it good for our cause to let Germany choose the point of attack. On the 30th of June we had sent from this country more than 1,000,000 men. The present prospect is that during July and August we will send at least a half-million more. Obviously, some of these men are not sufficiently well trained to go into immediate action, but they have had some training here in this country and apparently learn very rapidly in France; so that the increase of Allied numbers must be going on more rapidly than any possible increase in German strength, and I shall be quite heartbroken if we continue through this summer with the present tug-of-war and no big drive made by our people."

On July 8 Pershing, further to impress the War Department with the gravity of the situation, sent a cable showing the comparative strength of the armies facing each other on the Western front.[2] He declared the Germans had 3,557,000 to Britain's 1,044,000, and France's 1,333,000, or a total, counting the 25,000 which had been sent by Italy, of 2,402,000. France and Britain had available for 1918 1,293,000 more, and Germany 340,000 more, which still gave Germany a preponderance. Counting our million, however, the Allies now had the superior numbers, which we were increasing at the rate of 400,000 a month. The German strength was, of course, only an estimate, which post-War records were to prove to be an exaggeration.

Ludendorff, whose hope of a victory had lain in winning a decision before the arrival of the Americans in force, was now preparing his fifth offensive. He wrote in his book: [3]

"The contingent that the United States sent to France in April, May, and June was, according to the information obtainable, estimated at fifteen divisions. At the moment there might be twenty American divisions in all in France, more than I had believed possible, and not only had our March superiority in the number of the divisions been canceled, but even the difference in gross numbers was now to our disadvantage, for an American division consists of twelve strong battalions. In those parts of the line where we had hitherto been fighting with [American] divisions which had already been in France some time, we had remained masters of the situation, in spite of our inferiority in numbers. . . . But the fact that these new American reinforcements could release English and French divisions on quiet sectors weighed heavily in the balance against us. This was of the greatest importance and helps to explain the influence exerted by the American contingent on the issue of the conflict. It was for this reason that America became the deciding factor in the War."

While we crowded the transports with our men from the camps, the War Department must determine through all the agencies of the Staff departments and the War Industries Board our ability to carry out the 100-division program for 1919. The Foch-Pershing cable for the 100 divisions arrived in Washington at a time when we were straining all our efforts to send 300,-000 men a month to meet an emergency, when the congestion in French ports was requiring an eighty-day turn-around of cargo ships, when the future was dark as to how we were to supply the men we were sending, and when the problem of priorities in production to meet the demands of the A. E. F. and our Allies for munitions was increasingly acute. The Allies, besides, were pressing us to send troops not only to northern Russia and Siberia and Italy, but also to Macedonia.

This new demand—for 100 divisions—contemplated transporting across three thousand miles of sea, through the submarine zone, an army larger than Germany ever had in the field and twice as large as the combined British and French armies; and after we should land this immense host in France we should have to transport and maintain it at a distance from the ports greater than the average distance of the British, French, and German armies from their munition plants and sources of supply. In brief, America was expected to do far more in ratio to population and distance than the nations which—in defense of their very homes and their national integrity—had been able to do at the top of their exertions, and when Britain and France had had all the world's munition power at their service, including our own, before we entered the War. The War Department's position was further complicated by the whispering gallery which was fed by travelers' tales and gossip from the Allied missions. The same busy tongues that, a year ago, were saying we must have half a million men in France by the summer of 1918 were now declaring that we ought to send 5,000,000 overseas immediately.

STILL THE WHISPERING GALLERY COMPLAINS

There was no satisfying Colonel Harvey, who wrote in his weekly:

"Transpose the letters in BAKER and you have BRAKE— and that is what our Pacifist Secretary of War has been from the beginning of the great conflict, both before and after we engaged in it, and what he is today. We cannot bear in mind a single contribution made by him to winning the War. . . . Anything, anything for an excuse for doing nothing."

It was not Colonel Harvey, however, but the *Deutsche Tageszeitung* that wrote, after its disappointment over the failure of the fourth German offensive and of the Austrian offensive:

"Today, on the anniversary of the American day of independence, the Entente will fill the world with resounding phrases about their [Americans'] help. America herself will produce a world of bluff in the form of phrases, threats, and assertions—all bluff, pure bluff, celebrated in Paris by reviews."

Other German papers were boasting of submarine successes and saying that the Americans could not swim nor fly, and that therefore our mob of conscripts herded on transports would never reach France. When Ludendorff knew how time was crowding him to the wall, any disparagement of our effort might aid morale for his fifth offensive—which was also to be his last.

Easy as it was to write the Foch-Pershing cablegram, sound and proper as it might be, there was also the entering factor that Foch, the soldier and withal the Frenchman, thinking in terms of man-power for his dispositions, did not, as Pershing has remarked, concern himself much with tonnage and supplies.[4] It is not surprising that the great tactician thought in terms of continental armies with short railroad systems, rather than overseas armies.

The main purpose the War Department had in mind was to keep up the present rate of troop shipments to meet the crisis of the summer of 1918, which would be building up a maximum for 1919, even if it were not equal to the 100-division program. Baker had cabled Bliss July 1: [5]

"Possibilities of compliance are being studied here. Many questions of material and industrial output are involved, and no immediate determination can be made. It is of great importance that no expectation be held out to comply with this enlarged program until studies are completed. Meantime, it is highly desirable that the July rate of shipping of troops from America be maintained through August. If military representatives will so recommend, the British will no doubt continue the use of their shipping, upon which we must depend in this matter."

March sent a cable of the same tenor to Pershing on July 2: [6]

"The 100-division program is being studied, and it is considered by the President and Secretary of War of the greatest importance that no expectation be held out by you to representatives of foreign armies that the United States will be able to carry out such a program until you are informed so from here. We intend to keep up the increased program through August provided shipping can be definitely obtained from Great Britain. Before that time consideration must be given to question of shipping, material, and the industrial output of the United States, concerning which conferences will be held with representatives of the Shipping Board, War Industries

Board, War Trade Board, and other civilian agencies initiated for the purpose of handling such matters by the President."

With reference to the tonnage for the 400,000 men a month and their supplies for the 100-division program, which he advocated urgently again in the same cable, Pershing said on July 6, 1918: [7]

"In private conversation with M. Clemenceau and Lloyd George, July 3, the latter affirmed Great Britain's intentions of providing all the shipping possible, showing that they fully appreciate the situation."

Enlivening on this subject is a passage in a letter from Bliss to Baker on July 3 about the meeting of the Supreme War Council on the previous day. André Tardieu, the French High Commissioner in Washington, who was now in Paris, presented a study he had made of the tonnage necessary for the 100-division program; but the premier of the maritime nation which supplied the shipping had something to say about this to the representative of the nation which had no shipping to offer. "This seemed greatly to irritate Mr. Lloyd George, who said that the question of tonnage did not concern the French, but only the British and Americans." When Tardieu said he had nothing to do with allocation but was only throwing light on the problem, "Mr. Lloyd George insisted that there was nothing to do but to await the study to be made in Washington." Then we would know how much tonnage America could supply, and "the British government would consider to what extent it could make up the deficiency." At a later meeting Lloyd George called attention to the fact that 150,000 of the 250,000 American soldiers shipped during the previous month had come in British transports. He said the whole thing could better be worked out by experts rather than discussed by the Supreme War Council; and Bliss said the United States, in the meantime, would make no promises. But he had already written to Baker, as soon as the 100-division program was proposed, that, as 2,500,000 tons of deadweight shipping would be required to maintain one million men in France, "such a force [100 divisions] could be contemplated only for a campaign of 1920, and God knows we hope the War will not last that long." It will be recalled that as early as April Bliss had written to Baker that if the Germans wanted a "show down" in 1918 they could force it, and now there could be no doubt that this was their plan.

WAS THE 100-DIVISION PROGRAM IN OUR POWER?

Time was to justify Bliss' previous conclusion that an army which seeks a decision promptly by continuing to attack another army can usually have it, and if the Germans put all their strength into action in the summer of 1918 they would have a decision. But at the moment his prophecy was already ancient history in the files; and, as he remarked in one of his letters, he had been wrong often enough not to take his own forecasts too seriously. On July 8 Baker wrote to Bliss:

"March and I are studying together the 100-division program, but are finding it full of burrs. The latest one presented to me is that all the ports in France, and all the berthing space there, if devoted to the exclusive use of America, would not, on present calculations, be adequate for the 100-division program. Other shortages which are causing us anxiety are wool and artillery. And if it turns out that we are going to have to resume the shipment of horses in any large numbers, the ocean tonnage problem gets a new complication. As you know, our intention has for some time been to develop 100 divisions by 1920, but to push that consummation ahead a whole year is not easy, to say the least, even if it should turn out to be possible with the maximum aid from the British and French. I note in one of your cablegrams the suggestion that General Foch and General Pershing have even a larger program than those under consideration for America. I am not willing to believe that anything is impossible, no matter what it is, but at present it looks as though I would need Aladdin's lamp for the 100-division program, and just what additional magic the larger program [the 110-division] will require, I do not know."

It was the demand for the 100-division program that helped to bring to a head the proposal from Washington (with which I shall deal later) to send General Goethals to co-ordinate supply at home and in France under one head, "The port situation, I confess," as Baker wrote to Bliss, "seems more or less insoluble at this end, and yet every estimate we get from France is hopeful, if not optimistic."

When the appeal for the 100-division program was first received, Baker considered going abroad himself in order that he might talk with the statesmen of the Allies, the shipping experts, and all concerned, so as to procure more direct information which he could better organize for his purpose than by depending upon cables; but, as he wrote to Bliss, he had decided that "it is better to let you work this out for us and for me to stay here until the legislation needed for it is safely through the Congress. In addition to the billions of dollars that will be required, a change in the draft ages will be necessary."

On July 6, 1918, Baker wrote to Pershing:

"When the 100-division program came it occurred to me that we ought to study the situation with the view of determining the maximum amount we can do. I have the feeling that this war has gone on long enough, and if any exertions on our part or any sacrifice can speed its successful termination even by a single day, we should make it. We are therefore now having studies made to show the things necessary to be done for three possible programs: involving 60, 80, and 100 divisions respectively by the first of July, 1919."

When the study was concluded it would "be possible to take up with those governments [the British and French] a frank exhibition of the possibilities, and to arrange for concerted action among us which will lead to the increase in our effort which you and General Foch recommend." The letter goes on:

"In the meantime, I have asked the British Government to continue the troop ships which they have had in our service during June through July and August, and have told them frankly that we are considering an enlargement of our program which may require for a time at least the uninterrupted service of all the ships which we have been using. If we are able in July and August to match the performance of June, it will mean another half-million men in France, as the June embarkation figures from this country show slightly more than 279,000 men. Our own ships carried during that month something more than 100,000, which is, of course, doing better than our part as we originally calculated it. I think it highly important that neither General Foch nor the British and French Governments should assume our ability to carry out an enlarged program until we ourselves have studied it. . . . One of the happy effects of the recent accelerated shipment of troops has been that we have outstripped our promises and, if I judge correctly the effect of this in Europe, it has been most agreeable and heartening.

"There is no disposition on the part of the United States to shrink from any sacrifice or any effort, and yet experience has taught us that, great as our capacity is in industry, it takes time to build new factories, get the necessary machine tools, and bring together the raw materials for any large increase in our industrial output. . . . The Operations Committee of the General Staff is pressing forward the necessary studies. These involve, of course, questions of clothing, small arms, ammunition, transportation, and training. As soon as these programs are worked out we will, in consultation with the War Industries Board, determine how far manufacturing facilities already in existence or possible to be created can supply the necessary material, and how much assistance we shall have in the way of heavy artillery and transportation from the British and the French."

WHERE WERE WE TO FIND THE SHIPS?

In a cable of July 19 Pershing complained that the tonnage which had been assigned to the A. E. F. would be inadequate to care for even thirty divisions by September. He thought that the shipping situation was being badly handled. Far more shipping should be spared for direct army use. "I request and recommend that at least 500,000 deadweight tons of vessels now employed in other trades be withdrawn and placed in other services. . . . Out of 530,000 deadweight tons of Dutch vessels requisitioned, only 344,000 tons had been assigned to direct army transport." [8]

All the Shipping Board's new tonnage ought to be immediately turned over to the Army, including "all new wooden and composite ships." It was such appeals, after the Caporetto disaster, that had led to sweeping the seas for ships, to requisitioning of neutral ships, and to the pooling of shipping by the new Inter-Allied Maritime Council. Indeed, shipping resources had been drawn on to their limit. Further tonnage for the Army was dependent upon the output of the shipyards of Britain and the United States. The Navy, which was building the North Sea barrage, must have its quota; there must be shipping allowed for the transport of raw material to Europe and for us in our manufacture of munitions, for all the trade of the world in its part in feeding the maw of war. The civil workers of the Allies as well as the armies must have food from the world's granaries. The Bethlehem Steel Company turned over its great ore vessels to the Army because they could carry locomotives on their wheels to France; but another method must be found to carry the ore for the making of locomotives and other steel products.

In his cable of July 19 Pershing had also said: "The tonnage mentioned can be unloaded promptly through ports here without delay." March conceivably had a grin over that, perhaps accompanied by the rapier look. Delay in unloading ships at French ports continued. It was hard to see eye-to-eye across three thousand miles of ocean when the Chief of Staff was so busy embarking two divisions a week and the Commander-in-Chief, as chairman of the reception committee, was so busy disembarking and billeting them.

The War Department had to be sure that it could have not only the supplies for the 100-division program and the ships to transport the men and supplies, but also the men trained and equipped for embarkation, when the withdrawal of all new levies from civil life meant so much less in industrial man-power. We could do no more than put all the women to work in the men's places.

At the rate of 400,000 a month we should more than exhaust the capacity of our cantonments in four months. This meant only four months' training. Pershing, who in a previous cable had asked that we draft immediately 2,000,000 men, in a letter of June 18, after the fourth German offensive had been repulsed and the Austrian offensive arrested, asked that we increase the number by five hundred thousand. He thought that since the French put up with the billeting in their houses of the soldiers of their own and foreign nations, the Congress should pass a law authorizing billeting in the United States. But French and German recruits had always been put in barracks for their initial training, even during the War: they had never gone back and forth between billets and drill-grounds. The proposal meant a revolution that would break down the whole training system, even if the Congress gave its consent.

HUMAN CHESSMEN—REPLACEMENTS

Since the emergency rush of troops had begun Pershing had frequently complained about the state of their training, and also that sometimes the divisions were not up to their maximum strength. On June 17, 1918, March had cabled to Pershing: [9]

"By reason of the increased number of troops shipped every month, the length of time portions of them have had in training camps at home has been correspondingly diminished. At the last minute the final combing out of each division always leaves a number of vacancies, which have to be filled by transfer of men from other divisions; and the instruction which a division has is not homogeneous, but there are in each division a number of men, sometimes numbering several thousand, who have less instruction than the rest."

The combing was inevitable as a result of the demands for skilled labor by the Shipping Board and other industries that were trying to speed up production to meet the same emergency that called for an army in France clear beyond Allied or even

A GERMAN VIEW
OF THE A. E. F.

AN AMERICAN VIEW
OF THE A. E. F.

WAR CARTOONS

Pershing's expectations; and also for the increased number of special units Pershing required for rapid dispatch to France. March cabled Pershing on June 19: [10]

"All divisions have been filled to maximum strength at their stations before shipment. Many men are absent without leave at time of sailing, others are necessarily left behind for various reasons, and others are rejected at eleventh hour. Casuals are shipped as soon afterwards as possible. See my weekly report of personnel shipped. Nearly every transport carries casuals of second and third corps."

Also, soldiers might become ill, even in the Allied emergency of the spring of 1918.

In his letter of July 6 to Pershing Baker said:

"The troops which we have recently sent you have admittedly been of an uneven quality, chiefly because we have made up deficiencies in divisions about to sail by taking men from other divisions, with consequent disorganization of those divisions from which men were repeatedly taken; and when we got to a place where we could no longer carry out this process, fairly raw men had to be used in order to keep divisions from sailing short. The plan inaugurated by General March of having replacement divisions in this country, from which deficiencies could be supplied without robbing other divisions and disorganizing them, seems to me to solve the problem, and the divisions which come to you in August and September will, I am sure, show highly beneficial results from this policy."

In theory casualties in divisions at the front should be replaced by men from replacement depots. Staff perfectionism might consider the soldier replacement as it would that of guns, rolling kitchens, rifles, or gas masks. But the soldier replacement was a human being subject to human psychology which the statesmanship of war had to consider carefully in undertaking to dispatch—in high zeal—one, two, three, four, five million young Americans of no previous military experience across three thousand miles of sea to fight in a war for a cause which might become something of an abstraction to numbers of them as individuals after a few weeks under the top-sergeant. It would become still more of an abstraction if the gang spirit, the pride of company, of battalion, of division were removed and they knew they were to be nondescripts separated from their buddies to go among strangers. Some staff experts in their studies might think that the really scientific army required that casualties in a division should be replaced from a warehouse of human chessmen; but the Regular at home who had the responsibility for training learned the value of developing the competition of *esprit de corps* among battalions and companies as well as among divisions; and in France the method became so intensified that it sometimes led to jealousies that interfered with friendly co-operation on the battle-line.

On this vital subject of psychology, another part of Baker's letter of July 6 should have particular attention in view of my future references to the Meuse-Argonne battle:

"We have discovered two things about training in this country which apparently nobody knew or thought of before we went into the War. First, that while it may take nine months or a year to train raw recruits into soldiers in peace-time, when there is no inspiration from an existing struggle, it takes no such length of time now when the great dramatic battles are being fought and men are eager to qualify themselves to participate in them. We are certainly able to get more training into a man now in three months than would be possible in nine months of peace-time training. And second, we have learned that to keep men too long in training camps in this country makes them go stale and probably does as much harm by the spirit of impatience and restlessness aroused as it does good by the longer drilling. The men in our training camps are champing at the bit, and this applies not only to the officers, who naturally want their professional opportunity, but to the men as well. Indeed, one of the difficulties in America is to make people content with the lot which keeps them here for any length of time, so impatient are we all, military men and civilians alike, to get to France where the real work is being done.

"As a consequence of these discoveries, I feel that we will be perfectly safe if we have a million men in training in the United States at all times. That will enable us to feed them out to you at the rate of 250,000 a month and bring that number in by draft at the other end, which will always give us an adequate supply of men who have had as much training as they can profitably secure here in the United States. The finishing touches in any event will have to be given in France, and I think you will find that men who have had four months' training here are pretty nearly ready for use in association with your veteran and experienced troops, and that no prolonged period of European training, for infantry at least, will be found necessary. This makes the problem very simple from the point of view of the draft and the training camps. A number of the camps originally established by us have now been developed for specialized technical uses, but we still have a large number —and I think an adequate number—of camps which can be enlarged without great expense; and there seems little likelihood of our being obliged to resort to the billeting system, although of course we should not hesitate to do it if the need arose."

THOSE SUPER-DREADNAUGHTS OF THE AIR

It is interesting to note that while the capacity of the nation was being analyzed for dispatching and maintaining the gigantic force and for insuring support of the Congress and the people, the proponents of an enormous aerial offensive in place of the use of so much man-power were not idle at home. Baker wrote to Bliss in his letter of July 8, 1918:

"You no doubt have seen in the newspapers a rather spectacular newspaper agitation which has been stirred up in this country for the building of aircraft which can fly across the Atlantic and still have enough vitality to be useful in war when they arrive on the other side. A British general, Brancker, has come over here in the interests of what he calls the 'aerial offensive.' His general thesis is that, in addition to army and navy aerial programs, an entirely independent aerial offensive ought to be planned against Berlin by the building of super-dreadnaughts of the air, launching them from England and sending them over in great squadrons to bomb inland German cities. Of course America is to be looked to for supplying a large number of these great machines. We are in the midst of the discussion with him, and much will depend upon the practicability of his suggestions; although, for my own part, I am more concerned for the immediate moment to get the aircraft program which we have in hand in some state of advancement, so that it can properly support our forces in France. This seems to me to be the first stage. It just happened by accident that an impudent American named W——, who seems to be the American representative of Mr. H——, was here in America at the same time that General Brancker was, and they both allowed themselves to be interviewed in the newspapers to the effect that as the question of ocean tonnage would seriously limit the transportation of aircraft, it was necessary to develop machines which would cross the Atlantic independently. On Brancker's part this was of course merely a daring speculation; on W——'s part, a piece of impudence in the interests of Mr. H——, who, it seems, desires to be invited to the United States, set up in a factory, and financed, while he builds H—— machines here, on the gratuitous assumption that America cannot build airplanes without Mr. H——'s personal presence and guidance.

"The independent aerial offensive has its strong points. To that extent it is better than Mr. W——'s. So far, however, the whole thing is in the initial stages of discussion and I merely apprise you of the existence of the suggestion because, if it ever gets to the stage of practicable consideration, I shall want to have your judgment about it all, as a part of the larger program. I am coming more and more to have a horror of dissipating our energies, rather than concentrating them, and this applies not only to our military forces but to our industrial energies. The sun-glass which converges all the scattered rays it can collect upon a single point seems to me to be a very excellent strategic symbol, and I think if I were ever able to help in the establishment here of a post-graduate war university, I would adopt the sun-glass as the seal of the institution. I do not know whether I have told you about my plans for this university or not, but if I have not I will some time. They are very fascinating, but unhappily they deal with the next war, and their consideration can, I hope, be postponed for some time without imperiling the national safety."

The fluctuations in the A. E. F.'s directions as to priorities as our divisions were being moved on Foch's checkerboard did not make the War Department's task any easier. For instance, it was not so simple as moving a pin on a map to comply with the request as late as June 27, 1918, that the forty-three squadrons of air personnel to be embarked during June and July be sent direct to England, when some of them were already on ships bound for France.[11]

AMERICANS IN AGAINST THE FINAL OFFENSIVE

While we continued to load every available transport with troops, to press every available cargo ship into our supply service, and to analyze our capacity for carrying out the 100-division program, the offensive was still with the enemy. Foch knew that the rapid arrival of American reinforcements set the time element in his favor as surely as it was against the Germans. Pershing had developed new confidence in his soldiers. After such convincing proof of our fighting quality as we had given at Cantigny, Belleau Wood, the Marne bridgehead, and Vaux, Foch not inclined to keep our new divisions long in quiet sectors but put them in battle action. For he had the authority as generalissimo to move divisions at will. He had sent the British divisions to the Aisne; and was to send a British division to relieve our 1st after the drive of July eighteenth. He was bringing more American divisions to the battle area, where they faced the provocative military insult of that vulnerable, balloon-like salient which the third German offensive had sunk in the Allied line.

Ludendorff had made laborious preparations for his fifth offensive, which did not come until July 15. By this time there were 300,000 Americans in the Marne area or in available close support. Although off their regular line of communications, they were being well supplied. Three American divisions had a part in meeting the offensive, whose line of attack extended from east of Rheims to Château-Thierry, the right wing having to force a crossing of the Marne. The 42nd, on its way to the salient after a restless month in further training which had not staled it, was in against the full impact of the blow east of Rheims as a part of Gouraud's army which shattered German hopes in that direction. Just east of Château-Thierry the 3rd—which had been only four months in France and had 124 guns against 336 German guns—won its sobriquet "The Rock of the Marne" by a most brilliant action which drove the Germans, who had made a lodgment on the south bank, back across the river with heavy losses. On the right of the 3rd, units of the 28th (Muir) Pennsylvania National Guard, were in close-quarters action sharing the honor of the enemy's repulse.

So the fifth German offensive had failed. This was reassuring to the War Department, which called 400,000 more men in the draft in July to fill the places of the departing divisions. Even before the start of the German offensive that widened the salient, Foch's plan for closing it was on the way to execution. On July 18 our 1st Division, now under the command of Major General Charles P. Summerall, and our 2nd, now under the command of Harbord, were a part of Mangin's army in its attack against the bottleneck of the salient. Behind the rolling barrage of their guns they struck the enemy by surprise, and made their own "race to victory" in superb rivalry, as they sent columns of prisoners to the rear. I saw this operation. Its success seemed incredible after we had been so long on the defensive. Our two pioneer divisions continued their drive until, near Soissons, sheer exhaustion called for a halt, as Ludendorff rushed reinforcements to check the sudden reversal of German fortunes.

Our 26th (Edwards) advanced from Belleau Wood as a part of the general movement to force the issue. Fresh American divisions succeeded our exhausted divisions. When the 3rd, the 26th, and 28th were worn down, the 42nd, the 4th (Hines) (which had been with the British and two months in France), and the 32nd (Haan) (five months in training in France including two months in tranquil trenches) continued the advance—

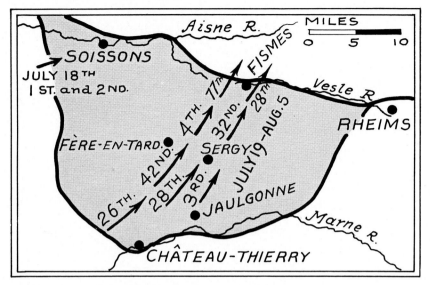

AMERICAN DIVISIONS IN THE MARNE SALIENT

CHATEAU-THIERRY RECOVERED FROM THE GERMANS

conquering German machine-gun nests in the test of open battle, storming the heights of the Ourcq, and working their way up the valley of the Vesle. Yet another division, this time a National Army division, the 77th (Duncan), which had been with the British and four months in France, was to know front-line service in the Allied counter-offensive that had closed the salient and taken Fismes by August fifth.

EIGHTY DIVISIONS OUR LIMIT IN FRANCE

These successes should have somewhat consoled Pershing for the bad news he had from Washington. On July 25 the War Department, on the basis of all the information it could gain, decided that it would undertake the 80-division program— which meant, according to March's understanding of Pershing's estimate, about a million men fewer than Baker, on his second trip to France, was to find that Pershing had in mind. But the War Department had approved the 80-division program only in the sense that it could deliver the men and material to our ports. It was not yet sure of the necessary shipping. On July 28 Baker wrote to Bliss:

"When you have ascertained, by conference with your British associates, what we can expect in the matter of assistance with tonnage cargo, the situation will be clear. That, and the capacity of the French ports, are our greatest impediments.

"The work of the Shipping Board in this country is progressing rapidly; Mr. Schwab seems to have imbued the whole industry with his vitality and spirit, and the shipyards of the country are ringing with rivet-driving contests, so that the estimates of tonnage hitherto made by the Shipping Board are quite likely to prove conservative and rather under than over the output. I think we have all, however, come to appreciate one quality of the American mind more than we did when we began these war preparations. Our people are entirely satisfied if we tell them that we are going to do 50,000 tons, and then actually do 60,000; but they will be in a horrible temper if we tell them, on the same outlook and with the same facilities, that we are going to do 100,000 and then do 99,000.

"There has, therefore, grown up in all of the departments and bureaus a remarkable conservatism of statement, which I think is real and general enough for me to communicate to you so that you can rely more or less confidently upon estimates from America being carried out. I rather gather by the statements made by Mr. Lloyd George, in your account of the Supreme War Council's deliberations, that the British were expecting to be called upon for large tonnage contributions. From such calculations as we have been able to make, we will not need this assistance beyond the first of January, at which time, unless submarine destruction exceeds present rates, we will have pretty nearly caught up with our Army's needs, even though we maintain the accelerated rate of troop shipment which has been preserved through June and July."

So the mad dream of Hog Island by a nation that before the War had been so largely dependent on foreign merchant marines was actually coming true.

Our approval of the 80-division program came ten days after the final German offensive, a week after our two pioneer divisions had participated in the first Allied counter-drive of 1918. Between July 18 and August 5 the Allies had closed the Marne salient, and forty thousand German prisoners had been taken.

On July 24, the day before our approval of the 80-division program, Foch drew up a memorandum: "The defeat of the Germans must first of all be exploited thoroughly on the field of battle itself. That is why we are pursuing our attacks without pause and with all our energy." And in Foch's own italics, *"The moment has come to abandon the general defensive attitude forced upon us until now by numerical inferiority and to pass to the offensive."* [12] His statement at the time about numerical inferiority, though not correct, was of course quite sincere and based on Allied intelligence reports. The Allies already had superior numbers on the earth and in the air.

Foch's next offensives had three primary objects: to free the Paris-Avricourt railway in the Marne region; to free the Paris-Amiens line; and to free the Paris-Avricourt in the Commercy region, which he had already designated for the American army in its Saint-Mihiel battle. The closing of the Marne salient had freed the eastern section of the Paris-Avricourt railroad. In this operation the schooling of our men, of our platoon, company, battalion, and regimental leaders, and of our division staffs, had been the better because the action was so swift in pressing every advantage and overcoming resistance with repeated attacks. There were incidents of heroic persistence worthy of our best traditions; and incidents belonging to a new tradition that began with our plan for our part in the War with the 10,000,000 men registering themselves of their own free will in a spirit that was self-expressed rather than impressed.

"They ain't calling us Wops now!" said a little Italian-American. The doctor who had passed him as a recruit had found his arches all right; but now, under the heavy pack, they were breaking, and he was suffering that cruel pain which only one who has tried to walk with a falling arch can understand. He could not keep up on the march. I told him to shift his pack and rest beside the road until an ambulance came. But he said: "I gotta keep up with the gang. I gotta show I'm an American." So he plodded on toward the shellfire under which his battalion was advancing.

GERMANY'S "BLACK DAY"—THE TURN OF THE TIDE

Now to continue with the picture "over there" and to allow it to become personal. It happened that on the "black day," August 8, I saw the British in their offensive, and also men of the Canadian Corps whom I had known when they had had their baptism of fire in Flanders, now in another success that seemed incredible in the rapidity of its advance in the open, and in the number and ease with which prisoners yielded to skilful battalions, which became the more eager with success after their long period of stonewalling. It chanced that elements of our 33rd Division, which had been only six weeks in France, were in training with the Australians on August eighth. They advanced in company with their veteran instructors. Now I knew that the signs I had seen on July 18 were not local but symptomatic of a change in the morale of the German army.

Ludendorff wrote: [13]

"It was in this sense that I discussed matters with my staff; and while still occupied with those thoughts the blow of August 8 fell upon me. August 8 was the black day of the German army in the history of the War. . . . Knowing that the next measures must be purely defensive, General Headquarters had ordered a gradual withdrawal of our lines in the plains of the Lys and the evacuation of the bridgeheads on the Ancre and the Avre."

On August 8, too, the second of Foch's primary objects was gained in the freeing of the Paris-Amiens railroad. His own comment on Ludendorff's black day follows: [14]

"The enemy, taken wholly by surprise by the violence and rapidity of the attack, fell back in great confusion, abandoning a large quantity of material. . . . More than thirteen thousand prisoners and three hundred guns were taken on the first day."

Therefore, as he said in his orders for the next day, "Move fast, march hard, maneuver to the front, support firmly from the rear with all the troops you have."

And it happened that on August 8, the day before he had received the communiqués of the Somme victory, Baker said to Bliss, in writing of our own part in the turn of the tide:

"The whole attention of the country for the last week has been centered on the great battle. Maps of the Soissons-Rheims salient are on every street corner, and the location of the line is marked from day to day while crowds gather around to enjoy the spectacle. As yet we have no casualty lists, and the heavy price which this great success must entail is not yet disclosed, but I think our people understand and will wear myrtle cheerfully while our boys are so bravely wearing laurels. These are times when one wishes he had the power of Le Sage's Devil-on-Crutches to sail around through the air, taking off the tops of houses and seeing what people were doing inside. Personally, I should like to sail through Germany at the present moment on such an expedition and see how Hans and Gretchen are explaining to one another the rapid progress which the All-Highest is making forward by moving backward.

"Surely if there is anything in the psychology of people, that of Germany has been built on the tradition of invincibleness, and when the head of the dynasty turns out not to be able to fulminate success, depression and disillusionment will be swift and terrible."

FOCH'S "DISQUIETING" APPEAL TO BLISS

On August 8 for the first time in four years the offensive was with the Allies. Thenceforth from front line to the councils of state and munitions works the Germans must do the guessing and conform to the Allies' initiative and tactics. Foch had the mass of maneuver and the element of surprise in his favor.

The British continued to recover the old Somme battlefield, the French to make successful advances. On August 20 Mangin's French army struck toward the Ailette, taking two hundred guns and eight thousand prisoners. By the 26th the British had taken twenty-six thousand more prisoners. Three days previously Foch had been made a Marshal of France for his victories.

From August 8 to August 15 the British took thirty thousand prisoners, and the total taken since the turn of the tide had been one hundred thousand. On August 13 at Spa, Ludendorff offered his resignation and urged peace, but the German government did not accept it for fear of undeceiving the people.[15] But Pershing did not know of this, which is another instance of the influence of military secrecy, when on August 17 he was pressing again for one hundred divisions by July 1, 1919, "as the very least force that will insure victory in 1919." [16]

As we already had 1,300,000 soldiers in France, it might seem that the eighty divisions would be enough; but I turn, as the next in the sequence of documents about our program for 1919, to a letter written by Bliss to Baker on the 27th which tells more graphically than the cables of the "disquieting" result of his visit to Foch's headquarters. "I do not want to dictate the following and therefore I shall have to ask you to put up with my own handwriting," said Bliss. "The military representatives of the Supreme War Council had been asked each to submit his recommendation to Foch as to the sound military policy on the Western front for the remainder of the present year and for the coming year. On the afternoon of the 26th the military representatives were at Foch's headquarters in answer to his summons. He had their papers on his desk, which he had found to be in substantial agreement that 'every effort must be made by the Allies to beat the Germans thoroughly and crushingly on the Western front next year.' "

Foch then said, to quote Bliss, that

"the British and French divisions must be maintained at at least their present strength through the next year at all costs; that one hundred American divisions must be in France by July 1, 1919; and that tonnage must be provided, at any sacrifice, to enable the United States to do this.

"He constantly reiterated that it was man-power that he wanted; that he wanted as much artillery, tanks, and aviation as he could get, but that it was man-power and again man-power that he wanted."

Foch held this view, Bliss reported, in "the full light of the success he is now meeting in his present offensive against the Germans." Pershing was in accord with him, Foch said, and he would make this statement before the next meeting of the Supreme War Council.

In his memoirs Foch was too engrossed with his tactics in the ensuing weeks to mention this call on August 27 for one hundred American divisions. The German resistance was breaking at a vital point in front of the British even as he called for man-power and yet more man-power, while Ludendorff's man-power continued to wane in spirit and numbers. By the 30th the Germans held only one bridgehead west of the Somme. The next day the British recovered Péronne. On September 2 the French Tenth Army had the heights of Crouy and had reached the high road from Soissons to Coucy-le-Château. In Foch's own words:

"At the other end of the battle-line the British First Army, continuing its broadly conceived operations, recommenced its attacks. On September 2, after violent and stubborn fighting, it broke through the Droucourt-Quéant line, and passed on several miles in the direction of Marquion." [17]

Several miles for the Allies on that trench-locked Western front—such gains were becoming regular events. But let Foch continue.

"After this smashing blow the enemy began to retreat along the whole front between the Somme and the Sensée reaching new positions behind the Tortille and the Nord Canal in front of the Hindenburg line. Thus at the beginning of September, victory had passed to the Allied banners."

In the Ypres salient the Germans had had to yield all their gains of April. Indeed, within six weeks the Allies had won back all the ground lost in 1918, and much more.

Meanwhile, after the closing of the Marne salient, Pershing's divisions had begun their movement toward their own sector. They were to have their own first battle as an American Army to reduce the Saint-Mihiel salient which Foch, Pétain, and Pershing agreed would give us a most favorable opportunity for an impressive American victory. Baker was to see the battle; but only as incident to the main object of his second visit to France, which was to secure shipping for the 80-division program, while Pershing was to continue to insist upon an even larger program. I shall tell later how America rose to her supreme height in the War in preparing to train, transport, and maintain that mighty host in France in 1919, which the Commander-in-Chief had set for the year of decision against the enemy.

But now, in my dogged devotion to continuity of subject— or at least a phase of a subject—rather than chronological miscellany, I shall turn, in the next two chapters, away from the masters of military chess-play to the War Department's interest in the individual himself who had gone from civil life to the camps and cantonments and then to France.

XXXII

JUSTICE

THE demand for justice is as old as Humanity. It represents the deepest feelings of a man toward his superiors, of the citizen toward his government, of the private soldier toward his officers. In the World War four million youth became subject to military courts under military law; with few exceptions the officers were as new to the Army as the men themselves. Some officers were bound to be weak, some too severe, some without a sense of steady equity in command, and all capable of errors owing to temperament and circumstances. But orders must be obeyed or there was debate instead of unity of action. The enterprise upon which the nation embarked on April 6, 1917, was military. War had taken charge of the justice among nations and the justice within armies.

"The administration of justice is a compromise between speed and certainty," as Baker said in a memorandum to Judge Advocate General Crowder. It was inevitably difficult in a hastily formed army "to establish such processes as will throw around every man in the Army, whether private or officer, the surest safeguards and protections which can be devised against either error of law or passion or mistake of justice at the hands of those who try him, involving either his property, his honor, or his life."

Lack of discipline had been responsible for many of the misfortunes of our previous wars, including the ravages of disease among the troops. Baker was determined to support discipline as a fundamental principle in the prompt preparation of so large a force in the requisite uniformity of training and action. He said: [1]

"Under ordinary circumstances, discipline is developed in an army by the admission of a relatively small number of re-

cruits into a veteran organization, and the new men acquire
their sense of discipline from their contacts with older men
who have gradually become disciplined soldiers. Under war
conditions new men are gathered in vast numbers into fresh
military units in which there are few, if any, men who have
had any experience as soldiers. There is therefore no barrack-
room communication of discipline from the older men to the
new men, but the whole idea of discipline descends like an
unfamiliar thing which in the hurry of mobilization nobody
has time to explain, but which the officers feel must be rigidly
enforced because these new men must learn quickly what in
peace-time they would learn gradually. Many of the officers
in a new unit in war-time have themselves only had six weeks
or two months of officers' training, and their administration of
discipline is unseasoned by experience. They are therefore
afraid to pass over any defect or dereliction, with the consequence that they are themselves administering very recently
acquired knowledge to other men to whom the whole situation is strange and little understood.

"I am inclined to think that more explanation of the imperative necessity of discipline was made to our soldiers by
lectures and in other ways than has ever been done for the
recruits in any other army; but when all was done that could
be done, there was still a large proportion of the men who
did not understand the vital necessity of unquestioning ob-
servance and of rigid discipline. Of course, these men understood it later when they came into actual fighting, where the
safety of the cause and of one's associates plainly depends upon
every man's doing his task without stopping to inquire the
reason for it. In the early stages, however, of the making of
our Army, or any other new army, there necessarily grows up
a disbelief in, and resentment of, discipline which seems excessive and unreasonable."

There were echoes in the Congress of the view that our Articles of War were archaic. The articles were rewritten by Acting
Judge Advocate General Samuel T. Ansell, with modifications
by Colonel John H. Wigmore, Dean of the Law School of North-
western University, a reserve officer in the Judge Advocate General's office. But the purpose of the revision had already been

secured owing to the war-time conduct of the department and
the settled policy

"that the Judge Advocate General's office would review
all sentences with a view to establishing uniformity to the extent of moderating those most grossly excessive, and that immediately upon the declaration of peace, a comprehensive and
fresh revision of all sentences would be undertaken with a
view to reducing them to their normal peace-time limits as
soon as the disciplinary needs of an actual state of war were
relieved."

Since the number of court-martial cases was astonishingly
small, as I have stated, the number that came up for review was
small. Many of these, especially when a precedent was involved,
were referred to Baker. Drunkenness in an officer was a serious
offense which set a bad example to his soldiers, when drinking
by anyone in uniform was against the law. Almost invariably
the offender offered the extenuating circumstance of the unexpected effect of a cocktail or two upon a man of abstemious
habits. In these cases, when the sentence was dismissal, Baker
seemed to be a little harder on mature men of higher rank than
on lieutenants. The members of a court-martial recommended
that a certain major, who had made a "spectacle" of himself, be
granted clemency because "never being accustomed to the drinking of intoxicants he had taken drinks on an empty stomach
prior to joining a dinner party at the hotel." With reference to
the commutation recommended, Baker wrote: "If this officer is
confined to the limits of the camp for six months, it will be
known throughout the camp that he is so confined; that his offense was drunkenness, and no fine distinctions will be drawn
by the junior officers as to why he was not dismissed." His influence would be broken.

Baker would not condone absolute insubordination; but veterans who were young officers in the training camps may read
with interest his reasons for clemency in one instance where a
"kid" second lieutenant had been sentenced to dismissal from
the service.

"It seems that there had been some laxity in the matter of saluting officers in Camp J——, and a certain Captain C—— was sent out on special inspection duty to take the names of officers who failed properly to salute their superiors. Captain C—— met the accused, whom he had been watching for some time on the street, and, noting the fact that he did not lower his hand smartly to the side, but only partially so when he made the salute, spoke to him, saying that his salute was deficient and that he should lower his hand completely to his side. The accused immediately began to defend his mode of saluting, and a controversy arose which resulted in the Captain's asking the lieutenant his name. The lieutenant more or less jestingly gave him a wrong name, apparently regarding the whole matter as an instance of very exacting conduct on the part of a slightly higher ranking officer. When he later learned that Captain C—— had been assigned to this special duty of correcting deficient salutes, he sought him out and gave his correct name and apologized.

"He was wrong in not saluting properly, in arguing with a ranking officer on the subject, and in frivolously giving a wrong name; but all of these reasons put together do not seem to me to constitute ground for a dishonorable dismissal from the military service of the country in time of war, and I feel quite sure that a reprimand administered to this young officer by his Division Commander will accomplish the curative purpose of establishing in him a wholesome respect for discipline, and at the same time will save for the service an officer whom the Government has been at a good deal of pains and expense to educate."

In order that the reviewing authority should be safeguarded, Baker sent Brigadier General E. M. Kreger, of the Judge Advocate General's Department, to France, where he was stationed at G. H. Q. to keep justice in the A. E. F. in touch with home justice and to go over cases in which heavy penalties had been imposed. Eventually, after the War, all the cases in which sentences were still being served were again reviewed. To quote Baker:

"This policy was carried out with only one modification, which was the reduction of long-term sentences. Sometimes the reductions were in successive stages in order to hold out the hope of further reduction as a stimulus to good behavior in the disciplinary prisons. Before I left Washington every sentence imposed during the War had been revised, and every sentence which could by any possibility be regarded as excessive had been reduced to peace-time standards." [2]

FOUR SENTENCES TO DEATH

But there was one sentence in which review could not wait until after the War—death. This brings us to the famous cases of four soldiers, whose names, however, I shall not give, because no good purpose would be served by doing so now. The Commander-in-Chief in France, the Chief of Staff, and the Judge Advocate General in Washington, confirmed the verdict of the court-martial for the extreme penalty. In transmitting the four cases to the President, Baker wrote on May 18, 1918:

"As I find myself reaching an entirely different conclusion, and disagreeing with the entire and authoritative military opinion in the cases, I beg to set out at some length the reasons which move me in the matter.

"The cases must be divided into two classes, and I will first deal with the two young men convicted of sleeping while on duty. [These two cases, he found, were] substantially identical in their facts. The accusations were laid under the 86th Article of War, which reads: 'Any sentinel who is found . . . sleeping upon his post . . . shall, if the offense be committed in time of war, suffer death or such other punishment as a court-martial may direct.'

"In both cases a corporal inspecting along a front-line trench found these young men standing in the proper military position, leaning against the trench, with their rifles lying on the parapet of the trench within easy reach of their hands. Each man had his head resting on his arm, and his arm resting on the parapet. The offenses were committed, in the A—— case on the night of November third and fourth, and in the B——

case on or about the fifth of November. In both cases the testimony was exceedingly brief, and showed that the night was dark and cold, that the soldiers had their ponchos and other equipment on, and in one case it was a fair inference that the poncho was drawn over the ears and trench helmet in such a way as to make it difficult for the soldier to hear the approaching steps of the corporal. In each case the corporal laid his own rifle upon the parapet, and took that of the soldier, carrying it away with him, and instructed the other sentinel, the men being posted in this outpost duty in twos, to shake the soldier and tell him to report to the corporal for his gun. In each case the corporal shamed the soldier for his neglect of duty, and pointed out to him the fact that not only his own life but those of others were at stake, and that he should be more zealous and alert.

"In neither case does either the corporal or the fellow-sentinel swear positively that the accused was asleep. I confess that on all reasonable grounds, taking the circumstances into consideration, it seems to me entirely likely that both men were asleep; but it is important to note that in neither case had the accused stepped away from his proper military post to sit down or lie down; both being found standing at their post of duty in what is admitted to have been a correct military position; and if they were asleep their heads literally nodded over on to their arms without any intentional relaxation of attention to their duty so far as can be gathered from any of the surrounding circumstances.

DOUBLE SENTRY DUTY AND NO SLEEP

"These soldiers are both young. A—— enlisted into the Regular Army by volunteering on April 18, 1917, having had no previous military experience, his age at that time being 19 years and six months. He was, therefore, slightly more than 20 at the time of the alleged offense. B—— enlisted on May 11, 1917, without previous military experience, his age at that time being 18 years and 11 months. He was, therefore, at the time of the alleged offense, slightly under 20 years of age.

"From the testimony it appears that both of these young men had been posted as sentinels doing what is called double sentry duty, going on duty at four P. M., and remaining on duty until six A. M., with relief at intervals by other sentinels during the night, but with no opportunity to sleep during the night because of there being no place where they could secure sleep. It further appeared that neither of them had slept during the day before, after having spent the previous night on gas sentinel duty, although both had tried to sleep during the day preceding the night of the alleged offenses but found it impossible because of the noise. In each case the commanding officer who forwarded the charge and recommended trial by general court-martial added to his endorsement as extenuating circumstances the youth and failure of the soldier to take the necessary rest when off duty on the first occupation of trenches.

"It is difficult to picture to the eye which has not seen it the situation in which these young soldiers were placed. In the month of November the section of France in which these soldiers were stationed was cold, wet and uncomfortable in the extreme. No sort of shelter of any comfortable kind could be provided near the trenches, because any such shelter attracts enemy observation and fire. Throughout one long night they performed duty as gas sentinels. During the next day, when they perhaps ought to have sought more rest than they did seek, they found it difficult to secure any sleep because of the noise and discomfort of their surroundings. As a consequence, on the night of the alleged offenses they had reached the place at which exhausted nature apparently refused to go further, and without any intentional relaxation of vigilance on their parts they dozed in standing positions at their posts of duty.

"I am quite aware of the gravity of this offense, and of the fact that the safety of others, perhaps the safety of an army and of a cause, may depend upon such disciplinary enforcement of this regulation as will prevent soldiers from sleeping on sentinel duty; and yet I cannot believe that youths of so little military experience, placed for the first time under circumstances so exhausting, can be held to deserve the death penalty, nor can I believe that the death sentence ought to be imposed in cases which do not involve a bad heart, or so flagrant a disregard of the welfare of others and of the obligation of a soldier as to be evidence of conscious disloyalty.

"In both of these cases the reviewing Judge Advocate quotes

with approval some observations of General Upton who in his work on military policy points out that the action taken by President Lincoln in the early days of the Civil War in pardoning or commuting sentences in cases of death penalty, led to the need of greater severity at a later period in the interest of discipline; but the cases which General Upton had in mind were cases of desertion in the face of the enemy involving cowardice, and cases of substantially treasonable betrayal of the nation, and I can see no persuasion in them as an example. Rather it would seem to indicate that the invocation of this opinion of General Upton indicates a feeling on the part of the reviewing Judge Advocate that, while these particular cases might not be deemed on their own merits to justify the death sentence, nevertheless as a disciplinary example such action would be justified. I am not, of course, suggesting that any of the military officers who have reviewed these cases would be willing to sacrifice the lives of these soldiers even though innocent; but I do think that if these cases stood alone no one of the reviewing officers would have recommended the execution of these sentences; their recommendations being, in my judgment, soldierly and in accordance with the traditions of their profession, and based upon a very earnest desire on their part to guard the safety of their commands, and the lives of other soldiers; but, nevertheless, to some extent influenced by the value to the discipline of the Army of the examples which their execution would afford.

"I have not sought to examine the learning of this subject, and therefore have not prepared a history of the death penalty as a military punishment; but I think it fair to assume that it arose in times and under circumstances quite different from these, when men were impressed into armies to fight for causes in which they had little interest and of which they had little knowledge, and when their conduct was controlled without their consent by those who assumed to have more or less arbitrary power over them. Our Army, however, is the army of a democratic nation fighting for a cause which the people themselves understand and approve, and I had happy and abundant evidence when I was in France that the plain soldiers of our Expeditionary Forces are aware of the fact that they are really defending principles in which they have as direct an interest as anybody, principles which they understand, approve and are willing to die for.

"I venture, therefore, to believe that the President can with perfect safety to military discipline pardon these two young men; and I have prepared and attached hereto an order which, if it meets with your approval, will accomplish that purpose, and at the same time, I believe, upon its publication further stimulate the already fine spirit of our Army in France. Such an order as I have here drawn would be read by every soldier in France and in the United States, and coming from the Commander-in-Chief would be a challenge to the performance of duty, quite as stimulating as any disciplinary terror proceeding from the execution of these sentences. In the meantime, public opinion in this country would, I believe, with practical unanimity approve such action on your part. . . .

"The Judge Advocate General in reviewing these cases called the attention of the Chief of Staff to the fact that four cases of sleeping on post arising in the same regiment at approximately the same time resulted in acquittal of the accused on substantially the same evidence as that recited in the A——— and B——— cases above reviewed, and that in six cases similar offenses committed elsewhere in France had led to very moderate penalties."

PARDONED—AND AFTERWARD FOUGHT BRAVELY

The President pardoned both young men. Both fought bravely afterward, one being killed in action.

In reviewing the two other cases Baker said:

"The charges are substantially identical in that each of them is accused under the 64th Article of War of having 'wilfully disobeyed any lawful command of his superior officer.' The facts show that on January 3, 1918, these two young men in broad daylight in the theater of war, at a place back of the actual line, were directed to bring their equipment and fall in for drill. Each refused, whereupon they were warned by the lieutenant who gave the order not to persist in their refusal on the ground that grave consequences would ensue. They were not warned that the penalty of disobedience was death;

but were advised earnestly to comply. Both persisted in their refusal. Each gave as his reason for refusing that he had been drilled extensively the day before, that they had gotten cold, the weather being extremely severe, and that they had not yet recovered from the effects of that exposure.

"Both pled guilty at the trial.

"It is perfectly obvious that this order ought to have been obeyed. It was a proper military order, and it seems to me inconceivable that such obstinate refusal on so trivial a matter could have been made with any consciousness that the death penalty was the alternative. Nevertheless the disobedience was wilful, undisciplined, and inexcusable, and it ought to be punished with a suitable punishment.

"The Judge Advocate General in reviewing these two cases limits himself again to the technical correctness of the proceedings; but in a subsequent memorandum says: 'In addition to the foregoing, the study in this office reveals a number of cases which have come in from France where men have been convicted of wilful disobedience of orders under circumstances which do not distinguish them as to the locus of the offense from the cases of C—— and D——, who were sentenced to death. The sentences in the cases referred to run from a few months' to several years' confinement.'

"In other words, the Judge Advocate General reviewing generally the state of discipline in the Army in France, and the steps taken to enforce it, reaches the conclusion that up to the time of the trial of these cases the offenses of which these soldiers were convicted had been regarded as quite minor in their gravity. The Chief of Staff in commenting upon this memorandum of the Judge Advocate General is able from his own recollection to add that the wilful-disobedience cases lately tried in France did not occur in the actual theater of war, making at least that much of a distinction. But the case still remains one in which suddenly a new and severe attitude is taken without the record disclosing that any special order had been made notifying soldiers that the requirements of discipline would call upon courts-martial thereafter to resort to extreme penalties to restore discipline.

"Both C—— and D—— are young. The record shows that C—— enlisted on February 3, 1917, without previous military

experience, his age at that time being 18 years and 1 month.
D—— enlisted on February 17, 1917, without previous military
experience, his age being 19 years and 2 months. Each of them
at the time of the commission of the alleged offenses was, therefore, less than 20 years of age.

"The record in the D—— case shows that there had been
previous shortcomings on his part in the matter of obedience.
That is to say, he had once failed to report for drill, for which
he was required to forfeit 15 days' pay; a second time failed
to report for drill, penalty not stated; and a third time failed
to report for fatigue duty, for which he was sentenced to one
month at hard labor and to forfeit two-thirds of his pay for
two months. He seems, therefore, to have found it difficult to
accommodate himself to the discipline of the life of a soldier,
and his offense hereunder reviewed is aggravated by this previous record.

"By a very extraordinary coincidence this record discloses
the fact that these two soldiers were members of a company
commanded by Captain D. A. Henckes. It is from the captain
of his company that the soldier most immediately learns discipline and obedience. The captain sets the example, and in-
culcates the principles upon which the soldier is built. Now
this particular Captain Henckes, although for many years an
officer in the Regular Army, was himself so undisciplined and
disloyal that when he was ordered to France with his command, he sought to resign because he did not want to fight
the Germans. Born in this country, and for twenty years an
officer in its Army, under sworn obligation to defend the
United States against all her enemies, domestic and foreign,
he still sought to resign; and when the resignation was not
accepted, and he went to France, the Commander-in-Chief was
obliged to return him to this country because of his improper
attitude toward the military service and his country's cause in
this war. He was thereupon court-martialed, and is now serving a sentence of twenty-five years in the penitentiary for his
lack of loyalty and lack of discipline.

"I confess I do not see how any soldiers in his command
could have been expected to learn the proper attitude toward
the military service from such a commander. I do not suggest that the shortcomings of Captain Henckes be made an

excuse for their disobedience, but these mere youths can hardly be put to death under these circumstances, and I, therefore, recommend that the sentence in each case be commuted to one involving penal servitude under circumstances which will enable them by confinement in the Disciplinary Barracks at Fort Leavenworth to acquire under better conditions a wholesomer attitude toward the duty of a soldier. Orders accompanying this letter are drawn for your approval which will carry out the recommendation here made.

"In view of the fact that both C—— and D—— had been previously guilty of minor offenses as disclosed by the record, the penalty suggested is three years' confinement."

The President concurred in Baker's recommendation.

PERSHING'S APPEAL FOR MORE POWER IS REFUSED

Soon after Baker had sent his review of the four cases to the President, he was writing on May 11, 1918, to the President about Pershing's demand for fuller power in executing the death sentence without review by Washington:

"General Pershing, as the Commanding General of the Army in the Field, now has authority by virtue of the provisions of Article 48, paragraph D, of the Articles of War, to execute sentences of death in the cases of persons convicted in time of war of murder, rape, mutiny, desertion, or as spies, without referring such cases to the War Department for revision or to you for approval. In a cablegram recently received from him he points out that General Haig and General Pétain are each entrusted with a much larger authority in the enforcement of the death penalty, and suggests that an amendment be made in the 48th Article of War enlarging his power in the premises. The other offenses for which the death penalty are permissible are attempted desertion, advising or aiding another to desert, misbehavior before the enemy, subordinates compelling commander to surrender, improper use of countersign, forcing a safeguard, corresponding with or aiding the enemy, misbehavior of sentinel, assaulting or wilfully disobeying superior officer, failure to suppress mutiny or sedition.

"You will understand that the death penalty is permitted in

the last-enumerated cases but may not be executed by the
Commanding General of the Army in the Field without reference to the War Department and to you. My own judgment is that the power of the Commanding General ought
not to be enlarged in this regard, and I am not disposed to ask
Congress to amend the Articles of War as suggested by General Pershing. . . .

"If you do not concur in my judgment in this matter I will
be glad to lay General Pershing's request before the appropriate committees, but I do not desire to take that course unless
such regulations, if passed by Congress, would be in accordance with your judgment in the case."

The President agreed with Baker's view.

XXXIII

"THE INVISIBLE ARMOR"

In every hour not occupied by drill in the camps and cantonments in the United States there were opportunities for relaxation and entertainment in the hostess houses that had superseded the cribs of the Mexican border. Baker said that he not
only wanted our soldiers well armed, clothed, and fed, but he
wanted them to go to France taking an "invisible armor" which
would be made up of

"a set of social habits replacing those of their homes and
communities, a set of social habits and a state of social mind
born in the training camps, a new soldier state of mind, so
that when they get overseas and are removed from the reach
of our comforting and restraining and helpful hand, they will
have gotten such a set of habits as will constitute a moral and
intellectual armor for their protection overseas." [1]

Life had become quite settled and conventionalized for the
soldier after a few weeks in a training camp. But from the minute he started for France he became a buffeted traveler who
from one day to another never knew what his next destination
would be. On the closely packed transports he slept and ate in
shifts. In France he saw nothing of those American railroad
cars on the lines of communication. He rode in the "forty and
eight"—forty men or eight horses—box cars. His home was in
the billet or the dug-out where he spent the night.

There were cafés down the street that sold beer, wine, and
cognac; and the restrictions of the home camp area, which had
left him dependent upon "complacent sweethearts," did not
exist. We were guests in a land of different customs, laws, and
civilization, and our hosts' attitude toward our policy involved
a problem in Allied relations quite as delicate and vexing as
preserving the integrity of our Army or allocating shipping.

The French considered that our ideas ran counter to human nature; and Fosdick in his official report on the whole subject said:

"The position taken by the American Expeditionary Forces in regard to the problem of prostitution is unique among the armies of Europe on both sides of the battle-line. In the French and British armies and with the German and Austrian troops, licensed houses of prostitution have been generally permitted under supervision of army medical staffs. General Pershing has from the start refused to tolerate this approach to the problem, and has insisted upon a policy of repression as opposed to the system of reglementation in vogue in the other armies. . . . The following official papers will undoubtedly have considerable historical value in the future."

Pershing understood Baker's views on the subject; he had had experience of the conditions on the Mexican border and appreciated the results that the War Department policy had achieved. As soon as our soldiers began arriving in France the Commander-in-Chief issued an order reminding each soldier that it was a vital necessity that he maintain himself in the best physical condition.[2] . . . "A soldier who contracts a venereal disease not only suffers permanent injury, but renders himself inefficient as a soldier and becomes an incumbrance to the Army. He fails in his duty to his country and to his comrades."

The effects of the scourge were to be explained to the soldiers by the medical officer of his command; there were to be fortnightly inspections; prophylactic stations for treatment after exposure were to be established; soldiers must report for treatment; and those contracting the disease were subject to court-martial and a forfeiture of pay. A later order on September 9, 1917,[3] required commanding officers to follow the general orders of the War Department in providing entertainment, sports, and all manner of recreations; regimental infirmaries were to be established for the isolation and treatment of the disease, and also receiving hospitals would be near shops where the victims might perform manual labor; the syphilitic register was to be carefully kept; the case of any officer contracting the disease was to be reported immediately to General Headquarters; and any infected women who were located were to be taken to hospitals.

An order of December 18, 1917,[4] was even more explicit about the duty of commanding officers in enforcing the prophylaxis regulation: No man was to leave a transport until he had been inspected for disease; all recognized houses of prostitution were "off limits"; and "soldiers are forbidden to buy, or accept as gifts from inhabitants, whiskey, brandy, champagne, liquors, alcoholic beverages, other than light wines or beer"; and all places where the forbidden liquors were sold were "off limits." On the subject of light wines Fosdick had written to Baker as early as September 22, 1917:

"We are beginning to get letters of protest from around the country in regard to the use of wine by American troops in France. These letters assert that the same protection supplied by the enforcement of Section 12 of the Army Law [which forbade the soldiers to drink any alcoholic liquors] should be afforded our men abroad.

"This is a question which in my mind is going to take sheer statesmanship amounting to genius to handle. I am myself pretty well acquainted with France, and as a practical measure I do not see how we can very well forbid the use of wine. It is served in every restaurant and café as we serve water. Dr. Martin of the Council of National Defense says that such use is outrageous and is constantly on my coat-tails to get the War Department to do something about it. I am confident that measures can be taken to protect the troops abroad from venereal disease, although I confess I am not quite clear in my mind as to just what measures should be taken. But this question of wine is a different matter.

"I write you at this time because of the presence on my desk of a large number of letters which I don't know how to answer."

To this Baker answered on the 24th, setting Fosdick's doubts at rest:

"The use of the French light wines by our soldiers must be regarded as a very minor evil in comparison with a great many things which we have to combat. It seems incredible that any great amount of wine-drinking should grow up among our men, but of course no sort of police regulations that we could enforce in France outside of the limits of our own camps could reach the question.

"It seems to me the only answer you can possibly make to the kind of letters to which you refer is that we are in the constructive steps of fighting the greater evils, and that this one will be limited as far as our military power can reach."

CLEMENCEAU FAVORS LEGALIZED PROSTITUTION

The "off limits" rule and our policing of towns where we had many soldiers, especially ports, inevitably led to friction with the French. In some cases the mayors reported the complaints of their constituents about loss of trade. At the outset of Fosdick's report, which he considered might be of "historical value in the future," is printed Clemenceau's letter which expressed officially through the French premier the views of the French government on the subject:

"The presence on French territory, especially in certain important centers, of American troop agglomerations brings up questions of social hygiene which it is of great importance to solve to the best interest of the health of the Allied troops and of the civilian population.

"Regarding more specially the propagation of venereal diseases, the methods followed so far by the American Commandant do not seem to have given good results. In fact, total prohibition of all regulated prostitution in the vicinity of American troops has had for result, in spite of the measures of prophylaxis and discipline taken by the American authorities, the increase of venereal diseases among the civilian population of the neighborhood.

"Consequently, I should be very much obliged if you would again call the attention of the American High Command to this serious question.

"In this respect, it is certain that clandestine prostitution offers to men more numerous and more dangerous temptations than does regulated prostitution. The latter, in its strictest form—*i. e.*, the house of prostitution—if it does not exclude completely, at least reduces substantially, the dangers of unrestrained prostitution. Owing to the administrative and sanitary control by the public authorities it offers the maximum of security, reducing the risk of contagion to the minimum.

"Should the American High Command see this question in the same light, I would put my services at his disposal for initiating if necessary, along with the Minister of the Interior, the creation of special houses of this kind.

"I beg of you to communicate to me as soon as possible the reply of the American Commandant."

A long memorandum by Medical Inspector Simonin, Assistant Director of the Social Hygiene program of the French Surgeon General's office, supported Clemenceau's view. M. Simonin had read the regulations which "the Honorable Secretary of War, Mr. Baker," had devised for our home cantonments, and which received the support of the Congress. He said:

"The strikingly original characteristic of the American theory is the repressive measure at the head of this program, *i. e.*, 'the total suppression of all prostitution in the zone of the cantonments.' The second item is the repression of clandestine prostitution, which the above prohibition can, alas, but increase. . . .

"The plan depends upon anti-venereal education and the distraction resulting from physical exercises and amusements to turn away young men from their sexual pleasures. . . .

"Mr. Baker has moreover constituted a commission on camp sanitation to exercise constant vigilance, not only for the elimination of recognized houses of prostitution, but in order to drive clandestine prostitutes from the streets, lodging houses, and hotels. . . .

"In absolute contrast to the above is the secret note of January 15, 1916 (No. 1061–5), French Headquarters, relative to the prevention of venereal disease, which contains the following paragraph:

" 'The multiplication of public houses should be discreetly

favored and their inmates examined at least every two days by the military physician.' "

He notes that although on June 22, 1916, the French Academy of Medicine had recommended inspection and teaching soldiers the value of continence, six months later, as the result of further experience, the Academy had "requested the opinion of the Under Secretary of State for Health, on the propriety of favoring the establishment of houses of toleration well supervised in the 'centers of furlough (*herbergement*) for the American Army at the front.' " [5]

M. Simonin concluded:

"This policy seems very little in accord with the regulations of the Honorable Secretary of War in Washington and qualified to surprise him not a little."

In answer to our proposal to apply the home regulations to Saint-Nazaire, the entry port for our troops in the early period of the A. E. F., the local French authorities proposed the extension of licensed prostitution to meet the increased demands and suggested that the French would be agreeable to establishing prophylactic stations in the houses.

"But our Allies, faithful to the principles emanating from the Secretary of War, Mr. Baker, have declined the proposal and have persisted in their original plan, so that the situation at Saint-Nazaire on January 1, 1918, is as follows: (1) licensed houses are declared out of bounds by the American Commander; (2) licensed street-walkers are also forbidden the American troops; (3) sentinels placed at the entrance of streets inhabited by licensed street-walkers prohibit access to all quarters which are known or suspected to contain such women.

"The object of the Americans is to prevent their soldiers from having sexual relations. To attain this they bring into play every means for retaining the soldier in his camp by giving him all possible distractions.

"Starting from the principle that chastity is possible, they have decreed continence officially, and they entrust to religion and ethics the task of maintaining morality in man and of keeping him always master of his passions. They rely also on violent physical exercise to afford distraction and reduce desire. . . .

"America has the noblest aspirations for official morality. Can she give similar guaranties for individual morality? . . .

"According to the reports of police commissioners, the number of rapes and attempts at seduction has never been so great as during this period."

M. Simonin insisted that there had been a spread of clandestine prostitution at Saint-Nazaire and that our soldiers were bringing infection from America instead of getting it in France.

COLONEL YOUNG ANSWERS M. SIMONIN

The French hygienist did not go unanswered. Our expert on the subject was Colonel Hugh H. Young, the eminent urologist of Johns Hopkins, who had gone to France with Pershing's pioneer staff. He and his associate, Colonel Edward L. Keyes, another eminent expert, wrote a joint memorandum:

"The attitude of the French Government reflects that of the French people. They firmly believe that regulated houses of prostitution offer the best means of preventing the spread of venereal diseases and of discouraging prostitution among the civil population, at the same time protecting innocent women and children from rape.

"The total absence of reliable vital statistics in France makes the refutation of their arguments by an appeal to facts in this country almost impossible."

But Young said that every serious study, including Dr. Abraham Flexner's on "Prostitution in Europe," had shown that the licensing system fails of its purpose. There had been altogether four charges of rape against Americans at Saint-Nazaire. In a case of conviction there had been a sentence of thirty years' imprisonment. The majority of American soldiers who were infected upon arrival in France were members of hurriedly organized labor-battalions which had not been subject to inspection and our regulations at home. But once our home organization was in full working order, inspection upon departure and arrival had put an end to this source of danger, as our statistics proved.

"We have not received the slightest co-operation from the French authorities with reference to fighting venereal disease at Saint-Nazaire. In fact, all the efforts, and particularly those of the Mayor, have been most antagonistic. He has tried in every way to get people to say that it would be better to open the houses of prostitution and have the miserable condition of our troops as it was some months ago. The Mayor has tried in every way to get a wedge in so that our men can be allowed all kinds of liberty while in this port. When you think that transports of 12,000 to 15,000 men used to come through this port and stay here as long as ten or fifteen days and that an average of $20 to $30 was spent by each, you can easily see how much the town loses by our methods. . . . To give an idea of how much money the prostitutes made under the old method, one Madame deposited in one bank in one month 75,000 francs.

"If a saloon is caught it is closed for a short time, but it re-opens and goes on just the same. . . .

"I wrote a prescription for 7½ grains of cocaine and sent the worst-looking man we could find to get it. He priced a few articles, then got in a corner and presented the prescription. It was filled without protest. This druggist was suspected of selling cocaine to Negroes. The man was arrested in the store by the French police, and the drug was taken away from him and found to be cocaine. The French said that this was not good proof and would do nothing about it. Since then two other prescriptions were filled without a word of inquiry by the druggist, but were not reported because it was thought useless. The French here also sell firearms to Negroes and then liquor and cocaine."

M. Simonin might naturally assume that the experts were unfamiliar with European ideas and convictions about social hygiene. Fosdick, however, had made extensive studies of European city governments in this as well as every branch of administration; and his policy for our Army at home and abroad had been worked out after most serious study.

Young proceeded in scientific logic to prove the superiority, on purely practical and physical grounds, of the strange new system from America:

"The sanitation of venereal diseases as it has been developed in the United States is presented to the French in a practical manner for the first time. They have not had an opportunity of studying the basis upon which it is founded nor have their minds been subjected to the experiences whereby the United States has gradually come to accept the repression of all forms of licensed vice as the only solution of the problem of venereal disease. . . . They believe our attitude to be founded upon a prudery of which they feel themselves incapable, and to be essentially a question of morals. As a matter of fact, the attitude of the A. E. F. is essentially a matter of hygiene.

"It is our belief that our efforts are bearing fruit and that if the French Government will in any region or throughout a territory occupied by the A. E. F. either co-operate heartily with us or, better still, place the policing of a certain region entirely under the control of the American authorities, these will be glad to abide by the results obtained. . . . If, in a subsequent reply, the French Government alleges certain definite facts as a foundation for its allegations, these facts may then be discussed. Until then it would seem wise not to indulge in casuistry."

THE RECORDS SUPPORT OUR POLICY

In a paper which Young prepared on the subject he referred to the French and British armies which had remained for long periods at the front where there were no women and where the force of circumstances required continence:

"No one has ever suggested that these troops were not in fine fighting trim, or that their morale had been diminished by their excellent morals. One of the best preparations for the zone of the front in which troops have to follow enforced continence, is to have troops in training, habituated to getting along without sexual indulgences. This long-drawn-out war of the trenches has exploded another old-time fallacy, *i. e.,* that the soldier must be a libertine in order to be a fighter."

As the number of our troops in France increased and we had control of more towns through the sheer fact of our numbers, the accumulating records left no doubt that prophylaxis regulations, when supported by instruction and the threat of courts-martial, were highly successful, and that cases appeared principally among troops on the move through towns where we had no military police or prophylactic stations. A motor-truck company that "ran wild" had six times as many cases as one that was well regulated. The non-effective rate from the disease, which had been 5.62 in our Army in 1916, was reduced to 2.13 in the A. E. F. "Instead of now [June, 1918] filling three one-thousand-bed hospitals with venereal patients as had been expected by this time and planned for in the United States, there are no venereal hospitals, and only about three hundred beds occupied by venereal cases, and these largely in regimental and field infirmaries."

The campaign of education and discipline went beyond prevention of the disease by prophylaxis. In the words of Colonel Young: "Is this [continence] at all possible in armies? There are many who scoff at the idea. What do our statistics show in this regard?" He thought that the record he quoted was sound because the use of prophylaxis was proven to be practically universal in the American Army. The record for seven weeks among seven thousand men of all branches of the service showed only fifty-six men who had come for prophylaxis, and one case of disease.

The battle for American control by commanding officers against the local French authorities continued throughout the War. An example in point was the town of Blois. I quote again from Colonel Young's paper:

"The Provost Marshal toward the latter part of January placed the houses out of bounds. Immediate protest was made by the French authorities, and the houses were opened to American soldiers. . . . Then a house was taken over by the

Americans and run entirely for the American soldiers. French soldiers and French civilians were not admitted. . . . The women were examined two or three times a week by an American medical officer."

Word of this arrangement reached our G. H. Q., which immediately ordered that it be discontinued.

"The method now in vogue is that one of the military police meets each train; every woman coming into Blois is observed, and if suspicious, a detail is sent to see where she goes and to watch her movements. If it is found that she is soliciting she is immediately reported to the French police and if not registered is always run out of town. If registered, as a rule the French police turn her loose. The women found soliciting on the streets are arrested by the American military police and turned over to the French. As a rule they are turned loose again if they have cards, but they are promptly arrested again by the Americans, and as a result of these frequent arrests most of them leave town. During the past month over 150 women have thus been forced to leave, and the A. P. M. reports that there are only about 10 or 12 women *en carte* now and that clandestine prostitution has been greatly reduced. The houses are kept strictly out of bounds to American soldiers and officers; and both soldiers and officers, if seen with women, are apprehended by the police and both woman and man arrested. Women seen going to houses with men are also arrested along with the men. As a result there has been a tremendous transformation of vice conditions in Blois, and the better French people have begun to appreciate it immensely. I am told by the A. P. M. that he frequently receives letters from them notifying them that women of questionable character are occupying certain houses or apartments, and asking investigation, which is promptly given. . . . Certain politicians and owners of saloons and houses of prostitution are crying out greatly against it, but the better element of the population are outspoken in approval."

There were only one-third as many cases of disease to the thousand under the American as there were under the French method.

On no subject were our people at home more badly mis-informed than on sex-hygiene in our Army. The "frankness" so much in vogue in the writing of war novels has left a false impression, which, in the interest of fairness to the men and to history, should be corrected by candid quotations from official documents. Our people, under the influence of these novels, wonder whether many soldiers did not return from the A. E. F. with a permanent taint that they might pass on to future generations. This fear might be warranted if our policy in sex-hygiene had been the same as that of armies in the days when the "God-given passion" was recognized as the proof of manliness, when there was little attention paid to sex-education, safeguards, or preventive medicine, and when the nature of the scourge was too abhorrent to be mentioned in print.

Some of our returning soldiers boasted the more of their amours because these had so slight a basis of experience. As a matter of fact, many of them, easily the great majority, knew enforced if not voluntary continence all the time they were in the A. E. F.

XXXIV

HIGH TIDE

WHILE our soldiers were closing the Marne salient and forming their battle-line at Saint-Mihiel, new draftees must take the
place of the trained men who were leaving the cantonments at
the rate of ten thousand a day. Three hundred and seventy
thousand recruits were summoned in May, 300,000 in June,
and 400,000 in July, making a total of more than a million in
three months.

Provost Marshal General Crowder, his assistants, and the
draft boards were to have no relief from the treadmill until
Armistice Day. Their labors became both more arduous and
more thankless in the second year of the War, after the primary
enthusiasm for the draft had worn down to the quick of its
machine realities.

Meanwhile the revised draft regulations which had been put
into effect in the early winter of 1917–18 had been fortunate
preparation for the wholesale demands for man-power after
the German offensives began. They had corrected mistakes in
administration that experience had developed. The draft boards
were expanded for broader and more detailed examinations
in classifying personnel. The nation's lawyers volunteered for
the legal advisory boards to give aid to any who needed it among
ten million men in answering the new and complicated ques-
tionnaires and to advise the district boards about exemptions.
If people had not been too busy in the War to be litigious,
clients would have gone without legal advice. Doctors who
were too old to serve in the Army—while they had to look after
the patients of their absentee colleagues—volunteered for the
medical advisory boards which examined several million men,
so the government would know the tasks for which each man
was physically as well as mentally best fitted.

Until May, 1918, not more than 200,000 men had been drafted in a single month. Alarms on the Mexican border as well as in Europe accounted for the 373,000 in May. The ground the first and second German offensives had gained influenced the Congress not only in passing the Overman Act and the Sedition Act, but in its attitude toward the government's further control of the nation's man-power. The unexpected demands for troops in France meant the early exhaustion of Class I of the available men for the front, the depletion of Class II, and the invasion of Class III.

"WORK OR FIGHT!"

One year after the passage of the first selective act came the "Work or Fight" order. Many labor leaders opposed it, but again Gompers' statesmanship prevailed in answer to the appeal of the crisis. This meant that no man who had a low number in the drawing should remain idle. He must either go to work or go to war. The deferred classes, including those who claimed that they had dependents, must prove that they had some constructive occupation, or be put to work. This was a further burden for the draft boards during the May rush to the camps, at the same time that they were combing the draft lists for skilled mechanics for the shipyards or other specific industrial service. Then the Congress, on May 20, authorized the registration of all young men who had become of draft age since the first registration of June 5, 1917. So these had their day, three-quarters of a million of them in all, when they took their turn in line, each an individual unit who must be duly examined by the draft boards.

Another drawing similar to that of a year ago decided the order in which they should be called to service. Meanwhile the volunteer system still ran parallel to the draft. The Navy, the Emergency Fleet, and the Marine Corps were making their appeals to men to enlist. Crowder found this disturbing to a proper draft organization, which would classify all our man-power and dispose of it in the true sense of selective service [1]— after Pershing, in his alarm over the success of the third German offensive, had asked for 2,500,000 men continuously in training at home, and that the Congress authorize billeting. On August 24, two weeks after Germany's "black day" and the turn of the tide on the Western front, the Congress amended the Selective Service Act to enroll all youths who had become twenty-one since June 5, 1917, which added another chore in registration for the draft boards.

Then, on August 31, the Congress passed an act discontinuing volunteer enlistment and requiring all services to depend upon the draft for man-power; and on August 31, which was three weeks after Germany's "black day," when the tide turned definitely against her, the Congress met Pershing's request for the extension of the draft age by including all men between eighteen and forty-five. This meant more than another chore—a huge burden indeed—for the draft boards. All the members who were under forty-five now had to set down their own answers to the questionnaire which they had so often assisted younger men to fill in. But they and their older colleagues already knew their parts so well, they had been so well drilled by the succession of detailed orders and interpretations from Washington, that they were prepared to make a routine election-day business on September 12 of the registration of more men to the number of thirteen million. As Crowder said, all the able-bodied man-power of the nation was now at the government's disposal.

It was work or fight for all. The decision as to who should work and who should fight rested with the exemption boards as the very foundation of a fair and systematic administration of the draft. Baker's part as the buffer between the boards and the demands for class exemptions had its supreme test through the heat of Washington's second war-summer.

"I have made arrangements," he wrote to the President, "which keep medical students and a selected number of engineering and technical students in schools." These and other specialists might be more valuable in the home effort than on the battle-line. But his reply to the President, who was naturally interested in safeguarding scholastic instruction, said that many teachers had volunteered for the army, "which is a thing we have no right to discourage and could not have prevented. . . . So far as primary schools are concerned, they are so largely in the hands of women that the total number of men withdrawn from them must have been exceedingly small." The President did not demur at the decision.

Baker made one industrial class exemption, which was put in the draft regulations. "The request of Mr. Hurley [of the Shipping Board] stands on different ground," Baker wrote to the President. "In view of the urgency of the shipbuilding program, I think it ought to be regarded as in a class by itself, and men ought to be furloughed to the Emergency Fleet Corporation almost without delay so that every man who can be used effectively in shipbuilding will be so employed."

We might have millions of men in the final stage of training and all the arms and ammunition for them; but without transport to France they would be helpless against the enemy. Deferred classification for shipbuilding became as fundamental a military measure as the exemption of medical students to safeguard the public health and to provide medical officers for our expanding army. We might get on with fewer teachers but not without shipbuilders and doctors, if our army were to reach France and be supplied after it arrived, and if soldiers' wounds were to be bandaged.

STANDING BY THE DRAFT BOARDS

But what had been granted to one chief other chiefs thought they were equally entitled to. In the universal and increasing shortage of labor, every branch of war activities saw its own as the prime need. How were we to harvest the crops when farmhands were being sent in such numbers to the cantonments? The Woman's Land Army, under Mrs. Dorothy H. Hubert, the national director, sent its members to the farms and made high sport of their new experience in honest sunburn and blistered hands. We harvested the crops. Secretary of Agriculture Houston's organization had fulfilled his promise made just before our entry into the War, and there was enough food, even if there were not enough ships to transport it.

In answer to Fuel Administrator Garfield's request for direct exemption of coal-miners, Crowder said that an affirmative decision would "drive many registrants, quite as essential and indispensable to the nation, into the ranks of the coal-miners." Not a few registrants, who were not skilled mechanics, had stated that they were qualified as shipbuilders.

McAdoo was particularly insistent in behalf of railroad employees. Baker wrote to the President, who was the final resort of appeals, quoting figures to show that the district boards in their review of industrial cases had taken into consideration the importance of fuel and transportation.

"So far as I am able to judge, the draft as already operated cannot be said to have borne heavily upon industrial workers. The total industrial population engaged in coal-mining in 1917 was 600,148 men. Of these, 225,109 were registered as of draft age. Of that number, 74,109 were called for examination before local boards, but many of them were exempted and the actual number drafted for service was only 18,710, or 3.12% of the total number so engaged.

"With regard to railroad operatives, the experience of the first draft discloses that out of a total industrial population of 1,236,867 persons engaged in steam railroading only 277,-000 were registered, only 87,780 called for examination, and only 22,089 called for military service; or, in other words, the draft took only 1.76% of the railroad operatives, which seems to me to be a very small number."

On the advisory committees of the district boards there were members representing the industrial interests, labor, and agriculture, and also one who knew local industrial and commercial conditions. Baker depended upon these to do justice even when department heads in Washington asked the President to exempt chief clerks. He wrote to the President that if chief clerks were exempted "by a simple designation of their title it would be found that there are many chief clerks in minor offices of the various Departments scattered throughout the United States who are young, replaceable, and not specially trained nor technically indispensable."

THE GANGWAY TO FRANCE

ALL THE SOLDIERS THE SHIP CAN HOLD

The President stood by Baker and the principle that every registrant should go before the boards; and Baker in turn stood by Crowder. Chiefs of Staff and assistant Chiefs of Staff of the Army, assistant Secretaries of War, bureau chiefs, and members of the War Industries Board might change, but Crowder remained Provost Marshal General, the indomitable spirit flashing from his eyes as his frail body passed along the corridor to the Secretary for a decision on some moot point. He might not lead in action any of the men he drafted, but his honest hand was still on their shoulders when they went overseas; and among his assistants who shared his spirit and industry in marvelous team-play were Colonels J. H. Wigmore, J. S. Easby-Smith, and John Evans, and Major Reuben Clark. One of these, Evans, had made so signal a success in organizing the first draft in his native State of Colorado that Crowder brought him to Washington, where his ability would have a wider scope.

In order to close the subject of the draft while I am on it, it may be mentioned that altogether 23,908,576 men were registered, or not quite half all our male population of all ages. Their World War history and qualifications, and their 999 different occupations, were docketed by 4,648 local boards. The men were examined physically by 1,319 medical boards, and their applications for exemptions considered by 155 district boards. Of the 1.41 per cent that failed to respond to the call to register, more than one-half were apprehended. The cost for each accepted draft man in the World War was $11.34 as compared with $227.31 in the Civil War.[2] Of the 4,000,000 men who were in the military service first and last in 1917-1918—forty times the number upon our entry into the War—thirteen per cent were in the Regular Army, ten per cent in the National Guard, and seventy-seven per cent in the National Army.[3]

There had been some alarm about the attitude of our Negroes toward the draft. Soon after our entry into the War, German propaganda became very active in promising that a German victory would assure them freedom from racial disabilities, and even a section of the Southern States for their independent rule. Baker brought Emmett J. Scott, Booker Washington's former secretary, to Washington, where he was assigned the special task of keeping touch with his own people. In all 2,290,000 Negroes were drafted. Their response was excellent. Few claimed exemption.

German propaganda spread reports that our Negro troops in France were being pressed into the front line and sacrificed. But investigation proved the reports to be unfounded. The 15th New York Volunteers served in the battles in Champagne, July–September, 1918. There were two Negro draft divisions, the 92nd and the 93rd. The 92nd was with the French in the Meuse-Argonne, and later in line as a part of Bullard's 1st Army in preparation for the offensive toward Metz, which the Armistice interrupted. Regiments of the 93rd were also with the French in various parts of the line, and in the Meuse-Argonne. Selective service sent Negro longshoremen from the levees and wharves of the South to French ports where, in vigorous competing teams, they were invaluable in handling cargo. Other Negro labor battalions were doing their part from the rear of the Army to the farthest limits of the domain of the Services of Supply.

The public attention given to the draft and its success overshadowed the credit that was due to the early volunteers who answered their country's call by enlistment without waiting for registration and summons; the total of volunteers for all the armed services, before enlistment was stopped, was one million three hundred thousand.

AMERICAN TROOPS WANTED ON MANY FRONTS

Our man-power never lacked invitations to travel. Forwarding them to Baker became a matter of routine for Bliss, our representative on the Supreme War Council. To have accepted all would have scattered our troops on all the widely separated fronts of the Allies—with a single exception: Bliss found that Italy wanted no Allied contingents in Dalmatia lest this might interfere with the Adriatic becoming an Italian lake.

In some cases a remittance from our treasury would be acceptable in lieu of battalions. Bliss had only to say to a proposal to buy off Bulgaria from her alliance with the Central Powers that he considered it immoral and that we did not do that sort of thing. The memorandum of the proposal included for its support a quotation from General Bernhardi, Germany's military apostle of the ethical and pathological value of war. This did not seem quite in keeping with the cause for which the Allies were fighting.

One of the straws at which the Supreme War Council grasped was the possibility of an expedition from northern Turkey against the German divisions which had occupied southern Russia. It was reported that the Armenians and Georgians, if they had funds, could raise an army of one hundred and fifty thousand. The money could not be sent through any banking institution, diplomatic service, or by plane. It must go "as bullion in disguise."

Bliss looked up the latest optimistic figures to learn how large a force of armed Allied sympathizers existed in northern Turkey. Their numbers were as varied if not so large as Xerxes' host, being composed of Russian volunteers, Russian Armenians, Turkish Armenians, Greeks, and Syrians. Even, however, if the bullion should not be so thoroughly "disguised" as to vanish on the way to its destination, could it be distributed without starting a local war in one of the world-famous cockpits of racial jealousies? Granting that it could be, would factions preserve their unity in a campaign? Bliss concluded that the chances of raising a loyal Allied contingent of 150,000 men in northern Turkey were rather slim; and, in any event, its effect on the fortunes of war on the Western front would be considerably lessened by the fact that there were only two long and difficult roads by which it could advance. By one it would have to evade the Bolshevists, and by the other overcome hostile tribes, before trying conclusions with veteran German divisions.

The Allies might tell Bliss that the presence of American troops would assure a Balkan offensive, but he remained neutral in all the debates about the Salonica front. We would have no part in Mediterranean politics. Finally we acceded to the ap-

peal of the Italians, who thought our flag should be shown on
the Piave as well as the Marne. At first the Italians agreed to
send a ship of their own to bring a contingent from America.
In a realistic moment March cabled that this ought to be at
the expense of the Italians, "since they have recently proposed
to charge us $140 per officer and $40 per man for ambulance
sections sent to them at their own request." [4] When, however,
it was found that the inter-Allied Maritime Council had pre-
empted the ship Italy had in mind for the purpose, a regiment
was sent from the A. E. F. to the Italian front by rail.

Before the War was over, we had troops not only in Italy,
but in Russia and Siberia as well. Hope of regalvanizing Russia
as a factor on the side of the Allies would not die. The Kerensky
government, which the Bolshevists overthrew, had shared our
loans to the Allies, and received the advice of the Root-Scott
Mission, with its prestige of elder statesman and elder soldier.
To revive the interest of the Russian masses in the Allied
cause, propaganda proposed sending a solid train marked
"American Relief for Russia" each week from Vladivostok.
But all the welfare missions, all the publicists, found themselves only unheard voices speaking an alien tongue that could
not penetrate beyond the frontier of this enormous expanse of
chaos; and yet failure after failure only brought forth new
dreams among the visionaries, who thought that there might
be success with Lenin and Trotzky if there had not been with
Kerensky. Probably the mission of Mr. Yangoo might have
been as fruitful as its predecessors. In returning Mr. Yangoo's
letter to the President, the polite and ever considerate Secretary
of War said:

"Surely the suggestion is conceived in a handsome and helpful spirit, and yet I doubt very much whether a group of Philippine delegates would be able to comprehend the perplexities
and intricate cross-currents of feeling in Russia sufficiently to
be very helpful. Of course, no Filipinos speak Russian, and the
delegates would, therefore, be obliged to speak through interpreters; and in so vast a country, at present divided up into

so many localities with local differences of both race and party, I confess I do not see how they could be very weighty."

After the success of the third German offensive the gloom of the cables from France included alarm about the Russian situation. A new bogy had risen, that of German control of Russia through the Bolshevists as allies of the Germans. As a consequence, not only might more German divisions be released from the Eastern for the Western front, but also the Germans might even recruit Russian man-power for their army. It was difficult for Europeans to realize that Russia had no strength to spare for outside ventures from her revolutionary spasm; that the giant whose shadow had long lain over eastern Europe, Turkey, Persia, India, and China, had actually ceased to take any part in the World War.

ALARM OVER A NEW RUSSIAN DANGER

At one end of Russia was the port of Vladivostok, and at the other were Murmansk and Archangel—six thousand miles apart. In February and March, 1918, the British had occupied the port of Murmansk, which was the terminus of the new railroad from Petrograd; this with the approval of Trotzky for the Bolshevists. But by June he was demanding British withdrawal. This was the further unpleasant news at the time when the third German offensive had taken Château-Thierry, which served notice that the Bolshevists were against the Allies. The British answer to Trotzky was to hurry reinforcements under General Poole to Murmansk. Would America and the other Allies join in sending a quota to hold the port against the Bolshevists and to keep it out of the hands of the Germans?

In the turmoil of Russia, the Czech and Slav prisoners, with recruits from their races, and Russians loyal to the old régime, had formed an army resisting the Bolshevists and championing the cause of self-determination, which aimed at delivering subject races from their old masters in the new states of Czecho-Slovakia and Poland.

The Czecho-Slovak forces in Russia, in the summer of 1918,

were said to number one hundred thousand, in groups scattered over the five-thousand-mile stretch between Vladivostok and the Volga, which they held in rivalry with Bolshevik detachments and with remnants of the old Russian army in a patchwork of local half-governments. While the Czechs, short of supplies, stubbornly held out against the Bolshevists, German exploitation of Russia was hampered. Were not the Czechs a nucleus for reinforcement which might drive the Bolshevists from power and re-establish a Russian Eastern front? Their relief had the appeal of that of besieged crusaders for the Allied cause; and the route to it was from Russia's great eastern port of Vladivostok, which was seven thousand miles from our Pacific coast.

Ally Japan was near Vladivostok. She had taken no active part in the War except to join with the British in reducing the German protectorate of Tsingtau in China and in guarding the Pacific. Propinquity and her large army made it logical that she should send troops to co-operate with the Czechs. Her Korean and Manchurian railroad systems could easily feed men and supplies over the Chinese Eastern and the Siberian railway systems into Siberia, even as far as the Urals.

From the first Baker had been a "Westerner," convinced that the War must be won on the Western front. But the Supreme War Council, surveying the political and military situation as a whole, favored expeditions both to Murmansk and to Vladivostok, as Bliss informed Baker by cable on May twenty-sixth. On May 28, the second day of the Germans' astonishing advance toward Château-Thierry, Baker cabled to Bliss that

"intervention via Vladivostok is deemed impracticable because of the vast distances involved and the size of the force necessary to be effective. The expedition could serve no military purpose either in aiding the Allies on the Western front or in preventing the Central Powers from securing food and raw materials from Russia unless it penetrated European Russia, where its appearance would enable the German propagandists to persuade the Russian people that compensation at their expense and out of their territory was ultimately to be exacted. In this way and others Germany would be able to arouse Russian patriotic feeling and thus secure military and other aid from the Russians far outweighing any foreseeable advantage from so difficult an intervention. . . . The idea of compensating Japan by territory in Asiatic Russia is inadmissible."

COULD GERMANY DRAW ON RUSSIAN MAN-POWER?

Pershing also had been the sturdiest of Westerners. But he seemed to be in the process of revising his views nine days after Baker's dispatch to Bliss. The Germans were then in possession of Château-Thierry, French orders were prepared for the evacuation of Paris, and the undaunted Clemenceau was crying his determination to fight to the end before the Chamber of Deputies. In Pershing's cable of June 7, 1918, in which he called for 3,000,000 men in France, he evidently had in mind that they would have to fight the Russians on the Western front if we did not create an Allied Eastern front. I quote the whole dispatch as embodying the Commander-in-Chief's report for the enlightenment of the War Department on the Russian situation as he knew it: [5]

"There seems to be very real danger that Germany may recruit her man-power from among Russian peasants unless Allied Powers can counteract German influence. From several sources opinion is expressed that Russians look to United States for advice and possible aid. They are said to hate and fear Japanese without regard to class, and would resent Japanese interference. Information indicates that Russians might even unite with Germans against Japanese, but that they would welcome American assistance. Possibly they might not resent combination of Japanese and Americans and other Allies, provided definite agreement were made to withdraw all troops after the War. Opinions on this vary, but weight of opinion seems to be that Soviet party would resent Japanese interference under any guise.

"With the entrance of Japan into Russia it seems probable the German government would try to take advantage of such action to induce Russians to join Germany against Japan. The next logical step would be to fight the allies of Japan on the Western front. One well-informed authority believes that moral and financial aid and also military advice to the Soviet Government would be sufficient to stiffen resistance to Germany and prevent recruitment for the German army. Of course, this is the serious phase of the question. With Russia once in the conflict on the side of Germany, the man-power of the Central Powers would become relatively inexhaustible. I would earnestly recommend that this side of the question be considered without delay. No doubt the whole Russian situation is well known in Washington, but perhaps attention has not been called to the full meaning of this military menace."

In that desperate hour Pershing shared the view of many Allied statesmen and generals, who had suffered so much bad news that they read portents of more in every pessimistic suggestion. In one sense Pershing's apprehension, under the influence of the spectacularly successful third German offensive, was a singular tribute to the enormous prestige which the German army had established in the minds of the Allied military leaders; a tribute in that a commander who placed such value on thorough military training should consider German drillmasters so magically efficient and German propaganda so wizardous, that in a short time the two would be able to transform the demoralized Russian soldiers, who had rejected all forms of military discipline, into effective fighting legions against the skilful Allied veterans on the Western front. German experience of the Russian army, which the German army had beaten in battles against Russian odds of four and five to one, was the best reason that so quixotic a scheme would never receive the approval of the German staff.

SHOULD WE JOIN THE ALLIES AT MURMANSK?

Lord Reading had given our State Department a memorandum stating Lord Milner's reason why we should send troops to Murmansk. The President would not comply without Foch's approval.[6] Bliss had an interview with Foch on the subject on

June twentieth. The news at the time was very cheering. The fourth German offensive had been stopped, and the failure of the Austrian offensive in Italy had become apparent. Bliss told how Foch sent for his faithful Weygand and all the papers about Murmansk. Foch then stated that "the value of the occupation of the port was indisputable." He recommended sending French, Italian, and American battalions to join the British force. "The dispatch of one or two American battalions would not sensibly retard the arrival of American troops in France." A part of Bliss' cable related to the disputes over the leadership of the expedition. The French wanted command on land, leaving that on the sea to the British. Lord Milner "flatly demanded single command by the British."

The first object of the Murmansk reinforcement was to get possession of Archangel. At Archangel the Bolshevists were realizing a prolific opportunity in commandeering and selling to the Germans the vast stores of war material the Allies had deposited there for delivery to the Kerensky government, material that had never been moved. If Archangel could be taken, the Allied battalions would form a nucleus which would gather Russian volunteers in moving south to form a junction with the Czechs. Baker remained skeptical about any military adventure in Russia. In his letter of July 8 he wrote to Bliss:

"We have all been literally beset with the Russian question in its various forms. I have had repeated conferences with the British Ambassador, and in the last month it seems to me more people have come from Russia, each one knowing exactly the answer to the Russian problem, than happened in the previous year. Each one's solution is dictated by the occurrences which he saw in the little corner of Russia in which he happened to be stationed. Raymond Robins, who was a member of the Red Cross Commission there, is quite sure that the Bolshevists represent 'God in Russia'—at least to the extent of representing the only power which has achieved any recognition, and that the true course to follow is a frank acknowledgment of Soviet power, with Lenin and Trotzky as a part of it, so long as the Soviets continue to give them their confidence. On the other hand, most of the people whom I have seen from Russia profess to have allied themselves with what they call the Intelligentsia. To them, Lenin and Trotzky, and the Bolshevist power generally, are anathema, and any blinking look of recognition in their direction is playing directly into Germany's hands."

As for the Siberian expedition, Baker concluded that what really underlay the proposal, aside from diplomatic considerations, was the feeling that

"something must be done to break the deadlock that the Western front presents, and if it cannot be done on the Western front, then let's do it in Siberia or any other place. To me this is a very dangerous doctrine and a totally erroneous position. I do not see how this war can be ended by fretting Germany in other countries than her own. . . . I see no promise of salvation in an expedition of any composition or any size which cannot look forward to getting beyond Irkutsk. I mentioned to Lord Reading that Irkutsk was too many thousand miles from the Eastern front to be of any help. He said, 'It is nearer than Vladivostok,' to which I replied that that sounded to me like saying that a man was nearer the moon when he was standing on top of his house, in view of the fact that he would still be too far away to have any chance of getting there.

"She [Germany] is, I should think, more than willing to accept an immobile Western front, with a better chance in Russia—which she naturally has, approaching it from the densely populated side and by the shorter transportation haul —than would be possible to any sort of Allied action basing itself on Vladivostok or Harbin. Meantime, every man and every ship which is diverted from the Western front diminishes the aggregate Allied power there, and any expedition to any other part of the world increases the disposition on the Allies' part merely to hold the Western front and see what happens elsewhere."

It was in this letter that Baker said: "I shall be quite heartbroken if we continue through the summer with the present tug-of-war and no big drives made by our people."

Major-General JAMES G. HARBORD

General TASKER H. BLISS

Major-General G. W. GOETHALS

General PEYTON C. MARCH

On July 9 Baker cabled to Bliss: [7] "General March and I have been in conference with the President about the Murmansk expedition. As we understand it, the permanent military representatives are unanimous in recommending that the expedition as now proposed be duly undertaken. None of us can see the military value of the proposal and we assume that other considerations moved in favor of it. Please cable for the President fully your views, military and otherwise, on the subject."

BLISS' MILITARY AND PERSONAL VIEWS

In his answer by cable Bliss gave his military views and his personal views.[8] He said that entering upon any military plan was a compromise. But for compromise "any Allied action here would be impossible." Any general plan of intervention to be effective must include a large enough force moving southward from Murmansk and Archangel to control railroad communications between the east and the west in Russia. This could not be sent in and supplied from the outside. Any force sufficient for this would have to be Russian. A small Allied force might hold those northern ports during the winter, secure the stores, and win Russian sympathy by relieving distress through welfare activities. In case of general intervention it would be a mistake to give up the northern ports. We would be represented in a small force, but only our fair share.

In stating his personal view Bliss concluded: "It seems to me that our Allies want the United States to commit itself to expeditions to various places where, after the War, they alone will have any special interests. . . . We must fight somewhere, and originally we selected France and at the request of the Allies themselves."

The President, influenced by his desire that we should do our fair part and show our sympathy for the Russian people in their dark hour, consented to a regiment for Murmansk. Should we also send troops to Vladivostok? Baker's steadfast opposition to any further adventures in the uncertainties of Russia's immense territorial spaces is reflected in a letter written to him by

General Tom Bridges on July twenty-fifth. Bridges was a superb type of British officer, who had accompanied the Balfour Mission to America, and remained the chief British military representative in Washington, where he won a host of friends. He began his letter by saying that he had been struck by the wide divergence between Baker's and his own views in their talk of the previous day. Without assuming to criticize any actions of the American government, he wanted to restate his own position and make plain how strongly he felt about the Eastern situation.

The German conquest and exploitation of Russia seemed to him inevitable. It would release thirty or forty German divisions for the Western front. Germany might throw Trentino, Belgium, Alsace-Lorraine, Serbia, and Montenegro to the wolves in order to make peace with the other Allies. Then who would recover Russia from German domination? Unless Germany retreated on the Western and Italian fronts, the Allies would have to capture line after line of formidable works. America would have to bear the brunt of the campaign of 1919 at the cost of millions of casualties, and even this might prolong the ordeal of human misery at the risk of effecting only an inconclusive peace. Bridges would have a strong force of Allied troops join the Czechs, rally around them a reorganized Russian army, and, if necessary, accept the assistance of a large Japanese force.

This letter was a most logical presentation of the Eastern view by an able soldier who had known trench warfare in the Ypres salient in the days of the German army's prime. Its views, so contrary to those of that uncompromising Westerner, the British Commander-in-Chief in France, illustrated the differences of opinion within the fold of one Ally which, as late as the summer of 1918, continued to puzzle Washington in making its decisions. Bridges, who was about to return home, arrived after Ludendorff's "black day" when Haig's army had begun its final advance against an enemy whose morale had finally been broken by attrition.

But military logic yielded to other considerations, as the

White House looked across the Pacific toward Vladivostok. When the Allied statesmen sounded Japan, she accepted readily the suggestion that she intervene in Siberia. Lloyd George, too, was ready to send a British contingent to accompany the Japanese expedition. Should America stand in the way of an effort by her Allies to rescue the Czechs and to strike a blow at the common enemy through Russia? This time the European statesmen had found our tendon of Achilles in our detachment from world-politics beyond our own hemisphere. We might be aloof to the special interests of Britain, France, and Italy in Egypt, Asia Minor, the Balkans, the Adriatic, and the Mediterranean; but the Open Door in China touched a special interest of our own, even if it was not so much of a national shibboleth as the Monroe Doctrine. To the President the question had become one of high state policy which, in this instance, overruled the opinion of the War Department. If Japan went into Siberia, we must go.

THE PRESIDENT DECIDES FOR A SIBERIAN EXPEDITION

Major General W. S. Graves was given command of the expedition, comprising the 29th and 30th infantry regiments from the Philippines and 5,600 men of the new 8th Division on the Pacific coast, which had been brought to a high state of training under Major General John F. Morrison. So we were committed to two Russian ventures. The Allied force at Murmansk recovered the Allies' stores, but no Russian volunteers joined them for the southern march, and they were frozen in at the time of the Armistice.

On August 3 the British contingent for the Siberian expedition joined the Czechs at Vladivostok, and on the 12th the Japanese began disembarking. They were closely followed on the 16th by the first units of our expedition, whose adventures and part in world-politics I shall revert to later.

In passing, it is of parenthetic interest that Bliss reported to Baker on August 7 that in response to the pressure of "The League for the Regeneration of Russia," General Diaz had suggested that exiled Russian officers of the old régime be associated with our contingents operating in Russia. Bliss observed dryly that the officers' willingness might be construed as eagerness to get on the American payroll. He was sure that, though our taking them on would relieve the Allies of a burden, it would also make a lot of trouble for us, and informed all concerned at the Supreme War Council that "the policy of the United States is to conduct its own military operations with its own officers and men."

It was certain the State Department's move into Asia was anything but welcome to the group who met in a round-table conference every Wednesday morning at Baker's office, including March, the Chief of Staff, and such responsible chiefs of industrial war activities as Baruch, Schwab, Hurley, Ryan, and Franklin.

"I think you would get a better idea of the way we try to keep together," Baker said in a note to the President inviting him to be present, "and a better bird's-eye view of the situation than in any other way. The progress of the War is exhibited and explained in statistical form by a series of charts."

REACHING THE LIMIT OF OUR RESOURCES

Through the heat of that second Washington war-summer, key-men and their assistants had ample office space in the new emergency buildings; but the now established organization, centering at the Secretary's desk, met no less of a challenge in the 80-division program than it had in its formative days when Pershing had sent word, in July, 1917, that we must prepare to transport and maintain overseas an army of a million. Now another expedition was forth to "show the flag" in a port six thousand miles from home, with immediate demands for more ships and material, which might expand in proportion to Asiatic land distances.

Of the men who met at the round-table conference, no one understood better than Baruch, the Chairman of the War Industries Board, that every able-bodied man summoned to a training camp meant a further tax on our productive capacity which had been correspondingly reduced by the loss of the man's labor. Baruch had been called the "dictator of industry"; but the minutes of the Board demonstrate that his was the kind of leadership which democracy develops in a chairman of council and a referee in controversy, who does not depend upon the rigid exercise of official authority but upon method and personality.

Even price-fixing was not by arbitrary fiat but the result of consultation with producers, followed by a decision by Robert S. Brookings, that master of impartiality, as to what was fair. The Board held open court where producers' protests against inadequate prices might be heard. At one meeting John H. Kirby appeared in behalf of the Southern lumber interests with a lawyer to represent them. Baruch remarked that nobody had ever brought a lawyer to a meeting before:—but, all right— let him remain. Brookings said: [9]

"We feel, of course, that the industry is as much interested as we are. We are willing to have any number of meetings to try to get an agreement. We are at war and willing to concede just as much patriotism to the industry as we have."

That was spoken fair, as the saying goes, to start a discussion in which all arguments, including all resentments, were fully aired in many pages of the minutes. Concessions were met by concessions until an adjustment was reached that sent the lumbermen back to their sawmills in high spirits.

Price-fixing in steel, in which America had a world lead, was simpler than in medicines or surgical needles, for which we had depended upon Europe before the War; or in any article for which the raw material was subject to world market prices. Priority had its stern innings when such steel masters as Judge E. H. Gary, J. A. Farrell, J. A. Campbell, H. G. Dalton, W. L. King, E. G. Grace, and J. A. Topping appeared at a meeting of the Board. The interchange of views among those generals of industry was as intense as Pershing's with the Allied premiers and generals about the integral army issue.

Steel was king. "We must have the weight of metal," as Baruch said. Our Allies were all demanding steel, and at home all the munition plants competed with the demands of steel for rails, locomotives, and cars for the railroads, automobiles, and ship-plates. Hugh Chalmers, President of the Automobile Chamber of Commerce, came to a meeting of the War Industries Board in a highly indignant mood. He represented all the makers except Henry Ford, who was a lone fighter.

BUT FORD ALREADY HAD THE STEEL

"Our people have a great deal of feeling," he said, "about Ford's ability to get steel when they can't get it." It seems that Ford had been forehanded and accumulated a reserve of steel at his factory. He was making Liberty motors, and Baruch's "What ought we to do?" in the case got no answer. The Board would not attempt to take the steel away from Ford by force.

In answer to the statement that passenger cars were a luxury, Chalmers retorted, "You said to take a taxi and come to this meeting." If the Board carried out its proposed limitations on the automobile industry "you might as well appoint a receiver for the State of Michigan. . . . Our dealers are flat on their backs."

"That is one of the uncertainties of war," said Judge E. B. Parker, who was the ranking priority expert.

"This is your problem just as well as ours," said Baruch. "We don't want to be arbitrary. I don't want to say to any industry, 'You can't do this' and 'can't do that.' I know if you've got to close the automobile industry, you'll take your medicine."

When Chalmers talked of appealing to the country for fair play, Parker said: "I am willing to bet with you right now on the elections, if you please, as to whether they give the boys in khaki their supplies or the automobile industry theirs."

"We can't get the steel and can't give it to you," said Baruch.

After Chalmers had conferred with his colleagues of the industry, they accepted an allowance of steel and rubber for fifty per cent of capacity, which was their sacrifice in helping to win the War.

When Charles M. Schwab appeared at a meeting with the steel-makers, it was not only Schwab the steel man, but Schwab of the Emergency Fleet Corporation, who met his colleagues of the industry. Alexander Legge might report on behalf of the Allied Purchasing Commission that Italy wanted 25,000 tons of steel rails immediately; but Schwab was thinking of ship-plates. "Give us the steel and we'll give you the ships," said Schwab. "What are we to do?" asked Baruch, who had a way of letting the discussion run. "McAdoo wants rails and more rails." [10]

"Give us the fuel," said Gary, "and we will give you the steel."

"We want plates, and that in no wise interferes with the production of rails," said Schwab.

"Locomotives first," declared J. Leonard Replogle, who represented the Steel Division of the War Industries Board. George N. Peek, the finished products expert of the Board, had no concern in the discussion.

KINGS OF THE KING INDUSTRY

"Fifteen thousand tons additional a week for the next two or three months and I would be safe," Schwab said.

"You want 65,000 tons a week altogether for two or three months," said Baruch. "Priority is not a fixed thing. Something unforeseen might happen and the case would be reopened." After eighteen months' service through Caporetto and the German offensives, Baruch spoke with feeling about the unexpected.

"Mr. Schwab is a most convincing talker," remarked Mr. Porcher, who wanted rails, "and we ought to give Mr. Schwab anything he wants because he is Mr. Schwab and because of what he has done, but—"

And Schwab pictured shipyards stopping work for want of steel, leaving idle men to drift. "God knows," he said, "we have enough difficulties; but the worst difficulty is to lay these men off because we haven't got the steel to keep them going."

"I have an order for 27,000 cars from General Pershing, and here we are back in the old vicious circle," said Baruch. "The next draft will take 500,000 men, and we're looking forward to that." Hurley suggested that "we employ women," and Parker answered, "The industries are doing that right along."

Parker declared locomotive production must not be curtailed. The country could not produce the 1,400 locomotives by January 1 to meet the orders of the railroad administration. Since General Pershing wanted 510 locomotives, the United States must be content with an equal number. Replogle said that Hoover also wanted more tin plate for food cans. The chorus swelled against Schwab, who finally said: "Give me 40,000 tons and I won't bother you for thirty days."

Again, at a meeting on August 22 three weeks later, shortage of steel became still more ominous. There was a mention that the French were not using all their pig-iron from America, but allowing it to lie on their docks. Then: [11]

BARUCH: Whenever an army advances it means steel.

LEGGE: Whenever they make a retreat it means steel.

BARUCH: We hope that is behind us. Every place there is an Allied army there is a demand upon this country. We have additional demands for the Mesopotamian campaign. The whole Siberian project rests upon whether we can support the men there with material.

FARRELL: It is not a question of one thing or another: it is a question of everything in this case. [To Dr. Garfield] In the meantime you will give us 160,000 tons of coal a month more.

DR. GARFIELD: I will do the best I can.

FARRELL: You cannot make ifs in our business.

PARKER: He says he'll do it.

In all the range of industrial needs the War Industries Board was preparing on the Pershing basis for an immense American army to win the final victory in 1919. The Board's many

SHIPBUILDING AT HOG ISLAND

SHIPPING LOCOMOTIVES ON THEIR WHEELS

branches continued to sound the ends of the earth in its bargains for essential materials and to encourage production. Its building projects were speeded up by the spur of the 80-division program. The Muscle Shoals project, which was to be the subject of so much post-War discussion, was under way. Two great powder-plants were being hastened to completion.

The Allied missions had advised us, after our entry into the War, that the Du Pont plant, which had been expanded to meet the enormous market of explosives since August, 1914, would be equal to future demands. But Caporetto had brought a definite alarm about this supremely essential munition. Baker had found the Du Ponts' terms for constructing new plants and their price for the product too high. To conclude the controversy he called in D. C. Jackling, a mining engineer. Jackling said he did not know how to make powder, but he gathered experts and started the government plant at Nitro, West Virginia. Then the Du Pont Company, as agent for the government, started another at Nashville. We were determined to have enough powder even for a 110-division program.

When we were building shipyards and ships and powder-plants in the face of shortage of labor, private building operations, and even more school accommodations, must wait until after the War. Baruch wrote on September 11 to Mayor John F. Hylan, of New York: [12] "Out of New York's need for school buildings, which you have set forth to me in your letter, there flows a condition which is nation-wide, and which reaches the very front of our battle-line. . . . The case of New York is typical of the whole country. . . . The rule in one case must be and is evenly applied to all."

ALL WORK, NO FIGHT FOR WOMEN

Safeguards for the protection of women and children in industry, of which Baker, President of the National Consumers' League, had always been a strong advocate, must suffer in a period when "Work or Fight" was a rule applying to all in spirit if not in regulations. As he had said, he would not "break down those barriers which we have set up through years of patient labor against the enervation and dissipation of the child-life and of the woman-life and of the man-life of this country. . . . After the wastage of war has really come to an end there will be a solid ground gained here at home upon which further advance and social reconstruction can proceed." [13]

But now it was war, and the women were in the fight to make that solid ground for the future. Mrs. Shaw continued in her part as the veteran leader. Miss Mary Van Kleeck continued as the director of the "women in industry" service of the Department of Labor and of the Ordnance Department, and Mrs. Samuel B. Harding of that of the Council of National Defense. More than 1,000,000 women served in the Liberty Loan campaigns under Mrs. McAdoo's committee. Escape from responding with a larger subscription than you could afford was only possible by hiding in a cave—from which very likely you would be dug out and then publicly posted as a slacker. Women were acting not only as motor-car drivers but as street-car drivers and traffic police.

"Hooverizing" was not the only form of war economy to which a people used to prodigality were adapting themselves under the leadership of an early dollar-a-year man, A. W. Shaw, of the conservation division of the War Industries Board, who had associated with him George N. Peek, H. W. Dennison, and W. D. Simmons. Applying the "buy and carry" system for purchases meant fewer delivery wagons and a saving of labor. Traveling salesmen who commonly had eight or ten trunks were limited to two. Baby-carriages were standardized. Metal was conserved by eliminating brass, bronze, and copper caskets. Types of ploughs were reduced from 326 to 76; trace chains from 504 to 72; planting machines from 326 to 29; and hat manufacturers' samples from 4,000 to one hundred and forty-four. Bulky catalogues were no longer welcome in parcel post sacks. Seventy-five thousand tons of pig tin for canning foods were released by excluding tin from children's toy carts; and 30,800 gallons of varnish by leaving off the painted lines from rubber shoes. Ambassador Jusserand influenced the Parisian styles in favor of silhouette gowns for women; and there was more saving of tin by taking the rustle out of silk. To conserve leather in order that there might be Sam Browne belts for the officers in France, harness for artillery horses, and hundreds of other military purposes, women gave up high shoes, while the colors for shoes were reduced to three, and no new lasts were made.[14]

Not all of the economies of which I have given a few examples were practised in obedience to orders; many sprang from a sense of the hour's need, in order to meet the A. E. F.'s requirements three thousand miles from home. As these requirements became larger, more elaborate, and insistent, the supporting home force simplified its wants and stretched its energies. We had thrills which only strengthened our common purpose—as the Zeppelin raids had that of the British—when a German submarine sank a few ships along the Atlantic coast; though our troop transports, under naval convoy, were taking ten thousand men a day safely through the danger zone to increase our army in France.

XXXV

STILL THE CALL FOR MORE

IN the course of reading stacks of war documents I have gradually come to the conviction that by the summer of 1918 the home effort was better organized than that in France. There was less delay while boards considered a subject, less waste of motion in changes of plan, and authority was more confidently delegated and better co-ordinated. One reason for this may have been Baker's readiness to take responsibility, his inductive method of administration that kept self in the background: a method that he defines in one of his letters as "the secret of using enthusiasm in others when it is not exactly your enthusiasm." It had capitalized in team-play the ability of such men as Pershing, Bliss, March, Goethals, Gorgas, Frank A. Scott, Willard, Baruch, Gompers, Ryan, Stettinius, and Lovett. Another reason may have lain in March's slashing definiteness. But the great reason was democracy.

The door on the left of the Secretary's desk remained open to newspaper men and callers of the unofficial world as well as to Congressmen. Chiefs of the various War Department activities were aware not only that their labors were subject to public review but also that their reports might be checked up by other experts. In a land of organized industry we did not lack organizing talent; the trained men were available and had only to adapt themselves to war work.

By the summer of 1918 the talk about supermen had ceased. Walter S. Gifford, the pioneer of industrial preparedness, said there was no such person as a superman.[1] Gifford had been close to the progress of our effort until he went abroad in July, 1918, to serve on the inter-Allied Munitions Council. His intimate experience convinced him that democracy, which had seemed so footless in making war in the early spring of 1917, was the most efficient system in the end. It found itself in the concentration of authority in able leaders—not necessarily the ablest, but certainly able—who had won in competition and stern trials the co-operation of their fellows.

In the A. E. F. corrective criticism must proceed largely from the throne from which orders were issued. Pershing knew only through personal inspection or official inspectors whether performance was up to the reports made by his chiefs, and whether his policies and projects were being carried out in the wide area of his command. The "follow-up" section of his staff, which would keep him informed of actual in comparison with reported progress, was subject to many limitations.

GOETHALS NOT WANTED IN THE A. E. F.

Baker's letters and memoranda show that after the great exodus overseas had begun and the home organization was going well, his thought turned more and more to the A. E. F. and the problem of how to supply its rapidly increasing numbers. On June 6 he had written to Pershing:

"Our tables seem to show that the evacuations from the [French] ports from month to month are less than the cargo discharges there, so that there seems to be a constant increase in accumulated and unevacuated cargo at the ports which we use; and I am fearful that if we secured additional cargo ships we would simply add to the congestion of the ports, rather than add to your supplies. Of course, I know how seriously this whole question is being studied by you, and now that it looks more and more as though the American participation would have to be upon a larger scale than any of us have planned, I trust you will have your engineers give immediate and earnest consideration to the question of port capacity, as that may turn out to be the controlling feature in the whole business."

During the succeeding weeks there was no improvement in the evacuation of cargo in the French ports; and the slow turnaround of cargo ships had become so serious, in view of the rapid increase of our army in France, that in a letter to

Pershing on July 6 Baker suggested that Major General George W. Goethals should undertake the co-ordination of our whole supply system from the American sources to the front:

"The President and I have had several conferences about your situation in France, both of us desiring in every possible way to relieve you of unnecessary burdens, but of course to leave you with all the authority necessary to secure the best results from your forces and to supply all the support and assistance we possibly can. As the American troops in France become more and more numerous and the battle initiative on some parts of the front passes to you, the purely military part of your task will necessarily take more and more of your time, and both the President and I want to feel that the planning and the executing of military undertakings has your personal consideration and that your mind is free for that as far as possible.

"The American people think of you as their 'fighting General,' and I want them to have that idea more and more brought home to them. For these reasons, it seems to me that it would help if some plan were devised by which you would be free from any necessity of giving attention to Services of Supply; and one plan in that direction which suggested itself was to send General Goethals over to take charge of the Services of Supply, establishing a direct relationship between him and Washington, and allowing you to rely upon him just as you would rely upon the supply departments of the War Department if your military operations were being conducted in America, instead of in France.

"Such a plan would place General Goethals in a co-ordinate rather than a subordinate relationship to you, but of course it would transfer all of the supply responsibilities from you to him, and you could then forget about docks, railroads, storage houses, and all the other vast industrial undertakings to which up to now you have given a good deal of your time and, as you know, we all think with superb success. I would be very glad to know what you think about this suggestion. I realize that France is very far from the United States and that our reliance upon cables makes a very difficult means of communication, so that you may prefer to have the supply system as one of your responsibilities. I would be grateful if you would think the problem over and tell me quite frankly just what you think on the subject. The President and I will consider your reply together, and you may rely upon our being guided only by confidence in your judgment and the deep desire to aid you.

"One other aspect of your burdens the President feels can be somewhat lightened by a larger use of General Bliss as diplomatic intermediary. The President is adopting as a definite rule of action an insistence that inter-Allied military questions be referred to the Permanent Military Representatives. Our difficulty here has been that the British representative would present something for consideration without the knowledge of the French, or the French without the knowledge of the British; and when we took the matter up for decision we would sometimes find that the other nation felt aggrieved at not being consulted. As each of the Allied nations is represented at Versailles, the President is now uniformly saying, with regard to all inter-Allied military questions, that their presentation to him should come through the Permanent Military Representatives who, in a way, are a kind of staff for General Foch, and undoubtedly maintain such close relations with him as to make any proposition that they consider one upon which his views are ascertained. As the President deals in matters of military diplomacy with General Bliss, it would seem that he could with propriety relieve you to some part of the conferences and consultations which in the early days you were obliged to have with the British War Office and the French War Office, thus simplifying the presentation of inter-Allied questions to the President."

Stettinius, who was to be succeeded by Ryan as Assistant Secretary of War, had been mentioned for the post for which Baker had suggested Goethals; but Baker had concluded that as he was a banker without military rank, he would better represent us on the inter-Allied Munitions Council, which was more in line with the war work he had been doing. Goethals was in charge of transport and supply at home, and he was a Regular officer of adequate rank and sufficiently high prestige to command the militarized S. O. S., in which all the workers from civil life were in uniform.

"Mr. Stettinius will leave very shortly for Europe; I enclose you copy of a letter which I have given him, outlining the inquiries which I desire to have him make. You will find him a very considerate man in the matter of demands upon your time, as he is accustomed to dealing with busy men and not prolonging conferences beyond their useful limit.

"It seems not unlikely at present that I shall myself come over to Europe in connection with our enlarged military program. If we find that our ability to do the thing depends upon French and British co-operation it will be a good deal simpler to put the whole question up to the British and French Cabinets and get definite agreements of co-operation and concerted action. Cablegrams are of course inconclusive and uncertain, and I constantly find that even letters fail to carry just the spirit in which they are dictated. When I write you, of course I know that our personal relations and knowledge of each other are too cordial and entire to allow any sort of misunderstanding; but I haven't the same acquaintance with the British and French Cabinet officers, and with them the presumptions do not obtain which are always implied in our correspondence. I confess I am somewhat moved to this idea of the necessity for my going by my desire to go; it is a tremendous inspiration to see our forces and to look at the work which you and they have done."

HARBORD SAVES THE SITUATION

Now it happened that Pershing had determined, soon after his arrival in Paris, that Goethals was one of two of the men whom he did not want in France because their dominant natures made them insubordinate. The other was Leonard Wood.[2] Baker's letter started the Commander-in-Chief to writing very vigorously on the pad on which he blocked out important papers in pencil. This cable in answer was marked "RUSH RUSH RUSH RUSH" across the top:

". . . I very much appreciate your desire to relieve me of every burden that might interfere with the direction of military operations. However, there appears to be an exaggerated view concerning the personal attention required in handling the details of administration of this command. . . . The whole must remain absolutely under one head. Any division of responsibility or co-ordinate control in any sense would be fatal. The man who fights the armies must control their supply through subordinates responsible to him alone. The responsibility is then fixed, and the possibility of conflicting authority avoided. This military principle is vital and cannot be violated without inviting failure. . . . When it becomes necessary for me to be constantly at the front I shall retain general control through the General Staff. . . . General Kernan has worked very hard but has not all the qualifications necessary for success."

Kernan, who had been Pershing's choice to command the Services of Supply, was sent to Berne in charge of the mission to look after the interests of American prisoners in Germany. For his successor Pershing turned to Harbord, the first Chief of Staff of the A. E. F., the Harbord of Belleau Wood, who had just led the 2nd Division in the initial offensive in closing the Marne salient. The appointment of Harbord put the seal on Pershing's objection to Goethals. "With him in command of the Services of Supply I shall be able to devote myself to military operations," Pershing said in his cable; and in a letter to Baker he suggested that Goethals would be welcome on a tour of inspection in France. Within a few days after Harbord had taken charge in the S. O. S. all sections, from ports to regulating stations, were feeling the touch of a vigorous and harmonizing hand.

But we were still sending troops to France out of proportion to cargo. By September 1 we should have a million and a half over there. On August 16 Baker wrote to F. H. Goff:

"The strong likelihood is that I shall have to go to Europe just as quickly as certain necessary things can be done here . . . and so my chances for even a few days' absence from

Washington seem very slight indeed. I have no doubt I feel the responsibility for our million and a half men in Europe in a degree quite out of proportion to my personal ability to look after their fortunes; but every shipload of soldiers we land in France increases the complications of their supply and, quite confidentially, increases the complication of harmonious co-operation with our Allies. Under normal circumstances international relations every now and then flare up into disagreements, and when three great armies are kept steadily in battle for months, and the peoples of three great nations are constantly kept on the anxious seat, international nerves become painfully exposed and the possibilities of difficulty multiply.

"I have no doubt that a large part of Napoleon's success was due to the fact that he was constantly opposed by a coalition in which the separate interests of the members were constantly being pressed to the damage and possibly to the destruction of the common interest. The appointment of a commander-in-chief in France really rescued the whole Allied military and sometimes I wonder whether there ought not to be an inter-Allied dictator to settle all other inter-Allied questions and suppress individual national interests and desires until the great common object of destroying Germany's military power is safely accomplished. Of course, this is an entirely impracticable suggestion and, as a consequence, we have to resort to the only possible substitute, which is daily and hourly forbearance and composition."

Two days after this letter, on August 18, Colonel Harvey in his weekly wrote: "It is impossible that this pacifist has any realization of the responsibility . . . of guaranteeing our soldiers every safeguard." It was in this issue that the Colonel published a double-page cartoon in which Baker was shown on one page sitting in his chair, oblivious of the soldiers who were pictured in battle on the opposite page.

While Baker continued his routine between his office and Georgetown, the whispering gallery continued to center its fire on him personally, thus insuring protection of his colleagues from interference. One of the favorite hints of the whispering gallery, this being too impolitic for publication,

A CARTOON IN *HARVEY'S WEEKLY*

was that Baker was a Jew who had deserted the faith of his ancestors. It happened that he was born an Episcopalian, of English, Scotch, Irish, and German stock, long resident in America.

Where this story started is as immaterial as the origin of that other story, about Roosevelt, when all the races were claiming "Teddy" as their own, that he had Jewish blood. The word was even passed among those whom it pleased that Roosevelt's name had originally been Rosenfeldt. Possibly the legend was based on Roosevelt's having a Jew as a member of his Cabinet, on his preachment of the "square deal," and on his concern with a man as to what kind of man he was, regardless of his origin. This was a doctrine that Baker, too, had invariably applied in the melting-pot of Cleveland, and it became the gospel of the draft, in spite of the fact that Baker's father, in his rural world, was inclined to be anti-Semitic. But—well, if Baker was not a Jew, then certainly Mrs. Baker was—her maiden name had been Leopold. This name, however, is German as well as Semitic; and as she has fair hair, the report stretched the whispering gallery's license further even than in the case of her dark-haired husband.

A GRAVE SHORTAGE OF CARGO SHIPS

But the serious charge of the whispering gallery—on the basis of reports it had direct from France—was that Baker was not sending Pershing enough troops or giving him enough support. Meanwhile, the cargo situation became no better. We might be shipping some locomotives on their wheels—on the few ships that could accommodate them—but this did not mean we could manufacture, let alone transport overseas, enough locomotives for that 80-division program. Pershing cabled on August 17 in favor of his 100-division program that "we shall be able to force new tonnage into war service instead of debating the question beforehand with the shipping people." [3]

Yet on August 7 the War Department had been informed that, although we had the troops and material at the ports for the 80-division program, their transportation was uncertain.[4] After a study made by Sir Joseph Maclay, British controller of shipping, Lloyd George reported to Clemenceau: "I regret to declare that we shall not be able to continue our help as far as cargoes of merchandise are concerned, and that we shall probably have to cut down the tonnage assigned for troop transportation. . . . Every day Australia and New Zealand ask for help that we are unable to give them. . . . In Lancashire at least 40,000 cotton workers are idle because of lack of raw material; and to increase the cotton supply we have been forced to cut short our program for cereal supply." British, French, and Italian munition works were calling for coal while ships were delayed for want of coal; and war industry was generally hampered by heavy drafts of man-power to the front.

A confirmatory note of the gravity of the cargo outlook came from the A. E. F. in the middle of August when Pershing asked that troop shipments should wait on more S. O. S. troops and replacements. Harbord's persuasiveness could no more conjure transport material and labor battalions out of a hat than Baker could ships.

March replied on August 20: [5] "Six divisions are at port or en route or have been sent. Three had been planned for embarkation in September but will now be postponed to October if possible to provide other troops. All replacements called for by you are being shipped, but they are often delayed by quarantine. Cable your orders further in advance."

On August 6 Pershing asked for 202 air squadrons and 133 balloon companies by July 1, 1919.[6] He wanted 2,000 Liberty engines a month allocated to our Allies in addition to all required by our own Army and Navy. He insisted again that if only we made use of all available tonnage we could send all the railroad and port material necessary to care for one hundred divisions.

On August 26 March informed Pershing that it was impossible to ship immediately the eight regiments of cavalry which Pershing wanted immediately.[7] All were needed on the still troublesome Mexican border, "where Holbrook has asked for five more regiments. We have authorized Governor of Texas to organize six regiments of National Guard cavalry for border service and when they come in it may be possible to release Regular regiments for you. At present we have not enough horse boats to carry the draft animals and mules asked for by you, and tonnage is not in sight to carry horses for cavalry regiments and the forage for them. If Great Britain agrees to furnish tonnage for 80-division program we will include a request for horse boats among the cargo boats asked for and proceed with shipment of animals vigorously." Cable brevity did not permit reference to the time it took to transform a cargo boat into a horse boat.

The British had supplied troop transports, but not cargo ships. They wanted the men first; and cargo could come afterward. The figures at the end of the War showed that less than twenty-five per cent of cargo for our troops in France was carried in foreign bottoms.[8] Every man we sent to France was to need supplies not for a day or a week, but for as long as he remained there. The turn-around of troop ships had decreased in ratio until it was one-half that of cargo. The *Leviathan* and other fast liners were averaging twenty-seven days, while cargo ships were averaging seventy days. It was simpler for a soldier to walk on and off a ship than to load and unload supplies. Our forming of our own army was clearly connected with the cargo situation. The inter-Allied shipping control had scoured the seas for more tonnage, and all possible neutral ships had been requisitioned. Keels were being laid and vessels launched at Hog Island, but mass-production could not be expected for months yet. Our other shipyards were doing their utmost.

HIS SECOND TRIP TO FRANCE

Although our first contract ship had been built in six months and actual deliveries of contract and requisitioned ships had been 870,000 tons by July 1, 1918,[9] it was clear we should lack enough cargo ships until early in 1919 to meet the 80-division

program. The possibility of a real shortage of supplies faced
our army in France in December and January. This would
give the whispering gallery a cry that the War Department was
starving our men. If we were to have enough cargo ships they
must come from the British, whose mood had changed since
Haig's "backs to the wall"; and the threat to Paris of the third
German offensive called for the rapid dispatch of our infantry
and machine-gun personnel. British shipping circles had been
disturbed by reported talk from our side of the ocean that our
huge shipbuilding program would take the guerdon of the
sea away from Britain after the War was over.

Baker's general purpose, therefore, of familiarizing himself
with the whole situation abroad through first-hand observation
included the special mission of securing enough ships for the
service of our army. With him went Brigadier General Frank
T. Hines, our master of troop transportation: and also Ryan
of the Aircraft Board. Ryan could provide the thousand Liberty
motors for which both the British and French were asking, but
we had in mind certain material and aid in return for the gigantic 80-division program. It was before Baker started on this
trip that a subordinate came to him in high indignation against
a man who ought to be disciplined for having been overheard
to express hope that a submarine would get "Newty" on the way
across the Atlantic.

"All he wants is a new Secretary of War," Baker replied
cheerfully.

Colonel Harvey, who had welcomed Baker's departure on his
first trip to France as taking the brake off the War Department, saluted the advent of the second trip, under the caption
"A Grave Situation," with the remark, "Meanwhile Mr. Baker
deserts his post." Harvey also demanded in the same breath,
"From where are the ships to come?" He had evidently heard
that Pershing's 100-division program had not been approved,
and therefore the War Department was not giving the
Commander-in-Chief adequate support. In a later issue, after
Baker had arrived in France, Harvey wrote:

"He went up to see the big show as soon as he arrived, but probably did not stay very long for fear of getting lost or somebody inadvertently stepping on him. The last we heard he was inspecting hospitals, huts, etc., somewhere in Europe, and talking so softly and happily in his sleep, for publication, that maybe the President will either let or make him stay."

HE SEES THE BATTLE OF SAINT-MIHIEL

The "big show" was the battle of Saint-Mihiel, in which a dream came true. As far back as November 13, 1917, Pershing had written to Baker that he had an understanding with Pétain that the first offensive operation by our army would be against the vulnerable Saint-Mihiel salient, in order to assure a victory for us; and again in a letter on February 24, 1918, he hoped that our first test would not be too severe, although, as he observed, there was no telling what would happen in war.

Baker saw the object of the plan of early 1917 being achieved in action by eight divisions: three Regular—the veteran 1st (Summerall), the 2nd (Lejeune), and the 5th (McMahon), which had its first opportunity in France to prove it was trained in the Regular tradition; the two veteran National Guard divisions—New England's 26th (Edwards) and the "Rainbow" All-America (Menoher); and three National Army divisions—the 82nd (Burnham), 89th (Wright), and 90th (Allen), which had been formed from draft men who had gone to the cantonments a year ago. All eight divisions now belonged to the "United States Army." There were three corps: the 1st, under Major General Hunter Liggett; the 4th, under Major General Joseph T. Dickman; and the 5th, under Major General George T. Cameron.

Having caught the Germans unready in the early stages of evacuation, they swept through the barbed wire to take 16,000 prisoners and 443 guns, in addition to much material. Mont Sec, which had grimly looked down on so many of our soldiers in their early trench experiences, was now behind our lines. The Secretary of War was walking through the shell-torn town of Saint-Mihiel. For four years it had been in German possession. The Germans had exiled the able-bodied citizens, and the people who remained had had no news of the War or of world events except through the invaders. Women and children crowded around Baker with tears of joy and relief.

"Lafayette, we are here!" The home of President Poincaré and the ancestral home of the young adventurer who was Washington's aide were no longer occupied by the enemy. Colonel de Chambrun, a descendant of Lafayette, was accompanying Baker. When they came to the Lafayette house, Baker paused at the door, thinking that on an occasion so touching and intimate his companion would prefer to be alone as he noted what damage had been done.[10] When de Chambrun came out, he brought to Baker a steel engraving of Lafayette in memory of the significance of Saint-Mihiel day; it seemed a gift that the Secretary of War, who as an official was so punctilious in such matters, might personally accept.

Baker saw our artillery in action, the long lines of American motor trucks, with military police directing the traffic, and the American ambulances bearing the wounded back to the American hospital trains. These trains went on to the acres of American hospitals, which were preparing for the glut of casualties from the greater battles that our staff foresaw for the campaign of 1919. The doctors who had been trained under the régime of Surgeon General Gorgas at home, and then under Ireland, Surgeon General of the A. E. F., were having their taste of the realities of war no less than the infantry of the eight divisions. Miss Julia C. Stimson, who had been a pioneer in the first contingent of nurses which joined the British army in May, 1917, had no small command in all the nurses of the A. E. F.

Riding along the highways of France, Baker passed stretches of the American telephone and telegraph wires from America, strung on poles which American foresters had taken from French forests. Colonel Harvey was correctly informed: Baker did visit the huts and canteens which were a part of the "invisible armor" he would provide for our soldiers; and once

PIER BUILT ON THIS SIDE TO SPEED CARGO TO THE A. E. F.

GANTRY CRANES ON THE BASSENS DOCKS WE BUILT IN FRANCE

more he was inquiring if anything could be done so that the soldiers might get their mail more promptly.

The civil head of the army was making as thorough an inspection of the writing on the white paper of France as he had made on his first trip. From front to ports, with the call of "more" in his ears, he saw the projects which, in March, 1918, had been in the blue-print stage, or half-completed, now completed; new projects in the course of construction, while blueprints of others, not yet begun, were offered for his inspection. He met again Atterbury and pioneer Wilgus, of the transportation corps of the S. O. S., who had not enough locomotives, cars, rails, or repair shops, while he could connect their eagerness with the busy offices of S. M. Felton and Colonel F. A. Molitor in Washington, who day after day had tried to square requisitions from France with home production. And he met Brigadier General Edgar Russel, Chief of the Signal Corps of the A. E. F., who could not get enough equipment to satisfy the A. E. F., which sent 40,000 telegrams a day; and Baker could connect this with the efforts of Brigadier General C. M. Saltzman, chief executive officer of the Signal Corps at home, and his assistants, laboring their sixteen hours a day throughout the War in their battle with priorities to give just one branch of the A. E. F. what it wanted.

THE S. O. S. UNDER PRESSURE

A far less observant person than the Secretary of War could see, without waiting out a conference with the commander of the now huge army of the S. O. S., how Harbord's energy had given what was once called the "Service of the Rear" an *esprit de corps* of its own, and how—through his assistants, Brigadier Generals W. D. Connor, Johnson Hagood, and Edgar Jadwin, and Colonel Charles S. Symmonds, in command of the huge plant at Gièvres, and Colonels M. L. Walker and John P. McAdams—he had developed a team-play by every method known to the military and civil worlds. From Brigadier General Charles M. Dawes, the purchasing agent of the A. E. F., Baker could learn not only how, under pressure of the spring and summer crisis, unexpected resources had been developed in Europe to aid our army in the pooling of supplies as well as ships, but also what might be expected for the coming months. And the cry from every office, every dock, every railroad yard, every warehouse center of the S. O. S. for more and more material and labor battalions simply spelt more ships. Since the congested southwestern ports of France had forced some of our cargo through the Straits of Gibraltar to Marseilles, this meant the further delay of a still longer turnaround.

Baker listened to all appeals, listened even to one proposal that we change the style of our uniforms, now worn by 4,000,000 men; to which he replied that he did not think it worth while unless it would help to win the War.

ALLIED SUCCESSES CONTINUE—BUT PERSHING SKEPTICAL

And he had come to France to make sure of sufficient cargo vessels to serve our army for the coming winter. It was as an advocate that he appeared before the British shipping lords of the inter-Allied Maritime Council, when the Germans were in retreat, after Saint-Mihiel had been won, Soissons regained, all the German gains of 1918 recovered, and British shipping circles were disturbed about competition after the War. Soon the President, who had been gravely concerned about the situation, had assurance by cable that lawyer Baker had won his case.[11]

"The British have definitely allotted us 200,000 of deadweight tons, and these ships will be immediately diverted to us." And with the President's approval he was arranging that the British would continue to allocate the additional tonnage "necessary for constant maintenance of such American forces as are already in Europe from time to time."

It was Baker's fortune to be in France in two very dramatic periods. On his first trip his problem was the transport of manpower to meet the German offensives; on his second trip all his conferences had in view the program for 1919. It has already been related how Foch sent for Bliss on August 26, and said that he and Pershing agreed that "one hundred American divisions must be in France by July 1, 1919"; and then how the Allied successes in the following days led the General-issimo to write in his memoirs: "Thus, at the beginning of September victory had passed to the Allied banners." [12]

Now we may turn to the cables that were passing between Pershing and March while Baker was on his way to France early in September. Pershing was calling for the very combat divisions which had been at the ports when he canceled their sailings. On September 9 he demanded to know exactly how many troops he would have from month to month for the next ten months; and exactly how much material.[13] March cabled on the same day: "It is inferred that old system of phases has been abandoned and that troops will be in future scheduled by months in accordance with your monthly needs." [14] On September 11 Pershing cabled two pages of details for the next three hundred thousand troops.[15] On the 12th, in answer to Pershing's demand for more troops and more train-ing at home, March said that fifteen new divisions were train-ing at home and we planned to have eighteen training at all times. "This will give them all four months' training if not too many changes made in schedule." [16]

On September 13 Pershing called peremptorily for more motor transportation.[17] One of the results of forming the in-dependent American Army was that he had to supply motor transportation for the divisions that had been moved from the British front. Why were not more trucks shipped on the open decks of ships? But we must have them manufactured before we could ship them. Even America could not produce motor trucks fast enough for the A. E. F. in its rapid expansion of combat divisions which were all being hurried into active battle. Our victory at Saint-Mihiel on the 12th had released the last section of railroad, that of the Paris-Avricourt in the Com-mercy region, which Foch had in mind as an objective in his offensive program of July twenty-fourth. On the 17th there had been a sudden reversal of the situation in the Balkans when the Allies started a successful offensive. Within a week

Bulgaria was to sue for peace. Allenby's final drive against the Turks, which he had begun on the 19th, moved forward with giant strides. Haig was before the Hindenburg line. Fresh advances had begun in the Flanders area. By September 23 the enemy's ramparts were breaking on all fronts. Meanwhile, Baker, in consultation on the ground, found that Pershing was still insistent on a 100-division program and that the A. E. F.'s present idea of the amount of man-power involved in the 80-division program was different from the basis of all the computations by the War Department.

<h3 style="text-align:center">A DIFFERENCE OF A MILLION MEN</h3>

In a cable to March on September 23 Baker said that that 80-division program, as adopted and approved by the War Department, contemplated an "aggregate total force A. E. F. by June 30, 1919, 3,760,000, including wastage replacements of 400,000." [18] But he had learned that this meant nearly a million fewer men than Pershing had in mind. "Authorities here contemplate a total force by the same date of 4,700,000. . . . That is, the A. E. F. included sixteen depot divisions as a complement of the eighty." This was one way of getting the hundred on which the persistent Pershing had set his mind. Baker asked March to advise Pershing definitely "the details contemplated by the 80-division program as you interpret it. . . . I want personally as much information as possible before I leave." The addition of a million men and their supplies would leave us dependent on the British for shipping until well into the summer of 1919; and Baker's powers of persuasion in London had not yet got enough shipping to maintain the eighty divisions. According to the basis of reckoning of the A. E. F., a 100-division program would have meant 5,800,000 men in France, and the 110-division program about six and a half millions. Probably the inevitable increase of the S. O. S. forces would have brought the total of the 100-division program to more than six millions. March replied with characteristic definiteness to Baker's inquiry, and direct

to Pershing: [19] "It is impracticable to carry out such a program. The 80-division in France program [as worked out by
the War Department] is the official program, and you will give
instructions that rate of shipment and requirements be worked
out to correspond therewith. Should it be possible to exceed
it that will be done and you will be advised."

Meanwhile, Foch had grown confident with success. Employing the obvious tactics of swift alternating blows—which had
been practically the German plan in the spring of 1918—he
would give the enemy no time to meet one attack before he
delivered another. Haig had become equally eager to press
his advantages on the British front. From the first he had said
that it was a war of attrition and that the break might come
suddenly.[20] He had stonewalled in the Ypres salient; fought
the offensive of the Somme; pressed the Germans in their retreat to the Hindenburg line; hammered month on month in
the long battle of Passchendaele for yards and rods of gain;
stonewalled against the German offensive of 1918—ever having to adapt his plans to Allied crises. Now, after his mind had
been set so long on that stubborn line from Flanders to the
Somme, he still had the resiliency of spirit to profit promptly
by his perception that at last attrition was striking the sword
out of the enemy's hands.[21] The British Cabinet became
alarmed when he proposed to attack the redoubtable Hindenburg line; [22] but he went on boldly with his preparations.
Meanwhile, Foch had set for the Americans no relatively easy
task such as Saint-Mihiel, but a most wicked task—that of the
hammerhead in the long battle of the Meuse-Argonne, which
we began on September 26 as our part of an advance in con-
junction with Gouraud's army on a front of forty miles. On
the 27th the British, with two American divisions, the 27th
and the 30th, assisting, broke the stronghold of the famous
Hindenburg (Siegfried) line. The Belgian army left its
trenches in the common movement. From the Meuse to the
Channel the whole front was aflame.

Foch pressed in every division at his command to force the

Germans into a position where they could not re-form on the shorter Antwerp-Meuse-Strasbourg line for another long period of resistance.[23] On the 30th Ludendorff confessed privately to despair,[24] and on the 30th the German Chancellor resigned and the troubled Kaiser appointed as his successor Prince Max of Baden, a liberal. Since the beginning of their offensives on July 18, the Allies had taken 3,600 guns and 25,000 machine-guns. On October 1 Hindenburg told the German statesmen that a peace offer must be made immediately, because the German army was breaking. Three days later, when this was unknown to Foch but when he realized the rich harvest his combinations were yielding, Baker called at his headquarters.

FOCH SAID FORTY DIVISIONS; PERSHING SAID A HUNDRED

Baker remarked to Foch that Pershing insisted on 100 divisions, and then asked the Generalissimo's opinion as to how many divisions he must have to win the War in 1919.

"Forty!" Foch replied.

"I think I must have misunderstood the Marshal," Baker said to the interpreter. "Will you repeat the question and make sure that he understands that I am referring to divisions to be in France for use in 1919?"

When the interpreter repeated the question, Foch replied: "I understood the Secretary, and my answer is forty."

"But, Marshal, there are nearly that many divisions in France now, and General Pershing is urging upon me the necessity for 100 divisions in 1919."

"I win the War with forty," Foch replied.[25]

On his way to Brest to take ship on his return to America Baker learned how our 2nd Division had stormed Blanc Mont in Gouraud's action, which put the Germans out of artillery range of the Rheims Cathedral. Allenby had entered Damascus; and Ferdinand had abdicated as King of Bulgaria.

At Brest, before Baker embarked, Rear Admiral W. B. Wilson, in command of our naval forces in France, sent him a note saying that the local paper had just received a dispatch that

"Germany, Austria, and Turkey propose an armistice and declare themselves ready to negotiate for peace based on the 14 points of President Wilson."

The news rapidly spread. There was victory in the air, although a month was to pass before the Armistice was signed. As Baker ascended the gangway of his ship, hundreds of American soldiers were looking down on him. But he did not raise his head. Raymond Fosdick, who was with him, rounded on him after they were on board:

"There's no doing anything with you. Why didn't you raise your hand to them? They were spoiling for a chance to cheer somebody."

"I was afraid they *would* cheer me," Baker replied.[26]

What was a Secretary of War for? Not to be cheered, to receive the hurrahs, when our soldiers were fighting in the Meuse-Argonne.

The President answered the German peace proposals on the 8th, when Baker was at sea, saying the Allies would not consider a cessation of hostilities until the enemy had withdrawn from their soil. On that day the British took 200 guns and 10,000 prisoners. With the last of the fortifications of the Hindenburg line behind them they entered Cambrai. The British and Belgian forces were out of the old Ypres shambles and advancing on fresh battle-ground before Baker reached Washington, where the State Department had had word of Austrian moves for peace and the imminent collapse of the Austrian Empire.

At the close of a letter to Bliss on October 14, Baker said: "I reached New York yesterday morning and Washington this morning, to find the German peace proposals the sole topic of conversation; but the day has been too short to allow me to form any impression that it would be worth while to put in a letter as yet."

His part was not with peace negotiations, but was rather to keep up the home effort in support of our army fighting its way step by step up the troughs of the Meuse and Aire rivers, through the great forest and patches of woods, and over the knolls between the rivers under play of the shellfire from the Meuse heights.

The Fourth Liberty Loan campaign was under whip and spur. As soon as this reached its goal, a united drive of the welfare societies would have the field.[27] On October 13 Garfield, the Fuel Administrator, asked Pershing for a message on "the importance of coal connected with the military situation. Coal production indicates big shortage and drive on to spur production." On the 15th,[28] McAdoo sent the draft of a message for Pershing to sign, to the effect that the success of the Fourth Liberty Loan meant "triumphant victory for America's cause. America's soldiers on the battlefields of France rely upon America's home army to do its full duty."

NO PAUSE IN THE NATION'S EFFORT

While the signs of the enemy's collapse were clearly written on the map, Pershing's staff was thinking that if we wanted to be sure of that triumphant victory we had better send more soldiers, more guns, more rolling stock, more war material of all kinds. March cabled to Pershing on the 13th—the day Mangin's French army entered Laon—that we could not meet his order for one hundred and twenty twelve-inch howitzers before October, 1919, and that their construction was opposed by the Navy, the Shipping Board, and the railroad and labor administrations.[29] Our foundries were busy making fourteen-inch guns for the A. E. F.'s previous order. They had started eighteen-inch howitzers, but the A. E. F. decided a twelve-inch mortar should have preference. On the 15th—the day that the Germans were evacuating both Lille and Ostend, which had been in their possession for over four years—March cabled Pershing that we could not ship more than two thousand knocked-down railroad cars in November if we shipped ten thousand motor trucks.[30] Nor could we send gantry cranes and airplanes, which occupied so much space on board ship, or the animals he wanted. Would Pershing send a priority schedule in a long list of materials beginning with tractors and trailers and ending with aviation gasoline in barrels?

By this time Colonel Harvey had ceased to demand 5,000,000 men in France. He said the War was going quite well, in spite of Baker; indeed, the procession had long since left the Secretary of War so far in the rear that even he would now be unable to prevent victory. If the Colonel had seen a letter that Baker wrote after his return from France, *Harvey's Weekly* would have had further evidence of how the "chattering ex-Pacifist" twittered away his time on inconsequential things.

TO A DEAD SOLDIER'S FATHER

Baker had found opportunity in France, after he secured the ships from the British, to ride one hundred miles to visit the grave of the son of his friend, Dr. J. W. Kern, of Lexington, Virginia. He wrote to the father:

"I talked with the doctor in charge of the hospital and he told me some of the particulars of Dabney's last illness. He was brought in with a wound in the back of his head which he had received at Château-Thierry on the 21st of July. The wound was not necessarily fatal, but he developed spinal meningitis and died on the 31st of August, 1918.

"The inscription on the cross is as follows: 'First Lieutenant Thomas D. Kern, M. C. Company, 26th Infantry, died August 31st, 1918.' On his grave there lay the remains of a beautiful floral tribute tied with the associated ribbons of America and France, and in a kind of circlet of aluminum letters the following words appeared: '*Les officiers Français à leur camarade Américain.*' The floral tribute had, as the inscription says, been presented by French officers to their American comrade. My first thought was to bring away the ribbons with the aluminum letters for you and Mrs. Kern, but I decided not to do it for two reasons. In the first place, I felt that you would want there with him this evidence of the respect and affection of his French comrades; and, second, the French have a very strong feeling against taking away from a grave any flowers or ornaments once placed there, and I feared that the removal of the articles, even for the purpose of preserving thm in the boy's home, would be misunderstood.

"From the photographs you will see that the grave lies on a hill and nearby are a number of other graves of enlisted men. He was the only officer buried there at the time of my visit, but a newly made grave was open near his and a few days later another American officer was laid by his side. The cemetery is a piece of ground presented by the city to the American Army. The view is very beautiful and overlooks the mountainous region in which these great summer resorts like Chatel Guyon are located. It is a beautiful and quiet resting-place.

"Your boy was surrounded in his last hours with every attention that affection and sympathy could extend, and he had the benefit of the wonderful hospital facilities and the fine surgical and medical care which have been provided. No doubt James has sent you more intimate particulars of his last hours, but it was a pilgrimage of love and respect for me to go to his resting-place and have these pictures made; and while nothing can soften the tragedy of this loss to you and Mrs. Kern, it gives me a certain sort of happiness to be able to assure you that he was tenderly cared for, and that he rests for the time being in a beautiful and well-cared-for place in the very heart of the country where he made his sacrifice, and for whose liberty he and our wonderful American boys are fighting like heroes.

"I am sending several copies of the pictures, as they present various views and you may desire to send some to particularly near friends and relatives. In my own photograph album, which records the incidents of my trip, I am including a copy of these pictures so that I too can have a lively recollection of this beautiful and sacred spot."

CLICKING OFF THE CASUALTIES

One section of the War Department, which had had little to occupy it in the period of preparation, had now become grimly active. It was transcribing cablegrams from the A. E. F. which had nothing to do with shipping, or programs, or phases, but much to do with the call for replacements. Both March and Pershing held that all casualties should be sent in cipher lest they reveal to the enemy the identity and losses of units engaged.

BRINGING IN A WOUNDED MAN

Received at

2/1800 NA   Sept 6, 1918

      Agwar   50

Dahaar Farharj Ehfobjeyyr Hemekehhyd Yvvyzbagud Hebaffegug Unmok Nayer
Nywovfebim Yvvyzozhuk Yzbemhebam Egwuvfegil Unmok Samuel Suwuv Ashby
Ehfifgeyyr Ehkudrybum Ehlilyvvyz Dadakfezyp Unmok Alvion Ruth Upbimyvvyz
Ozhukyzbem Hebafegwuv Ickyc Benjamin Austin Upbimyvvyz Ozhukalraz
Hebafegwuv Fegubunmok William Pogym Stevenson Hepuvehjug Yvvixagkak
Ehmykgirip Fegadunmok Alley Mastroni Ehrexrybum Ehfolyvvyz Lahybfegef
Unmok Alexander Melnil Ehfifgeyyr Ehlulrybum.

1105AM.

LIST OF CASUALTIES RECEIVED IN CIPHER

"Sending casualty cablegrams partly in English and partly in code makes use of the same cipher table for confidential messages unsafe," March reported to Pershing, "as the publication of the casualties in the newspapers enables intercepted messages to be easily deciphered. A new code for casualties will be completed soon." [31] Men who had volunteered, men who had marched gaily forth to register for the draft, and had been lost in the fog over there, had become important enough as private soldiers to have their names put on the trans-Atlantic wire. Relatives were awaiting the lists in the same sort of anxiety that European countries had known for four years, the same that was felt in our own country (how well Mr. Randolph remembered it!) after Shiloh, Antietam, Fredericksburg, Gettysburg, and the Wilderness. For America, too, was now blood-deep in the War. Cable transmission instruments clicked, typewriters clicked with the names after they were deciphered, and though lights might go out in other offices the clerks here kept on with their gloomy task into the night.

Dr. Frederick Keppel, now Third Assistant Secretary of War, who had conducted the noonday rounds in the Secretary's reception room in the spring and summer of 1917, was assigned to look after the casualty section. Members of Congress acting for relatives of soldiers, and relatives on their own part, crowded the corridors and the offices asking that special inquiry be made about some one of the hundreds of thousands in the anonymity of over there, where Foch moved the chessmen of three nations and Pershing drove the spurs into the flanks of his soldiers, and a man who was dead or who occupied one of the cots in the rows on rows in the hospitals had become "expended" in the military sense. And the machines clicked on with the names that the A. E. F. was sending as fast as it could from the front, where the thought was on more able-bodied, trained, living men to step into vacant places in the ranks.

Those who had wondered whether we should ever get into

the War in earnest, whether all the divisions in training and chafing to board a transport would ever reach France, had their answer in the casualty reports of divisions that seemed to have left home only yesterday. There was nothing to do but to wait for the lists. Each report would be checked off for accuracy or there might be unnecessary anguish and a cruel reason in an individual example as a basis for scoring official carelessness and callousness. Sometimes individual cables were ahead of the official. There was the case of a father and son who were both in the A. E. F. The father served in an office in Paris, the son in combat. Thinking the official message had already gone, the father sent this message to the mother, "In life and in death we rejoice in him"—which was the first word of the son's death that she received.

We were as fresh to the sacrifices as we had been to war preparations sixteen months ago. The nation was in no mood for compromise after all the expenditure of effort and money as the bills for the supreme price were coming in. But our mechanistic age had not affected the Spartan character of some parents. I quote from a letter written by John O. Tardy, a farmer of Murat, Virginia, to Judge S. J. Graham, then Assistant Attorney General, who sent a copy to Baker:

"I have two boys in France fighting for their country and humanity. A few days ago, I received a telegram from the War Department, that one of them, Corporal Jackson R. Tardy, Company L, 38th Infantry, A. E. F., was killed in action on July 15th. I think the Red Cross Bureau or some other bureau will get particulars. I would like to get particulars. Please give this to the proper bureau. This boy was just 23 years old, the other one is 19. It is sad to lose one's boys, but I would rather my sons were dead soldiers in France than to be alive and slackers at home. My boys volunteered. I have four boys at home aged respectively 17, 15, 13, and 11. I will encourage them to go as they become old enough."

Distance was against us in reporting casualties, most poignantly against us, when the other nations might send theirs by mail to be delivered the next morning. The cables could not keep up with the toll the enemy was taking as he pressed in divisions to prevent our army in the Meuse-Argonne from cutting off his retreat.

XXXVI

THE MEUSE-ARGONNE BATTLE

BEFORE the ordeal was over more than a million men were fed into the treadmill between the western edge of the Argonne Forest and the heights of Verdun. The Meuse-Argonne battle has been misunderstood by America as well as by Europe. Our people saw the map-pins of victory advancing slowly in our sector and rapidly from Champagne to Flanders. The British and French, absorbed by the march of their own veterans to victory, hardly realized that the American Army was fighting.

Military speculation will long continue as to the probable result if our fresh divisions, instead of beginning a new battle, had been put in line at Saint-Mihiel to continue pressure in that direction. Would we have reached Metz? To many of us who were at Saint-Mihiel the answer lay in the soft earth of the Woëvre under autumn rains, in guns and transport stalled in the mud.

But this is certain: Foch had decided for the new battle to the east of Verdun. He had invited our High Command to dream of a swift advance that would cut off two or three German army corps; of repeating, on the scene of that famous German victory, a Sedan in which the Germans would be the losers. Did he think we could succeed in so quickly reaching the goal he had set for us? At least, he was aware that he had given our young corps and divisions, acting as an independent army, a full and terrible opportunity for expending their ardor. He knew that the harder we fought the more enemy strength we would draw off from other parts of the front.

Our pioneer divisions, which had been in the easier task at Saint-Mihiel, could not be brought up in time for the "jump-off" on the first day of the greatest battle in numbers and gun-power in our history; nor could the 3rd Division, which had been the "Rock of the Marne," or the 32nd (Haan), which had qualified as veteran in red earnest with the French at Juvigny after its part in closing the Marne salient. The four pioneer divisions had averaged eight months before they entered an active battle sector. It was aften ten months of training, and after weeks of preparation, that the 1st had made its attack on a short limited objective at Cantigny; and the 2nd might have waited its ten months if Harbord had not met the occasion with an instant offensive into Belleau Wood.

The nine divisions in the first line of attack in the Meuse-Argonne had averaged three and one-half months in France. Only one was a Regular division, the 4th (Hines), under a most experienced division commander, who had been with the 1st through all the stages of its training. The 4th had been four months in France. All the divisions had been hurried into position against elaborate trench systems and deep fields of barbed wire of four years' standing.

Our Line officers had had no opportunity to familiarize themselves with the ground beyond the study of their maps. Some of the divisions had not their own artillery, but that assigned from other divisions. Co-ordination from transport to trenches must be impromptu, based on theory rather than on the practice of association; and over all was a staff facing a prolonged tactical maneuver in meeting each day's new situations over a long front for which its only experience had been the swiftly concluded action of Saint-Mihiel.

Two of the National Army divisions, the 79th (Kuhn) and the 91st (Johnston), had been only two months in France, hardly time enough to find their land legs and to be acclimatized. Neither had ever been under fire; they went in the trenches for the first time in a major action against these semi-permanent fortifications. The 79th had been singularly the victim of the changing phases, schedules, and programs, after Allied alarm over the successes of the German offensives had crowded three hundred thousand men a month on board transports, with the accompanying pressure on industrial effort and the disorganization of priorities in vicious circles.

As Camp Meade was on the industrial Atlantic seaboard the 79th had been subject to the drain for replacements, for shipbuilders and all kinds of skilled labor, while Pershing insisted that divisions arrive in France with full rosters at the same time that he called impatiently for special service battalions, which, as military organizations under military officers, must come from the cantonments. He could not tell a week ahead what he wanted in those days, but inevitably everything he wanted must be sent in a hurry. When the 79th was suddenly ordered to embark, it included ten thousand draft men who had had only a brief period of drill—not four months, nor three months, but many only a month, or a few days. Thus prepared, or unprepared, the 79th sailed for France. Then, one night, the 79th was marched to the front, and the next morning saw No Man's Land for the first time, which was also the fortune of the 91st from the Pacific coast. And the 79th was set the farthest objective of any division on the first day. It was to take the key position of Montfaucon on the top of a distant hill from which the Crown Prince of Germany had watched some of the Verdun fighting.

But the purpose is not to single out the 79th, or the 91st, or the 77th (Alexander), the melting-pot division, when its men, who knew no jungles except city streets, faced the Argonne Forest. Left to right the divisions were the 77th, National Army, the 28th (Muir), National Guard, 35th (Traub), National Guard, 91st, National Army, 37th (Farnsworth), National Guard, 79th, National Army, 4th, Regulars, 80th (Cronkhite), National Army, and 33rd (Bell), National Guard; with a regiment of the 92nd (colored under Ballou) operating with the French beyond the forest. In all the nine, just one Regular division!

A CRUEL TEST FOR YOUNG DIVISIONS

The nationalized Guard, after intensified training, was to answer the peace-time flings about "tin soldiers" and Senator Chamberlain's criticism of the Guard's general worthlessness; and the National Army was finally to answer all the prophecies that the draft would lead to home riots and bloodshed and that the draft soldier would be a slacking soldier. These fresh arrivals had not been through a Lorraine winter, drilled and drilled in the atmosphere of war, then advanced by degrees from very tranquil to moderately tranquil sectors and then to active sectors. They had not stood for hours in the pouring rain, lines face to face, waiting for the inspection by the Commander-in-Chief, who noted that their shoes were muddy.

As they looked out on the expanses of barbed wire and that old trench line, it was hardly worse than they had imagined it would be. They had not been fooling themselves after reading about this War for four years. Here was their job in front of them. After a night in which suspense gave little refreshing sleep, they had to drive through the wire and over the trenches and keep on going. Although there were broad stretches where the artillery did not cut the wire, they went through it, and the second as well as the first line of trenches and wire and into the open; and they kept on going and fighting. It was incredible that, in their inexperience, they should not have tied their formations into knots before they got through the wire, even if they had met little opposition. Their conduct was a tribute to their industry in training; a tribute to the manner of their training by the Regular officers who had to remain at home and had to conceal their heartbreaks and their consciousness of the stupid and utterly false conclusions a questioner might draw from their casual answers, "No, I did not get to France."

It turned out that in the assignment of the divisions harder problems had been given to those with no experience than to those with some experience. Of course the attack could not advance so far on the first day as the line the staff set on the maps supplied to field officers. The maps showed contours, but necessarily lacked information as to which bush concealed a German machine-gun nest, or where the German infantry would dig a line of foxholes and wait for targets in the open, or where a barrage of gas would be laid down as the German resistance formed and grew stronger with reinforcements.

The measure of success was dependent largely on the nature of ground and the resistance in each case, and partly on the gamble of the way that division commanders, their staffs, the brigadiers, and the colonels applied their training in the plans for action and in their execution under fire. The mishandling of a certain division would have been a burlesque if it had not been so murderous. Without reaching their objectives divisions advanced three, four, and five miles beyond the fortifications. It was an amazing achievement for men having their first baptism of fire—one of the great achievements of the World War.

As soon as the attack began, of course we had disclosed to the enemy that our objective was a vital artery of his communications—the Sedan-Mézières railway—which served his armies in western France, and which he required to cover his retreat.

Unless the German High Command had lost all its wits and its wisdom of experience and its understanding of the simplest strategic problems, it would not allow us to reach the railroad while it had a single corps west of our line of thrust. It was bound to continue to feed in artillery, infantry, and machine-gunners against us. As resistance strengthened the second day, and another hope of a miracle on the Western front had passed, the task before us was revealed as clearly as Little Round Top or Culp's Hill to the Confederates at Gettysburg, or the heights of Fredericksburg to the Federals. But these great Civil War actions had been over in a few hours, while this action of the Meuse-Argonne was to continue for weeks.

We had been allotted a battlefield that both the French and the Germans had found impracticable for a jump-off. Except on the west bank of the Meuse—our right—it had been undisturbed by the Verdun battles. Our left was in the Argonne Forest. If the Forest had been stripped bare of its trees, it would have presented a great ridge-like bastion cut by ravines, with irregular hills and slopes of a character which, even though bald, would have been formidable in defense. Its timber had nothing in common with the American conception of a park-like European forest, in which the ground opens between tree-trunks in lines as regular as in an orchard. If the Argonne had been without roads, the Red Indians might have been as much at home

VALLEY OF THE AIRE—THE MEUSE-ARGONNE BATTLE

in its depths as in the primeval Appalachians or Sierras. Under-brush grew as freely as in second-growth woods in our New England or Middle States; the leaves had not yet begun to fall from the trees.

At the foot of the Forest's irregular wooded slopes ran the little River Aire. On the other flank ran the Meuse, and beyond that rose the Verdun heights. Between these parallel walls of the battlefield, with the parallel streams to halt our move-ment, rose a whale-back with the highest point beyond Mont-faucon. Once we had ascended this, it was downhill to the rail-road. But the whale-back was not smooth. Its surface was more like the folds of a rhinoceros' hide. After you had taken one crest you were down in a fold and the enemy was above you. Guns out of the reach of our guns on the heights of the opposite bank of the Meuse swept our right flank where we were plotted to the gunners like flies on a tablecloth. There was a play of cross-fire not only in the valley of the Aire but elsewhere from ridges that formed more alleys within alleys. The many patches of woods on the whale-back were staggered in relation to the contours of the landscape, as a further provision by nature which skilful soldiers could utilize for defense.

A BATTLE OF SQUADS, PLATOONS, AND COMPANIES

Our army, its teeth set in the enemy's neck, could only keep on chewing toward the artery of the railroad. Many experts thought that its tactical direction was suffering from the same handicap that it had in the mobilization for the jump-off: the clumsiness of the big division, which the French staff had wished on us. With smaller divisions, which would have been more mobile, we might indeed have carried out our dream of a rapid advance. Once the knots in our transport had been untied, and we had corrected our lines, the staff might order another general attack, or a corps attack; but the battle was essentially one of squads, platoons, companies, battalions: a battle by the bar-rack groups at our training camps, its tactics in all the crochet work of detail devised by junior officers, against an enemy so veteran and skilled in this kind of fighting. So each unit knew only its part in the whole, the problems and the fire it faced; each man, indeed, knew only the world of his foxhole. It was Belleau Wood over again on a large scale, and fought with the same spirit against the enemy's counter-attacks. Rested divisions took the place of exhausted. It was my fortune to see each one when it was in action. The rotation began when the veteran 1st (Summerall), the veteran 32nd (Haan), and the veteran 3rd (Buck) relieved divisions that had paid the price to become veteran.

But before we could go farther we must have the east bank of the Meuse, which swept our left flank at right angles with blasts of shells. That item had been overlooked in the plan for the battle. The 29th (Morton) now appeared for its part. On July 17, when it had been only a month in France, the Commander-in-Chief, who had given the Regular 1st nine months' training before he put it in battle action, had informed Foch that the 29th was available at once.[1] This National Guard Division had had two months in quiet sectors before it was given the task, which it performed smartly, of clearing the way for the 33rd in crossing the Meuse. Now a new line was formed on the east of the Meuse to capture the high Borne de Carnouiller (Hill 378), from which the Germans sent their plunging fire upon the eastern slope of the whale-back. But while the Germans still had infantry and machine-guns, they were loth to yield the master height; and day after day, in the pocket of a valley, these two National Guard Divisions, the 33rd (which had been in the battle from the first) until October 21, and the 29th until the 31st, keep on attacking and slowly gaining.

So the struggle went on from forest to Verdun heights by driving in wedges, gouging, wrestling, and whittling. The advance of the British and French armies was aided by every German division that our pressure drew to protect the Mézières railroad line. By the middle of October we had practically cleared the Argonne Forest and the valley of the Aire to where it spread with the river's turn toward Grand Pré. The 42nd (Menoher) was now in. Three National Army Divisions, the 78th (McRae), the 82nd (Duncan), which had both been three months in France, and the 89th (Wright), which had been two months in France, replaced divisions that had been fresh when the second stage of the battle began. The 5th Regular (McMahon-Ely), which had been five months in France and had battle experience, also was put in.

On the 15th Pershing made a reorganization. Major General Charles F. Summerall was given command of the 5th Corps in place of Cameron. A major upon our entry into the War, at first chief of the artillery of the 1st Division, Summerall had won his way in action as a master of battle who had, in addition to his skill, the talent of natural leadership. He surely had speed and iron. Major General John L. Hines was given the 3rd Corps in place of Bullard; Major General J. T. Dickman, the 1st Corps in place of Liggett. Brigadier General Preston Brown, who had been the brilliant Chief of Staff of the 2nd Division at Château-Thierry, succeeded Buck in command of the 3rd; and Brigadier General Frank Parker, who personified the finest traditions of the Regulars, succeeded Summerall in command of the pioneer 1st.

Our Corps were grouped in two armies. Hunter Liggett was named commander of the 1st Army, which had the Meuse-Argonne sector; and the indomitable Robert L. Bullard, of the 2nd Army in the Saint-Mihiel sector. Both these major generals were promoted to be lieutenant generals. With 1,800,000 Americans in France, Pershing could feel that he was on terms of equality with Pétain and Haig, who also commanded groups of armies. If he had to go to Paris for diplomatic conferences, or look after other pressing problems of his great fief from ports to the front, he could confidently leave active charge of the battle to Liggett, deep student of tactics, former Chief of the War College, and organizer of our pioneer 1st Corps. We owe much to the able, equable, loyal, and modest Liggett.

But let us turn back to the cablegrams between the A. E. F. and the War Department during the battle. On October 2, three days before Marshal Foch had told Baker that he wanted only forty divisions to assure victory, Pershing cabled: [2]

"Our Allies and Marshal Foch understand our 80-division program to mean that by July 1, 1919, we shall have in France 80 combat divisions with all necessary corps, army and S. O. S. troops. . . . A minimum of 800,000 for the S. O. S. . . . 600,-000 replacements, which gives a total of approximately 4,770,000 personnel demanded by our 80-division program. . . . We must bring over approximately 3,000,000 men in the next nine months. . . . The needs of the American Expeditionary Forces and the order in which they should be met are best known here."

On October 8 Pershing wanted to be sure of 864 heavy howitzers by July 31, 1919, plus replacements.[3] On October 10 March reminded Pershing that the "number of men in the U. S. military program by July 1, 1919, had already been clearly stated to our Allies as well as to you."[4] The number in France by July 1, 1919, as March had said—in reply to a cable from Baker from France in the last week of September, at the time the Secretary learned the difference in estimates of the total personnel for eighty divisions—would be 3,360,000 men in France, with 1,500,-000 in training at home. This was the number for which the British had agreed with Baker to supply the necessary additional shipping.

"You will plan operations," March told Pershing, "upon the basis of the maximum strength in France stated in the foregoing." March also reminded Pershing that the Congress had not yet appropriated the money to carry out the War Department's estimates for the 80-division program. At the time, Congressmen were watching the rapid advance of the Allied armies and pondering the peace proposals of Prince Max, the new German Chancellor. In the same cable by March, from which I have quoted, appeared a sentence which revealed the reason why we could not meet all Pershing's demands instantly from camps to port and ports to France; the same reason that put many of the soldiers who arrived in France in hospital before they reached the front:

"If we are not stopped on account of influenza, which has passed the 200,000 mark, you will get the replacements and all shortages of divisions up to date by November 30."

Until September 14, 1918, there had been fewer than ten thousand deaths from disease in our New Army, with a death-rate of fewer than five a year a thousand men. As if there were not deaths enough in battle and from wounds and misery enough, a new horror, baffling to medical science, had stricken peoples and armies at home and abroad. Day after day the number of cases increased until barrack buildings were turned into hospitals, while many of the tireless doctors and nurses in home camps —working double shifts at the same time as their colleagues who were caring for the sick and wounded soldiers in France— themselves became victims of this swift destroying influenza-pneumonia pandemic. In the second week of October, when March sent his cable, it caused the death of four out of every thousand men under arms in the United States. From September 14 to November 8 there were 316,000 cases of influenza, and 59,000 cases of pneumonia. Our second winter of the War promised to be more dismal than the first. Pneumonia was responsible for eighty-three per cent of the deaths from disease in the Army in the World War, which was our first war in which deaths from disease did not exceed battle deaths.

THE INFLUENZA-PNEUMONIA PANDEMIC

On October 13 Pershing sent another peremptory call for hospital units.[5] In answer March explained, "Every effort being made to send you all medical personnel possible . . . 8 base hospitals, 1 evacuation hospital, 14 evacuation ambulance companies assigned to an early convoy."

While the machines continued to click off the names of casualties in the Army, the influenza had stricken the civil population as well as soldiers, delaying production, transport, and shipping. Pershing cabled, on October 19, that his supply of infantry and machine-gun replacements was exhausted, and he protested again that motor transport, medical personnel, and ordnance personnel were not coming fast enough.[6] On October 23 March cabled:[7]

"Epidemic has not only quarantined nearly all camps but has forced us to cancel or suspend nearly all draft calls. Continued shipments are consequently draining reservoir of men in this country. Only a few thousand replacements for November are in service. . . . Influenza situation has improved in the Army and in civilian population in Eastern United States. So we hope for early improvement in above conditions."

On October 25 March cabled: [8] "Every man at Fort Ogle-thorpe who is available for overseas duty is being sent. A personnel officer has just returned from investigation there. He took all men out of organizations far down on priority to fill organizations high on priority"—all who had not the influenza.

Now we may pause for a moment for a sidelight on Allied relations which forecast some of the difficulties that awaited the President when he went to Paris for the peace negotiations. On October 14 the sage Bliss wrote a significant note to March at the time that Pershing was calling for masses of replacements. Bliss spoke of a call from Stettinius, who had been arranging the munitions program for 1919:

"He tells me that he is now running up against a decided indisposition on the part of the British and the French to give us the help which they promised. This is not surprising to me because, from various little indications that have come to my notice, it seems to me somewhat evident that the European Allies will attempt to minimize the American effort as much as possible. They think that they have got the Germans on the run and that they now do not need as much help as they were crying for a little while ago.

"I think I told you some time ago that I had heard a gentleman in high position here say that the United States was building a bridge for the Allies to pass over; that the time for the United States to secure acquiescence in its wishes was while the bridge was building; that after the Allies had crossed over the bridge they would have no further use for it or for its builders. This may be true or not. I do not know. *Qui vivra verra.*"

And now we turn to an incident in which high politics were related to high command.

American lives in the American Army! and French lives in

French army! On October 21 Clemenceau wrote a letter to Foch which the Marshal says "had in view nothing less than to effect a change in the Chief of Command in the American Army." [9] The sardonic and incisive old Premier said he would not waste time in reviewing the "development of General Pershing's exactions" and "his invincible obstinacy," which had won out against Foch.

CLEMENCEAU WOULD RELIEVE PERSHING FROM COMMAND

"I am the head of the French army . . . I would be a criminal if I allowed the French army to wear itself out indefinitely in battle, without doing everything in my power to ensure that an Allied army which had hurried to its aid was rendered capable of fulfilling the military rôle for which it is destined. The French army and the British army, without a moment's respite, have been fighting daily for the last three months. . . . These two armies are pressing back the enemy with an ardor that excites world-wide admiration; but our worthy American Allies, who thirst to get into action and who are unanimously acknowledged to be great soldiers, have been marking time ever since their forward jump on the first day, and, in spite of heavy losses, they have failed to conquer the ground assigned to them as their objective. Nobody can maintain that these fine troops are unusable; they are merely being unused."

This letter was written after the French had recovered Laon; after the Germans had evacuated Lille, Ostend, and Zeebrugge, leaving large quantities of material behind them; after Count Czernin had gone to Switzerland to sue for peace for Austria-Hungary; and two weeks before Bliss' letter which noted the changed attitude of the Allies, who were now thinking less of how to win the War than of the reckoning after it should be over. We were still farther away from the day when only our financial and commercial aid was desired, and from the initial humble appeal for a few battalions to show our colors in France, followed, a few months later, by Joffre's statement to Baker that five hundred thousand was the largest American army the Allies would ever expect in France. The day after Clemenceau wrote his letter, Baker was writing to the President:

"More than two million American soldiers have sailed from the ports in this country to participate in the War overseas. . . . Our losses [at sea] have been exceedingly small considering the size of the force transported, and this is due to the efficient protection given American convoys by our naval forces. We also have been greatly assisted in the dispatch of troops abroad by the allocation of certain vessels of our Allies, principally those of Great Britain."

Tiger Clemenceau, in his zeal to get his teeth into the red meat of victory, continued in his letter to Foch:

"When General Pershing refused to obey your orders you could have appealed to President Wilson. . . . I took the liberty of differing with you. . . . You wished to prolong the experience. . . . Now that I have learned that you have taken direct command of General Pershing's troops, I cannot refrain from feeling that this trial should be the last of those we have been compelled to undergo. . . . If General Pershing finally resigns himself to obedience, if he accepts the advice of capable generals, whose presence at his side he has until now permitted only that he might reject their counsels, I shall be wholly delighted. [But, in the event that Pershing persisted in his obstinacy, it was] high time to tell President Wilson the truth and the whole truth concerning the situation of the American troops. Indeed, neither you nor I have any right to conceal it from him. The President of the United States has frequently declared that he was ready to conform to your judgment in all military questions. He will undoubtedly appraise at their true value, as he ought to do, both the patience you have long shown and the decision to which you have finally been led. . . . You will recognize that this state of affairs cannot continue any longer. For this reason, I would be glad if you could find it possible to send me an early answer."

It was the gossip about the supposed contents of this letter, when its very existence was a subject of doubt in staff circles, that led to rumors that Pershing was about to be relieved; that the time had come for a McClellan to go and for a Grant to be sought.

The air-raid in Paris the night after Baker's arrival there, on his first tour of our Army in France, led him to remark to Pershing that generals were mortal. Since, in a war where explosives were dropped so far behind the lines, our Commander-in-Chief was inevitably subject to many risks and might himself one day be on the casualty list, Baker asked him if he had ever considered who was best fitted to be his successor.[10] Pershing said that he had not, but would do so, and would give his answer. Pershing did not mention the subject again; so Baker brought it up before leaving France. Pershing replied that he had not been able to make a selection. Since time must not be lost in choosing a successor, to meet an emergency, Baker decided that he would make his own choice, which narrowed to Liggett, Harbord, and Summerall. His decision upon his first visit to France was reinforced by his observation on his second visit. It was for Harbord, who as the pioneer Chief of Staff, the fighting commander at Belleau Wood, and the reorganizer of the S. O. S., had risen ably to his responsibility in each part and had given proof of a poise, initiative, judgment, and perspective that fitted him for command of the whole.[11]

WHO WOULD HAVE TAKEN PERSHING'S PLACE?

Meanwhile, Baker never had any thought of relieving Pershing for any other reason than the one he had mentioned to Pershing himself. Pershing was his general; and he believed in his general and stood by him. As President Wilson had been an advocate of unified command from the outset, and had so steadfastly supported Foch's authority, an acute question of policy would have risen for the President and the Secretary of War if Foch had relieved Pershing or asked for his relief.

Clemenceau's letter was not brought to the attention of the President or Baker, who were too busy with real problems to borrow trouble over hypothetical ones. Yielding to Foch in the crisis of the German offensives was in quite a different category from yielding three weeks before the Armistice, when the Ger-

man army was already retreating. Even the combined appeals of
the Premier of France and the Generalissimo of the Allied
armies, on the threshold of victory for the Allies, would hardly
have influenced the President and Baker to relieve an American
Commander-in-Chief in what had become distinctly an American battle by an American army. However, Foch did not accept
Clemenceau's suggestion.

"Having a more comprehensive knowledge of the difficulties
encountered by the American Army, I could not acquiesce in
the radical solution contemplated by Monsieur Clemenceau,"
said Foch in his answer to Clemenceau in which he enclosed a
table showing that there were now forty-three American divisions in France. Of the thirty fit for battle ten were with the
British and French armies, twenty under Pershing. The other
thirteen were at bases or being disembarked. He said that by
manipulation he could shift more divisions from Pershing to
other armies if circumstances warranted it, and thus

"diminish the weaknesses of the [American] High Command
rather than by orders. These I shall give, to be sure, but the
High Command may not perhaps be in a position to have them
executed, since to do so would require corps and division commanders and staffs having the necessary experience. Moreover,
this crisis is of the sort from which all improvised armies suffer,
and which always impairs their achievements at the start.

"But there is no denying the magnitude of the effort made
by the American Army. After attacking at Saint-Mihiel on
September 12 it attacked in the Argonne on the twenty-sixth.
From September 26 to October 20 its losses in battle were 54,128
men [an understatement]—in exchange for small gains on a narrow front, it is true, but over particularly difficult terrain and in
the face of serious resistance by the enemy." [12]

WE LEARN WARFARE BY ATTRITION

Foch now planned to broaden the American field of attack by
an enlarged Franco-American maneuver which would clear its
flanks, especially on the right bank of the Meuse where the
German guns from the crests still had a cross-fire on the right

WEIGHING SHELLS IN A MUNITION PLANT

RESERVES OF SHELLS CLOSE TO THE BATTLE-LINE

of our advance between the two rivers. His directive raised the ghost of the limited objective which set a certain distance for a day's progress. Bitter experience in all the offensives, until the turn of the tide in the midsummer of 1918, had taught high commands that limited objectives against the trench system were the only way to prevent sections of the line that had easier going than others from being engulfed and massacred in pockets of cross-fire. While open-warfare conditions measurably prevailed elsewhere on the long line of battle, our own ordeal against the stonewalling of the enemy in the Argonne renewed the old lesson. We, too, were now having our battle of attrition.

When Foch saw the plans drawn up by the 1st American Army and the French Fourth Army for the new operation, he complained that their rigidity "might conceivably hamper the rapid exploitation of any success achieved. They indicated a return to the method of attack which consisted in marking beforehand on the map successive lines to be reached, and betrayed an exaggerated solicitude in the matter of alignment." In his directive calling for more energetic action he said:

"Important results such as we are pursuing in the present stage of the War, when we are confronted by an enemy whose exhaustion increases every day, can only be achieved by progress as rapid and deep as possible. Troops launched into an attack need not think of anything except the direction of the attack. . . . They must operate not against lines indicated *a priori* and suggested by the nature of the ground, but against the enemy; and once they have seized him, they must never let go of the grip."

Pétain, the commander-in-chief of the French army, changed his instructions to conform with the Generalissimo's orders, and "urged Pershing to hasten the launching of the offensive west of the Meuse."[13]

It was unpleasant enough for the American staff, when it was fighting its first great battle in command of a supposedly independent army, to have General Maistre, Foch's representative, at its elbow; and still more unpleasant to hear the reports of

Clemenceau's demand that Pershing be relieved and to have in Foch's directive an oblique reminder of their failure to carry out the offensive tactics which they had championed in criticism of the trench-defensive habits of the French. Franco-American military relations were never quite so brittle as after we had our integral army in action. It was as easy for Foch to write the words of his directive as it was for the sections of the American staff to write cables to the War Department asking for more motor trucks, more locomotives, railroad cars, port material, airplanes, replacements, labor battalions, cranes, or hospital units.

OUR ARMY AND THE BRITISH BEAR THE BRUNT

The French staff regarded our New Army with the same professional hauteur with which it regarded the British New Army. It seemed to have forgotten its cardinal errors early in the War: the mobilization east of Rheims; the early offensive into Alsace, which played into German hands; and the tragic lack of information about the Germans' preparation for their third offensive, which both the British [14] and the American staffs had forecast through their study of the German battle order. It might be worth while mentioning an instance where Haig's judgment was better than Foch's. After the turn of the tide, as Haig pressed his advantage, the British commander-in-chief and the Generalissimo had a sharp controversy as between two plans of future action.[15] Without enforcing his points by loud talk or gesticulation, Haig could be very insistent. Foch yielded to his view. Its wisdom was proven by the event and gallantly praised by Foch.[16]

The British had started with willingness to learn, and had the first-hand schooling of four years' battle experience. This may build as strong a staff organization, at a terrible cost, as that of a large professional army staff in peace-time, which, in turn, may be over-confident of its own excellence as a model for the staffs of all nations. It may be questioned whether in 1918 the British staff was not better than the French.

At the time Clemenceau wrote his letter there was already on file in the archives of the A. E. F. a dispatch from the commander of one of our pioneer divisions in which he said that if he had to fight in liaison with French divisions again, he would resign: for the French were too battle-weary, too canny as veterans, to keep pace with our vigorous attacks. The first Marne, Champagne, Verdun, and the disastrous offensive of the spring of 1917, had taken a toll of vitality from the French soldiers which could not be recovered during the War. It is hard to believe that a French army, though under a Pétain, a Gouraud, a Mangin, or a Degoutte, if it had been given the Meuse-Argonne offensive, would have gone so far or so rapidly as the Americans. However, Foch would hardly have ordered a French army to take the arrows in its breast, even for so important an object—not after so many appeals had come to our G. H. Q. in the summer and early autumn of 1918 for the presence of one division, or even a smaller American unit, with a French corps to renew French morale.

It happened that in the final three months of the War the American New Army shared the brunt of the action with the British New Army, now an old army. Legs growing more limber in open warfare, the British did not stop to count the cost of their progress. In no week, from August 8 until October 27, were their casualties fewer than 14,000, and twice they were over 40,000; they were to reach a total of 342,000 in the thirteen weeks of their triumphal sweep to the end of the War in which they took 200,000 prisoners and 2,080 guns.[17]

Haig had long since parted with all our divisions trained under him except the 27th (O'Ryan), and the 30th (Lewis), both National Guard, which shared the elation of a notable advance after each attack. Two of our divisions which had been in the early stage of the Meuse-Argonne, the 37th (Farnsworth), National Guard, and 91st (Johnston), National Army, were sent to Belgium, where they served under Degoutte. There, after storming ridges, taking difficult woods, and crossing the Escault River, they knew advances of as many as eight miles in a day.

But the spirit of our soldiers who remained in the Meuse-Argonne was that of the dogged persistence for small gains of the British New Army in its first great offensive of the Somme.

The veteran 26th had now entered the battle on the east bank of the Meuse.

In answer to Foch's whip, our staff, as it learned lessons in the severe school of battle, was to apply the whip in turn. It could round on haggard brigadiers and could issue orders for the attack to colonels who rounded on majors and captains, and so down the line, for not having reached the objectives set on their maps, no matter what the opposition. For failure the penalty was Blois, the soldiers' rebuke, and shame in relief from command in action. Staff brains reeled from fatigue as they issued more directives. Only the wearer of a wound tag might return from the front past the cordon of military police. All must fight or at least remain in the fighting zone until their units were relieved.

EXHAUSTION—A LITTLE REST—BACK INTO THE MILL

On the roads in the rear of the Army, past the lines of ambulances and trucks, groups of replacements were marching toward the battle area. They were the fresh man-power to feed into the mill which was destroying man-power so fast by wounds, death, and exhaustion. Animals must have time to get their land legs after a sea voyage; but no thought was given to the acclimatization of recruits from influenza-stricken cantonments, who were hurried out of the sardine-pack of the transports, where they had slept in shifts, into the sardine-pack of the "40 and 8" cars where they had no sleep at all. A day later, in the company of men who had recovered from wounds, they were filling the vacant places in the ranks of a battle-exhausted division in rest in dug-outs and ruined villages; and officers, fresh from home, were in the company of officers who had recovered from wounds, in putting the newcomers through a few days' drill adapted to the latest tactics at the front. So to be wounded meant that if you were to fight again, it would not be in the company of your own buddies. The soldier and the junior officer had now completely become pawns.

As soon as the division had had a little sleep and been fattened a little, all in its roster who could move on their legs, even those who had coughs that might indicate the first stages of pneumonia, were sent along the muddy trails toward the roar of battle under leaden skies that rarely showed a glimpse of the sun through the mists. It had been summer when our men went in to stop the Germans at Château-Thierry with flowers in their rifle barrels. It was now the stark, cheerless, chill, moist autumn of this region of France, with only withered grass and foliage on battlefields of lean grazing land. When the relief columns came to the point where the transport had its dead-line it was already dark; and dark before that if we were concentrating for an attack. Some of the platoons went to their appointed places in warrens dug on reverse slopes; others in cautious, softly stepping files, led by guides who knew the ground, went on until they came to the little pits where the outposts were lying, and other men went on to machine-gun posts which faced the enemy under the whipping of bullets and the bursts of shellfire and gas. They were the very spearhead of the nation's effort. The filthy, hollow-eyed, old tenants, feeling so very old in a few days, slipped out of their places as the new slipped in; and a shift in the operatives in the war factory was completed.

Officers located positions on their maps, received instructions from their predecessors. The processes were very different, indeed, from those of the days of stationary warfare in deep dugouts behind the walls of sandbags. Monotony was varied by patrols and alarms and broken by the order for an attack. Bloodstains, torn bits of uniform, meat-tins, and hard-bread boxes formed the litter around every foxhole where a man had dug in after another stage of progress. The young officers had to creep from foxhole to foxhole, keeping touch with their platoons. They and the men must not forget anything they were told. The rolling kitchens might try to reach the front line, but that only drew fire. There was no warm food. Those who had blankets found them a soggy shroud of refrigeration in the frequent chill rains and the penetrating mists. It was an army that shivered from cold, not from fright.

There must be no singing, no talking, lest that locate you for the enemy's veteran riflemen and machine-gunners. But there was no holding back the coughs. Men died of pneumonia as well as from wounds in the foxholes. It was a battle being won by the men; by the young reserve officers; and by the young West Pointers who had physical endurance and mental alacrity which readily adapted their sound fundamental training to new conditions. Something more human and personal than the will to win, which had been born of tradition and drilled into our platoons, supported the repeated charges from the old to gain a new line of foxholes: it was to have the agony over soon; to be dry again, to be warm again, to have a hot meal again. The 90th (Allen), National Army, which had been three months in France, came in for its share of the adventure. Before the battle was over the 1st, 3rd, 32nd, 42nd, and 79th were in twice, and the 80th three times. The 81st (Bailey) was to be in the final attacks.

The roster of our citizen army's achievements is incomplete without that of the 36th (Smith), National Guard, another division separated from the army family. It had had no trench experience, it had never been under fire, when it took over from the veteran 2nd, east of Rheims, on October 6, and drove on in the company of French veterans—drove on even when the German artillery, before its retreat, decided to fire all the shells in a dump into the Americans rather than have the dump captured; and after that, the 36th kept its formation against a rear-guard action of a fifteen-mile stretch in a single day. Democracy, summoning itself to war according to the rules of democracy, had come to France to fight, and it was fighting and trying to do everything according to the textbook of the Regulars.

Meanwhile, all the A. E. F.'s schools of training were kept at full blast during the battle to prepare for the campaign of 1919. Commanders whose divisions were about to go into the line for an attack had word to detach notably efficient officers from companies and battalions which had long been under their hands. These officers were to report at once to the staff school at Langres, or some other school in a quiet, academic atmosphere far in the rear, instead of entering the swiftly applied curriculum of battle action. One division commander, whose troops were about to go over the top, refused to send his officers to school.

After the big division came shattered out of the Meuse-Argonne ordeal, it must have the vacant places in its files filled to complete strength. Two divisions were broken up for replacements. The big companies must have a full roster, but they were often without a full complement of officers. Among these would be some fresh from the home training camps, each of whom would be expected to direct twice as many men as a veteran British or French officer, and this in a battle which was distinctly one of minor tactics.

VICTORY NEAR—AND STILL G. H. Q. PLANS FOR 1919

Now in those dramatic final days, we again turn to the cables between the A. E. F. and the War Department. We learn that March cabled Pershing on October 24 that we were producing 200,000 model rifles a month; [18] but six days later, on the 30th, Pershing was concerned lest we should not have enough rifles for 1919.[19] By this time Ludendorff had resigned from the army and the Kaiser had sought refuge from Berlin at the German headquarters at Spa, while Hindenburg appealed for German unity. On the 27th March asked Pershing to reconsider, at the personal request of Baker, the use of 7-inch naval guns which he had rejected, since we had "the guns, plenty of ammunition, and some caterpillar mounts, and can put them in the field in a relatively short time"; and the War Department had notified the Navy that they would be manned by the coast artillery, and received the Navy's assent. "The reason for your objection to them," March stated, "is not understood by anyone here." [20]

On the same day March said that Pershing's request for 194-millimeter caliber guns would require the construction of new plants, at the cost of millions, and production could not begin for a year; [21] and the War Department was reluctant to proceed with the project. On October 28, while the Italian offensive was in full progress beyond the Piave, Pershing presented his priorities for 350,000 troops in January.[22] There were to be six combat divisions and, among the other requirements, 18,000 for the air service, 13,000 army troops, and such items as three hundred casuals for pigeon service, five hundred cement-mill workers, five hundred cooks, twenty-four hundred clerks, typists, and stenographers. To the Chief of Staff in Washington the A. E. F. still seemed to be proceeding on the basis of the 100-division instead of the 80-division program. In reply, ten days before the Armistice, November 1, March reminded Pershing that if his schedule kept calling for more troops than could be transported, "it follows that we fall farther behind each month, with consequent derangement of priorities unless those of previous month are continued." [23]

By this time the Austrian commander had sent in his flag of truce to the Italian commander, and Austria was out of the War. Three days later the Italian dream of Trieste came true, when it was occupied by a landing party of Italian sailors. Our Army in the Meuse-Argonne was over the summit of the whale-back and speeding after the breaking enemy at a rate that ought to have satisfied even the impatient Clemenceau. But in his call, November 2, for 140,000 replacements by the end of the month, Pershing's cable said: [24]

"It is evident that necessary preparations were not made to meet our replacement needs. . . . Divisions in the United States should be stripped of trained or even partly trained men and . . . shipped immediately. Cannot this matter be given the consideration its importance deserves?"

LOOKING AHEAD TO POST-WAR PROBLEMS

In view of the Austrian surrender, Baker wrote, on the same day, November 2, a letter to the President, which envisioned a post-War danger:

"May I suggest for your consideration the possibility of your issuing a statement through Berne, or otherwise, in the constituent countries of the Austro-Hungarian Empire expressing the hope that the peoples of these nascent nations will observe orderly processes in these revolutionary days and refrain from acts of violence in order that their candidacy to admission in the family of nations will not be blemished at the outset by disorders which would tend to throw doubt upon their capacity

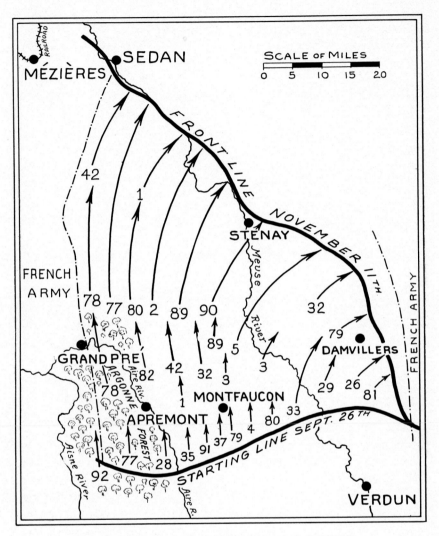

DIVISIONS IN THE MEUSE-ARGONNE BATTLE

for self-government in the eyes of the nations whose ordered civilizations have made this era of freedom possible for them."

And on the same day Baker wrote to Brand Whitlock, our Minister to Belgium, at a time when the Belgian people were welcoming in city after city the return of their King at the head of his advancing army:

"The scenes are now shifting, and an entirely different act in this great drama is about to be introduced. I pray earnestly that we may all be wise and farsighted and that we may remember the long interests of the future in the new order which we seem to have the chance to start. A great many evil beliefs and things have been uprooted; a great many iniquities, cruelties, and oppressions which victory would have covered now stand disclosed with no shred of excuse to cover them. I am sure if the human race can learn a lesson it ought now to read, in print as plain as that in a spelling book, the futility of aggregate wrongdoing under the guise of national aggrandizement. But the world will still be wearing mourning for this episode when you and I are called away, and neither of us will be permitted to see whether its days of wisdom will outlive the days of its repentance. Still I am one of those persons who are perhaps obstinately optimistic. I do believe the world is growing better."

Three days later, November 5, Germany chose her delegates to negotiate an armistice on the basis of President Wilson's terms. On the same day March reported that in October 242,-000 men had been shipped to France.[25] This completed the October program except for a part of the replacements, and the prospect for these was better. "Influenza not only stopped our draft calls in October but practically stopped all training. If nothing happens" he hoped to catch up with replacements by the first of the year. On the day he sent this cablegram some of our divisions had advanced five miles. In a cable of November 8,[26] he promised Pershing seven hundred selected captains and lieutenants immediately to replace the wastage of junior officers in battle. On that day one American division had advanced twenty-five miles. Our men were on the outskirts of Sedan: they had reached their goal. In a letter to Pershing, on November 8, Baker said:

"I am writing this note in the tense hours during which the representatives of the German government are supposed to be in consultation with Marshal Foch. Yesterday morning a premature announcement was made to the effect that the German representatives had met Marshal Foch and signed the Armistice, which led to very tumultuous outbursts of joy throughout the country. The streets of the cities all over the land were filled with throngs of cheering and singing people. . . . With full credit to our gallant associates of England, France and Italy, we Americans can have a full cup of happiness and pride from the effort our nation has made."

"CEASE FIRING!"

Our High Command, so intent on its own problems, had been slow to see the signs which had been so apparent since early October, that the end was near. To the last it had been looking forward to the battles of the following year for which the Meuse-Argonne was a preparation. Some of the enthusiasts at G. H. Q. foresaw Pershing at the head of the greatest army in Europe, upon which the Allies must depend for victory. Then he, and not Foch, might be Generalissimo.

But if the War had gone on, there were hard problems awaiting our Commander-in-Chief in the winter of 1918–19. Army opinion, although it salutes and is subordinate, can speak with the voice of command to its High Command. Young American reserve officers were learning that drilling a company of infantry was not so great a mystery as some of the keepers of the secret chamber would make it seem, and that so much inspection of buttons was unnecessary to preserve the spirit and the very soul of discipline in a veteran army.

But beyond the world of conventional military routine was another: that of battle tactics and of army organization, which are mastered only by prolonged application. It is vain to estimate how much worse off we should have been in France if Elihu Root, whose influence carried through the years to a battlefield in Lorraine, had not founded the General Staff, the War College, and the Leavenworth schools, and if Baker had not saved the General Staff; and it is equally vain to estimate how much better off we would have been if we had had an adequate General Staff and more graduates of Leavenworth before our entry into the War.

There were General Staff and Leavenworth men who could not rise to the mighty responsibility suddenly imposed upon them, and whose previous training seemed to some observers to assure only a pomposity blown-up with power; but both Leavenworth and General Staff training were worth while in the score of men to whom studies and industry in peace were the foundation of rapidly broadening capability in practice. These were indispensable and irreplaceable. They would have been the master hands upon whom Pershing would have depended in his reorganization of his Army in the winter of 1918–19 if the War had continued.

In that reorganization many highly placed and weary staff officers would surely have been given a well-earned rest; some division commanders would have been transferred to dug-outs at the rear, which were more comfortable than those behind the battle-line; old West Point graduates would have to yield to the young under the call of youth for action; we should have had, as the British army had in 1918, colonels and brigadiers who had known no military training when they answered their country's call; and as the result of youthful activities, we should have had a higher percentage of brigadiers on the casualty lists in 1919 than in 1918.

When Armistice terms were under discussion, Pershing, fighting his Somme with no Arras or Passchendaele to come, stood out for unconditional surrender; but here the civil hand of the supreme Commander-in-Chief in the White House, and his civilian Second-in-Command, waved the military hand aside. At the same time when our troops were attacking so fervently and in such numbers, our propaganda leaflets were falling into the German lines, to assure the German soldier who, after fighting so long, faced another fresh host, that he would receive from the President a fair peace to inaugurate a new world-era of international fellowship, which was not the kind for which Clemenceau would drive forward our men in the Meuse-Argonne. However, had that German army recovered the spark of desperate resistance, such as Lee's army exhibited often in its final campaign, we should have found ourselves with roads to build, our transport stalled, unable to fight further in the inclement winter weather; and when spring came, additional casualty-recording machines would have had to be installed in the War Department, and the cost of the War might have risen to a hundred million dollars a day. The drive-teams may have been just as well satisfied that they did not have to put over four or five more Liberty Loans; and our men of forty that they did not have to go to the cantonments.

But to me the outstanding feature of our part in the War—aside from High Commands, Medals of Honor from the Congress, Distinguished Service Medals and Distinguished Service Crosses, and Allied decorations bestowed on persons high and low—was the civilian's acceptance of all the discipline and the effort as the dictum of the experts who knew "the game"; and my regret is that some members of our High Command in France were so preoccupied with their heavy labors that they returned to America without yet knowing their own country or their fellow countrymen and women.

On November 11 the thunders and the killing of the World War ceased. Some of our units that had not reached the front, others that had the order to "cease firing" just as their guns were in position, might feel that the Armistice had robbed them of the experience for which they had so arduously trained, a sensation which the British and French, who had fought for four years, could not share.

After silence had come to the front, and the deepest world-wide rejoicing of all history in the real Armistice celebration was being voiced by the peoples, the War Department sent a cable on November 11 for the information of the A. E. F., saying that "all draft calls and special inductions into the service have been canceled." [27] No further personnel except medical and hospital would be sent; but, of course, the shipment of subsistence and clothing would be continued. "Further Sunday work and overtime work in production for the Army, Navy, and shipping contracts have been stopped." March assured Pershing that cessation of the shipment of combat troops after an armistice was signed was in keeping with international law and the traditional American policy. Should Pershing find that the military situation warranted further replacements he was to "take the matter up with Marshal Foch and the Supreme War Council, and their recommendations [were to] be obtained and transmitted to the War Department for consideration." At the same time Baker cabled to Stettinius:

"It is of course important to cut down expenditures as rapidly as possible. Please get into immediate communication with General Harbord and with General Pershing's headquarters and represent me in working out with them a program for the cessation of all construction and procurement which can be stopped without prejudice to the situation as it now is. Contracts in process of making, both in England and in France, should be suspended, and generally every effort made to narrow our obligations as far as possible."

Another cable on Armistice Day bade Pershing "report by cable as soon as possible all deaths, seriously wounded, and missing up to the time hostilities ceased. Send in English." [28]

XXXVII

WHAT DID NAMES MATTER?

OUR war machine, which had been gathering power for nineteen months, had its gears suddenly reversed when it was going full speed ahead. The first lot of the quarter of a million of new draft men, who would have been on their way to the cantonments on the very hour that firing ceased on all fronts, had word from Crowder which left them to celebrate the Armistice in any manner that they chose. Draft boards might pack up their papers and do some final chores in the ensuing months; lawyers and doctors of the legal and advisory boards might return to their practices. If they desired to continue in a war activity, they could volunteer to assist the "drive" teams, which were not to be demobilized until they had put over the Victory Loan to meet the loans to the Allies, and the cost of sending two million men to France, of fighting the submarines, and of building a mine barrage across the North Sea.

Soldiers who arrived in Brest harbor, to learn that the War was over this morning, were not disembarked, but returned on the same transport to the homeland where, in the period of rejoicing which is the last stage of enthusiastic war emotion, they were demonstratively welcomed as the first of the victorious men from "over there." These had seen nothing of France except a harbor; but the veterans of the Meuse-Argonne, who had no shelter except dug-outs and the cellars of ruined villages, had seen too much of one kind of life in France.

The largest number of men we had transported to France in a single month had been slightly over three hundred thousand. Even if we had at our service as many British ships, in addition to our own, as we had when the call for machine-gun and infantry personnel was so imperious, it would take more than six months to bring the two million back. Britain had lost nearly twice as much shipping as the rest of the world from submarine sinkings. British liners now had errands to do for their own country. They were seeking prompt reconditioning in order to recover their peace-time passenger lists, while trade routes were calling for carriers to renew the world's peace commerce, and industries were eager to replenish their coffers by early advantages in world markets.

Allied peoples were thinking of the care of their maimed, and of the debts they must pay, as they began life afresh in a world which they were sure would never be the same again; and the Allied statesmen were preoccupied with the division of territory that was to make a new map of Europe at the coming Peace Conference, which was soon to have the stage at Versailles in place of the Supreme War Council. The military representatives on the Council were occupied at the same time as our draft boards in packing up their papers, while they gossiped about another proposed international body of the future, the League of Nations. And all the soldiers in the dug-outs, in billets, or in the S. O. S., now that the War was over, wanted immediate demobilization, when demobilization must be a long and arduous process, for the good reason that it takes time to unwind a spool after it has been wound. But—what was a Secretary of War for, if not to "check out" a soldier from a dug-out into his home bedroom the moment the War was over?

Even for the men in the cantonments demobilization was not so simple as it appeared to those who said that you had only to give the boys railroad tickets, wish them good luck, and they would find their front doors. Forty thousand men could not be entrained from a cantonment on a single day. There were formalities required on leaving the Army as well as upon entering it: another medical examination for every man, and the final record to be made in careful detail for the acreage of World War personnel files now in the War Department.

Not all the reserve officers who were not in combat divisions could be discharged at once. They must assist in the demobilization of men and supplies. Some were held in uniform for many months. The dollar-a-year men were in a different class. While the captains of the High Command in France saw their power passing, the captains of industry saw their power returning. Soon they would be their own bosses again, in their own realm of business which needed their attention at once. They would not have to knit their brows again over supplying Pershing with 194-millimeter guns or rolling stock, and try at the same time to meet the demands of the Allied Purchasing Commission. The last session of the War Industries Board had a joyous official brevity: there were no more problems of priority or price-fixing to consider.

Baruch and some of the chiefs must remain some time to close up shop before they gave him a loving-cup. But many committees, representing every branch of production, every kind of raw material and of industrial technique, were almost as automatically dissolved as those of a municipal anniversary celebration after the celebration is over. They might well be proud of their achievement. The aviation dream was fulfilled in the production of 4,200 Liberty engines in October, 1918, more than the total of all the Allies, who had been complaining in the previous August that we were not allotting them enough. Our Ordnance Department had artillery in production, while the A. E. F. still had ample guns from the French foundries; our new Browning machine-guns were piling up in the warehouses of the S. O. S. waiting to be substituted, in the campaign of 1919, for those with which we were fighting the Meuse-Argonne. We had produced, in the period while we were in the War, more rifles than either Britain or France, as many machine-guns and automatic rifles as Britain, twice the amount of smokeless powder of France and Britain.

THE ROSTER OF INDUSTRIAL ACHIEVEMENT

It interests me to turn again to "The Handbook of Economic Agencies," of more than 500 pages, which listed all the different committees co-operating with the War Department in 1917–18. Each one represented a disciplined army of industrial effort under high pressure. Each name stood for technical and industrial experience in providing some of the sinews of war. We heard Baruch's name often; not so often that of Major Hugh S. Johnson, a Brigadier General at the end of the War, who represented the Army on the War Industries Board, after Brigadier General Palmer E. Pierce had gone to France; and even seldomer mentioned were W. R. Abbott, Chairman of the Public Utilities section of the Board; C. H. MacDowell, Chemical Division, nitrates, pyrites, and sulphur; Dr. E. R. Weidlein, chemicals; J. W. O'Leary, War resources and conservation; O. C. Howe, W. B. Eisendrath, C. F. C. Stout, H. W. Boyd, J. C. Byron, all of whom were expert in some branch of leather production; and Dr. L. H. Baekeland, John Johnson, C. E. Munroe, H. F. Moore, F. P. Underhill, of those who labored in the National Research Council.

A Secretary of War's dependence upon all the different activities—now in cold type in "The Handbook of Economic Agencies," which is hard to procure—must have been a factor in Baker's modest attitude toward the part which destiny had assigned him as the keystone of the arch of administration in our greatest national industrial enterprise. I run through the pages of the book as I would the roster of a combat division in France, imagining all the travail that the training, the equipping, the transport, and the direction of the division represented: Brass and Copper tubes, J. P. Elton; Brick War service, William Schlake; Building material, W. P. Gleason; Cast-iron pipe, N. F. S. Russell; Cement, J. R. Morron: and the Cotton Committees of the War Industries Board, T. W. Page, Chairman; R. S. Dwight, cotton battings; G. R. James, cotton linters; C. G. Brand, cotton distribution; J. Rousmaniere, cotton duck, and G. F. Smith, cotton and linen thread.

Now we may jump 450 pages, which include the procurement of about 30,000 articles, to wool. Here we find the Wool Division of the War Industries Board, Lewis Penwell, A. W. Elliott, and the Wool Stock Graders' Association, Edward A. Stone. If we turn back to clothing, we have the Clothing Division of the

War Industries Board, Lincoln Cromwell, and the divisions and branches under the Quartermaster's Department under A. L. Scott, L. R. Ach, Malcolm Donald, and H. A. Rosenthal. Names may slow the narrative for the reader, but in this case a glimpse at the personnel of the army of industry appeals strongly to the imagination if we remember that the clothing items for our army in 1917–18 included 9,500,000 overcoats, 22,000,000 blankets, 15,000,000 wool coats, 23,000,000 wool breeches, 34,000,000 shoes, 17,000,000 puttees, 6,000,000 gloves and mittens, 81,000,000 drawers, 85,000,000 undershirts and 85,000,000 stockings.

Incidentally, we made a total of 5,400,000 gas masks and 2,728,000 steel helmets. Samuel McRoberts, who had charge of all procurement for the Ordnance Department, and John H. Rice, whose concern was all carriages for ordnance from machine-guns to huge howitzers, had known harder work for the government than in building their own fortunes. But what did names matter when individuals were absorbed into the whole?

CAN WE HAVE SUCH TEAM-WORK AGAIN?

Names did not matter to the elderly workers on the draft boards, or to the young workers against the machine-gun nests; or to the men and women who found they were not so old that they could not do their bits; or among the members of the press, which showed it could be its own censor while it gave free advertising for the draft and the drives; or to the men who built the ships and loaded them, and painted their camouflage stripes; or to the four-minute men, the drive teams, and the men and women laboring to produce guns, rifles, and uniforms on time. In this the first war of populations, all aided whether they did chores or brought in the harvest. The members of the home guards and militia, who seemed such tyros to the doughboys, guarded bridges and munition plants, rounded up slackers, and gave an example of enterprise, while they carried on their occupations, thus releasing more men for the cantonments and heavy labor. To borrow a phrase from Harbord, I have not been trying to measure "relative excellence" in giving the few names

SELECTIVE SERVICE

that I have chosen at random. In his final report of the S. O. S. he said:

"Who can measure correctly the relative excellence and justly weigh the rewards for services that covered almost every field of activity from the highest type of staff work to the humble toil of the dock stevedore—each essential to the success of the whole? Every trade and profession known to our civilization contributed its members to this enterprise. Officers who had spent their lives in preparing for the command of soldiers in battle, cheerfully threw over the ambitions of years and forgot the bitterness of disappointment in their enthusiasm for this service; black men from the cottonfields of our South toiled on docks and in warehouses and built roads that no soldier might be unfed; lumbermen operated in the forests of the Vosges and the Pyrenees; millionaires contributed their great business experience and captained new industries; lawyers of eminence protected the interests of the country; chiefs of the great railroad organizations of America brought their unexcelled men and methods to the success of the transportation service; tremendous engineering problems were solved by leaders in that profession; the distant markets of other countries were searched by trained buyers to save precious tonnage; men labored under earth and water, and met dangers in air and under the seas; officers and soldiers from the battle-fronts restored only to partial health contributed their shattered strength and maimed bodies to this work; the best medical and surgical skill of the world organized and administered hospitals on a scale never before seen; the great welfare organizations ministered to the morale and entertainment of the Supply Army; salvage services were organized on an immense scale; leaders in the world of electricity covered France with a network of uninterrupted communications; kings of finance, diplomats, linguists, artists, artisans of all arts, experts and organizers of all phases of industrial life caught the step and marched with the Services of Supply. Without the excitement and glamour of combat service, often unobserved, sometimes unrecognized, and seldom adequately rewarded, these men quietly and unselfishly contributed their part to the winning of the World War. . . . They worked as a great team which was only striking its stride as the War ended."

In the S. O. S., working under the Regular chiefs, aside from Atterbury and Wilgus, and wearing khaki, were Hugh Cooper, the engineer, who later was at Muscle Shoals and then built dams for the Soviets; Hugh B. Moore, who was Atterbury's right-hand man, in shipping; George T. Slade, liaison officer between French and American transport; John O'Neill, the chief long-shoreman of the S. O. S.; John P. Jackson, who looked after labor; Dr. Haven Emerson; Dr. Frederic Washburn, in charge of the evacuation hospitals; William B. Greeley, who was the Chief Forester of the S. O. S.; and Arthur D. Hill, expert on that troublesome subject of claims, rents, and requisitions.

On Armistice Day Baker wrote to Frank Scott, who had broken his health in the ordeal of the early days as the pioneer organizer of our war industries:

"You know, from your own service, how much the best-minded and best-hearted business men of America have helped in making possible the triumph of this day. Our country has been more at one in the past year than in any year I can remember, and I trust that the new understandings which have been created will cement us all together for the work of the future, which will not be less dignified or important than that which has been brought to its conclusion today, and which will be harder to do because the setting will be less heroic."

XXXVIII

MUSTERED OUT

CROWDER, without compromising his conscientious scruples too much, could tell the Secretary that he had a mind to take a night off without work. March might postpone his regular morning tennis game until seven-thirty. Baker confessed in letters to friends something he had not confessed since our entry into the War: now that it was over, he had moments when he felt a little tired. With peace, the right to be a little tired became an established privilege of war-workers.

President Wilson had informed Baker immediately after the Armistice that he was to be one of the Peace Commissioners. But the sudden resignation of McAdoo as Secretary of the Treasury, leaving post-War finances and the "unscrambling" of the railroads to a successor, developed a new situation, which Baker recognized in a letter to the President on November 23:

"Of course, with you in Europe neither I nor anybody else is necessary to the presentation of America's case, but here at home, particularly during your absence, I can perhaps be helpful in conferences with the remaining members of the Cabinet. The next two or three months are likely to present situations of uncertainty of opinion and hesitancy on the part of business and labor in process of readjustment, and while no fresh legislative policy perhaps needs to be worked out, I am persuaded that the country would feel more concerned about your own absence if two members of the Cabinet were with you now that the Secretary of the Treasury's post will have to be filled by a man new to those responsibilities.

"I trust you will understand the spirit of this suggestion, but I am really deeply concerned not only to have your own stay in Europe made as free from anxiety as possible but to have the situation here kept on the even balance, and public feeling and opinion kept in sympathy with both the things you are doing abroad and the policies of the economic and political readjustment here which you desire to have our peace-time establishment take.

"May I not suggest for your consideration the possibility of making General Bliss a Peace Commissioner? And then after the conferences have gone so far that you feel you are able to return here, and leave the details to be reduced to writing for signature, if you then thought it wise I could be sent over to join the Commissioners at the wind-up."

In a letter to Thomas L. Sidlo, his law partner, on November 25, Baker referred to the President's response to his suggestion that he should not be included in the Peace Commission. He said that the President

"thought about this for three days, and this afternoon came over to my office to tell me that he has been trying to see some other way out, as he was very anxious to have me with him, but he felt the strength of my suggestion so much that he was obliged to adopt it, although very reluctant to do so. He was genuinely fine about it, and I am so sure that this is the right thing to do that I have a real sense of relief tonight about the whole matter."

Bliss was chosen as our military representative in the Peace Conference. That Cabinet wheelhorse, D. F. Houston, Secretary of Agriculture, became Secretary of the Treasury. Walker D. Hines, who had been McAdoo's assistant, took over the administration of the railroads.

THE SOLDIERS WHO WERE FARTHEST FROM HOME

Baker was not to be in "at the wind-up" of the Peace Conference, but was to devote himself to demobilization. A large portion of his files is occupied with its details. Aside from the A. E. F. there was the detachment at Murmansk in northern Russia, now frozen in for the winter. There were also the soldiers of our Siberian expedition. Their position had become still more insistently a State Department matter after the Armistice was signed.

The State Department had given Major General W. S. Graves, in command of the expedition, an *aide-memoire* stating that its object was "to render such aid as may be acceptable to the Russians in the organization of their own self-defense." In a memorandum on October 25, 1918, Graves said, "This limiting phrase 'as may be acceptable to the Russians' of course hampers all activities. I think, however, it is a very wise limitation." He found that the officers of our Intelligence Department sent for service in Siberia were not hampered in the same way and were difficult to handle, "energetic, competent and very ambitious though they are." He hoped they might be useful in learning how best to distribute supplies which we were sending in the generous quantity in keeping with American welfare policy, and as a part of our propaganda in the regeneration of Russia. In no one of our war policies were we more steadfast than that those whom we fed would become our friends and the friends of civilization. To quote Graves again:

"The Russians cannot be depended upon to do things according to our ideas . . . when all Russians are uncertain as to what political faction will be on top when a government is established in Russia. . . . The Japanese have more troops at practically every station occupied by United States troops than I have. . . . I have been practically sewed up to the railway line between Vladivostok and Harbarovsk."

General Ivanoff Rinoff, Minister of War for the new Omsk government, told Graves that the Japanese were evidently in Siberia to stay, were driving Russian troops out of their barracks, and backing Kalmikoff, who was a robber and murderer, in his depredations and assassinations. But Graves concluded by saying, "My relations with Japanese Headquarters have been very cordial, and they have always, apparently, desired to co-operate with me in matters lying within our respective authorities."

The Japanese Foreign Minister informed our Embassy in Tokyo, "If the Americans advance, we must advance hand in hand with them." [1] Before the President left Washington for the Peace Conference, Baker wrote to him on November 27, 1918, with reference to the embarrassment of the presence of our troops in Siberia as follows:

"I know how fully your mind is informed and how much you have thought about the subject, but I confess I myself feel it with increasing anxiety. . . . We sent about seven thousand men on agreement with the Japanese that they would send a like number. They immediately notified us that they would increase their expedition up to one division, or about twelve thousand men. From then until now they have increased their force until it is in the neighborhood of seventy thousand men, and they are apparently still dispatching troops into Siberia. In the meantime they have seized the Chinese Eastern Railroad and the report is that they are co-operating with one group of Russians, supplying them with money and aiding them in acquiring supremacy over other groups of Russians and thus building up a pro-Japanese faction among the Russians themselves."

The seizure of the connecting Chinese Eastern Railroad by the Japanese did not facilitate the task of John F. Stevens, the eminent engineer, who had been sent to Siberia to carry out the dreams of those who had faith in regenerating Russia as an ally, in reorganizing the Trans-Siberian Railway. Baker continued in his letter:

"Two reasons are assigned for our remaining in Siberia. One is that having entered we cannot withdraw and leave the Japanese. If there be any answer to this it lies in the fact that the longer we stay, the more Japanese there are and the more difficult it may be to induce Japan to withdraw her forces if we set the example. The second reason given is that we must have a military force to act as guardians and police for any civil relief effort we are able to direct toward Siberia. I frankly do not believe this, nor do I believe we have a right to use military force to compel the reception of our relief agencies.

"I do not know that I rightly understand Bolshevism. So much of it as I do understand I don't like, but I have a feeling that if the Russians do like it, they are entitled to have it and that it does not lie with us to say that only ten per cent of the Russian people are Bolshevists and that therefore we will assist the other ninety per cent in resisting it.

"I have always believed that if we compelled the withdrawal of the Germans and Austrians we ought then to let the Russians work out their own problem. Neither the method nor the result may be to our liking, but I am not very sure that the Russians may not be able to work it out better if left to themselves, and more speedily, than if their primitive deliberations are confused by the imposition of ideas from the outside.

"I dread to think how we shall all feel if we are rudely awakened some day to a realization that Japan has gone in under our wing and so completely mastered the country that she cannot be either induced out or forced out by any action either of the Russians or of the Allies.

"It may be that you prefer to discuss this question when you get abroad and seek some concert of action on it with the Great Powers there, but my own judgment is that we ought simply to order our forces home by the first boat; notify the Japanese that in our judgment our mission is fully accomplished, and that we limit our assistance to Russia hereafter to an economic aid, in view of the fact that our enemies have been required by the Armistice to withdraw their armed forces from Russian territory."

Our troops were not to be withdrawn from Siberia until April, 1920, and were to go as far as Lake Baikal, 2,000 miles from Vladivostok and 9,000 miles from Seattle. All the Czechs who did not wish to remain in Russia were rescued.

It is not in the province of this narrative to consider the ensuing futile campaign of the White Russian army against the Soviets, Japan's demands upon China, her ultimate evacuation of Shantung, and her return of the Chinese Eastern Railroad to China. But the President, when he went on board ship, bore among his documents a long sheaf on the Russian and the Far Eastern situations, and they were among his handicaps in his battle for the League of Nations. An interesting sidelight on the feeling of devoted friends of the President, who were sounding opinion in Paris over the effect of his coming, appears in a letter written by Ralph Hayes from Bruges, November 18:

"The announcement of the President's visit has raised various emotions here. The man in the street is jubilant. Keppel thinks that Jove should not come down from Olympus. Bliss believes that the problems of the green table will have been so much preadjudicated and predetermined, or will require so very much time in their solution, that the President's presence at some or all the actual conferences will not maximize his influence. The feeling is quite general. I believe that if he does come he ought not to stay too long."

SUPPLIES SO VITAL IN WAR NOW WASTE

Since Baker was not going to Paris he had to depend upon Stettinius, the American member of the Inter-Allied Munitions Council, to act for him in looking after the disposition of the two billion dollars' worth of American property in France until a liquidation commission should be formed. "He is a man of great exactness and of an almost terrifying sense of responsibility," Baker had written to Bliss when Stettinius was sent abroad in the summer of 1918. Stettinius, whose son was in the Army and had been gassed, had no second thought about doing his duty when summoned in war's aftermath, as well as in war. Baker wrote to him:

"I am anxious to have you know how grateful I am to you for staying there, and how much comfort and consolation it is to me to know that you are on the ground. . . . I have a notion that if we plan to put a few locomotives and cars on a returning transport and start them for the United States, the attitude toward us would entirely change and there would immediately be a disposition to talk business on proper lines, rather than pursue the suggestions which I have heard to the effect that we ought to present these vast properties to various people without compensation. I merely make this suggestion for your consideration, and if it appeals to you perhaps General Harbord would be willing to act on it at once. . . . I think it entirely likely that the best place for a good deal of this material is Europe, where it can be used in relief work of various kinds, but I would like to make a spectacular demonstration of the fact that we do not have to give it away or sell it.

"I understand that the French and British are canceling orders over here right and left. Mr. Baruch tells me their cancellations are coming in rapidly and cover all kinds of supplies. There would seem to be no reason, therefore, for our acting out of any international comity here, or why should we not cancel quite freely over there and save all the money we can in prospective international purchases. . . . The whole problem is so vast and complex that I frankly do not see how I can hope for a comfortable time in having it all adjusted without asking this service at your hands."

Stettinius found that Loucheur, the French Minister of Munitions, was appealing against the cancellation of contracts because it would throw many men and women out of employment.[2] On November 25th Stettinius cabled to Baker [3] that he had notified Loucheur that the United States would no longer participate in the sessions of the Inter-Allied Munitions Council. "I have no apprehension of difficulty with the British respecting either cancellations or principles or amounts of settlements. As to France situation is more difficult."

André Tardieu, French High Commissioner, backed Loucheur's insistence that we go on with our artillery contracts in France in order to keep the French in work. Stettinius replied that if the French wanted to continue the manufacture of war material for political or economic reasons, this was their affair. He proposed to pay the French all we owed them and no more. Meantime Stettinius, co-operating with Dawes, the purchasing agent for the A. E. F., brought Loucheur and Tardieu around to the sane view of not promoting further war waste by continuing the manufacture of now unneeded armament and munitions. Edwin B. Parker, the veteran of the War Industries Board, was appointed as head of the Liquidation Commission, which took over the task from Stettinius. Henry H. Hollis and Homer H. Johnson were the other two members, with Dawes making a fourth. It was to be a long and tiresome business, liquidating all the French claims, large and small, against the United States Government. The French insisted they did not need the piers, the shops, the warehouses, the spur tracks around the ware-

houses beyond centers of population, and the various equipment—invaluable though all had been when the cables of the
A. E. F. were desperately calling for more, but now in many
cases as superfluous as the paper napkins and old newspapers
on the green after the picnic is over. But food need not be
waste, not in hungry middle Europe. The great S. O. S. organization, which had been formed to subsist the A. E. F., needed
only the word from Hoover, the American Food Administrator, to become the efficient distributor of relief to the victims
of war.

As for the residue which it was not worth while to ship
home, Baker wrote to Pershing on August 3, 1919, that if we
were to undertake the retail sale of the property "and its distribution, it would require the building up of a vast organization; and the cost of guarding the property [which was estimated as high as one million dollars a month] until disposed
of would be a serious item. We would undoubtedly have to pay
the French import duties, great depreciation would take place
in the property, and in the end we would find ourselves with
all the most salable property disposed of and a great accumula-
tion of stuff on our hands for which it would be difficult to find
any sale at all."

The Liquidation Commission found that the only way was
to accept a flat price from the French government, which, in
turn, realized little on its purchase, except as an act of enforced
philanthropy, because the peasants broke into many of the
warehouses and pilfered their contents. Dawes satisfied the
country with the Commission's work by his "Hell and Maria"
dissertation before the Senate Committee.

Our shipping account with the British was settled much
more simply. The British had transported more than half our
troops to France, and we had carried quantities of material for
them in our vessels. In each instance accurate records of the
service had been kept, but no attempt had been made at a
reckoning during the War. When Baker was in London in the
spring of 1919, he found that Lord Reading, who had charge
of the matter for the British, was ill in bed. Lady Reading said

that her husband wanted to see him, but admonished him not to talk about business. As Baker was about to leave the room, Lord Reading expressed his regret that they could not settle the shipping business at this time:

"I am sorry, too, as I had hoped we could do it in a single sentence."

"Pray, what is the sentence?"

"That neither nation ought to make a profit out of the service it has rendered to the other, and our experts should proceed on that basis."

"I think that does settle it. If you will instruct your people to act on that principle, I will so instruct ours."

Brigadier General Frank T. Hines, in charge of our transportation, met the British experts. They struck a balance, and a check for $75,000,000 was transmitted by our government to the British government.

The shortage of shipping which had handicapped us in the War led us to complete the ships on the forest of ways at Hog Island and other yards, in order to replace the wastage of submarine destruction, and in the hope that we might re-establish our merchant flag in its former majesty on the seas of the world. However, we had no need for the two new powder-plants. Labor, which was employed in building new munition plants, soon had occupation in catching up with normal civil demands after the War's recess in civil construction. But employees in the munition plants, and employees who waited until peace-time machinery had replaced war-time machinery in many factories, must compete with demobilized soldiers for jobs. We might store guns, rifles, powder, gas, and gas masks as Army reserves; but the disposal of the immense stocks of subsistence supplies had an angle which brought many delegations to the Secretary's reception room.

The Army owned all the wool in the country and part of the cotton. What would be the effect on the markets of the country if all this wool and cotton and all the immense store of canned goods the War Department had accumulated, were suddenly released? Business men were appealing to Baker not to flood the commodity markets by a sudden dumping, which would be a calamity of itself, and a disaster if, at the same time, all the 4,000,000 men who had been under arms should flood the labor market. War stocks of men and goods ought to be fed out slowly as an aid to stabilization. But, in face of the enormous government expenditures and the prospect of heavy taxes to pay the interest on the huge war debt, Congressmen were appealing to Baker to realize promptly on war supplies to the last cent.

Assistant Secretary Crowell created a sales department with E. C. Morse in charge. Morse was a hard bargainer. In one instance he sold a warehouse full of hams to a purchaser who had not seen them, and who found they had gone bad. At first Morse insisted that as the purchaser had taken the risk he must meet the contract, but in this case he was not sustained. We had enormous supplies of raw silk from China for powder bags. Morse succeeded in cleaning and dyeing the silk and selling it for a good price.

BACK TO THE FREE WILL OF THE CIVIL WORLD

The same critics who had raised their voices in skepticism about the draft, who had cried out in the spring crisis of 1918 that we had not soldiers enough, and who had sped those who were going as knights fighting to save the world for democracy, were now alarmed, as they cited Civil War precedent, over the prospect that the restless veterans might become a disorderly factor in the nation's life. The statesmanship of war had another problem in restoring to the free will of the civil world the four millions who had had to submit their wills to the command and initiative of others. The longer a man had been in the Army, the harder the transition.

When Baker and March visited the demobilization camps, they found that Major General Grote Hutcheson had built up such an excellent organization at Battle Creek that the commanders of other camps were sent there for indoctrination in his methods.[4] The first consideration was the demobilized

BAKER WITH FRENCH SCHOOL CHILDREN

RAYMOND B. FOSDICK

Surgeon-General W. C. GORGAS

soldier's health. Must the government care for him a while longer, or permanently? If he was disabled there must be vocational training in some occupation for which he was fitted; and if he was a psychopathic case, assistance in recovering mental strength and equilibrium. The man who was well had the counsel of an employment officer. A lawyer, of the legal advisory boards, was at his service if he chose. He was advised to go home though restlessness beset him; but if he would not, if new visions had come to him in seeing salt water for the first time, and in the training camps and in the trenches, then he was all the more in need of advice, and of aid to a change of occupation.

The homeland seemed very strange to the veteran of the A. E. F. His neighbors had been in civil life all the time. They were talking about their work in munition factories and in the drives. They did not understand his state of mind as the result of what he had been through, and he himself was inarticulate in expressing his experience in everyday terms to them. It was as though he had stepped out of another incarnation whose habits were still upon him. He was greeted with, "Now we must all get to work!" when he did not know yet just how to work—but only how to drill and drill, march and march, face shellfire and man foxholes.

"One-hundred-per-cent Americanism" was the slogan of the moment. Even that seemed unnecessarily vocal to him after his return from overseas, where in that intimate soldier clan of his buddies, his platoon, and his company, he had been fighting off homesickness at the same time he was fighting for America. One soldier I knew, who had the Distinguished Service Cross, was buttonholed and asked in the street whether he was a one-hundred-per-cent American. All these manifestations were not new in post-war psychology, which again required statesmanship in making the proper arrangements to insure that the demobilization of the nation's youth should be as successful as its mobilization was.

Meanwhile, the Allied captains were the acclaimed celebrities of victory parades in London and Paris: General Pershing at the head of his veterans, who marched with West Point precision, as an example of American training and discipline; Marshal Foch riding beside the senior Marshal, "Papa" Joffre, and junior Marshal Pétain at the head of proud *poilus;* and Haig leading the survivors of the long British drama of attrition, in which they had served under him for more than three years. When his government asked Haig about honors for himself, he replied that he wanted none unless they were shared by his generals and until his soldiers were cared for.[5]

But one civil chieftain, whose heart had been so keenly set on serving in France, was not to be over there in the hour of triumph with his volunteer division. He had lived to see 2,000,-000 American soldiers in France, 24,000,000 draft men registered, the War won, and his controversy with Baker buried in the newspaper files. In a letter to Pershing upon Theodore Roosevelt's death, Baker said:

"You will, no doubt, be greatly distressed at the news, and will look back, as we all do, across many years of history-making eventfulness, in which the Colonel has played a prominent and often determinative part. About many things my disagreements with him were fundamental, but like all Americans I had a sympathy for his irresistible energy and courage, and when all is said and done few Americans have lived so much and so hard as he has."

HOW OCCUPY OUR WAITING SOLDIERS IN FRANCE?

Pershing had a problem in how to occupy his soldiers now that there was no fighting. French veterans had been all the time in France among their own people, and had only a few hours' train ride to reach their homes; and the British a short rail journey and the Channel crossing to be in Blighty. Our soldiers must mark time in a land of strange habits and tongue, while they waited for transportation. However, if Foch could have had his way, they would have had no idle hours after the Armistice. How they would have received the Generalissimo's final directive cannot be recorded, as it never was brought to their attention. He wrote to Pershing:

"The American Army has, like the French army, a great part of its units at rest. Those units which are stationed near the devastated regions or near those that are encumbered by trench systems, etc., could render precious service to our population. I do not doubt that your sentiments will lead you to continue to give France, during the period of the Armistice, the aid which you have so generously given her during the War. I am equally convinced that your troops will put all their soul into repairing, as far as they are able to do so before leaving France, what has necessarily been destroyed during the course of the operations.

"The work which would be asked of the troops would be of the same nature as that to which they have become accustomed during the campaign. The nature of the various classes of work and the methods of execution are set forth in the note herewith."

Thus the Generalissimo would have our soldiers put to labor in filling in trenches, clearing the battlefields of débris, and reconstructing ruined villages. It is needless to say that Pershing, in cabling this letter on November 28 to Baker, did not accompany it with an approval of the plan.[6] Baker replied: [7]

"No soldiers of the United States can be retained in France for any other than strictly military purposes. No part of their duty to their own government as soldiers would justify our government in requiring them to perform such labor for such purpose."

The thorough Commander-in-Chief would keep his diminishing host subject to war discipline, and thus out of mischief, until the last man had gone home. The military police continued to round on an officer or man who had a button unbuttoned. The Training Section, with an immense force of soldiers still at its disposal, would continue extensive and intensive drill and tactical lessons for long hours, in order to profit by the errors of the Meuse-Argonne. It was hard for the A. E. F. staff to have to close all the special schools which had been in full blast at the time of the Armistice, turning out graduates for the campaign of 1919.

Our men, in the long winter nights in their billets in French villages, and in their day's drilling in the mud, had a conviction that, with the winning of the War, their part as citizen soldiers was finished. It was puzzling; why should they still be put through the military paces? And each one wondered when his turn would come for a day in Paris. The French had strongly advocated these excursions for the money they would bring to shops and restaurants. Our soldiers agreed with the French view, if it did not receive the warm support of Pershing at first. It seemed hardly fair that an American veteran should not complete his adventure overseas by seeing Paris, where he found that he must make up for the brevity of his visit by an intensive application, which was not difficult, as a release from the intensiveness of the military routine to which he had been subjected from the day he went to camp.

PROMPTER MAILS—BUT NO LESS DRILL

One happy result of the Armistice was that he was receiving his mail more promptly. The Post Office Department had originally set out to conduct the mail service of the A. E. F. Baker made a special study of it on his first visit to France; then the A. E. F. took charge, and one reform after another was tried. Mail bags still came on ocean liners, but when all were troop transports, which had to pass through the submarine zone, no one was more wroth over belated letters from home than the officers of the staff. General Bliss was jubilant when he received a letter within eleven days after mailing from Washington. Always the service was being "improved." Major General J. T. Chamberlain, the Inspector General of the Army, wrote as late as September 7, 1918: "The mail problem has not yet been satisfactorily solved, but it is improving, and more satisfactory conditions appear to be in sight." In order to have mail delivered promptly you must have a settled address; and our soldiers in France, as our divisions were switched here and there, hardly had that.

And the intensive drill continued. Disturbing reports were being brought in to the War Department about the rigorous routine and the harsh punishments inflicted on offenders. On

February 3, 1919, Baker sent this cable to be delivered "confidentially and personally" to the Commander-in-Chief:

"I get reports from various sources that our soldiers in Europe are many of them living under conditions of very great hardship, and that there is no group which has as its special problem relieving as far as possible the depressing conditions surrounding them. Earnest and sympathetic men tell me that the effect of this is a great depression of morale, and a feeling on the part of many soldiers of bitterness toward the A. E. F. and the War Department for permitting these conditions to go unremedied. I realize how impossible it is to fight the mud and rain of France, and that many soldiers must endure hardships for the present; but would it not be wise to select a group of officers and civilians to work together on this problem so that conditions may be relieved as far as possible, and also so that the soldiers will see direct evidence of the interest which you and I have in their comfort and happiness? I think it would be better to have civilians associated with the military men than to have a group entirely of officers, and would suggest that the most intelligent and effective Red Cross, Y. M. C. A., Salvation Army, and Knights of Columbus representatives be chosen and asked to associate themselves with Mr. Fosdick as my personal representative, and yourself. His large experience both here and abroad will make him acceptable to them and useful both to us and to the soldiers in producing a better state of mind.

"Among the accounts given me are many which deal with discomforts growing out of strict adherence to minor regulations, in spite of conditions which would seem to justify abatement of them. For instance, men at Brest are not allowed to turn up collars of their raincoats in spite of constant downpour of rain. A committee of both civilians and military men of the kind I suggest would evolve many suggestions which the military men could at once see were regulated through normal military channels."

This started Pershing on an extensive inspection. He made no reply to the cable until February 23, 1919. He said then that the intensive program of military instruction had been virtually finished and athletics and amusements were being substituted.

Leaves were being more freely given. The recently granted authority to make promotions would increase contentment. He had recently inspected eight divisions and found their morale excellent. "I shall without cessation keep up my efforts to improve the living conditions of our splendid troops." In a letter of March 12, in reference to Baker's cablegram of February 3, he said that the only purpose of the intensive military instruction had been to keep up morale. The men he had seen were well contented. He could not believe that any criticism of "the management over here" was worthy of serious attention.

But now there was ample space in ships for the allotment of cargo for the welfare societies, whose part was far from finished but rather amplified. At last the plan of having a hut wherever we had soldiers' billets might be carried out. There could not be too much entertainment or too many American delicacies for the homesick man of the A. E. F. Among the men who shared with Raymond Fosdick the administration of the great work throughout our part in the War were: Malcolm L. McBride, Fosdick's right-hand man: Joseph E. Raycroft, in charge of athletics; Lee F. Hanmer, of music; Joseph Lee and Howard Braucher, in the Community Service; John P. Myers, W. Prentice Sanger, Major Bascom Johnson, Colonel Jason Joy, and Brigadier General Palmer E. Pierce, pioneer liaison officer between the army and industry—who had nine jobs before he went to a combat division. But another provision for the waiting soldiers of the A. E. F., which particularly interested the Secretary of War, looked to another kind of welfare. It was the Army Education Commission under Brigadier General Robert I. Rees and Professor John Erskine. Aside from the divisional schools, men who had left college before graduation or wished to continue collegiate studies had the doors of the British universities and the University of Beaune in France opened to them.

By the middle of January Representative P. P. Campbell, of Kansas, who was interested in the 35th Division, introduced a resolution which promised that the conduct of the A. E. F. would be subjected to a thorough inquiry. On January 20, 1919,

Baker sent a cable to Pershing in which he spoke of the dis-
cussions going on in the country "about the operations, handling, and general conduct last year of the forces under your
command. . . . I am not concerned especially by the critical
aspects of the discussion, but I think that it is important that
the facts should be promptly available for our people." He suggested that Pershing send over officers familiar with the different branches of the A. E. F. who would have the facts and
records ready for the press and the Congress.[8]

LEAVING THE RECORD TO HISTORY

In a letter on the same day to Pershing, in which he referred to the reports that were current and especially about
the treatment of the National Guard, Baker said:

"My own philosophy of life has always been that the truth
has the means of defending itself, and that attacks based upon
misunderstanding or misrepresentation never get anywhere;
and so I have every confidence that even if we do nothing about
it, the present situation will not prove serious. Indeed, I think a
good deal of the gossip and comment to which I am referring is
really aimed at me. I am not fearful that the sane judgment of
American people will permit itself to be misled long.

"So far as this affects you and the A. E. F., however, I have a
different feeling. You are far away and you have not the means
of answering and exposing these comments, and I want you to
do all that is humanly possible to prevent this kind of injustice
from detracting in any way from the feeling of gratitude and
appreciation which the American people ought to feel and do
feel toward you and the A. E. F. for your work in France."

We might pause, with reference to Baker's remark in this
letter that much of the gossip and comment was aimed at him,
to say that the opinion of many of his countrymen at the time,
and after he left office, was expressed in an article in the 12th
edition of the Encyclopedia Britannica:

"The charge that he was a pacifist was often made against him,
and his career as Secretary condemned throughout the United
States as lacking in energy, foresight, and ability, and especially

for his failure to prepare adequately in the months immediately preceding the American declaration of war."

This brought such a storm of protest from those who had served near him that the article was revised to meet the criticism. But he refused to share the indignation of his friends. He wrote to F. H. Goff :

"I am not so concerned as I should be, I fear, about the verdict of history. For the same reason it seems to me unworthy to worry about myself, when so many thousands participated in the World War unselfishly and heroically who will find no place at all in the records which we make up and call history."

Now I resume the thread of the narrative again. On January 27 Baker cabled Pershing that he and March had gone before the Rules Committee and convinced the members that an inquiry should not be made at this time, and so Pershing need not send the officers until requested. On February 5 Baker suggested to Pershing by cable that, in case Congressmen or others asked him whether he was willing to have an investigation, "it would be wise for you to reply in substance that you welcome every investigation which can be made when all the records and all the persons who have knowledge of these transactions have returned to the United States and are available." On February 23 Pershing replied that all criticisms could be fully and completely answered and he considered any statement by him inadvisable as the ground had been amply covered by Baker's statement to the Congressional Committee. He had replied to the only Congressmen who asked him about the investigation that the matter was entirely in the War Department's hands.

SOLDIERS WANTED HOME—NOT VICTORY PARADES

At this time there were a million and a half soldiers still in France. But by April, 1919, we had the shipping to bring them home faster than we had ever sent them; and Baker had affairs in such shape that he could go to France a third time. One day Representative Martin Madden, of Illinois, and a number of other members of Congress were with him reviewing a division. Congressmen had been interested in victory parades, one to be staged by each returning division in the region from which it was drawn. The cost of travel and subsistence and the time occupied after the division's return were items to be considered in the plan, not to mention that many of the men were replacements who came from other localities. Baker said he was in favor of the parades if the men were—which he doubted, in spite of the Congressmen's convictions to the contrary.[9] "We'll find out," said Baker, who passed the word to Pershing that the men be allowed to remain on the field at ease after the review. Baker and the Congressmen circulated among the groups and found that in nine cases out of ten the men were quite definite in their feeling that they had had glory enough. They wanted "no more parades," no formalities that would delay their being mustered out, as they eagerly awaited their turn to entrain in France for the last time on the way to the deportation camp at Brest.

There they had a feeling that they were confined in a corral, in spite of all the entertainment provided. That seaport town, which had the low attractions of the crib district of the Mexican border, was out of bounds for them, in spite of the mayor's protest in the interest of his constituents. Every soldier, before he went on board a transport, was clean in body and in clothes. He had been examined, and was to be examined again on his arrival, to make sure he did not bring home either "the scourge of armies" or any other communicable disease. This feature of the plan of 1917, which had its inception in the lessons learned on the Mexican border, also had its share in making the victory more than merely one of arms.

With fifteen thousand men arriving home every day, and being sent back to civil life at that rate, the Regular officers, who had been made generals and colonels for the War, had no divisions, brigades, and regiments left to command. This brought up a problem with which the Sam Browne belt was closely connected. Originally the belt had two straps over the shoulders to enable British officers the more easily to carry revolver, canteen, maps, and other things needed on active service. With a single strap, it had passed from the British to the other Allied armies, to be adopted in turn by the A. E. F. as the symbol of commissioned rank. The belt was regulation in France, but not in the United States. March was against it and Pershing for it. The requirement that the officer surrender it at the gangway, when it had acquired a fine "tone of time" after veteran service, constituted "another insult from March." This did not matter much to the reserve officer who was about to lose all his insignia, but often the Regular officer had immediately to yield his general's stars for the colonel's eagles or major's leaves of his peace-time rank.

OFF WITH THE SAM BROWNE BELT

On August 19, when Pershing himself might be soon returning in his Sam Browne, Baker wrote a letter to him which is worth quoting for other reasons than its direct references to the belt:

"So far as its value in the field is concerned nothing can be added to your information, but the attitude of America toward it, I feel very sure, you have not had full opportunity to realize. The soldiers themselves do not like it. On the returning transports when the officers have taken off their belts, they have been greeted with cheers. I returned on the *George Washington* with General Haan, and a large number of other officers. The ship's band, one night, paraded around the deck, led by some of the junior officers, bearing signs of a jesting and jocular character pertaining to the death of Sam Browne. As the band went by, officers joined the procession, taking off their belts and carrying them in their hands. The several thousand soldiers on the ship saw the procession, and cheered far into the night, and when General Haan himself joined the procession and took off his belt the cheering was quite wild.

"I do not know why it is, but there has grown up among the soldiers a feeling that many officers fail to realize the difference between the enlisted men of the old Army and the volunteers and drafted men of this Army. Perhaps some officers did fail to realize it, but of course the fact is that the Army we formed for this War was a cross-section of the life of the country, containing in its ranks men of fortune, education, and culture, who would never under any circumstances have enlisted in the old Army as it was prior to the emergency. . . .

"Our own decision not to have the belt in this country was only in part dictated by these sentiments; though all of them were present to our minds every time the question arose. In addition, we constantly faced a growing leather famine, and the use of the leather necessary to make the belts, when stated in the number of pairs of shoes which could be made of it, seemed quite indefensible. . . . It will be very easy to add the belt to the uniform if after canvassing all the sentimental and other reasons it seems the wise thing to do."

Pershing's reply was that the belt had now become the sign of commissioned rank in all armies, that it gave a neat appearance and led an officer to stand straighter; for West Point had no sympathy with the Sandhurst British officers' stoop, which had at first been associated with the belt. Pershing's view was to be accepted, and the Sam Browne belt, far from being unpopular, was to be worn by uniformed men in private services, which might be construed as robbing it of some of its Army distinction.

Pershing returned to have his home victory parade. Bliss and March might not retain the four stars that they wore on their shoulders in war-time: Pershing retained his in the Regulars, on active service, as "The General of the Armies" by act of the Congress, which refused to provide the grade of lieutenant general for Harbord, Liggett, Bullard, or Crowder. There was to be one general, for Pershing's life, and the next in rank the major generals. He was given spacious offices in the old State, War, and Navy Building; his choice of officers to aid him in writing his reports; and provided, aside from his General's pay, with every allowance within reach of the law, while he devoted himself, as head of the Battle Monuments Commission, to supervising the memorials to be erected on the battlefields of his army.

It seems worth while to make this final quotation from another letter of Baker to Pershing in the summer of 1919:

"When this incident is all over, I want it to be a lesson for all future time in the way to fight a war, which I should conceive to be this: Select a commander in whom you have confidence; give him power and responsibility, and then (this, of course, is for the civilian official) work your own head off to get him everything he needs and support him in every decision he makes."

A STERILE INVESTIGATION

And the civilian's part included facing the investigation of the Department's conduct of the War after it was won. I anticipated that I should have a long chapter on this subject; but on no other subject has my reading of the documents yielded so small a result for the time spent. The Congress kept faithfully at its search in response to the expectation that corruption would be disclosed. In 1921 $2,700,000 was appropriated to continue the investigations under President Harding when Harry M. Daugherty had become Attorney General. A select committee of the House of Representatives took evidence in thirteen States and held hearings in France. The Department of Justice, the Inspector General of the Army, and a joint board of survey had the subject in hand for three and a half years. The testimony before the House Committee alone amounted to twenty thousand pages. On the day before Thanksgiving, 1925, the Associated Press in Washington sent this dispatch:

"The last of the war fraud indictments were wiped off the criminal records today."

The following were the convictions: a man in Texas was sentenced to two and a half years for stealing a motor truck and afterward paroled; a second got eighteen months; a third was fined $100 for pilfering government property; and the fourth was guilty of a falsehood in applying for a passport. And, after all this costly investigation by the succeeding administration, which had no reason to be partial to the War administration, all other indictments were quashed. I have not mentioned the names of some important men who were subjected to charges of which they were subsequently cleared. The Hughes investigation recommended courts-martial for two highly placed reserve officers; but an Army board of review decided that the evidence did not warrant their being brought to trial. Mr. Randolph, for whom life was again normal in the corridors of the War Department, could say, at the conclusion of the investigations, that his third war had come to an honorable end; and he might also recall, with understanding sympathy, the words that Mr. Dooley had put into the mouth of Russell Alger after the Spanish War, when the Secretary advised Chauncey Depew thus: "But, oh, Chanse, don't iver aspire to my job. Be sicrety of war, if ye will; but niver be sicrety of A war!"

The big American war fortunes were made out of munitions, ships, and supplies before our entry into the War. The price-fixing system of the War Industries Board was generally effective except in certain instances over which control was difficult. The Board might require 50,000 tons of steel bars in a hurry. One plant that was all set to make steel bars could produce 10,000 for a smaller cost than other plants which had to make adjustments before they began production of the remaining forty thousand. But the government received back a large proportion of profits through the excess profits tax.

There were more trials for Baker after the summer of 1919 than demobilization, the sales of surplus war supplies, the reorganization of the Army on a peace basis, and the regular routine, which included maintenance of the Army of Occupation in Germany. He wrote to his law partner, Joseph C. Hostetler, on October 7, 1919:

"We have all been so much concerned about the President, since he returned ill from the West, that I feel a year older than I was two weeks ago. Unhappily none of us know much about his illness as the doctors are telling us little more than they put into the bulletins, but most of the stories afloat are obviously wrong. The President's mind is clear and active as usual. He writes us notes and would write more if the doctors would let him, so I suppose his nervous condition is just bad enough to make the doctors fear collapse unless he can get rest and sleep and enough digestion to nourish him. Each day now is better than the one before it, so it should not be long until the doctors are willing to take a more positively reassuring tone. So far they look serious and say: 'The President is very sick, he must rest, he is better than he was'—and there they leave it."

The President had broken down on a tour of passionate appeal to bring the nation into the League of Nations which he had fathered. He would send down notes from his sickroom to the Cabinet meetings that were held when he was unable to be present.

HIS BIT IS FINISHED

In the bosom of the law firm Baker expressed his views on political ethics to Hostetler on March 12, 1920:

"I see that Davis has resigned. I admire him for it. He is right in his feeling that he cannot do his duty as Mayor while canvassing to be nominated for Governor. In fact I have long believed that whenever a man holding one job begins to want another job, he should resign the one he has. I should apply this to cabinet officers, generals and others! Perhaps I am able to pronounce such a judgment because I am clean as a mountain spring from desiring any job."

And again he was writing to Hostetler in an equally characteristic vein:

"I knew that pneumonia and empyemia were consequences of the 'flu,' but had no idea that an income-tax return was a part of the evil results! This is my first day out of bed since Saturday and the doctors predicted that I would feel confused and dizzy —evidently they understood about the income-tax return. I have read the thing through twice. It certainly is not poetry, for it does not rhyme; and it certainly is not prose, since it conveys no ideas. What language *is* it in? . . . When I think how glad I am to pay this income tax—really glad—as it is the only substitute allowed me for the service of a sterner sort done by the soldiers, I cannot forgive my Government for making my happiness so complicated and difficult. They take all the pleasure out of being honest so as not to be thought stupid.

"They explode another long-held theory of mine too. All my life I have believed tariff and other indirect taxes to be bad because a man did not know what he was paying and had no sense of a stake in the Government because he knew what it was costing *him*. I used to say, with other tax reformers (not Bill Matthews!): 'Now if we had a scientific system of taxation, an income tax, a citizen would know, and his patriotic interest would be aroused in affairs by his knowledge!' An afternoon spent with this return, however, makes me wonder whether a specific duty paid at the port of entry or an *ad valorem* filched by the Collector of Customs does not leave you freer from confusion of mind and spirit, after all."

On March 23, 1920, he was rejoicing in a letter to Hostetler that Dr. Thomas Salmon, the psychiatrist, who did such great service in France, had said that our Army was "the most sober, the most sane, and the least criminal body of its size the world has ever seen." On June 21, 1920, he was already looking forward to his return to Cleveland:

". . . Not an apartment of state with rooms en suite (and bill en bitter!) but a modest room with bath, as befits a man whose conscience is clear enough to enable him to sleep easily in simple surroundings and whose purse is light enough to excite the compassion even of an inn-keeper."

His essential ambition, however, was for "a roof to keep out the rain, a few more windows to lock at night, and an additional dozen frail porcelain gods and goddesses which my romping babies may break!"

On Christmas Day, when he made it a custom to write to his friends, he wrote to Hostetler:

"The calendar says that there will be but seventy days from Christmas until, in our several parts, the Baker family enact *Paradise Regained*. . . . I used to know an old man who spent his time trying to prove that the earth is flat. All of us wise ones laughed at him, but I realize now that he probably had held public office! He held office too long, apparently, and never got over it. But when I get away I shall put the thesis in this form:

'The earth is a large, round, joyous place, with peaks near home and certain dreary flat surfaces in and about all public offices.' "

He wrote to Hostetler on January 15, 1921: "Both you and Tom ought to feel free to do anything you want to do after I get back, and let me carry whatever added burden I can to make up for the way you have carried it while I have been away on this assignment."

On March 4, 1921, his bit in the War was finished; and so, inevitably, was the political career of a man who had spoken so many No's in the course of his service as Secretary of War. For sixteen years he had been in public office. When he returned to Cleveland and his friends, the "roof to keep out the rain" was a small rented apartment; for he was penniless, and would have been in debt if he had not received a small inheritance while he was in Washington which enabled him to carry on respectably as a Cabinet member.

At last he could practise his profession and strive to earn a competence for his family. He was not the only man in the War who found that his talents were not in eager demand upon his demobilization. Immediately after his return to his Cleveland office, he certainly had no need for Dr. Keppel, who had shepherded the press of callers in April, 1917, in Washington. As he listened to the footsteps in the hall, one after another they turned into his partners' offices. But he was in a high mood over making a start in life when he wrote to Fosdick in answer to congratulations upon return to "our learned profession," that " 'Lawyer Baker,' after the formalities of 'Mr. Secretary,' appeals to me with a charm I should find it difficult to describe."

REFERENCES

XIX

1. Bliss to the author. 2. Letter, Baker to Pershing, September 10, 1917. 3. Pershing letter to Baker, November 13, 1917. 4. Order published October, 1917, A. E. F., from Pershing's official report, 1920. 5. Foreword, "Memoirs of Marshal Foch," courtesy of Doubleday, Doran & Company. 6. A. E. F.–S–454. 7. "My Experiences in the World War," Pershing. 8. A. E. F.–S–42. 9. S. O. S.–S–18. 10. A. E. F.–R–429. 11. A. E. F.–S–271. 12. A. E. F.–S–372. 13. W. D.–R–345.

XX

1. To National Woman Suffrage Association, December 14, 1917. 2. Newport News, Virginia, September 3, 1917. 3. Speech at Cleveland, October 17, 1917. 4. To the New York Southern Society, December 12, 1917. 5. To the Chautauqua representatives. 6. To the National Consumers' League, November 14, 1917. 7. To The National Woman Suffrage Association, December 14, 1917.

XXI

1. To the Republican Club of New York. 2. David F. Houston to the author. 3. Daniel Willard to the author. 4. The *New York Tribune,* September 17, 1917. 5. Ralph Hayes to the author. 6. To the author. 7. Raymond Fosdick to the author. 8. A. E. F.–S–387. 9. "Ordnance and the World War," Crozier. 10. *Congressional Record,* 56–2. 11. The *New York Times,* January 14, 1918. 12. Minutes, General Munitions Board, April 3, 1917. 13. "Panama, Past and Present," Farnham Bishop. 14 & 15. The *New York Times,* January 24, 1918. 16. The *New York Times,* January 26, 1918.

XXII

1. *Congressional Record,* 56–2. 2. A. E. F.–R–695. 3. "The Victory at Sea," Admiral W. S. Sims. 4. A. E. F.–S–277. 5. A. E. F.–S–445. 6. A. E. F.–S–616. 7. To the author. 8. A. E. F.– S–673. 9. A. E. F.–S–666.

XXIII

1. Quoted in "The American Reinforcement," Frothingham.

XXIV

1. W. D.–S–558. 2. Letter, Pershing to Baker. 3. "Luden-dorff's Own Story," Ludendorff, courtesy of Harper & Bros. 4. Quoted in "It Might Have Been Lost," Lonergan. 5. Telegram of Colonel Wagstaff, British liaison officer at American G. H. Q. 6. Quoted in "It Might Have Been Lost," Lonergan. 7. W. D.–R–487. 8. A. E. F.–S–555. 9. W. D.–R–705. 10. "Ludendorff's Own Story," Ludendorff. 11. "British Official History of Naval Operations." 12. "My Experiences in the World War," Pershing. 13. "Ludendorff's Own Story," Ludendorff. 14. "Grandeur and Misery of Victory," Clemenceau. 15. "My Experiences in the World War," Pershing. 16. Letter from Bliss to Baker, May 11, 1918. 17. "At the Supreme War Council," Wright. 18. "Ludendorff's Own Story," Ludendorff. 19. "Memoirs of Marshal Foch." 20. "Sir Douglas Haig's Command," Dewar. 21. "Memoirs of Marshal Foch."

XXV

1. Quoted in "It Might Have Been Lost," Lonergan. 2. "My Experiences in the World War," Pershing. 3. "Out of My Life," Hindenburg. 4 & 5. "Memoirs of Marshal Foch." 6. To the author. 7. Joint Note No. 18, Supreme War Council. 8. Baker through Bliss, S. P. C. to W. D.–S–67. 9. S. P. C.–R– 39. 10. "Memoirs of Marshal Foch." 11. W. D.–S–820. 12. A. E. F.–R–1004. 13. W. D.–S–1036. 14. Lord Reading's dispatch, quoted in "It Might Have Been Lost," Lonergan.

XXVI

1. Major General W. S. Graves to the author. 2. A. E. F.–R–874. 3. A. E F.–R–1301. 4. A. E. F.–R–1344. 5. Bliss to Baker, April 10, 1918.

XXVII

1. A. E. F.–R–1267. 2. A. E. F.–R–1301. 3. A. E. F.–R–1381. 4, 5, 6, 7, 8. "The American Air Service," Sweetser. 9. A. E. F.–R–699. 10. W. D.–R–319. 11. W. C. D.–9754–58. 12. A. E. F.–S–67. 13. A. E. F.–S–659. 14. John D. Ryan to the author. 15. Ryan to the author. 16. Baker to the author.

XXVIII

1. Bernard M. Baruch to the author. 2. Baruch to the author. 3. Baker, lecture to the War College, May 11, 1929. 4. To the author. 5. To the author. 6. Raymond Fosdick to the author. 7. "Frontiers of Freedom," Baker's War Speeches. 8. King to the author. 9. Baker files. 10. A. E. F.–S–527. 11. Baker-Pershing correspondence. 12. A. E. F.–S–954. 13. W. D.–S–1159. 14. Pershing to the author. 15. W. D.–R–1086.

XXIX

1. A. E. F.–S–101. 2. A. E. F.–S–1223. 3. "A History of the Great War," Buchan. 4. Supreme War Council, June 3, 1918. 5. A. E. F.–S–1235. 6. A. E. F.–S–1219. 7. A. E. F.–S–1279. 8. A. E. F.–S–1285. 9. "Out of My Life," Hindenburg. 10. "Ludendorff's Own Story," Ludendorff.

XXX

1. A. E. F.–S–65. 2. A. E. F.–S–280. 3. A. E. F.–R–390. 4. A. E. F.–S–366. 5. A. E. F.–R–492. 6. A. E. F.–S–311. 7. Raymond Fosdick to the author. 8. To the author. 9. Bliss to Baker, Jan. 22, 1918. 10. Pershing to the author. 11. "Life Story of Leonard Wood," Hagedorn, in the *New York Tribune,* 1931.

12 & 13. Kirke Simpson, Associated Press, to the author. 14. "Life Story of Leonard Wood," Hagedorn. 15. Graves to the author. 16. New York *World*, December 14, 1930. 17. Pershing to the author. 18. A. E. F.–S–1484. 19. A. E. F.–S–1485. 20. A. E. F.–S–1778. 21. A. E. F.–S–1331. 22. Baker to the author.

XXXI

1. W. D.–R–1369. 2. A. E. F.–S–1428. 3. "Ludendorff's Own Story," Ludendorff. 4. "My Experiences in the World War," Pershing. 5. Am. S. W. C., Versailles–R–66. 6. A. E. F.–R–1640. 7. W. D.–R–1423. 8. W. D.–R–1487. 9. A. E. F.–R–1543. 10. A. E. F.–R–1566. 11. W. D.–R–1637. 12. "Memoirs of Marshal Foch." 13. "Ludendorff's Own Story," Ludendorff. 14. "Memoirs of Marshal Foch." 15. "Ludendorff's Own Story," Ludendorff. 16. W. D.–S–1608. 17. "Memoirs of Marshal Foch."

XXXII

1 & 2. Baker to the author.

XXXIII

1. Talk to National Conference on War Camp Community Recreation Service, Washington, October 23, 1917. 2. A. E. F., General Order, No. 6. 3. A. E. F., General Order, No. 34. 4. A. E. F., General Order, No. 77. 5. Cabinet du Ministre, Section des œuvres militaires diversées, December, 1917.

XXXIV

1. "The Spirit of Selective Service," Crowder. 2. Report of Provost Marshal General, 1919. 3. "The War with Germany," Ayres. 4. A. E. F.–R–1475. 5. A. E. F.–S–1253. 6. Baker's letter to the President, June 20, '18. 7. W. D. to Am. S. W. C.–S–68. 8. Am. S. W. C.–S–148. 9. Minutes, War Industries Board, July 9, 1918. 10. Minutes, War Industries Board, August 1, 1918. 11. Minutes, War Industries Board, August 22, 1918. 12. Report of War Industries Board, 1921. 13. Speech to National

Consumers' League, Baltimore, November 14, 1917. 14. "Industrial America in the World War," Clarkson.

XXXV

1. To the author. 2. Pershing to Felix Frankfurter. 3. W. D.–R–1608. 4. W. D.–R–1567. 5. W. D.–S–1859. 6. W. D.–R–1623. 7. W. D.–S–1877. 8. "The War with Germany," Ayres. 9. "The American Merchant Marine," Admiral W. S. Benson. 10. Baker to the author. 11. A. E. F.–S–1718. 12. "Memoirs of Marshal Foch." 13. W. D.–R–1675. 14. W. D.–S–1926. 15. W. D.–R–1676. 16. W. D.–S–1935. 17. W. D.–R–1686. 18. W. D.–R–1717. 19. W. D.–S–1982. 20. To the author. 21. "Field Marshal Earl Haig," Charteris. 22. "Sir Douglas Haig's Command," Dewar. 23. "Memoirs of Marshal Foch." 24. "Ludendorff's Own Story," Ludendorff. 25. Baker to the author, from memory. 26. Fosdick to the author. 27. A. E. F.–R–2046. 28. A. E. F.–R–2050. 29. A. E. F.–R–2047. 30. A. E. F.–R–2054. 31. A. E. F.–R–2104.

XXXVI

1."My Experiences in the World War," Pershing. 2. W. D.–R–1742. 3. W. D.–R–1767. 4. W. D.–S–2040. 5. A. E. F.–S–1785. 6. W. D.–R–1812. 7. A. E. F.–R–2088. 8. A. E. F.–R–2101. 9. "Memoirs of Marshal Foch." 10 & 11. Baker to the author. 12 & 13. "Memoirs of Marshal Foch." 14 & 15. "Field Marshal Earl Haig," Charteris. 16. "Memoirs of Marshal Foch." 17. "Sir Douglas Haig's Command," Dewar. 18. A. E. F.–R–2094. 19. A. E. F.–S–1850. 20. A. E. F.–R–2108. 21. A. E. F.–R–2108. 22. W. D.–R–1848. 23. W. D.–S–2134. 24. W. D.–R–1861. 25. W. D.–S–2150. 26. W. D.–S–2162. 27. W. D.–S–2174. 28. A. E. F.–R–2170.

XXXVIII

1. No. 137, Tokyan Milstoff, November 25, 1918. 2. S–594, Stettinius to Baker. 3. "The Journal of the Great War," Dawes. 4. Baker to the author. 5. "Field Marshal Earl Haig," Charteris. 6. A. E. F.–S–1933. 7. W. D.–S–2274. 8. A. E. F.–R–2521. 9. Baker to the author.

INDEX

Abbéville conference, II. 170
Abbott, W. R., II. 387
acetone for coating airplane cloth, II. 180
Ach, L. R., II. 388
Adamson Act, I. 97-99
Advisory Commission, I. 50, 60; personnel, I. 61; I. 62, 63, 94, 95, 96, 102; no money, I. 102, 104, 105; I. 108, 128, 260; on war risk insurance, I. 268-270; on aviation, I. 285; II. 201
A.E.F., I. 92, 110, 122; co-operate with British or French, I. 153-155; 156; plans for, I. 167; first contingent, I. 178, 181, 182, 247-248; its numbers as ordered by Pershing, I. 249-251; size of divisions changed, I. 253-257; divisions named, I. 356-357; in action, I. 382-383; discipline, II. 4-5; technical heads all Regulars, II. 9-10; its supply difficulties, II. 10 ff.; relations with French authorities, II. 11-12; its confusing demands for supplies, II. 16-19; reports as to its numbers, II. 50-51, 151;

problem of keeping its integrity—see integral army; author's conjectures as to result if A.E.F. had opposed German drive, spring, 1918, II. 134-137; question of reinforcing Allies, II. 144-146; its airplane requirements—see aviation; first action, II. 215; in 3d German offensive, II. 216 ff.; Belleau Wood, II. 222; examples of its requisitions, II. 249-250;

numbers in France, July, 1918, II. 253; replacements, II. 264-266; training needed, II. 266-267; in 5th offensive, II. 269-270; join in closing Marne salient, II. 272;

numbers as planned in 80-division program, II. 346; demobilization, II. 384-386, 400-402; post-War discipline overseas, II. 402-406; its training schools closed, II. 403; their mail, II.

404; education continued, II. 406; Congressional inquiry into management of A.E.F., II. 406-408
Aeronautical Society, II, 173
A.F. of L., I. 225, 259, 262, 265, 267
Agriculture, Department of, I. 3
Aguinaldo, I. 161
Ainsworth, General Fred C., I. 3, 68, 69
Air Service—see aviation
Aircraft Production Board, I. 286, 288; in connection with aviation scandal, II. 173; II. 175 ff.; cable message describing Board decisions, II. 179-180. See also aviation
airplanes—see aviation
Aisne line, II. 216
Alexander, Maj. Gen. Robert, II. 358
Alger, Russell A., I. 3, 8, 32, II. 413
aliens, I. 86, 100-102, II. 158-164. See also foreign-born citizens and espionage
Allen, Maj. Gen. Henry T., II. 230, 341, 376
Allenby, Maj. Gen. Sir Edmund, I. 385; II. 32, 118, 346, 348
Allied councils, commissions, etc.—see Inter-Allied
Allied reserve, II. 128, 129, 130, 134, 141
Allied stores of material at Archangel, II. 317
Allies, I. 21, 110 ff.; missions, I. 112-113, 115, 146-147, 149, 150; II. 47
loans to, I. 115, 124, 125 (see also war debts); lack of unanimity, I. 146, 149, 150, 168, 174, 373 ff.; I. 381; II. 320; first conference in Paris, I. 347; need of co-ordination, I. 373-376; to support of Italy, I. 391; conference (Nov., 1917), I. 375, 391-393; relations with U. S. in shipping, I. 403-404; their shipping needs, I. 406; in shipping conference, I. 408-412; their prospects for 1918, II. 117; opinions on "Eastern" question, II. 118-119;

of having a dictator, II. 336; allegation that he is a Jew, II. 336-337; purpose of 2nd trip, II. 340; sees Battle of Saint-Mihiel, II. 341 ff.; visits Lafayette's house, II. 342; inspection, II. 342-343; sees S.O.S., II. 343-344; secures allotment of British shipping, II. 344; gets A.E.F.'s idea of 80-division program, II. 346, 364; talk with Foch on 100 divisions, II. 348; hears news of armistice proposal, II. 348-349; episode at gangway, II. 349;

letter to dead soldier's father, II. 351-352; receives copy of one from a father, II. 354; II. 368; discusses Pershing's possible successor, II. 369; no thought of replacing Pershing, II. 369; II. 377; to President on possible disorders in new European states, II. 378-379; to Whitlock on futility of war, II. 379; to Pershing on premature Armistice news, II. 380; cables Stettinius to stop work and contracts, II. 383; to Pershing to report casualties and deaths, II. 383; to Frank Scott on American business men's service in the War, II. 390;

confesses he is tired, II. 391; to President on wanting to stay here for post-War adjustment rather than go to Peace Conference, II. 391-392; to Sidlo on President's acquiescence, II. 392; suggests Bliss as Peace Commr., II. 392; to President on troops in Siberia, II. 394; argues for bringing them home, II. 394-395; on Bolshevism, II. 394; to Stettinius on returning our material from France, II. 396-397; to Pershing on selling this, II. 398; his conversation with Lord Reading on Anglo-American settlement, II. 398-399; visits demobilization camps, II. 400; on death of Roosevelt, II. 402; to Pershing on keeping troops overseas to clean up, II. 403; study of mail problem in France, II. 404; to Pershing on post-War morale of our troops, II. 405; and on criticism of the conduct of the War, II. 407; comment on Baker in *Encyc. Brit.* revised, II. 407-408; to Goff on leaving the record to history,

II. 408; suggests Pershing's policy in case of investigation, II. 408; makes 3rd trip to France, April, 1919, II. 408-409; in connection with victory parades, II. 409; to Pershing on Sam Browne belts, II. 410-411; on the way to manage a war, II. 412; his concern about the President's health, II. 413-414; on an office-holder who runs for another office, II. 414; on income-tax forms, II. 414-415; on Dr. Salmon, II. 415; on returning to his Cleveland home, II. 415-416; on being only a lawyer once more, II. 416

Baker, Newton, I. 77, 79-81, 158, 200
Baker, Mrs. Newton D., I. 364, 365, 368, II. 337
Baldwin, Spencer F., I. 269
Balfour, Arthur, I. 112, 146, 154, 155, 249, 374, 401
ballast for our ships returning, II. 86
Ballou, Maj. Gen. Charles C., II. 358
Barber, John E., I. 400
barracks, I. 234
Barrette, Brig. Gen. John D., II. 3, 248
Barry, Maj. Gen. Thomas H., I. 101-102, 161, 162, 240; II. 41, 230, 232, 234, 241-245
Barth, Brig. Gen. Charles H., II. 248
Bartlett, Gen., II. 50, 228
Battle Monuments Commission, II. 411
Baruch, Bernard M., I. 61, 103, 107, 349, 353; II. 38, 40; made new head of War Industries Board, II. 83-84, 200-202; II. 204, 322, 323-326, 327, 330, 386, 387, 397
Battle Creek demobilization camp II. 400
bayonet types, I. 272-273
Beatty, Lord, II. 121
Beaune, University of, II. 406
Belgium, II. 379
Bell, Maj. Gen. J. Franklin, I. 161, 162, 240, II. 163, 228, 230, 232, 234, 241-247
Bell, Maj. Gen. George, Jr., I. 306, II. 358
Belleau Wood, II. 223-225, 357
Belmont, August, I. 269
Benét-Mercié gun, I. 275, 276
Benson, Admiral W. S., I. 376, II. 84, 85

293; his orders about venereal cases, II. 293; on danger of Germany's drawing on Russian man-power, II. 315-316; II. 330, 331; his "follow-up" section, II. 331; does not want Goethals, II. 334-335; II. 338, 341, 345; on number of divisions wanted, II. 346-348; II. 350; reorganizes for Meuse-Argonne, II. 363; cables troop requirements, II. 363-364, 366; rumors about replacing him, II. 368; II. 377; states numbers of troops wanted in January, 1919, II. 377-378; calls for replacements, II. 378; his possible problems if War had continued, II. 380; wants unconditional surrender, II. 381; II. 383; post-War discipline of A.E.F., II. 402-406; II. 407, 408; in Washington, II. 411

Pershing-Milner agreement, II. 169

Pétain, I. 151, 251, 381, 382, 384, II. 67, 108, 119, 123, 124, 133, 139, 141, 216, 277, 290, 341, 371, 373

Petrograd, I. 385, 387

Philippines, I. 2, 4, 26, 32, 59, 165, 166, 210, II. 232, 246

Phillipp, Governor E. L., I. 336-338

Pickett's Charge, II. 136

Pierce, Franklin, I. 2

Pierce, Brig. Gen. Palmer E., I. 107, 120, 121, 154, 181, 353, 378, II. 63, 152, 387, 406

plans for winning the War presented to War Dept., I. 113-114

Plattsburg camp, I. 46-47, 59, 162, 165, 310

Playground and Recreation Assn., I. 310

Plummer, Maj. Gen. Edward H., II. 228, 230

Poincaré, I. 90

Poinsett, Secretary, I. 185

Polk, Frank, I. 139

Pope, Gen., I. 157

Pope's peace note, I. 361-363

Porto Rico, I. 26

Post Office Department, I. 3

Pratt, Francis C., I. 105

preparedness, I. 3-4, 5, 6, 7-8, 10, 39 ff.; various plans, I. 42-46; Plattsburg camp, I. 46-47; industrial, I. 47-50, 52; Natl. Defense Act, 58-60; for Army, 62; for Navy, 62-65.

Presidential campaign and election (1916), I. 21, 71, 73, 78

Princeton, I. 224

prices, I. 129-131, 179, 259, II. 323; on mine-production, I. 179; in steel, II. 323

priority, I. 129, 135, 353; II. 11, 14, 84, 324-326

"profiteering," II. 413

pro-German activities—*see* espionage

prohibition, II. 25

propaganda, I. 38, 39, 40, 41, 43, II. 159; ours among German troops, II. 381-382

Proper Military Policy for the United States, I. 42

prophylaxis.—*see* venereal disease

prosperity during War, I. 258

prostitution—in Army on Mexican border—*see* venereal disease; overseas, II. 292-303 *passim;* attitude of French authorities, II. 292-293; Clemenceau on licensing, II. 295-296; our policy criticized by M. Simonin, II. 296-298; defended by Col. Young, II. 298-301; method used in Blois, II. 301-302

Prostitution in Europe, Flexner, II. 298

Public Information, Committee on, I. 112, 290, II. 35-36, 75, 164, 189, 190-191

public, mood of—on our entry into War, I. 123-124, 126; in response to draft, I. 206-207; on Baker's answers to Senate Committee, Jan. 10, 1918, II. 60-61

Pullman strike, I. 29

punishment in the Army—*see* discipline

Purchase and Storage, Division of, II. 58

Quartermaster Corps, 247. *See also* Sharpe, Henry G.

Quartermaster Dept., II. 54-55, 388. *See also* Sharpe, Henry G.

railroad cars for A.E.F., II. 12, 88, 350

railroad employees and the draft, II. 308

railroad strike, I. 97-99

railroads, U. S.,—govt. control of, I. 133-135, II. 29-30; congestion and

on draft exemption, I. 325-326; II. 208, 244

Tuscania, II. 85

Tuttle, M. C., I. 235, 253

typewriters, I. 128-129

Underhill, F. P., II. 387

unified command, II. 128, 140-141, 144, 146; Baker describes to President, II. 148-149; resolution creating it, II. 150

uniforms—alleged shortage of, II. 57; wool for, II. 59; proposed change in, II. 344

unions—*see* labor

Upton, Brig. Gen. LaRoy S., II. 225, 286

U. S. breaks off relations with Germany, I. 84; declares war, I. 90

U. S. Public Health Service, I. 317-318

U. S. Shipping Board—*see* Shipping Board

U. S. Steel Corporation, I. 130

Van Deman, Brig. Gen. Ralph H., II. 46, 158

Van Der Voort, William H., I. 105

Van Kleeck, Mary, II. 35, 328

Vardaman, Senator J. K., I. 57, 87, 88, 90

Vauclain, Samuel, I. 105, 245

Vaux, II. 225

venereal disease, preventing it in the Army, 296 ff.; its ravages, 297; compulsory prophylaxis, 297; conditions on Mexican border, 297 ff.; investigation by Fosdick, 297; Baker's position, 302-304; preventive measures, 305; new policy, 305-307; offset by recreation—*see* recreation

overseas, II. 292-303 *passim;* Pershing's orders, II. 293; teaching and prophylaxis, II. 293; hospitalization and registration, II. 293-294; connected with problem of prostitution, II. 295 ff.; no co-operation from French authorities in our efforts to control, II. 299; our policy vindicated by health records, II. 300-301; examination for, on demobilization, II. 409

Vera Cruz, I. 16, 28

Verdun, I. 4, 151, 384

Vesle, II. 271

Vickers gun, I. 276

victory parades, II. 401-402, 409

Villa, Francisco, I. 12, 13, 17, 18, 20, 21, 24, 162

Viviani, I. 112, 146

Vincent, J. G., I. 294

Vladivostok, I. 111, II. 312, 313. *See also* Siberian expedition

volunteer divisions, objections to, I. 203-204

volunteer workers in Washington, I. 135-140

Wadsworth, Senator James W., jr., II. 53, 57, 59-60

Walcott, Dr. Charles D., I. 285

Waldron, Col. S. D., I. 286, II. 194

Walker, Col. M. L., II. 343

Walsh, Patrick, II. 90

"War Cabinet," II. 167-168

War College, I. 36, 38; its "war games," I. 40, 41, 57, 65, 152; I. 42; its "Proper Military Policy," I. 61; its hypothetical plans, I. 62-63; I. 92; its plan for the draft, I. 93, 188; I. 250; its tables for cantonment accommodations, I. 254-255; aviation plans, I. 288, 290-291; plan for identifying spies, I. 357

War Council, II. 2-3

war debts, cancellation of, I. 153

War Department, I. 2, 3, 4, 8, 9, 11, 12, 16, 20; its activities subject to Congressional orders, I. 45; inadequate funds, I. 91, 93-94, 115, 118-120; given funds, I. 121; I. 132, 140-141; its records of officers, I. 159; its War policy, I. 178 (*see also* Baker, Newton D.); attacked—*see* Roosevelt, Theodore, *and* Harvey, George B.; defended by Baker before Senate Committee, I. 150-153, 168-169, II. 53-60; criticized by Chamberlain in Senate speech, II. 68-69; its policy described by Baker to Senate, II. 72 ff.; its task in carrying out the 100-division plan, II. 256-257; agrees to undertake 80 divisions, II. 271-272; after Armistice, cancels draft calls, etc., II. 382-383; investigation of its conduct of the War, II. 412-413

War Industries Board, I. 50, 106, 131, 353, 378, 379; II. 200 ff.; 258, 324-